FANATICISM

FANATICISM

On the Uses of an Idea

ALBERTO TOSCANO

VERSO
London • New York

First published by Verso 2010
© Alberto Toscano 2010
All rights reserved
The moral rights of the author have been asserted

1 3 5 7 9 10 8 6 4 2

Verso
UK: 6 Meard Street, London W1F 0EG
US: 20 Jay Street, Suite 1010, Brooklyn, NY 11201
www.versobooks.com

Verso is the imprint of New Left Books

ISBN-13: 978-1-84467-424-4

British Library Cataloguing in Publication Data
A catalogue record for this book is available from the British Library

Library of Congress Cataloging-in-Publication Data
A catalog record for this book is available from the Library of Congress

Typeset in Fournier by Hewer Text UK Ltd, Edinburgh
Printed in the US by Worldcolor/Fairfield

For Nina

Contents

Who writ the histories of the Anabaptists but their enemies?

Richard Overton

They claimed the rights of the human race; but they asserted them like wild beasts.

Voltaire, *Essai sur les mœurs*

They saw nothing but a question of *philosophy* and *religion* in what is really a question of *revolution* and *politics*.

Robespierre

Not everything that is irrational can be dismissed as stupidity.

Ernst Bloch, *Heritage of Our Times*

Introduction

There are few terms in our political vocabulary as damning as 'fanatic'. Beyond tolerance and impervious to communication, the fanatic stands outside the frame of political rationality, possessed by a violent conviction that brooks no argument and will only rest, if ever, once every rival view or way of life is eradicated. A fanatic, Winston Churchill once quipped, 'is someone who can't change his mind and won't change the subject'. He or she is also a subject who will not change, an intransigent, incorrigible subject. Though one might hazard explanations as to the elements or sources of fanaticism, fanatical action itself, lying outside the domain of negotiation, is most often viewed as undeserving of the assumption of rationality that commonly governs our evaluation of social and political behaviour. Those who refuse dialogue, so the reasoning goes, are unworthy of our understanding. Here our 'powers of empathy', our 'ability to reach into another's heart', find it impossible to 'penetrate the blank stares of those who would murder innocents with abstract, serene satisfaction'.[1]

Fanaticism, Hegel declared, is 'enthusiasm for the abstract'. The question of abstraction is at the core of any political and philosophical reckoning with fanaticism. It is abstraction, and the universality or egalitarianism that attaches to it, which separates the figure of the fanatic from that of a mere madman, and into the bargain lends fanaticism its allure of extreme danger. The apparent anti-humanism of fanaticism is often the vehicle for a humanism, that is, a political universalism that trespasses

---

1 Barack Obama, 'Preface to the 2004 edition', in *Dreams from My Father*, New York: Crown, 2004. I thank Bart Moore-Gilbert for bringing these lines to my attention.

ethnic or social boundaries – though such humanism may be anything but humanitarian.[2] Similarly, though fanaticism defies explanation and dialogue, it is also frequently identified not with the absence but with the excess of rationality. Homing in on the question of abstraction – which is the foremost legacy of Marx's reflections on religion – permits us to complicate the common perception of fanaticism as simply the encroachment of religion into a supposedly secularized public sphere; it also allows us to engage those treatments of fanaticism, especially under the rubric of political religion, which regard it as an irremovable potential within religion itself, and a driving force in 'totalitarian' movements like communism. To consider fanaticism under the heading of the politics of abstraction is to give ourselves the means to follow this notion in its numerous shifts across seemingly disparate intellectual domains, historical periods and geographical areas. In this way, we can open the critical and historical interrogation of this term to a broader reflection on the contemporary relationship between universal emancipation and abstract universality, a relationship nicely encapsulated in a question posed by Jacques Derrida: 'Should one save oneself by abstraction or save oneself from abstraction?'[3] Rethinking the history and politics of fanaticism is not simply a way of resisting the invidious calls for a defence of the beleaguered West against its irrational adversaries; it also allows us to confront the impasses and hopes of a radical politics of emancipation and egalitarianism – a politics that over the centuries has frequently been smeared with the charge of fanaticism.

This book explores the enigmatic and unstable conjunction, under the banner of fanaticism, of a refusal of compromise and a seemingly boundless drive to the universal. Sometimes, the accusation of fanaticism is levied at those who inflexibly, intolerantly and sometimes

---

2   As Faisal Devji notes in his galvanizing and counter-intuitive treatment of Al Qaeda's sacrificial humanism: 'for many [jihadi] militants today, turning humanity from victim into agent provides not so much the justification as the very content of their violence . . . bringing a global humanity to the fore'. Faisal Devji, *The Terrorist in Search of Humanity: Militant Islam and Global Politics*, London: Hurst, 2008, 30, 17.
3   Jacques Derrida, 'Faith and Knowledge: The Two Sources of "Religion" at the Limits of Reason Alone', in *Religion*, J. Derrida and G. Vattimo (eds), Stanford: Stanford University Press, 1998, 6.

insanely defend an identity or a territory. As we will see, nineteenth-century British pundits, imperial administrators and counter-insurgency experts characterized the rebels they encountered from India to the Sudan as 'fanatics', grudgingly recognizing their partisan valour and local solidarities while arguing for their elimination. At other times, it was not resistance to dispossession but the unconditional affirmation of universal rights, or of a universal human nature beyond any hierarchy or distinction, which was deemed fanatical. The hugely influential polemics against the French Revolution composed by Edmund Burke, Hippolyte Taine and many others fit into this category. Their writings turned the Jacobin into the very archetype of the modern fanatic: a reckless innovator 'possessed with a spirit of proselytism in the most fanatical degree'; zealously attacking religion 'in the spirit of a monk'; laying waste to custom, property and manners, decreeing laws and parcelling out territories – all in a frenzy of abstraction forcing upon human affairs 'the monstrous fiction' that they could be handled like mathematical theorems or geometrical objects.[4] Burke's vitriol against the 'tyranny of the politics of theory'[5] sets the template for treating all advocates of radical equality as dangerous fanatics – most evidently in the nineteenth-century attacks against American abolitionism, but also throughout the history of the workers' movement in its socialist, anarchist and communist strands. Warnings against philosophical 'fanaticks', spreading the 'political metaphysics' of unconditional equality and the Rights of Man,[6] were often accompanied by a conspiratorial sociology preoccupied with the explosive alliance between deracinated intellectuals and impulsive mobs.[7]

---

4 Edmund Burke, *Reflections on the Revolution in France*, L. G. Mitchell (ed.), Oxford: Oxford University Press, 1993 [1790], 110, 37.

5 Conor Cruise O'Brien, 'Edmund Burke: Prophet Against the Tyranny of the Politics of Theory', in Edmund Burke, *Reflections on the Revolution in France*, F. M. Turner (ed.), New Haven: Yale University Press, 2003 [1790].

6 Burke, *Reflections on the Revolution in France*, 58.

7 For Taine, 'Jacobinism is no more than a doctrinal disease arising from a combination of ideology and social maladjustment; and Enlightenment rationalism was a utopian abstraction which might have remained relatively innocuous had it not intersected with the interests of psychopathic and marginal lawyers without briefs, doctors without patients, untenured holders of useless university degrees, and so on.' See Patrice

The anti-revolutionary critique of fanaticism promoted a remarkably enduring model of explanation and polemic, depicting the social
implementation of philosophy – understood as an atheistic, abstract and
universalizing doctrine – as the very essence of fanaticism. In what is
perhaps the founding gesture of the counter-Enlightenment, it turned
the *philosophes'* attack on religious fanaticism against the politics whose
very groundwork they had laid – asking, for instance: 'Is this horrible
fanaticism not a thousand times more dangerous than that inspired by
religion?'[8] Burke did not mince his words:

> These philosophers are fanaticks; independent of any interest, which if it
> operated alone would make them much more tractable, they are carried
> with such an headlong rage towards every desperate trial, that they would
> sacrifice the whole human race to the slightest of their experiments. . . .
> Nothing can be conceived more hard than the heart of a thorough-bred
> metaphysician. It comes nearer to the cold malignity of a wicked spirit
> than to the frailty and passion of a man. It is like that of the principle of
> Evil himself, incorporeal, pure, unmixed, dephlegmated, defecated evil.[9]

Coldness was the very predicate chosen by Herder to identify philosophy's dangerous fanaticism, for which he employed the term *Schwärmerei*,

Higonnet, 'Terror, Trauma and the "Young Marx" Explanation of Jacobin Politics', *Past
and Present*, 191 (2006), 125. Mme de Carrière, mentor to the liberal Benjamin Constant,
asked 'What are the constituent parts of Jacobinism?' Her answer is emblematic: 'the
manipulation by a few fanatics and by a horde of ambitious men of the envy of the poor
who want to be rich' (quoted in Higonnet, 137). On the sociology and political economy
of Burke, who linked the activism of revolutionary intellectuals to the destructive effect
of financial speculation, with both destroying custom, religion and any fixed standard
of value, see J. G. A. Pocock, 'Edmund Burke and the Redefinition of Enthusiasm: The
Context as Counter-Revolution', in F. Furet and M. Ozouf (eds), *The French Revolution
and the Creation of Modern Political Culture*, Vol. 3: *The Transformations of French Political
Culture, 1789–1848*, Oxford: Pergamon Press, 1989.

8   Madame de Genlis, quoted in Darrin M. McMahon, *Enemies of the Enlightenment:
The French Counter-Enlightenment and the Making of Modernity*, New York: Oxford
University Press, 2001, 45. A very useful survey of this strand of thought, also cover-
ing unalloyed reactionaries like De Maistre and Rivarol.

9   Edmund Burke, 'A Letter to a Noble Lord', in *Further Reflections on the Revolution
in France*, D. E. Ritchie (ed.), Indianapolis: Liberty Fund, 1992, 314.

coined by Luther to castigate the theologies of peasant revolt. For Herder, philosophy and fanaticism became synonymous: 'If it was a philosopher who named our century the age of philosophy, perhaps he understood thereby the century of cold *Schwärmerei* and *schwärmender coldness*. . . . The *Schwärmer* wants to be the greatest philosopher, and the greatest philosopher is the greatest *Schwärmer*.'[10] Underscoring the link between abstraction, confusion (swarming), and mass behaviour (swarming, again), critics of the Enlightenment like Herder or Lessing posited a close and dangerous link between the philosopher and he who '*schwärmt* for the rights of man', to use Lessing's expression. Such thinkers identified 'a perverse dialectic between unrestrained subjectivism and collective frenzy – or, perhaps better, between the implosion of the individual self and the explosion of the collective self'.[11]

In so doing, they mined the linguistic and etymological resources of the family of terms that we are investigating here under the rubric of fanaticism. Where *Schwärmerei* denotes confusion, unrealism, and a menacing multitude, a swarm,[12] while enthusiasm (*Enthusiasmus*, *enthousiasme*) evokes a

---

10   Johann Gottfried Herder, 'Philosophei und Schwärmerei, zwo Schwestern', quoted in Anthony J. La Vopa, 'The Philosopher and the *Schwärmer*: On the Career of a German Epithet from Luther to Kant', in *Enthusiasm and Enlightenment in Europe, 1650–1850*, San Marino, CA: Huntington Library, 1998, 92. Also: 'In the emotionalism of revolutionary politics, as in religious fervor, individual introversion and collective frenzy entered a frightening dialectic' (105). Testifying to the resilience of this schema for the understanding of the link between theory and politics, Perry Anderson characterized 'the fashionable philosophy of Parisian irrationalism', with its central notion of Desire, as a 'subjectivist *Schwärmerei* that followed disillusionment with the social revolt of 1968'. See *Arguments within English Marxism*, London: New Left Books, 1980, 161.
11   La Vopa, 'The Philosopher and the *Schwärmer*', 98. I originally came to the topic of fanaticism by considering the writings of one of the philosophical inheritors of this debate, the young Schelling. See my 'Fanaticism and Production: Schelling's Philosophy of Indifference', *Pli: The Warwick Journal of Philosophy* 8 (1999).
12   Coleridge emphasized the link between the cognitive and collective dimensions of *Schwärmerei* in a memorable passage: 'A debility and dimness of the imaginative power, and a consequent necessity of reliance on the immediate impressions of the senses, do, we well know, render the mind liable to superstition and fanaticism. Having a deficient portion of internal and proper warmth, minds of this class seek in the crowd *circum fana* for a warmth in common which they do not possess singly. Cold and phlegmatic in their own nature, like damp hay, they heat and inflame by co-acervation; or like bees they become restless and irritable through the increased temperature of collected multitudes. Hence the German word for fanaticism (such at

divine inspiration that finds its Greek sources in Plato's philosophy,[13] fanaticism proper (*Fanatismus, fanatisme*) derives from the Roman term *fanum*, referring to a consecrated place (the opposite of this being the profane, and the act of disrespecting the *fanum*, profanation).[14] In particular, *fanatici* was the name given to the followers of the Cappadocian goddess Comana, introduced to Rome as Bellona. 'In celebrating the festival of the goddess they marched through the city in dark clothes, with wild cries, blowing trumpets, beating cymbals and drums, and in the temple inflicting wounds upon themselves, the blood from which they poured out as an offering to the goddess'.[15] Without engaging in genealogical fallacies – as we'll see there are many uses of fanaticism that bear little relation to this cultic model[16] – in this origination we can see the sign not just of an inaugural

least was its original import) is derived from the swarming of bees, namely, *schwärmen, schwärmerey*.' Samuel Taylor Coleridge, *Biographia Literaria*, New York: William Gowans, 1852, 163. For an astute and original treatment of *Schwärmerei* and swarming with reference to Freudian and Lacanian psychoanalysis, see Justin Clemens, 'Man is a Swarm Animal', in *The Catastrophic Imperative*, D. Hoens, S. Jöttkandt and G. Buelens (eds), Basingstoke: Palgrave, 2009.

13 Margot and Rudolf Wittkower, *Born Under Saturn*, New York: New York Review of Books, 2007, 98.

14 On the principally French and German histories of fanaticism as both *Fanatismus* or *fanatisme* and *Schwärmerei*, see Werner Conze and Helga Reinhart's impressive entry 'Fanatismus', in *Geschichtliche Grundbegriffe. Historisches Lexicon zur politisch-sozialen Sprache in Deutschland*, Vol. 2, O. Brunner, W. Conze and R. Koselleck (eds), Stuttgart: Klett-Cotta, 1975. Following translations of 'fanaticism' into non-European languages and intellectual traditions, or investigating autochthonous concepts that have similar uses would be a very interesting project, though one that lies well beyond my competence. It is interesting to note that the modern term used to translate fanaticism into Arabic, *ta'assub*, is derived from the term *'asabiyyah*, which denotes bonds of tribal solidarity and partisan feeling, and is discussed in Ibn Khaldun's crucial fourteenth-century universal history, the *Muqaddimah*. In 1879, al-Afghani wrote that the 'fanaticism (*ta'assub*) of those who adhere to the same religion and concur on the principles of the creed is expressed in a balanced agreement that avoids injustice in actions that regard the community, does not offend those who are different and does not undermine their protection'. In this definition, 'fanaticism' is obviously not the simple antonym of tolerance. See Biancamaria Scarcia Amoretti, *Tolleranza e guerra santa nell'Islam*, Florence: Sansoni (Scuola Aperta), 1974.

15 William Smith, 'Fanum', in *Dictionary of Greek and Roman Antiquities*, W. Smith, W. Wayte and G.E. Marindin (eds), 2nd ed, London: John Murray, 1890.

16 For instance, in a symptomatic misunderstanding that linked religious frenzy to psychopathology, modern authors invented a Greek etymology for the term, linking it to notions of fantasy. Dominique Colas, whose *Civil Society and Fanaticism* provides a

link with religion, but of a preoccupation with the religion of the other (Bellona was not the state cult, but had been brought back by legionaries from their Anatolian campaigns) and with unchecked violence. The description of the cult's vital by a Roman contemporary foreshadows many of the portraits of indomitable religious 'fanatics', from Canetti's account of the Persian Muharram in *Crowds and Power* to Voltaire's tableau of theological possession in the *Dictionnaire Philosophique*: 'Once set in motion by the transports of Bellona, in her frenzy she fears neither the heat of the fire nor the blows of the whip. With a double-edged hatchet, she violently wounds her arms, sprinkling the goddess with blood, yet feeling no pain. Standing, her side pierced by a dart, she prophesies events which the powerful goddess makes known to her.'[17] It is from the Roman Empire too that a frequent synonym for fanatic, *zealot*, derives. This was a specifically political term, deriving from the religiously motivated Jewish resistance against colonial Rome in Palestine. In terms redolent of two millennia of counter-insurgency literature, Josephus, chronicler of the Jewish rebellion, speaks of nationalist and spiritual enthusiasm as a surrogate for military weakness, of 'animal courage for which no numbers were a match', of men joining battle 'with their passions in command'.[18] Political violence and intransigent emotions are certainly one of the concerns of this book, but my principal focus will be on the various configurations taken by the idea of fanaticism in philosophy and theory, with particular attention to its shifting polemical uses and what they might reveal both about the critics of fanaticism and about the types of political behaviour that elicit this accusation.

---

very useful if ideologically strident survey of the term's uses, notes this semantic spillover: 'even before the appearance of *fanatique*, a pseudo-Greek double, *phantastique*, has been used by Calvin for the Anabaptists as the equivalent of the Latin *fanaticus*. There was in fact a kind of indistinct competition between the two French terms, *phantastique* (occurring first in the texts) and *fanatique*, and between the two spellings, *ph-* and *f-*, with the latter gradually taking over'. Dominique Colas, *Civil Society and Fanaticism: Conjoined Histories*, trans. A. Jacobs, Stanford: Stanford University Press, 1997, 12.

17   Tibullus, quoted in Robert Turcan, *The Gods of Ancient Rome*, London: Routledge, 2001, 116.

18   Josephus, *The Jewish War*, trans. G. A. Williamson, ed. and rev. E. M. Smallwood, London: Penguin, 1981, 249. See also the appendix on 'Bandits, Terrorists, Sicarii and Zealots', 461–2.

Philosophically, the response to fanaticism is broadly divided between thinkers who regard it as the outside of reason, the persistent threat of pathological partisanship or clerical irrationality, and those who instead perceive some unconditional and unyielding abstract passion as intrinsic to a universalizing rationality and an emancipatory politics. Very roughly, this is where the difference between Voltaire's *Lumières* and the *Aufklärung* of Kant and his epigones (or between the pre- and the post-revolutionary Enlightenment) is to be located. While the former treats philosophy as the nemesis of fanaticism, the latter views fanaticism as a potentiality inherent to reason, and even regards political enthusiasm as inextricable from a rational or universalizing politics. In revisiting, through the prism of fanaticism, a critical and dialectical lineage that travels through Kant, Hegel and Marx — but also through Sigmund Freud, Ernst Bloch and Alain Badiou — this book will go on to examine the recent calls for what we might term an 'Enlightenment reloaded', urging us all to *écraser l'infâme*, whether in the guise of Islamic militancy or Christian fundamentalism. The present fortunes of the term 'fanatic' as a political epithet can be linked to this nostalgic and sloganeering turn to a certain image of the eighteenth-century Enlightenment, in particular to its diagnosis and excoriation of religious intolerance as the principal motor behind political violence, social destabilization and intellectual backwardness.[19] Today's 'rentiers of the Enlightenment',[20] showing neither the intellectual inventiveness nor the political courage that marked the practice of the *philosophes*, think it enough to broadcast denunciations of irrationality and demands for a muscular secularism

---

19   See, among many others, Amos Oz, *How to Cure a Fanatic*, Princeton: Princeton University Press, 2006 (on the Israel/Palestine conflict); Alain Finkielkraut, 'Fanatiques sans frontières', *Libération*, 9 February 2006, and Fernando Savater, 'Fanáticos sin fronteras', *El País*, 11 February 2006 (both responding to the so-called 'cartoon controversy' following the Danish publication of caricatures of Mohammed); André Grjebine, *La guerre du doute et de la certitude. La démocratie face aux fanatismes*, Paris: Berg International, 2008; Walter Laqueur, *The New Terrorism: Fanaticism and the Arms of Mass Destruction*, Oxford: Oxford University Press, 1999. The recent pleas for atheism in the books by Christopher Hitchens and Richard Dawkins are also in many ways based on this model.
20   Isabelle Stengers, *Au temps des catastrophes. Résister à la barbarie qui vient*, Paris: La Découverte, 2009.

– all the while deeming the immanent philosophical and social critiques of the Enlightenment, as well as the historical reflections on its colonial and imperial uses, to be irrelevant. The prevalence of demonizing and superficial treatments of fanaticism is among other things a symptom of the incapacity of our broader intellectual culture to incorporate the lessons of the different waves of critique, the mutations and supersessions of Enlightenment that constitute the legacy of nineteenth- and twentieth-century critical political and philosophical thought. One of the aims of this book's detour through political and philosophical history is to undermine this lazy and pernicious reliance on a one-dimensional Enlightenment, together with some of its corollaries: in particular the relegation of extreme or unyielding political behaviour to the domain of psychopathology, and the often related culturalization of political fanaticism as a manifestation of the Arab mind, Asiatic despotism, Hebrew theocracy or what have you. As Edward Said noted apropos of terrorism (the contemporary magnet for talk of fanaticism), such essentializing visions 'serve the purpose of . . . institutionalizing the denial and avoidance of history', and obscure political understanding by 'a kind of metaphysical purity of horror'.[21] If it is true that 'no other epoch but ours is defined by its campaigns against its primitive rebels',[22] investigating the intellectual and emotive frameworks that govern the perceptions of insurgent ideologies can contribute to orienting ourselves in an otherwise opaque present.

There is a certain irony in approaching fanaticism historically, since one of the abiding features of its employment as a term of abuse is that it is frequently presented as an ahistorical or even anti-historical phenomenon. To describe an agent or an action as fanatical is to lend them a kind of monolithic invariance. Among the most striking aspects of the uses of fanaticism as a political trope is the reliance on analogy, simile, homology. Whether it is the short-circuit between Lenin, Hitler and Thomas

---

21   Edward W. Said, 'The Essential Terrorist' and 'Michael Walzer's *Exodus and Revolution*: A Canaanite Reading', in *Blaming the Victims*, Edward W. Said and Christopher Hitchens (eds), London: Verso, 1988, 149, 176. For a caustic and illuminating survey of imperialist uses of left-liberal anti-fanaticism in the recent period, see Richard Seymour, *The Liberal Defence of Murder*, London: Verso, 2008.
22   Gopal Balakrishnan, *Antagonistics*, London: Verso, 2009, 71.

Müntzer in Norman Cohn's seminal *The Pursuit of the Millennium* (aptly translated into French as *Les fanatiques de l'apocalypse*),[23] Michel Foucault's sympathetic analogies between the 'spiritualization of politics' in the Iranian Revolution and the figures of Cromwell and Savonarola,[24] or Hegel's pairing of Mohammed and Robespierre in *The Philosophy of History*, the discourse on fanaticism often seems to suggest that when it comes to the politics and subjectivity of unconditional conviction we can ignore chronology and geography.[25] While liberals, authoritarians or even radical reformists may come in all sorts of guises, it appears that fanatics not only do not differ from themselves, since their conviction seems impermeable to dialogue, they also do not really differ from one another (even if, in religious or civil wars, they may be uncompromising adversaries). Whence the repetitiousness of much writing about 'fanaticism', so often resorting to lists and descriptions, copious inventories of cruelty, intolerance and monomania that postulate, but rarely analyze or define, an invariant core. Not just zealots, but their critics, too, seem to be 'embosomed in . . . monotony'.[26] So, is there no history of fanaticism, or only, at most, a catalogue of its crimes and delusions? It is not so easy to answer in the affirmative, for a number of reasons. To begin with, there is the widespread conviction, voiced by Rousseau, Kant and Emerson among others, that any true human achievement, any historical

---

23   Norman Cohn, *The Pursuit of the Millennium*, 2nd ed, London: Mercury Books, 1962, 307–19. For some interesting critical comments on the limits of the analogy between Stalinism and religious extremism, see Richard Stoker, 'Fanaticism and Heresy', *New International*, 14: 1 (1948), 31.

24   Michel Foucault, 'Tehran: Faith Against the Shah', in Janet Afary and Kevin B. Anderson, *Foucault and the Iranian Revolution: Gender and the Seductions of Islamism*, Chicago: University of Chicago Press, 2005.

25   This can also be true of those rare political actors and thinkers who reclaim fanaticism as their position. As Joel Olson writes about the abolitionist Wendell Phillips: 'Placing [Toussaint] L'Ouverture alongside great figures of history like Mohammed, Napoleon, Cromwell, and John Brown, Phillips acknowledges that L'Ouverture "had a vein of religious fanaticism, like most great leaders".' Importantly, Phillips also had criteria for differentiating between them: 'Yet L'Ouverture is greater than Cromwell and Napoleon, for their genius was limited by military exploits or tainted by racism.' See Joel Olson, 'Friends and Enemies, Slaves and Masters: Fanaticism, Wendell Phillips, and the Limits of Democratic Politics', *Journal of Politics*, 71: 1 (2009), 93.

26   William James, *The Varieties of Religious Experience: A Study in Human Nature*, New York: Macmillan, 1961 [1902], 278.

act, requires, if not fanaticism proper, than at least its nobler cousin, enthusiasm. Furthermore, for many the drastic and 'fanatical' denial of a history understood in terms of gradual change or development, a denial that may take millenarian or messianic forms, is the *conditio sine qua non* for a properly modern experience of historical and political time as a time of breaks and anachronisms, discontinuities and irreversibilities.

One of the perhaps more obvious motivations for undertaking this conceptual and historical inquiry is the relatively recent rise in discourse about fanaticism. Though end of history narratives such as Francis Fukuyama's relegate fanatical drives to the 'zones of history' within an otherwise post-historical liberal order, many essayistic and journalistic treatments of the question, though they may note the technological instrumentalities of contemporary religious radicalism, treat fanaticism as anti-historical, anachronistic, atavistic: the revenge upon global modernity of peoples without history, but impassioned by transcendence. This is one of the paradoxes that I will try to investigate: the disruptive force of fanaticism lies in its explicit refusal of history as a domain of gradualism and mediation, combined with its *de facto* interruption of history as a naturalized dimension of predictable combinations. The pervasive uncertainty as to whether fanaticism is anti-historical, or a revenge of history, indicates profound tensions in our conceptions of change and action.

Whether by a ruse of reason or a heterogenesis of ends, the violent severance from the rhythms of custom – or from the time of deliberation and negotiation – would thus be what permits the unfolding of a notion of politics that harbours an unelimimably utopian, even transcendent dimension. Fanaticism here points towards a type of action that is, as I've suggested, at once sub-historical and supra-historical, but also towards forms of subjectivity that, for related reasons, oscillate between the anti-political and the ultra-political. When the accusation of fanaticism is used to disqualify or reject certain modes of political behaviour or allegiance from the normalized and normalizing vantage-point of a liberalism at once gradual and eternal, it is often difficult to tell whether we are dealing with the refusal to allow other forms of life now separated from the political to trespass into its realm (as in the secular critique of fanaticism), or whether the real problem is that of an excess of politics.[27] Indeed, it could be argued that fanaticism lends itself so well to a symptomatic inquiry into a hegemonic liberalism because it exposes a fundamental ambivalence in liberalism's apologetic discourse about the place of politics. An investigation of fanaticism can therefore prove instructive, both to the reflexive liberal and to those whom liberalism might be tempted to class as fanatics.

To reiterate: the superiority of a post-Kantian critical tradition when it comes to dealing with fanaticism lies in its commitment to exploring this vital ambivalence or dialectic, allowing us to reflect on how our conception of politics cannot be sundered from potentially ultra- or anti-political notions of absolute conviction, just as our notions of history collapse into mere developmentalism or naturalism if they expunge the kind of discontinuity and transcendence that marks fanatical or millennarian politics. David Hume's contention that political enthusiasm, unlike superstition, can be incorporated into a pacified polity provides an interesting and unimpeachably liberal corollary to our argument.[28] Though he judges both to be corruptions of religion, for Hume superstition and enthusiasm belong to different affective constellations: the first derives from weakness, fear, melancholy and ignorance; the second, though it shares ignorance with superstition, has its sources in hope, pride, presumption and a warm imagination. This clinical catalogue explains why, despite its epistemic deficit and unlike superstition, for Hume enthusiasm shares with 'sound reason' and philosophy an

---

27   For a philosophical statement of the exclusive alternative between liberalism and fanaticism as moral and political stances, see R. M. Hare, *Freedom and Reason*, Oxford: Oxford University Press, 1963. Liberalism stands on the side of a pluralist and tolerant morality of interest, while fanaticism (exemplified by or even equated with Nazism) represents an aberrant mode of moral evaluation, concerned only with the content of ideals and overriding the interests even of the fanatic himself. 'The enormity of Nazism is that it extends an aesthetic style of evaluation into a field where the bulk of mankind think that such evaluations should be subordinated to the interests of other people. The Nazis were like the emperor Heliogabalus, who, I have been told, had people slaughtered because he thought that red blood on green grass looked beautiful' (161).

28   This is why for Pocock he represents 'the last man to welcome the experience of the revolutionary dialectic'. J. G. A. Pocock, 'Enthusiasm: The Antiself of Enlightenment', in *Enthusiasm and Enlightenment in Europe, 1650–1850*, 22.

antinomian resistance to 'priestly power'. 'All enthusiasts', he writes, 'have been free from the yoke of ecclesiastics.' Enthusiasm is portrayed by Hume as having a developmental arc, beginning with violent fury and progressing towards moderation, as can be seen among Anabaptists, Levellers and Quakers. Its 'presumptuous boldness of character . . . begets the most extreme resolutions', producing 'the most cruel disorders'. But enthusiasm's 'fury is like that of thunder and tempest, which exhausts itself in a little time, and leave[s] the air more calm and serene than before'. The rejection of an official authority that would structure and prolong religious fury is what allows enthusiasm to 'cool', but also what counter-intuitively makes it a 'friend' of civil liberty: 'As superstition groans under the dominion of priests . . . enthusiasm is destructive of all ecclesiastical power. . . . Not to mention, that enthusiasm, being the infirmity of bold and ambitious tempers, is naturally accompanied with a spirit of liberty; as superstition, on the contrary, renders men tame and abject, and fits them for slavery.'[29] Such a comprehension of the virtues of what William James called the 'partisan temper'[30] is of course something alien to the vast majority of today's self-avowed liberals, for whom fanaticism is simply the absence of progressive history and the foe of consensual politics, an atavistic regurgitation proving, if proof were needed, the enduring urgency of enforcing secularism and securing Enlightenment.

For such sworn enemies of intolerance, fanaticism is something to be exorcised in order to move from an intransigent politics of conviction to a pluralist ethics of responsibility. But whether fanaticism has its own history, or indeed whether it plays a motive function in historical change, can we think of a history without fanaticism? Some indications for an answer are provided in a text written almost a hundred years after Hume's essay, one that also deals with the entanglement between the violence of religious sentiment and the politics of emancipation. 'Hegel's *Philosophy of Right* and the Politics of Our Times' was published in 1842 in the oppositional journal *Deutsche Jahrbücher* by the Young Hegelian

---

29   David Hume, 'Of Superstition and Enthusiasm', in *Essays Moral, Political and Literary*, Eugene F. Miller (ed.), Indianapolis: Liberty Fund, 1985, 75–8.
30   James, *The Varieties of Religious Experience*, 272.

and collaborator of Karl Marx, Arnold Ruge. Reflecting on the key problem of his time, the relationship between Church and State, Ruge declared that religion manifests itself as *desire* (*Lust*) for liberation, while fanaticism represents an 'intensified religion', or rather a *passion* (*Wollust*) for liberation that is born from a prior failure, from a blockage of the routes to emancipation. As in much of German political and philosophical thought, the French Revolution and Terror loom large, with their 'insane' but comprehensible attempt to crush the obstacles to freedom. In his phenomenology of the fanatic's 'practical pathos', Ruge shows himself to be one of our contemporaries. As he writes: 'when there is something to explode, one goes up in smoke with it, so that ultimately, while not sparing oneself, one also sacrifices others *horribly* to one's purposes'.[31] But while many of our talking heads might read this pathos (or pathology) in abstraction from its context of motivation, for Ruge it was a consequence of the failure to incorporate the passion for liberation into the mechanisms of the State. That is why he declared that 'as long as there are batteries to man and positions to defend with one's life, we will have no history without fanaticism'.[32]

Against the comforting idea that fanaticism is an irrational aberration, to be vanquished by some combination of pedagogy and coercion, this book wants to stay true to Ruge's recognition of the threads that tie fanaticism to emancipation.[33] To this end, it considers a series of

---

31   Arnold Ruge, 'Hegel's *Philosophy of Right* and the Politics of Our Times', in *The Young Hegelians: An Anthology*, Lawrence S. Stepelevich (ed.), Cambridge: Cambridge University Press, 1983, 236. The older Ruge would anticipate twentieth-century theories of political religion and castigate communism for combining 'religion of the spirit and fanaticism in the deed'. See Conze and Reinhart, 'Fanatismus'.

32   Ibid.

33   The fact that this book is not written from a prior acceptance of liberal democracy as the only legitimate horizon of politics sets it apart from historical and diagnostic works like Colas's *Civil Society and Fanaticism* (itself more of a continuation of anti-fanatical discourse than a study of its operations); Josef Rudin, *Fanaticism: A Psychological Analysis*, trans. E. Reinecke and P. C. Bailey, Notre Dame: University of Notre Dame Press, 1969; André Haynal, Miklos Molnar and Gérard de Puymège, *Fanaticism: A Historical and Psychoanalytical Study*, New York: Shocken, 1983; Michèle Ansart-Dourlen, *Le fanatisme. Terreur politique et violence psychologique*, Paris: L'Harmattan, 2007. Dourlen's relatively nuanced estimation of the Jacobins, her attention to Sartre's theory of 'fraternity-terror' and her interest in Reich's mass psychology of fascism make her book a useful contribution, despite its over-reliance on political psychology.

historical episodes or conjunctures in which political and philosophical thought delved into the threat, ambivalence and possible promise contained by the figure of the fanatic. Though fanaticism is rarely, if ever, an object of political affirmation,[34] serving almost invariably as a foil against which to define the proper path of politics, like its kin enthusiasm it is also 'a foil that [is] difficult to control' – both because it comes to inhabit as a possibility any politics of conviction wedded to 'abstractions' such as equality and emancipation, and because anti-fanatical politics so often finds itself justifying a kind of counter-fanaticism, in which the supposed partisans of reason and Enlightenment inoculate themselves with the virus affecting their enemies and justify their acts with the prose of counter-insurgency. Just think of Richard Nixon's notorious 'madman theory', according to which the enemies of the US 'should recognize that we are crazed and unpredictable, with extraordinary destructive force at our command, so they will bend to our will in fear'. [35] The most powerful inquiries into fanaticism, and the ones more

---

34 Despite its inspiring reclamation in the practice of American abolitionism, the most glaring case of a positive political use of the term fanaticism – Nazism – speaks against any simplistic contrarian rush to assert its qualities. In his brilliant and harrowing philologist's notebook on what he called the *Lingua Tertii Imperii*, Victor Klemperer noted that under Nazi rule, the words *fanatisch* and *Fanatismus* were 'used as frequently "as there are notes on a violin or grains of sand on the beach"'. Klemperer argues that 'the complete transformation of fanaticism into a virtue', hidden away in Rousseau's defence of civic fanaticism in *Emile*, was fully realized as it became a 'key National Socialist term', appearing in 'literally every single one of the countless pledges of allegiance to the Führer'. While before 'the Third Reich no one would have thought of using the word "fanatical" in a positive sense', under National Socialism, which 'is founded on fanaticism, and trains people to be fanatical by all possible means, the word "fanatical" was, throughout the entire era of the Third Reich, an inordinately complimentary epithet'. Victor Klemperer, 'Fanatical', in *The Language of the Third Reich: LTI – Lingua Tertii Imperii: A Philologist's Notebook*, trans. M. Brady, London: Continuum, 2006, 52–6. Later chapters will provide some orientation around this vexed question of the affirmation of fanaticism: while the Nazis' reclamation is directly targeted against the legacy of the Enlightenment, the abolitionists had reappropriated a political insult coming from a Burkean, pro-slavery, and in many respects *counter*-Enlightenmental camp. Where that of the Nazis was a fanaticism of vicious hierarchy, that of the abolitionists was one of unconditional equality.

35 Noam Chomsky, *Rogue States*, London: Pluto, 2000, 20. The neo-conservative thesis, that Western liberalism must fanaticize itself in order to combat the fanaticism of radical Islam, is at the core of Lee Harris's *The Suicide of Reason: Radical Islam's Threat to the West*, New York: Basic Books, 2007.

likely to allow us some distance from facile condemnations, are those that recognize the considerable if unsettling affinities between political behaviour stigmatized as fanatical, and rational, emancipatory politics.

By situating the current concern with passionate commitments in terms of the polemical history of fanaticism, this book aims to enhance the conceptual horizons of debates that rarely move beyond static juxtapositions between conviction and responsibility, fervour and reasonableness, decision and deliberation.[36] Indeed, part of my purpose is to mine a set of theoretical debates and controversies around fanaticism so as to reconstitute a political vocabulary capable of accommodating both enthusiasm and abstraction as inextricable elements of any politics of emancipation. In this regard, every chapter of this book should be read both as a critical excavation of the place of fanaticism in a discourse of demonization, and as a search for conceptual elements that might help us to reconstruct a theory of political abstraction not so easily dismissed as mere fanaticism.

Neither a history of fanaticism properly speaking nor a systematic theory of it, this book thus seeks to read the dark adventures of this idea with its mind on a present in which it has once again come to be used as term of abuse or political smear word – rarely, if ever, with the kind of depth or even the insight shown by the great reactionaries of yesterday. But it also intends, by a kind of counterpoint, to explore these various episodes of denunciation in order to contribute to the thinking of an egalitarian politics, one that will undoubtedly continue to be perceived by its detractors as an abstract and dangerous passion.

---

36   In this sense, I appreciate Sophie Wahnich's suggestion that emotions in politics should be considered 'not as ahistorical instincts but as historical variables articulated with a social history of beliefs, expectations and hopes'. *La longue patience du peuple. 1792. Naissance de la République*, Paris: Payot & Rivages, 2008, 38.

1

Figures of Extremism

Always, everywhere, John Brown was preaching the primacy of the act.
'Slavery is evil,' he said, 'kill it.'
　'But we must study the problem . . .'
　Slavery is evil – kill it!
　'We will hold a conference . . .'
　Slavery is evil – kill it!
　'But our allies . . .'
　Slavery is evil – kill it!

Lerone Bennett Jr., *Tea and Sympathy:*
Liberals and Other White Hopes

The fanatic enters the horizon of politics as an enemy, an inscrutable, intransigent and alien enemy. The elimination of the fanatic is closely linked to the administration of the social and cultural terrain from which he has sprung. Accordingly, though it is never clear whether there is a discourse of the fanatic, there is no shortage of discourses on fanaticism, on its causes, its modalities, its remedies. This was especially true in the latter half of the nineteenth century, a period in which imperial liberalism's twin struggles against the lower classes and the subject races attained remarkable intensity, and in the process lent the notion of fanaticism a number of novel applications. It is to this period that I will now turn, to explore the theoretical debate on the figure of the fanatic, or of passionate and partisan conviction, as manifest in twentieth-century politics and particularly in the retrospective judgments on the 'age of extremes'. This will provide a broader context for the historically-informed theoretical inquiry into the idea of fanaticism that will occupy later chapters. In both instances, the capacity of liberal thought to identify, and demarcate itself from, fanaticism will be at stake.

Part I: Fanaticism in the Age of Empire

SLAVERS AGAINST FANATICISM

Few but the most hardened contemporary adversaries of liberalism would tax it with support for slavery. *Prima facie*, a doctrine founded on the safeguarding of individual negative freedoms, the autonomy of civil society and the limitation of governmental prerogative would seem to recoil before the most unequivocal curtailing of rights and liberties imaginable. And yet, as recent critical histories have underscored, during its intellectual and political apogee, advocacy for liberalism was often accompanied by apology for human bondage.[1] The neutralization of this glaring contradiction took place, according to the Italian historian and philosopher Domenico Losurdo, through various operations of demarcation of the 'sacred space' of civic and commercial freedoms from the 'profane space' of oppression, racism and imperialism, on which the very viability of the sacred space often rested. In this view, whether by geographical or racial means (the latter often being combined with social antagonism into varieties of 'class racism'), classical liberalism developed as a democracy for the master-race (or class); a *Herrenvolk* democracy that would only slough off many of its most unsavoury characteristics through the struggles that pitted capitalist liberalism against social movements for workers' equality, and imperialist liberalism against anti-colonial, anti-racist and national liberation struggles. Though this thesis jars profoundly with the dominant self-image of contemporary liberalism, it appears as a persuasive and powerful way of reconciling its doctrines and its concrete historical unfolding, without succumbing to the facile historicist thesis according to which liberalism simply and gradually grew in extension (to the propertied middle classes,

---

1   The comments in this paragraph relate primarily to Domenico Losurdo, *Controstoria del liberalismo*, Bari: Laterza, 2005. But see also Ellen M. Wood, *Democracy Against Capitalism*, Cambridge: Cambridge University Press, 1995.

then to the lower classes, then to women, then to people of colour . . .) while retaining an intact original inspiration – a thesis refuted by the presence, alongside and against really-existing liberalism, of radical and egalitarian movements already demanding that which much of mainstream liberalism would only later concede.

One of the principal characters in Losurdo's counter-history of liberalism – indeed the one who prompts him to make the apparent paradox of pro-slavery liberalism into the guiding theme of his revision of accepted wisdom – is the Southern political thinker and twice Vice-President of the United States, John C. Calhoun.[2] In his writings and speeches, especially his notorious February 1837 speech in the US Senate where he described slavery as a 'positive good', the figure of the abolitionist as a 'fanatic' appears repeatedly. Calhoun relates the ominous and contagious threat of anti-slavery agitation by the 'fanatical portion' of the North's population to the classical liberal concern with the limitation of government power. Abolitionism is repeatedly described as 'incendiary', and intriguingly seen as a movement from below – from the ignorant and impoverished, to the pulpit, and finally to the House. It was given much of its impetus, according to Calhoun, by the extension of the powers of the central Government, effectively signalling the end of federalism in favour of a 'great national consolidated democracy'.[3] Now that the abolitionists of the North rightly estimate that the Government has the power to act, they immediately conclude that it is their inexorable responsibility to terminate the 'peculiar institution'. A fundamental commitment to racial supremacy, depicting slavery as the ideal social configuration in the South, is thus combined with an impeccably liberal argument about the necessary limitation of government and the legislative autonomy of states. As Calhoun declares: 'I fearlessly assert that the existing relation between the two races in the South, against which these blind fanatics are waging war, forms the most solid and durable foundation on which

---

2 Losurdo, *Controstoria del liberalismo*, 3–9. On the broader issue of the 'twin birth' of liberalism and slavery, and the nature of US and British liberalism in the eighteenth and nineteenth centuries, see Chapters 2 and 4 of Losurdo's book.
3 Calhoun, *Union and Liberty: The Political Philosophy of John C. Calhoun*, R. M. Lence (ed.), Indianapolis: Liberty Fund, 1992, 582.

to rear free and stable political institutions.'[4] Calhoun's political doctrine explicitly linked fanaticism to crisis.[5] The argument for preserving the 'liberty' of the slaveholding South is accompanied by a Burkean link between the fanatical 'spirit of abolition' and the financial 'spirit of speculation'.[6] Calhoun's apologia for the institution of slavery is explicitly framed in terms of a contrast with the socially destabilizing effects of capitalist exploitation and class struggle in the North and in Europe, and is aimed at averting 'the conflict between labor and capital'.[7] But the ultimate accusation against the 'blind fanatics' concerns the unconditional character of their demand, which threatens the institutional order of differences and the social basis of customs upon which the South rests. As Calhoun declares to the Senate:

> If we do not defend ourselves none will defend us; if we yield we will be more and more pressed as we recede; and if we submit we will be trampled under foot. Be assured that emancipation itself would not satisfy these fanatics – that gained, the next step would be to raise the negroes to a social and political equality with the whites; and that being effected, we would soon find the present condition of the two races reversed.[8]

Whence the note on which the speech ends, typical of so many critiques of fanaticism, whose corollary is more often than not a call for some variety of anti-fanatical fanaticism: in order to avert the levelling, divisive spirit of abolitionism, the southerners must 'unite with zeal and energy in repelling approaching dangers'.[9]

A year before Calhoun's 'positive good' speech, an anonymous book – later to be ascribed to another Southern politician, Colonel William Drayton – was published, with the striking title *The South Vindicated*

---

4   Ibid., 474. See the remarks on Calhoun's take on fanaticism, in the context of the emergence of a trans-Atlantic radicalism, in Losurdo, *Controstoria del liberalismo*, 162.

5   Calhoun, *Union and Liberty*, 67.

6   Ibid., 466.

7   Ibid., 474–5.

8   Ibid., 475.

9   Ibid., 476.

from the Treason and Fanaticism of the Northern Abolitionists.[10] Mainly comprising an elaborate and copiously footnoted comparative history of slave societies by way of justification for the 'peculiar institution', *The South Vindicated* is of interest to us over and beyond its role as an index of fanaticism's use as a political smear word. At a deeper level, it also attests to some of the constants in anti-fanatical rhetoric. Echoing Calhoun in his view of abolitionist fanatics as agents of division and disturbance, worrying the national wounds, which the nation's constitution and institutions had sought to heal, Drayton also cleaves much closer to previous philosophical characterizations of fanaticism. Alluding to fanaticism as a disturbance in cognitive faculties, Drayton writes of 'fanatics – who mistake the promptings of their overheated fancy – the vapours that rise from the molten lead of their seething brains – for the dictates of inspiration': a vision that goes back to Plato's treatment of enthusiasm in the *Ion*, which played a very prominent role in the aesthetic, political and religious controversies of the eighteenth century. Drayton combines this with a widespread medicalization of fanaticism, when, despairing of their corrigibility, he contends that 'the tranquillizing chair or strait jacket is the only effective argument' against fanatics.[11] Contagion, another mainstay of the discourse on fanaticism, is likewise a dominant feature of the 'abolition conspiracy', with its perversion of the Christian faith – fanatics are 'constantly fulminating religious denunciations' – and its targeting of women, whose emotional susceptibility to the inflammatory exhortations of the abolitionists occupy Drayton at some length. But at the heart of Drayton's asseverations there lies what

---

10   It turns out that Drayton was a friend of Edgar Allan Poe, who met him during his time in South Carolina and dedicated to him a book of his short stories. The attribution of a very favourable and intensely pro-slavery anonymous review of Drayton's book in *The Southern Messenger*, which Poe edited at the time, has been cause of much controversy. For a recent survey and analysis of this incident, and of Poe's views on race, see Terence Whalen, *Edgar Allan Poe and the Masses: The Political Economy of Literature in Antebellum America*, Princeton: Princeton University Press, 1999, Chapter 5.
11   William Drayton, *The South Vindicated from the Treason and Fanaticism of the Northern Abolitionists*, Philadelphia: H. Manly, 1836, xiv. This approach is also very prominent in Drayton's psycho-pathological portraits of abolitionist leaders. See *The South Vindicated*, Chapter 13.

we have already identified as the principal stake of the debate on fanaticism: abstraction. In *The South Vindicated* we find a remarkable crystallization, outside the domain of philosophy proper, of the notion of fanaticism as a key weapon in the rhetorical arsenal of an anti-egalitarian (but in its own way liberal) political thought:

> [B]y applying abstract but cherished axioms, without reference to consequences, [the abolitionists] urge a course which could never bear the test of cool and practical examination. It is the misfortune of our country that we reason from abstractions. We establish the principle that all men are created free and equal; and following it out, without regard to consequences, often infer that a community of goods is required by a rigid respect for the rights of man. It was this delusion, this proneness to rush recklessly on in the course marked out by some dreamy abstraction, which plunged revolutionary France into the reign of terror.[12]

As a politics of abstraction, fanaticism is to be condemned for its unconditional character ('without regard to consequences') and its refusal of measure and moderation. Though the broader principles that inspired the French Revolution may be sound, they become fanatical when 'pushed to extremes' and detached from any calculation of utility and feasibility. As so often, 'common sense' is pitted here against 'the misty abstractions of fanatical enthusiasts'.[13] Considering the link Drayton draws between the abolitionists' fanaticism and the Terror, it is little surprise that 'the splendid and philosophical mind of Burke'[14] looms so large in this defence of Southern slavery against the rising tide of abolitionism. Not only did Burke explicitly praise the 'spirit of liberty' in the slaveholding South,[15] he provided the definitive verdict

---

12   Ibid., 80.
13   Ibid., 81.
14   Ibid., 107. The gap between the extremism of principles and the customary and fallible circumstances of the empirical existence of rights was a mainstay of Burke's argument. For example: 'The pretended rights of these theorists are all extremes; and in proportion as they are metaphysically true, they are morally and politically false.' Burke, *Reflections on the Revolution in France*, 62.
15   Drayton, *The South Vindicated*, 108. See also Losurdo, *Controstoria del liberalismo*,

on the French Revolution as the precursor of abolition. Besides being 'the first and most devoted champions of abolition',[16] the French revolutionaries, as Burke presciently recognized, also heralded the unlimited extension 'without regard to consequences' of abstract rights, with chilling political effects. As proof of the dangers of this terrorist heritage of egalitarianism, Drayton turns to the question of women – so easily swayed by the incendiary religious rhetoric of the abolitionists, yet so at risk from the 'negroes' saturnalia of blood and lust' which will inevitably follow emancipation. As Burke showed, it is the Jacobins 'from whom the fanatics derive their notions of abolition, [who] directly undertook to assure the rights of woman. . . . To such lengths will these abstractionists carry their insane zeal'.[17] 'Abstractionists': this term lies at the core of the Burkean tradition of anti-fanaticism and its excoriation of a politics whose putative disregard for consequences bears frightful omens for a social order of hierarchy, difference and division. Among the effects of the abolitionists' refusals of measure and gradualism is something that Drayton's reader, he thinks, might greet with incredulity, considering it 'impossible that human delusion, even under the impulses of a heady fanaticism, can turn into absurdities so gross and disgusting' as the following: 'they might give us a black president'.[18] Like so many of his contemporaries on both sides of the Atlantic, Drayton will treat the Haitian revolution as the bogeyman to wave in the face of anyone insensitive to the dangers that lurk within political universalism:

39–40. The reference is to Burke's 1775 speech on conciliation with America. See Edmund Burke, *The Writings and Speeches of Edmund Burke, Vol. III: Party, Parliament, and the American War, 1774–1780*, W. M. Elofson and J. A. Woods (eds), Cambridge: Cambridge University Press, 1996, 122.

16 Drayton, *The South Vindicated*, 171.

17 Ibid., 181 (note). The last sentence relates specifically to the equal right of divorce that, in Burke's commentary, the French revolutionaries drew from their fanatical extension of the rights of man . . . to women. (Cf. Burke on 'women lost to shame' in *Reflections on the Revolution in France*, 69.) Drayton also goes back to 'the days of Cromwell' (179) to find analogies for the disruptive fanaticism, at once political and religious, incarnated by the abolitionists.

18 Ibid., 155.

[France's] principles were generally sound; but pushed to extremes, and followed without regard to practical results, they led to consequences at which the world even now turns pale. It was the prevalence of the spirit alluded to [of fanaticism and abstraction], which induced the French policy towards St. Domingo; and not only lost that colony to France and to the world, but rendered it a Phlegethon, in which evil spirits held, for years, their carnival of blood.[19]

In Calhoun and Drayton we experience the powerful rhetorical and political uses to which the idea of fanaticism was put in defending slavery against the threat of an uncompromising egalitarianism. In *The South Vindicated* we can also observe the endurance of some key aspects of the discourse on fanaticism which have persevered into the present, as I will suggest in the second half of this chapter. These include the warnings about egalitarian and universalist abstraction, the threat of religious agitation, the analogies across political domains, the pathologization or medicalization of the fanatic, and the role of women. Criticism of abolitionism as an excess of intransigence, if not an outright aberration, was by no means limited to the advocates of slavery. Abraham Lincoln himself referred to the great abolitionist militant John Brown in the following terms: 'An enthusiast broods over the oppression of people until he fancies himself commissioned by Heaven to liberate them.' Referring to Brown's raid at Harper's Ferry, Lincoln continued: 'He ventures the attempt which ends in little else than his own execution.'[20] The philosophical movement most closely identified with the United States, pragmatism, has also been seen to emerge in partial reaction to the violence and upheaval of the Civil War, regarded as a trauma in which the abolitionists' politics of principle 'marched the nation to war

---

19   Ibid., 80. The Phlegethon is a flaming river in the underworld of Greek mythology; in Dante's *Inferno* it is a river of blood where men of violence and tyrants are boiled alive. For the place of Haiti in anti-egalitarian liberal discourse and in the antagonistic formation of a radical tradition, see Losurdo, *Controstoria del liberalismo*, Chapter 5.

20   Lincoln, cited in *Chicago Defender* editorial (1959), in Benjamin Quarles (ed.), *Allies for Freedom & Blacks on John Brown*, Cambridge, MA: Da Capo, 2001, 125.

to the brink of self-destruction in the name of an abstraction'.[21] But what of the abolitionists themselves? What was their response to being stigmatized as blind fanatics, fulminating wildly in the mists of abstraction?

FANATICS AGAINST SLAVERY

As Joel Olson has recently shown, in work that makes a rare contribution to what he terms a 'critical theory of zealotry'[22] – a theory in which the consideration of fanaticism challenges the limitations of liberal political theory – the epithet 'fanatic' was worn as a badge of pride among the radical wing of the abolitionist movement.[23] Moreover, it was incorporated into a theory and practice of political rhetoric, agitation and action. Crucial figures like William Lloyd Garrison and Wendell Phillips were 'self-defined fanatics'. What did this entail? Explicitly working against the grain of a contemporary common sense that expediently identifies fanaticism and terrorism, as well as in contradistinction to political theories that expel intransigence beyond the hallowed bounds of democracy, Olson shows how the political posture and affective rhetoric employed by the abolitionists implied an understanding of politics that challenges

---

21   Louis Menand, *The Metaphysical Club*, London: Flamingo, 2002, 374. Menand notes the consequent impossibility, from within a pragmatist framework, of grasping a politics of principle: 'Pragmatism explains everything about ideas except why a person would be willing to die for one' (375). It is strange but telling in this respect that he nonetheless chooses to talk of the 'antipolitics' of abolitionism (20).

22   Joel Olson, 'The Freshness of Fanaticism: The Abolitionist Defense of Zealotry', *Perspectives on Politics* 5: 4 (2007), 686. The title is taken from the letter of an abolitionist, Abby Kelley, where she writes: 'We should pray to be preserved in the freshness of our fanaticism.' For Olson, such a critical theory means disputing the 'pejorative tradition' in the understanding of fanaticism, which treats 'zealotry as an individual, moral, or psychological defect rather than as a political activity engaged in by actors seeking to transform the public sphere' (685). Though I am less sympathetic to Olson's reliance on Schmitt's friend/enemy distinction as a mode of political antagonism, and my polemical concerns transcend the questions of liberal political theory, the spirit of this book resonates with much of what Olson has articulated against the 'pejorative tradition' in his recent articles. Indeed, Olson's project, to be developed into a book entitled *American Zealots*, is to my knowledge the only theoretical treatment of fanaticism whose intellectual agenda is comparable to the one advanced in this book.

23   For an interesting example of the reclamation of the term 'fanatic' by an abolitionist Democrat, see William Leggett's 'Progress of Fanaticism' (1837), in *Democratic Editorials: Essays in Jacksonian Political Economy*, Indianapolis: Liberty Fund, 1984.

some of our core presumptions about the political. Where deliberation
and consensus, or at the very least agonism and compromise, seem to
demand that principles test themselves against practicability and rival
opinion, the 'immediatists' in the abolitionist camp rejected the very
possibility of anything short of unconditional emancipation and total
equality. This did not mean mere intolerance, or a refusal of dialogue,
nor did it necessarily involve, as the stereotype goes, the theological
demonization of pro-slavery advocates or slaveholders (they were, for
instance, allowed at abolitionist meetings). Rather than a question of
blind possession or 'misty abstraction', the political style of abolitionism
was founded, alongside an ethical rejection of compromise, on a sober
estimation of the strategic weakness of deliberative politics when it came
to ending slavery. The fanaticism of the abolitionists was thus both a
matter of passionate conviction and of meditated strategy, combining
the attractions of symbolism and affect with the instruments of power
and calculation. The radical abolitionist was a 'reasonable zealot', for
whom means and ends could not be sundered.[24] Drawing lines and exacerbating divisions – the very activities that pro-slavery anti-fanatics like
Drayton and Calhoun railed against – was part and parcel of the abolitionists' practice. In Wendell Phillips, abolitionist 'talk' was to inflame
an 'insurrection of thought', and to force fence-sitters and moderates to
choose sides. Such talk was not aimed at deliberation or consensus, but
sought instead 'to forge a new public opinion, one that is abolitionist
and antiracist, and through it to win the struggle between friends and
enemies, slaves and masters, apostles of justice and traders in human
flesh'.[25] Viewed through the lenses of radical abolitionism, fanaticism
is 'the political mobilization of the refusal to compromise'.[26] Though
unquestionably illiberal and intolerant, if we assume certain parameters for political deliberation, fanaticism, in its attack on the accepted

---

24 Olson, 'The Freshness of Fanaticism', 691. Olson has also expanded this reflection in a provocative comparative study of John Brown and the anti-abortion militant
(and murderer) Paul Hill, 'The Politics of Protestant Violence: Abolitionists and Anti-
Abortionists' (unpublished). As he writes: 'Religious violence is both symbolic and
strategic because it merges means and ends.'
25 Olson, 'Friends and Enemies, Slaves and Masters', 90.
26 Ibid., 83.

frameworks of politics, can also serve an indispensable emancipatory function. In other words, the lesson of abolitionism as fanaticism is that 'there can be democratic potential in the fanatical encouragement of intractable conflict'.[27] But Olson's inquiries into American zealotry also point to another dimension of political fanaticism, which we will touch on in response to Sloterdijk's attack on Left *ressentiment*: solidarity. Fanaticism, especially conceived of in terms of its justifications of political violence, often takes the form of a passionate identification with the suffering and the oppressed in which sympathy turns into ontology, an ontology where antagonism is written into the very being of political subjects and the recipients of their solidarities.[28]

In this connection, it is significant that W. E. B. Du Bois's biography of John Brown spoke of him as 'the man who of all Americans has perhaps come nearest to touching the souls of black folk'. In a memorable passage, Du Bois takes up a number of the themes in the arsenal of anti-fanatical discourse (religious conviction, intransigence, the French Revolution), combining them in an elegy of the politics of abstraction as a deeply human politics:

> Was John Brown simply an episode, or was he an eternal truth? And if a truth, how speaks that truth to-day? John Brown loved his neighbor as himself. He could not endure therefore to see his neighbor poor, and unfortunate or oppressed. This natural sympathy was strengthened by a saturation in Hebrew religion which stressed the personal responsibility of every human soul to a just God. To this religion of equality and sympathy with misfortune, was added the strong influence of the social doctrines of the French Revolution with its emphasis on freedom and power in political life. And on all this was built John Brown's inchoate but growing belief in a more just and more equal distribution of property. From this he concluded – and acted on that conclusion – that all

---

27 Ibid.
28 See Olson, 'The Politics of Protestant Violence'. Olson notes the profound political ambiguities of these fanatical identifications, which span Brown's 'black orientation' (to cite Quarles) and Paul Hill's apocalyptic solidarity with the unborn. In both instances, the ontological character of conflict and oppression mean, according to Olson, that any violent act is experienced as a form of self-defence.

men are created free and equal, and that the cost of liberty is less than the price of repression.[29]

But the plea for fanaticism as unconditional universalism that we can hear in these lines, and which pervaded the thinking of 'immediatist' anti-slavery militants, remains, for all of its instructive and inspirational value, isolated. On several fronts, the nineteenth century saw the development of a plural, social-scientific and governmental discourse of fanaticism, one that prolongs some of the Burkean themes encountered in the likes of Calhoun and Drayton and focuses above all on immunizing the state, or the Empire, against destabilizing and antagonistic movements. In the imperial arena, particularly among the British, the development of racializing theories of religiously-driven political resistance sees fanaticism becoming a key term in the attempts to manage anti-colonial politics.[30] In a European context, this entails the pathologization of movements for radical social change – principally anarchism, but also emergent forms of feminism. An inquiry into nineteenth-century efforts to govern and police fanaticism can enrich our understanding of the strategic uses of the idea of fanaticism, laying some of the groundwork for a more conceptual inquiry into the philosophical and theoretical uses of the term.

---

29   W. E. B. Du Bois, *John Brown*, D. Roediger (ed.), New York: The Modern Library, 2001, 225. Thoreau's 'A Plea for Captain John Brown' (1860) had already spoken of Brown's 'immortal life'. See Henry David Thoreau, *Civil Disobedience and Other Essays*, New York: Dover, 1993, 47.

30   The use of fanaticism as a term with which to brand opponents of imperial and colonial policies was not exclusive to the British. Reversing Catherine II's eighteenth-century policy of tolerance and 'Islamization', and explicitly relying on the *Lumières'* understanding of religious *fanatisme* as a key threat to political order and unity, Russian Tsarist administrators employed it to identify Islamic political movements in Central Asia. See Abdel Khalid, *Islam After Communism: Religion and Politics in Central Asia*, Berkeley: University of California Press, 2007, 37. Stigmatization of participants in anti-colonial movements as 'religious fanatics' was also present, for instance, at the very beginning of the twentieth century in US 'counter-insurgency' rhetoric in the Philippines, with strong parallels to the current 'war on terror'. See Reynaldo C. Ileto, 'Philippine Wars and the Politics of Memory', *positions*, 13: 1 (2005), 223. In the context of his visits and reports on France's colonization and warfare in Algeria, Tocqueville also identified fanaticism as a key concern in terms of the prevention of anti-colonial uprisings. See Losurdo, *Controstoria del liberalismo*, 229–37.

FANATICISM UNDER EMPIRE

In their encounters with the armed resistance of religious groups, colonial administrators in India's North-Western Frontier Province wrote of 'Hindustanee fanatics', 'enthusiasts' and 'Muhammadan bigots', with a mixture of fright and admiration for their valour and virility.[31] In the twenty years after the 1857 Mutiny, the information-gathering and knowledge-processing apparatus of the Empire tried to deal with the threat of Wahhabism, both in the Anglo-Afghan Wars and internally, as a potentially subversive response to the repression of the Sepoy rebellion. Following Ranabir Samaddar, we can situate the rhetoric of fanaticism within the broader development of 'bio-political' modalities of rule by the occupying colonial administration. Here government 'meant the physical tasks of watching, disciplining, deploying, annihilating, besides the paltry task of the welfare of the bodies and the minds of the colonised'.[32] Relying on non-Wahhabi Muslim informants, administrators wrote of the Wahhabis as 'a fanatical, dangerous sect, daily increasing in numbers and power, having for their object the overthrow of the existing Government, and for their creed the double assurance that the slaughter of an infidel, or death received at his hands, is a certain passport to happiness in a future life'.[33] The Wahhabi threat was not primarily perceived in terms of their numbers or strategy; the unconditional intransigence and transcendent authority of their 'fearless speech' played

---

31   Charles Allen, *God's Terrorists: The Wahhabi Cult and the Hidden Roots of Modern Jihad*, London: Abacus, 2007, 13–14. This sensationally titled history is typically aimed at drawing lessons for the 'post-9/11' present from the record of colonial encounters and analyses, exemplifying a widespread and unsurprising identification between contemporary Anglo-American commentators and their colonial precursors. Allen advocates in his conclusion a preventive response to the grievances that stoke the flames of fanaticism (Palestine, Iraq), echoing some of the colonial administrators' own responses to religious fanaticism.

32   Ranabir Samaddar, *Emergence of the Political Subject*, New Dehli: Sage, 2010, 45.

33   Letter from the Acting Collector of Kurnool to the Secretary of the Board of Revenue, 26 April 1866, quoted in Samaddar, *Emergence of the Political Subject*, 43. Samaddar hints at the class differences behind certain aspects of religious sectarianism: 'The rich and cultivated Muslims loathed the Wahhabis, in exactly the same way as the latter hated the rich, corrupt, wealthy, and established Muslims.' Among the other interesting elements in Samaddar's account are the parallels made by the administrators between the suppression of Wahhabis and that of Irish Fenians.

a key part.[34] But what was especially menacing, according to Samaddar, was the manner in which they provided anti-imperialism with a kind of racial ontology, albeit not one congruent with the occupiers' understanding of race: 'It was the raw arrogance of counter-racism, inevitable under colonial conditions, that struck at the root of the legitimacy of colonial occupation.'[35] Indeed, we could regard fanaticism as a kind of cipher for the seemingly intractable problem, thrown up by the practices of imperial occupation and colonial exploitation, of governing subject peoples who could draw on a reservoir of religious virtue and oppositionalism against the forces of a secular modernity that they could only enjoy, at best, in a derivative or subordinate manner. The duplicitous universalism of imperial occupation was confronted with another brand of universalism, one of a theological and antagonistic kind, in which death and sacrifice played a signal role.

Though evidently marked by the exigencies of governing particular populations in specific political conjunctures, the colonial use of the idea of fanaticism displays many stable features. The Mahdist revolt in the Sudan in the 1880s led a wide swathe of British opinion to turn to the notion of a 'dervish fanaticism' to account for the fearlessness and ferocity of their opponents, whose motivations were viewed as religious. The Marquess of Salisbury wrote of Arabs 'fighting in their own country, skilled in their own warfare, and animated by that formidable mixture of religious fanaticism and military spirit which the religion of Islam seems alone to have the secret of conferring upon its votaries'. Like Calhoun in his Senate speech of 1837, British Army officers would seek to identify

---

34   The mixture of admiration and trepidation at the steadfastness of the Wahhabis is evident from one of the reports quoted by Samaddar: 'The Wahabee movement is in the nature of revival. They seek to re-establish the pure doctrines of their religion. They reject the intercession or worship of Saints, and all forms and ceremonies. They worship God alone as a Sprit and deny any divine characteristics to Mohamed himself. So far, no exception can be taken to their tenets, and they contrast favourably with their co-religionists. The only danger is that being earnest men they may seek to carry out in full all the precepts of their religion, including that of the *"jehad"*, or direct hostility to every other creed. Experience shows that a very dangerous spirit exists amongst the members of this sect . . .' *Emergence of the Political Subject*, 62.

35   Ranabir Samaddar, *Emergence of the Political Subject*, 84.

the 'fanatical portion' of the population.[36] Fanaticism is here revealed as an element in a kind of spontaneous anthropology, which 'explains' martial virtues and practices, even evincing a peculiar kind of respect, but also justifies policies of no quarter. The *Daily Telegraph* could thus declare how

> Under the influence of certain powerful motives they rise easily to abso-lute heroism and none more potent than religious fanaticism. A romantic chivalry towards women makes the Arab prize very highly their appro-bation of his personal courage, and his poetry incites him to exploits of veritable knight-errantry. . . . Indeed the Bedouin considers nothing manful but violence, nothing so honourable as war.

The naturalization and racialization of 'fanatical' anti-colonial violence could accordingly allow British soldiers to depict their own stagger-ing brutality as unavoidable: 'they are the pluckiest fellows I've ever seen . . . We shot & bayoneted all wounded as it was not safe to leave them as they speared or knifed everyone they could reach.' And another wrote of how his 'trusty claymore found its way to the hilt into several black devils. I clove a piece out of one of their heads just as one does an egg for breakfast . . . I was mad with rage and fury . . . I fought like a demon & only wanted to kill, kill, kill those awful plucky demons.'[37] As mentioned before, the notion of fanaticism (here in the figure of the 'plucky demon') often triggers a profound mimetic impulse: *because* the adversary is a fanatic I cannot but counter his madness with my own, pre-empt his cruelty before it is visited upon me.

Throughout these colonial writings we encounter the problem that still preoccupies today's commentators and administrators as they strug-gle with the realities of contemporary anti-imperial fanaticism – that of explanation. Those wishing to quell seemingly religious insurgencies are embroiled in 'causative controversies', where the aetiological question

---

36 Quoted in Edward M. Spiers, 'Dervishes and Fanaticism: Perception and Impact', in Matthew Hughes and Gaynor Johnson (eds), *Fanaticism and Conflict in the Modern Age*, London and New York: Frank Cass, 2005, 20, 21.
37 Ibid., 22–3, 25.

— why the uprising? — is inextricable from the political, administrative and military question of how to respond. To take the case of India again: was the British Empire to operate on the assumption that disturbances of the peace had purely militant-religious sources, or was it to look to ulterior, principally socio-economic causes? On the one hand we have administrators communicating to their superiors thoughts such as the following: 'I have been unable to trace the insurrection in Beerbhoom to any thing but fanaticism.'[38] On the other, those who think that religion is merely an expedient mode for the organization and manipulation of a discontent whose source lies elsewhere will say that fanaticism 'flourishes only upon sterile soil'.[39] This explanatory antinomy has yet to go away, as analysts and pundits debate whether religious militancy is the *ultima ratio* for insurgent anti-occupation politics, or whether the task at hand is to 'drain the swamp' of poverty and social discontent.

But the same problem is also one of the foremost conundrums for contemporary critical thought. Whereas a causal approach to fanaticism, scoping out 'root causes', often indicated the presence of a broadly reformist or governmental (rather than simply antagonistic or exterminatory) approach in colonial agents, much of the thrust of postcolonial theory and subaltern studies has been to refuse the reduction of religious consciousness in insurgents to some other, principally socio-economic

---

38   Quoted in Ranajit Guha, 'The Prose of Counter-Insurgency', in *Subaltern Studies 2*, R. Guha (ed.), Delhi: Oxford University Press, 1983, 35. Guha bases his critique of elitist theories of religious subaltern consciousness on the difference between reports written in the heat of insurgency, and retroactive explanations of the uprisings. The former treat religiosity as a mobilizing cause in its own right (as one of the reports has it: 'These Sonthals have been led to join in the rebellion under a persuasion which is clearly traceable to their brethren in Bhaugulpore, that an Almighty & inspired Being appeared as the redeemer of their Caste & their *ignorance & superstition* was easily worked into a *religious frenzy* which has stopped at nothing'); the latter suggest that religion is merely an instrument for the manipulation of benighted plebs. As Guha comments: 'The insurgents are regarded here as a mindless "rabble" devoid of a will of their own and easily manipulated by their chiefs' (35). As we shall see in the next chapter, he thinks that the model of history adopted by nationalist and Marxist historians replicates this condescension towards the insurgents.
39   William Logan, quoted in Ronald J. Herring, 'From "Fanaticism" to Power: The Deep Roots of Kerala's Agrarian Exceptionalism', in *Speaking of Peasants: Essays on Indian History and Politics in Honor of Walter Hauser*, W. R. Pinch (ed.), New Delhi: Manohar, 2008.

dimension. Whether in a sociological or a Marxist vein, such a reduction would relegate the consciousness of the oppressed to the domain of illusion or false consciousness, thereby subordinating them to the will and intellect of their disenchanted and manipulative leaders, or of historians and theorists treating their case in retrospect. For Ranajit Guha, viewing religion as a matter of manipulation or propaganda is tantamount to 'denying a will to the mass of rebels themselves and representing them as instruments of some other will', and testifies to 'the failure of a shallow radicalism to conceptualize insurgent mentality except in terms of an unadulterated secularism'.[40] I will return to this problem. It suffices for the moment to note the issue that Guha brings into relief: the question of fanaticism, understood in this instance as the insurgent religious consciousness of the colonized, is one in which the political and the epistemological are closely entwined, where frameworks of explanation are difficult to separate from political commitments and prescriptions.

THE PHYSIOGNOMY OF SUBVERSION

To conclude this preparatory survey of some figures and problems of fanaticism in the Age of Empire, I want to turn to the incorporation of the notion of fanaticism into the political and sociological criminology of the nineteenth century. As has been widely argued, both the shock of the Paris Commune – signalling, despite its brutal repression, that social upheaval and a radical alternative to capitalism could irrupt in the midst of the imperial metropolis – and the diffusion of radical ideas and actions (especially in the guise of anarchist terrorism) played an important role in the emergence of the social sciences as attempts to prevent or channel social antagonisms. It is perhaps not surprising that the fanatic, as a figure of pathological politicization, should also be found in this context. The much-maligned originator of modern criminology, Cesare Lombroso, makes a particularly interesting use of the term.[41] Yet, for all

---

40   Guha, 'The Prose of Counter-Insurgency', 38, 37.
41   For a detailed and insightful reconstruction of the political and scientific context of Lombroso's criminal anthropology, especially its link to the challenges posed by Italian unification, see Daniel Pick, *Faces of Degeneration: A European disorder, c. 1848–c. 1918*, Cambridge: Cambridge University Press, 1989, 109–52. Pick concludes that: 'The purpose of Italian criminal anthropology can be found, then, in the attempt

his positivist insistence on identifying, where possible, the congenital and pathological determinants of all forms of crime, political included, Lombroso's handling of fanaticism shows him to be a far more complex figure than his metrological obsessions with ears and brows might let on. Lombroso is significant for his explicit recognition that the secular polities of the final quarter of the nineteenth century were no longer affected by explicitly *religious* fanaticism. But even if the adjective disappears, the noun remains: surveying the turbulent social landscape of his time, Lombroso will encounter 'monoideist' fanaticism (the tendency to exaggerate ideals), along with the 'lively desire to feel and suffer' that one might associate with religious martyrs.[42] We even encounter the transhistorical analogies with seemingly unrelated fanatics – in this case Hassan-i Sabbah's Assassins – so typical of the discourse on fanaticism.[43] But the phenomenology of earlier forms of intransigent conviction – in any case perfectly explicable on scientific grounds for the Italian criminologist – has passed over into a new form of fanaticism: 'economic or social fanaticism'.[44]

Given Lombroso's notorious inclination to postulate biological origins for social deviance, it is notable that for him the bearers of 'altruistic fanaticism' – though they may reach pitches of 'delirium' – cannot easily be reduced to the status of 'born criminals'.[45] In fact, political criminals proper are 'the opposite of the criminal type'.[46] Lombroso articulates one of the peculiar constants of discourse on fanaticism, or on political and ideological extremism more broadly: the notion that 'fanatics'

---

to construct an ordered language for the containment of disorder and, through that language, to formulate the definition of a political subject by elaborating ever more closely the criteria for political exclusion' (139).

42   Cesare Lombroso, *Les anarchistes*, 2nd ed, trans. M. Hamel and A. Marie, Paris: Ernest Flammarion, 1896, 116; Cesare Lombroso, *Criminal Man*, ed. and trans. M. Gibson and N. H. Rafter, Durham, NC: Duke University Press, 2006 [1876–97], 314.

43   Lombroso, *Les anarchistes*, 127.

44   Lombroso, *Criminal Man*, 313.

45   Lombroso, *Les anarchistes*, viii–ix. Lombroso also has some interesting reflections on what we could somewhat facetiously call a geography of fanaticism: 'The convergent points of valleys are also the points of convergence of populations which follow the route traced by their political, moral and industrial needs. It is also there that one will find the greatest number of innovators and revolutionaries' (172).

46   Lombroso, *Criminal Man*, 313.

may also embody commendable or indispensable values and virtues. In *Criminal Man*, Lombroso writes of these 'passionate souls, whose ranks include history's most noble figures . . . the pioneers in the struggles for political, religious and social liberty'.[47] Determining the border between political excess and actual pathology leads the Italian criminologist into some rather peculiar differentiations, motivated by his own reformist political proclivities. Thus the fanaticism of Russian nihilists is absolved from anatomical aetiology, while French and Italian revolutionaries and anarchists – whose ribald songs, calligraphic idiosyncrasies, sexual fetishes and abnormal ears Lombroso records in inadvertently comical and novelistic detail – are condemned for their degeneracy. The likes of Vera Zasulich are thus admired for the beauty and harmoniousness of their 'anti-criminal' physiognomies, while Marat is identified as macrocephalic and Louise Michel disparaged for her 'muscular physiognomy'.[48] The difference between necessary revolutions (likened to organic crises) and pathological revolts is thus strangely projected onto the distinction between, on the one hand, political passions born of free will and ideas (which in this account seem to be irreducible to necessity), and, on the other, biological compulsion.[49]

But though Lombroso deems many of the anarchists to be born degenerates who 'hide under the mask of political passion their criminal tendencies', or 'political hysterics and epileptics',[50] it is nonetheless the case that his suggestions for social therapy are not principally eugenic or penal in character. Like the colonial administrators who opted for socio-economic accounts of fanaticism, Lombroso proposes (alongside punitive measures, which in any case are to be both lenient and flexible for political criminals)[51] to deal with the root causes. It is in this light that

---

47   Ibid., 314.
48   Lombroso, *Les anarchistes*, 101–2; Lombroso, *Criminal Man*, 313.
49   See Lombroso, *Les anarchistes*, 38–40. The section is entitled 'Revolution and Rebellion'.
50   Ibid., 55, 59.
51   Demonstrating an enlightened sensitivity almost entirely absent from today's debates on amnesties for political prisoners, Lombroso suggests that political crimes should be retried at five-year intervals, to ascertain if society's overall outlook has caught up with those of the subversives or revolutionaries, whose crimes would thus be nullified. Lombroso, *Les anarchistes*, 155.

he also wishes to oppose his reformist socialism both to anarchist insurrectionalism and to the blinkered corruption and incompetence of existing governments. The analogy he draws between religious and political
fanaticism is suggestive:

> The sole remedy against our political criminals who are such from acci-
> dent, from passion, from imitation, or from poverty, consists in reme-
> dying the economic uneasiness in the country, since this is the true basis
> for anarchy. We have to-day an economic fanaticism, as we formerly
> had a political fanaticism. It is imperatively necessary that we should
> open a vent for this economic fanaticism with economic reforms, as we
> have opened one for political fanaticism with constitutional and repre-
> sentative government, and for religious fanaticism with freedom of
> worship.[52]

One of the more intriguing aspects of Lombroso's treatment of the question is the link he draws between violent political conviction and novelty.
The political criminal is in fact curiously exempt from a condition that
according to Lombroso affects the majority of the population: hatred of
the new, or misoneism. Fanaticism, whether congenitally founded or
purely political in origin, is a kind of neophilia.[53]

The question of fanaticism also emerges contemporaneously in
another influential criminological paradigm, partly congruent with that
of Lombroso: that of Gabriel Tarde, an author who has found new favour
in social theory. Despite a not dissimilar political temperament, Tarde
distances himself from the hypothesis of the 'born criminal', arguing that
the conditions of social organization and communication – embodied
especially, at the end of the nineteenth century, in the mounting significance of the press in shaping political sentiments and movements – make
it necessary to employ explanations that combine the sociological and

---

52   Cesare Lombroso, *Crime, its Causes and Remedies*, trans. Henry P. Horton,
London: W. Heinemann, 1911 [1899], 329–30. Elsewhere, he writes: 'The most radical
remedies would be those which diminish the exaggerated centralisation of property,
wealth and power and which would give a guaranteed livelihood to all those who have
the intelligence and the force to work.' Lombroso, *Les anarchistes*, 210.
53   Lombroso, *Criminal Man*, 315; Lombroso, *Les anarchistes*, 158–9.

the psychological, giving relatively short shrift to biology, heredity or climate (and 'race' in general). Tarde is also concerned with the problem posed by the virulence of 'criminal sects', anarchism in particular. But his explanation centres on categories of collective action, in particular on crowds and publics conceived in terms of the fundamental forces of desire, belief and imitation. It is not in the individual that the sources of insurrectionalism are to be sought, but in a particular circulation of affects and ideas, aided and abetted by their material support in new forms of communication. Tarde thus elaborates on Gustave Le Bon's influential theses on crowds. The crowd manifests both irrationality and repetition. Its 'intense collective life' is 'a terrible alcohol for the brain'. The crowd is fascinated and stupefied by its own spectacle. Its activity is sterile and ultimately identical, from Müntzer's peasants to the mobs of the Terror, and on to contemporary riots.[54] 'Today's *dinamitards*', writes Tarde, 'simply take up the nightmare of the millenarians.'[55]

But Tarde devotes his most original reflections to the new collectivities of the age of newspapers: publics. Where crowds are affected by the tumultuous but relatively short-lived contagion effected by physical proximity and horde behaviour, publics – or 'spiritualized crowds' – are much weirder entities. On one level Tarde suggests – and his epigones in the public relations industry would make much of this – that publics, with their dispersion, immateriality, and action at a distance, may neutralize the physical threat to order and stability posed by crowds. On another, he realizes that publics are a kind of *pharmakon*, an antidote to the frenzies of multitudes that might provoke auto-immune reactions of sorts, presenting dangers far greater than those of crowds, with their spatial and temporal finiteness. What he calls 'hate publics' are hence more threatening than raging crowds, since 'the public is a far less blind and far more durable crowd, its more perspicuous rage accumulates and sustains itself over months and years'.[56] Though Tarde, more suspicious of group action than Lombroso, thinks that all collectivities are

---

54   Gabriel Tarde, *L'opinion et la foule*, Paris: PUF, 1989 [1901], 55 (on the inebriated crowd), 58 (on the spectacle), 159 and 181 (on Müntzer and the Terror).
55   Ibid., 177.
56   Ibid., 62.

menacingly prey to the passions and inevitably harbour 'a deplorable susceptibility to the excitations of envy and hatred',[57] he argues – referring to the spread of both anti-Semitism and doctrines of social revolution – that publics as immaterial crowds are a specific danger of the 'new democracies', pushed this way and that by the guile of demagogic writers who are, of course, capable on a whim of crystallizing dispersed publics into baying, 'acephalic' mobs. But though he too refers to fanaticism as a kind of political monomania, a pathology of excessive conviction, his real concern is with forms of social 'hypnotism'.[58] Manipulation and susceptibility, rather than steadfastness and intransigence, make up his paradigm. Fanaticism is here a matter of ideas, but these don't take the form of incontrovertible principles, so much as currents and imitations that come to incite people as they act collectively. Viral contagion, not personal possession, is the model.

Tarde's work also foregrounds the gender element of fanaticism, to which I have already alluded. Whereas Lombroso had noted the higher proportion of women among political criminals – that is, among criminals whose actions are not a function of biological defects and for whom, as we saw, Lombroso has a peculiar type of respect – Tarde focuses not on pure conviction but on frenzied susceptibility. Writing at a time when the idea of 'female crowds' might very well have suggested the first stirrings of the suffragette movement, Tarde repeatedly underscores the particularly fierce, 'fanaticized' character of women acting in concert. And though he talks of male and female crowds, male and female publics, Tarde suggests there is something specifically female about the manipulable irrationality and inconsistent passions of collectivities.[59] There is an echo here of the eighteenth-century discussion of the exclusively feminine phenomenon of the *convulsionnaires* of St Medard, which linked religious fanaticism, the group behaviour of women and 'nymphomania'; and which juxtaposed the comparably irrational, but

---

57   Ibid., 69.

58   See for instance his essay on 'hate crimes' in *Essais et mélanges sociologiques* (1895), where he writes of fanaticism in terms of '*idées fixes*, self-immolation to a disastrous and homicidal ideal'.

59   Tarde, *L'opinion et la foule*, 50, 58, 163.

possibly creative inspiration of the *fureur prophétique*, to the paradoxical sterility, criminality and shamefulness of the *fureur utérine*.[60]

Part II: Fanaticism in the Age of Extremes

INTENSITY IN POLITICS

Behind discussions of contemporary fanaticism, generally marked by an exclusive and tendentious focus on religious and especially Islamic fundamentalism – as well as by the revival of much of the imperial discourse on fanaticism surveyed above – there often lies another theme: that of the supposed demotivation and demobilization of liberal democracies, their passive nihilism. This age-old theme, crystallized in Fukuyama's reflections on the Last Men of triumphant global liberalism, has both Left and Right variants.[61] What interests me here is not so much the diagnosis of the neutralization of politics under liberalism, but the related attempt to develop theories of political passion. Contemporary concern with militant enthusiasms is of course related to a preoccupation with civic apathy and depoliticization, which some have evoked in terms of the rise of post- or sub-politics. But it also expresses a renewed interest in the question of fanaticism, understood as a collective

---

60   Mary D. Sheriff, 'Passionate Spectators: On Enthusiasm, Nymphomania, and the Imagined Tableau', in Klein and La Vopa (eds), *Enthusiasm and Enlightenment in Europe*, 56–8. See also, in the same volume, Jan Goldstein, 'Enthusiasm or Imagination? Eighteenth-Century Smear Words in Comparative National Context', 40. In different guises, the idea of a specifically feminine 'fanaticism' continues to haunt the theoretical imagination. Peter Sloterdijk – adopting Medea as paradigm – writes of how 'feminine psychism is precisely the one that travels at a frightening speed the path from pain to madness, and from madness to crime'. Sloterdijk, *Zorn und Zeit*, Frankfurt: Suhrkamp Verlag, 2006, 81. Alain Badiou in turn writes, in a Lacanian vein, of the passion of the real as a kind of 'ontological passivity' which is the other side of militancy and commitment, an active abandonment to what is happening. He thus speaks in *The Century* of how he has 'come to notice that women attune themselves more profoundly than men to thus uprooting abandonment, just as, inversely, they are terser and more obstinate when it comes to caution and conservatism. The feminine is that which, when it ceases to be the domestic organization of security and fear, goes furthest in the termination of all cowardice.' Badiou, *The Century*, Cambridge: Polity, 2007, 126.
61   For the former, see Simon Critchley, *Infinitely Demanding*, London: Verso, 2009. For the latter, see Grjebine, *La guerre du doute et de la certitude*, as well as Harris, *The Suicide of Reason*.

and transformative (and consequently often violent) enthusiasm for the abstract.

According to Michael Walzer, liberalism has traditionally advocated as one of its central planks a limitation and domestication of the passions. More precisely, it promotes a supersession of strong political emotions, whether civic or martial, by the non-antagonistic passions of commerce:

> it is by recognizing interest that liberalism accommodates itself to the passions while still excluding the fiercer forms of attachment and strug-gle. The politics of interested individuals and competing interest groups allows for conflict but stops well short of civil war, and it explicitly sets the warlike passions, and implicitly the affiliative passions, beyond the pale.[62]

This contrast between interest and passion is also one between bour-geois liberals and their adversaries – an aristocracy obsessed with valour and conquest, in a first moment, and then, after the integration of the aristocracy into a liberal capitalist order, on to the present-day plebeian, proletarian and subaltern classes, stereotypically possessed by unreason-able and antagonistic collective convictions.[63] Walzer, whose reflections on passion and politics take their cue from Yeats's oft-quoted lines from 'The Second Coming' – 'The best lack all conviction, while the worst are full of passionate intensity' – notes that the opposition between noble conviction and the intensity of the mob remains within an aristocratic or reactionary framework, while a liberalism of mere interests tends to erode both convictions and intensity.[64]

---

62   Michael Walzer, 'Passion and Politics', *Philosophy and Social Criticism*, 28: 6 (2002), 627. Walzer is here relying on Albert Hirschman, *The Passions and the Interests*, Princeton: Princeton University Press, 1977.

63   Walzer judiciously notes that after Marx it is increasingly implausible to treat working-class interests as irrational.

64   From Walzer's vantage point, Yeats's lines are therefore not to be interpreted, as Žižek does, as 'an excellent description of the current split between anaemic liber-als and impassioned fundamentalists', where '"The best" are no longer able fully to engage, while "the worst" engage in racist, religious, sexist fanaticism'. This juxtapo-sition belongs to a Right-aristocratic concern with mob passions and not to the strictly liberal framework of interest versus passion. However, Žižek does immediately correct

This is our contemporary conundrum, for Walzer: current debates about religious fundamentalism, nationalism and other forms of 'fanaticism' are driven by a basic question about the place of passion in politics. The average liberal will perceive all forms of political passion as unmediated commitments and collective identifications, either-ors refractory to the cool politics of deliberation and compromise, a politics whose key affect and mediating instance is (commercial) interest. Against the interested exorcism and limitation of the passions, which he presents as an unwarranted evacuation of what is properly political, Walzer proposes a revisionist liberalism, one capable of accommodating agonism and even antagonism as ineliminable aspects of politics – as encapsulated in Ignazio Silone's remark that politics is about the choice of comrades. Along the way, Walzer's essay touches on a number of themes germane to our own investigation. First, hinting at the distinction between virtuous enthusiasm and pernicious fanaticism, to which we'll have multiple opportunities to return, he mentions the Emersonian adage (itself anticipated by Kant) according to which enthusiasm is a precondition for greatness, not just a threat to social peace. Walzer also underscores a theme that plays a signal role in many of the discussions of fanaticism: crisis. As he suggests, in times of normality the administration of things might indeed occlude the presence of political divisions; but 'when the old social hierarchies are challenged, coherence undermined, the world in pieces',[65] then taking sides, with passion and a degree of intolerance, appears non-negotiable. Walzer also notes that political movements which might elicit our admiration and solidarity (his list includes industrial workers' movements, suffragettes, civil rights activists and velvet revolutionaries) are always ones which manifest 'conviction energized by passion and passion restrained by conviction'.[66] And yet such movements were generally regarded by many of their contemporaries as intimations or instantiations of Yeats's 'blood-dimmed tide' of mob violence.

---

his endorsement of this passage, to note that 'the worst' too are devoid of true conviction. See Slavoj Žižek, *Violence*, London: Profile, 2008, 72.

65   Walzer, 'Passion and Politics', 623.

66   Ibid., 624.

Walzer's persuasive list of passionate convictions is juxtaposed to one of those inventories of fanaticism with which we've already become familiar: 'Who can doubt that Puritan repression, or French revolutionary terror, or Stalinist purges, or Nazi genocide, or contemporary nationalist massacres and deportations were and are the work of passionately intense men and women – and their passions the worst ones: dogmatic certainty, anger, envy, resentment, bigotry, and hatred?'[67] Well, following sundry studies into the organization of political violence, we can certainly doubt that 'passionate intensity' is an endemic and operational affect within the disparate situations metonymically linked by Walzer. More to the point, should passion itself be regarded as a primary *explanans* for any of these situations? For instance, there is good reason to think that the Stalinist purges of the 'Old Bolsheviks' were aimed at eradicating a certain form of passionate intensity, replacing it with the controllable, mechanical and unified conviction of dependent cadres. The rather broad analogies enlisted by Walzer also indicate that his argument, though clearly responsive to the *air du temps*, is relatively detached from any particular historical juncture. And, for all its disavowals of an essentialist definition of politics, it remains at a high level of generality, both descriptively and prescriptively.

THE PROBLEM OF THE TWENTIETH CENTURY

For a more historically specific inquiry into political passion, one that provides some crucial insights into the entanglement between militancy, abstraction and fanaticism, I want to turn now to Alain Badiou's *The Century*. Badiou's lectures on the characteristics and impasses of the twentieth-century subject are in a sense wholly concerned with fanaticism, that is, with unconditional and passionate subjective convictions that determine a radically transformative and unequivocally antagonistic stance against existing society. The intellectual dispensation Badiou is contesting – what he pointedly calls the Restoration – gains much of its pacifying plausibility from its denunciation of the twentieth century as an age in which abstract principles led to concrete disasters,

---

67   Ibid., 622.

as the desire for total transformation translated into massacres on an untold scale. Founded on a neo-liberal evacuation of strong political convictions, the Restoration is at one and the same time the euthanasia of political passions and the apotheosis of interest. In other words, seen through the prism of Badiou's text, the problem of the twentieth century is the problem of fanaticism. The central, if rather unexplored, concept of *The Century* is that of 'the passion for the real' (*la passion du réel*) as the affect and impetus that defines the subjects of that century. Passion for the real would indeed be a good translation into Lacanese of what the tradition of political polemic and philosophical diagnosis has variously termed fanaticism or enthusiasm. In particular, the passion for the real incorporates four key and interlinked dimensions of fanaticism – the refusal of representation, the negation of the world, antagonism as constituent of subjectivity, and the predominance of violence and cruelty – into an 'internalist' exploration of the twentieth century.[68]

The first of these is at the core of the accusation of fanaticism. Refusal of representation becomes especially prominent once the negation of direct access to God, being, or infinity beyond the finite cognitive capacities of human beings – the traditional philosophical retort against fanatics, enthusiasts and 'dream-seers' of all stripes – slides into the attack on a specifically political fanaticism that would seek to embody abstract principles (equality, virtue, morality, etc.) in collective life without passing through mediations, institutions or (parliamentary) representations. The elision of these two meanings of the critique of representation, particularly prominent in the French philosophy of the 1960s and 70s, is a constant in Badiou's philosophy, and it plays a crucial role in *The Century*. What distinguishes 'the real' from reality is the fact that reality is fashioned by representations, mediations, institutions, languages. In Lacanian terms, reality is on the side of the symbolic. Closely modelled on Hegel's account of the Terror, and implicitly on his treatment of

---

68 In an earlier book, Badiou employs the notion of fanaticism to denote those 'ultra-Leftist' and 'Gnostic' deviations that deny the significance of structure and assert the unlimited capacity of subjective force. See Alain Badiou, *Theory of the Subject*, trans. B. Bosteels, London: Continuum, 2009, 17.

fanaticism, the passion for the real is driven by the limited, inadequate and ultimately deceptive character of reality itself. Representations are not useful place-holders for an already intelligible and ordered reality, so much as 'masks of a real they both denote and conceal'.[69] But for this very reason, the fanaticism of the twentieth century is of a very particular type. Though it can never be content with representation and its limits, it is forced to confront the realities of artifice and semblance.

Learning from the theatrical didactics and dialectics of Brecht and Pirandello, but also reflecting on the fatal dramaturgy of the Moscow trials, Badiou tells us that in both art and politics, the twentieth century did not deem it possible to attain the real by inspiration or mysticism. Instead it was a period subjectively and tragically aware of the omnipresence of representation, the necessity of fiction. This is evident in the formal attempts, among which Brecht's 'alienation effect' is exemplary, to exhibit the gap between semblance and the real. This 'post-Kantian' awareness of the fact that representation cannot be so easily transcended is also the reason why the passion for the real presents itself as a process – of wresting the real from its represented or fictionalized reality – and not as a simple, instantaneous act. Semblance also obliges the passion for the real to work on surfaces, mistrusting the idea, cherished by much nineteenth-century thought, that truth is to be found in the depths. Twentieth-century fanaticism thus takes the forms, anticipated by Hegel, of suspicion and purification, not because it transcends representation but because it is compelled ceaselessly to negate it. As Badiou explains:

> the real, conceived in its contingent absoluteness, is never real enough not to be suspected of semblance. The passion for the real is also, of necessity, suspicion. Nothing can attest that the real is the real, nothing but the system of fictions wherein it plays the role of the real. All the subjective categories of revolutionary, or absolute, politics – 'conviction', 'loyalty', 'virtue', 'class position', 'obeying the party', 'revolutionary zeal', and so on – are tainted by the suspicion that the supposedly real

---

69   Badiou, *The Century*, 49.

point of the category is actually nothing but semblance. Therefore, the correlation between a category and its referent must always be publicly *purged*, purified.[70]

The fanaticism of the twentieth century is tragically bound to a representation or semblance that dooms the real to constant misrecognition. Unlike the religious fanaticisms diagnosed by the Enlightenment, it is not a fanaticism of certainty, whatever the perfunctory political psychology of anti-totalitarianism might suggest. This is because, unlike a transcendent, divine reality of which we can suppose knowledge or from which we can draw inspiration, the real of the twentieth-century avant-gardes is devoid of internal criteria for judgment. Accordingly, 'we are in the realm of suspicion when a formal criterion is lacking to distinguish the real from semblance'. Paradoxically, this explains the autophobic, and autophagic, character of modern militancy, since suspicion dictates that wherever conviction seems most real, there too we are to look for treachery and falsity. This kind of negation entails a destructive nihilism, since the only thing beyond the reach of purifying suspicion is nothingness: death.

Such a verdict might appear to bolster the dominant view of the twentieth century as a vast grave of ideals, as well as of the countless bodies those ideals led to their deaths. But Badiou, prolonging a gesture that we will encounter in the most philosophically challenging and politically vital engagements with the problem of fanaticism, chooses instead to proceed immanently, trying to divide this seemingly doomed and terroristic passion from within. He thus distinguishes between two varieties of the passion for the real: the first, which bears the features of Hegel's absolute freedom, is a passion for destruction, driven by a search for the real conceived of as authentic identity – class, Virtue, equality, and so on – a passion that can only be enacted in the struggle against semblance. The second is what Badiou dubs a 'subtractive' passion, one that, following the model of Malevich's painting *White on White*, establishes the gap between the

---

70   Badiou, *The Century*, 52–3.

real and semblance as a 'minimal, albeit absolute, difference; the difference between the place and what takes place in the place, the difference between place and taking-place'.[71] This passage from destruction
to subtraction, which Badiou also regards as a passage from destruction to formalization, remains rather enigmatic as a political prescription. It could, be argued though, that Badiou's indications regarding
'restricted action' a politics without a party are efforts in this direction.
But the attempt to identify a non-destructive fidelity to the real also
touches on another question which is germane to the problem of fanaticism, that of novelty. If the 'passion for the real is always the passion
for the new',[72] it is because radical novelty, as opposed to mere modifi-
cation, always involves some kind of rupture with representation and
mediation, some leap beyond a finite condition in which all happen-
ings are mere combination, variation or repetition. Fanatics have
often been depicted as dangerous innovators, and much of Badiou's
work can be fruitfully perceived as an attempt to recast the connection
between radical, or militant, novelty and philosophical thought.

One of the ways in which this immanent critique of fanaticism
expresses itself – holding on to the concern with the real, while seeking to avert a purely destructive form of purification – is as a redefinition of how we are to understand antagonism and partisanship, notions
that loom large in any political and philosophical inquiry into fanaticism. Among the elements of the passion for the real is the prevalence of
what Badiou calls an anti-dialectical Two, or a principle of antagonism
without synthesis, throughout the century. In its destructive variant,
this entails the presence, over and against any militant subjectivity, of
an enemy, 'another we'. In the struggle to discern and produce the real,
if the adversary is already a self-contained and formed subject, the only
possible consequence is conflict and destruction.

What Badiou calls the subtractive, or formalizing path, is instead
founded on the idea that while form (or principle) lies on the side of
the subject, its counterpart or exterior is a kind of formlessness, requiring formalization. As he notes, this is the kind of situation in which

---

71   Ibid., 56.
72   Ibid.

declarations might be made such as 'the apathetic must be rallied to the Party; the left must unite with the centre to isolate the right; the artistic avant-garde must find forms of address which are perceivable by everyone'.[73] Whence Badiou's recommendation that we 'resolve the conflict between formalization and destruction by means of formalization'.[74] So, where Walzer seeks to surpass the liberal ban on political enthusiasm by advocating the impassioned conviction of an agonistic liberalism, Badiou instead wants to assume the passion for the real, the fanaticism of the twentieth century, in order to think through forms of unconditional conviction which, while not accepting the demands of mediation and representation, nevertheless are not prey to the devastating mechanisms of suspicion and destruction which accompany a politics that can only experience truth, or the real, as endless purification. In order to complement these distinct apologias of passion politics, I want to turn now to a thinker, Peter Sloterdijk, who has recently sought to reflect on the political conundrums of the twentieth century and the prospects of the twenty-first – what he calls our post-communist situation – specifically through the prism of passion, and more specifically through the emotions of rage and zeal, whose relevance to any study of fanaticism is evident.

WHEN HISTORY REFUSES TO END

Sloterdijk's project in books like *Zorn und Zeit* (Rage and Time) and *God's Zeal* couldn't be more politically and methodologically at odds with *The Century*'s excavation and defence of the passion for the real. Badiou's recuperative intervention, his inquiry into the conditions for 'resurrecting' some of the driving spirit of the twentieth century in the face of its denigration, is indeed one of the main targets of the German essayist's recent attempts to prolong Francis Fukuyama's suggestion, in *The End of History and the Last Man*, that we view the liberal closure of the horizon of political transformation from the standpoint of *thymos*, the Greek term which denotes the combative passions of pride or valour. It is worth pausing for a moment on Sloterdijk's most obvious precursor

---

73 Badiou, *The Century*, 109.
74 Badiou, *The Century*, 110.

in this attempt to delineate a 'moral and psychopolitical interpretation of the post-communist situation'.[75]

Fukuyama, in his effort to enlist Alexandre Kojève's Hegelian reflections to generate an epochal vision worthy of a US state bereft of a nemesis, made much of the absence of a reckoning with the historical force of the desire for recognition in mainstream political theory. Fukuyama locates, first in Plato's *Republic* and later in Hegel's dialectic of lord and bondsman, this crucial supplement to those realist or rationalist doctrines of political action which are forgetful of the role of non-instrumental passions in motivating political action. Platonic *thymos*, for Fukuyama, 'constitutes something like an innate human sense of justice, and as such is the psychological seat of all the noble virtues like selflessness, idealism, morality, self-sacrifice, courage, and honorability'.[76] But *thymos*, as Plato himself noted, is also a deeply ambivalent disposition, in which selflessness is combined with self-regard, or even selfishness (as in the feeling of indignation), and commendable courage is accompanied by unjustified rage. Echoing Kant and Emerson on enthusiasm, for Fukuyama nothing great is done without *thymos*: without that jealous care for the dignity of oneself and one's chosen collectivity, no struggles for justice would ever emerge. Equally, such Platonic 'spiritedness' has its dark side, which spans the two sides of *thymos*: *megalothymia* and *isothymia*.

These thymotic desires – to be recognized as superior and to be recognized as equal, respectively – have frequently been regarded as social evils. While potentially a rightful demand for meritocracy and respect, of the kind that drives capitalist acquisitiveness, to be recognized as superior is politically translated into the desire for domination and adulation, the wish to subdue and to be acclaimed, glorified – the motivations of the Machiavellian prince. Imperialism is megalothymic. So is the aristocracy, and here Fukuyama's view of classical liberalism as anti-thymotic, which is to say anti-enthusiastic – something that he relates to its emergence against the religious-political fanaticism of the English Civil War – resonates with Walzer's reflections. *The End of*

75   Sloterdijk, *Zorn und Zeit*, 61.
76   Fukuyama, *The End of History and the Last Man*, 171.

History and the Last Man is less precise when it comes to *isothymia*. This appears as an effect of the liberal struggle against the hierarchical values of aristocracy, leading to an endemic demand to be valued as an equal. Accordingly, it is a rather deflationary if occasionally turbulent passion. But it also manifests itself as the levelling passion for equality.

In reflecting on what danger *thymos* might pose to a liberalism which has given birth to men 'with modern educations [who] are content to sit at home, congratulating themselves on their broadmindedness and lack of fanaticism'[77] – Last Men, that is – Fukuyama weighs up the threats from above and below:

> Liberal democracy could, in the long run, be subverted internally by an excess of *megalothymia*, or by an excess of *isothymia* – that is, the fanatical desire for equal recognition. It is my intuition that it is the former that will constitute the greater threat to democracy in the end. A civilization that indulges in unbridled *isothymia*, that fanatically seeks to eliminate every manifestation of unequal recognition, will quickly run into limits imposed by nature itself.[78]

An endemic and broadly anaesthetic liberal-capitalist mix of depoliti-cized *isothymia* and *megalothymia* is contrasted with a passion for equality that is by definition fanatical, and which Fukuyama links to commu-nism, a system which failed because of (human) nature – a nature synonymous with unequal endowments and enduring instincts.

The relation between nature and history is particularly interest-ing for our purposes. While fanatical *isothymia* is checked by nature, which regains its pre-eminence after communism, Fukuyama asserts that 'Nietzsche was absolutely correct in his belief that some degree of *megalothymia* is a necessary precondition for life itself'.[79] This is a key thesis of anti-fanatical and anti-egalitarian discourse: that the passion for equality is a kind of anti-nature. In Fukuyama, this 'natural' critique of uncompromising egalitarianism is combined with an account of the

---

77 Ibid., 307.
78 Ibid., 314.
79 Ibid., 315.

historical function of the passions. Both *megalothymia* and *isothymia*, in their political, rather than merely private, psychological or commercial forms, are depicted in *The End of History and the Last Man* as veritable agents of modernization and historicity. What is more, in a manner reminiscent of Hume's account of the historical virtues of enthusiasm, Fukuyama contends that even seemingly unsavoury and illiberal manifestations of *thymos* have a progressive historical role to play: 'It was a thymotic passion, the desire for recognition on the part of the aristocratic master, that started the historical process, and it was the thymotic passions of religious fanaticism and nationalism that have propelled it along through war and conflict over the centuries.'[80] Conversely, the closure of history is outlined in terms of the apparent exhaustion of the political or historicizing capacities of *thymos*. Being part of human nature, the sense of dignity and the desire for recognition cannot be obliterated, but Fukuyama's verdict is that their capacity to transcend the bounds of the liberal order is next to nil.

So what is to be done about *thymos*? Beyond history seems to lie the horizon of cultivation, of the post-historical (or even post-human) management and channelling of human nature and its emotive dispositions: a politics of 'nature itself' or 'life itself', beyond history-making enthusiasms and fanaticisms – a bio-politics or zoo-politics for a human animal bereft of greatness or project. In a way, this would return us to what Fukuyama regards as the original intuition in the Platonic concern with *thymos*, that 'a just political order requires both the cultivation and the taming of a *thymos*'.[81] Politics thus incorporates a clinical and logistical relation to *thymos*, a calculation of the right dosages and correct placements of passions, for which thymotic outlets function as 'grounding wires that bleed off excess energy that would otherwise tear the community apart'.[82]

This post-political horizon is shared by Sloterdijk, whose recent reflections closely plough the furrow of Fukuyama's famous essay. Sloterdijk too belongs to those intellectual clinicians of our historical moment

---

80   Ibid., 214.
81   Ibid., 183.
82   Ibid., 315.

who think that we must both affirm the defeat of militant passions at the hands of a global capitalism and contend with the jaded apathy that allegedly characterizes a completed liberalism, albeit one unsettled by the recidivism of religious zeal. Coming two decades after Fukuyama, and written as a provocation to the Left-leaning family of critical theorists, Sloterdijk's books on the politics of fanaticism stand out for the relentlessness with which he flogs the supposedly dead horse of communism. He seethes against the censorship still imposed on anti-communist views under the discursive cover of anti-fascism. His perorations against the 'fourth monotheism' or 'second Catholicism'[83] are aimed at bringing out the centrality of rage to the history of the West, from Homer's *Iliad* onwards – a history of which communism embodies both the culmination and the exhaustion. They also seek to lay out a genealogy of militant passion that might enlighten us about its current religious recrudescence and secular weakness. Having said that, there is something peculiar about Sloterdijk's vitriol towards those who allegedly cling to a radical politics of rage, namely 'Left fascists' loitering around the academy.[84] But a purely political characterization of Sloterdijk's endeavour would not get us very far. Aside from the tiresomely irreverent taunting of his *Linksfaschistisch* opponents with undigested chunks of *The Black Book of Communism* (contrast Fukuyama's rather more Olympian thoughts on the vanquished Soviet experiment), the flirtation with Gunnar Heinsohn's deeply suspect 'demographic materialism',[85] and the suggestion that the traditional ends of social democracy need to be met with some ill-defined project of psychosemantic and bio-political management, Sloterdijk's politics – viewed from the vantage point of classical political theory – remain heavily underdetermined.

This comes as no surprise, since Sloterdijk is adamant about abandoning the field of politics proper for that of cultural theory, psychopolitics,

---

83 Peter Sloterdijk, *God's Zeal: The Battle of the Three Monotheisms*, Cambridge: Polity, 2009, 40; Sloterdijk, *Zorn und Zeit*, 333.

84 This has been duly noted by Žižek, who wonders whether Sloterdijk's 'obsessive-compulsive urge to find beneath solidarity the envy of the weak and thirst for revenge' is not in fact 'sustained by a disavowed envy and resentment of its own, the envy of the universal emancipatory position'. See Žižek, *Violence*, 165.

85 See Göran Therborn, 'Nato's Demographer', *New Left Review*, 56 (2009).

or psychosemantics. These supposedly burgeoning areas of inquiry are meant to supplant the kind of political theorizing which has trapped us in a modernist understanding of modernity, tied to the imperatives of novelty and emancipation and incapable of dealing with the affective configurations and dynamics of cultures and religions. As transpires from his conclusions, Sloterdijk's gripe is not just explanatory but normative. He argues that only a new, Nietzschean integration of psychology, biology, cultural theory and philosophy will permit us to move to a 'civilizing' politics, a politics 'after zeal' and 'beyond resentment', to cite the titles of the conclusions to *God's Zeal* and *Rage and Time*. As diagnoses, explicitly inspired by Nietzsche, of the maladies of universalism, Sloterdijk's recent works can be read as 'classical' critiques of fanaticism. *Rage and Time* and *God's Zeal* do not just provide eclectic narratives and phenomenologies of the enthusiasm for the abstract, they also enjoin us to have done with the politics of abstraction and with the extremism of a principled universalism. When he writes of 'the dangerous nature of universalist militants' and of 'manic-activist or messianic-expansionist' missionary drives, Sloterdijk prolongs the Burkean critique of abstract politics. He argues that universalism 'remains uncontrolled if it lacks a critical organ to restrain the zealots' urge to absolutize their goals', for such an absolutization rapidly slides into a 'fascism of the good'.[86] But how are these fanatical affects, rage and zeal, linked to universalism? In order to answer this question, it is useful to consider how Sloterdijk's account of *thymos* diverges from that of his model, Fukuyama, and how his overall view of political passions sets him apart from Walzer or Badiou.

Sloterdijk expands on Fukuyama's call for politics to concern itself with *thymos*. He underscores the limitation of an erotic rather than thymotic psychoanalysis, one grounded on love not rage, which treats political affect as neurosis. He criticizes the blindness to the centrality of self-affirmation and valuation that inheres in the Christian-democratic ethos of humility. His approach, though, differs significantly from that of the State Department philosopher, in terms both of

---

86   Sloterdijk, *God's Zeal*, 3, 67.

the ontology and the historicity of political passions. While Fukuyama treats his thymotic inquiries as a complement to political theorizing in the realist tradition and, like Walzer, depicts the passions in a manner broadly congruent with their traditional philosophical characterization, Sloterdijk — whose idea of cultural theory resembles nothing so much as late nineteenth-century attempts, *à la* Gabriel Tarde, to create a spiritualist social science of affects and forces — gives the notion of *thymos* a naturalist inflection.[87] He calls for a political theory that would treat collectives as 'pride-groupings', with internal thymotic stresses and tensions, arguing that 'political actions are triggered by differentials of tension between centres of ambition'; he claims that there exist a plurality of self-affirming forces which are in turn conditioned by a symbolic dimension that gives the thymotic drives of groups their consistency. Rhetoric, or 'the doctrine of the direction of affects in political groupings', becomes central to the understanding of struggles for power, ultimately determined by forms of ambition. Importantly, recognition, and any post-Kantian understanding of subjectivity, loses ground to a cultural physics founded on the idea of 'conflict and interaction between thymotic centres of tension'. The idea of politics as a management of affect — already present in Fukuyama and foreshadowed in Tarde's micro-sociology of beliefs and desires — is here joined to the suggestion that we could envisage a kind of scientific project to manage cultures as 'systems endowed with moral ambition', for which one needs the 'self-stimulation of actors by the raising of thymotic resources like pride, ambition, the will to prevail, the propensity to be indignant and the sense of right'.[88] This reliance on psycho- and socio-biological themes can be accounted for by the idea, central to Sloterdijk's narrative and

---

87   In both *Rage and Time* and *God's Zeal*, Sloterdijk's primary source is Heiner Mühlmann and his 'radically new paradigm for the combining of cultural science and evolution theory into the debate', principally centred, in Sloterdijk's account, on its concept of 'stress'. Forms of fury and wrath 'in the spectrum of berserker enthusiasms' would be ways for a warrior to identify with the very energies that overcome him, while misrecognizing them as transcendent in origin. For this treatment of the 'natural religion of the impassioned . . . rooted in endogenous mechanisms that are open to psychobiological elucidation', see *God's Zeal*, 7-9.
88   Sloterdijk, *Zorn und Zeit*, 38.

to his political prescriptions, that what is required by the present post-communist situation, with its combination of a dispiriting capitalism and ultimately isolated but conflictual thymotic centres, is something like a civilizing process following the end of history.

In order to ground this thinking of the politics of the 'human zoo', Sloterdijk relies on the amalgamation of two seemingly disparate discourses.[89] On the one hand a pseudo-quantitative treatment of political passions as objects of measurable accumulation and intensification, a kind of political hydraulics or energetics;[90] on the other, a *sui generis* narrative about the secularization of contents previously borne by monotheistic religions into political projects, namely communism. It is at the juncture of these two accounts that the relation between political passion and historicity is played out, in a manner that differs importantly from Fukuyama's account of *thymos* as a modernizing agent. If for Sloterdijk a valorization of violent affect is formative of the culture of 'the West' – as he recounts in his treatment of Homeric heroism, with its vision of the warrior as the 'medium' or 'receptacle' for a rage that is one with him and his action – then what really allows the West's history to begin is the 'secularization of affects': the passage from a situation in which men are had by their passions, to one in which passions are had by men. In other words, the onset of the Nietzschean 'user illusion' that behind the deed and its feeling there lies a doer, a subject.

This entails the development of subjects who can enjoy a distance from their affects, the distance of hesitation (the rage of the Homeric medium was immediate, unreflexive). But this emergence of subjectivation does

---

89   Peter Sloterdijk, 'Rules for the Human Zoo: A Response to the *Letter on Humanism*', *Environment and Planning D: Society and Space*, 27, 1 (2009). This paper, originally delivered in 1999, triggered a virulent polemic, pitting Sloterdijk against Habermasians and others who accused him of toying with fascistic notions of breeding and selection. See Andrew Fisher, 'Flirting with Fascism', *Radical Philosophy*, 99 (2000).

90   I use the term 'hydraulics' advisedly, in the manner introduced by Gabriel Tarde in his book on crowds and publics. According to Tarde these resemble one another in being nothing like organisms, but rather develop as 'streams whose regime is ill-defined', whence his talk of 'currents of opinion' and 'social rivers'. See Tarde, *L'opinion et la foule*, 32, n. 1. The Nietzschean theme of an energetic reading of culture is evident in the definition of rage as 'an intensive form of the liberation and transfer of energy'. Sloterdijk, *Zorn und Zeit*, 89–90.

not 'civilize away' the role of rage. The civilizing process, the prolonged labour of *embourgeoisement*, does not win out so easily. Indeed, Sloterdijk thinks that revolutionary subjectivity is in one sense the modernization of the ancient dynamics of rage, turning the militant into 'a receptacle for the rage of the world'. This 'psychology of receptacles' is by no means limited to subjects alone. The crucial notion in *Rage and Time*, the very link between affect and history, is that of another container of feeling, the 'bank of rage'. This is a home for passions lying outside of the subject proper, permitting the various dimensions of *thymos* (pride, anger, *ressentiment* and so on) to *defer* their release. As Sloterdijk writes, a bank, understood in the psycho-political register, designates 'the sublation of local capacities for fury and dispersed projects of hate within an all-encompassing agency whose mission, like that of any authentic bank, is to serve as the receptacle and valorizing agency for deposits'.[91] Political history becomes the history of the forms of production, circulation and distribution, but most of all of the accumulation of thymotic forces, as such 'banks' allow affect a historical span and geographical range unknown to the ancients (the Communist International is perhaps the paradigm here). The notion of secularization thus takes on a different meaning, since the banking of rage, later to be transposed into a profane register by the anarchist and communist movements, is for Sloterdijk an invention of monotheism. From God to the Party, the political history of the West is a history of the management of deposits of rage, of thymotic capital, which is to say in strict Nietzschean observance that it is a history of *ressentiment*. And more specifically, of the management of the mass pain of humiliation and the yearning for vengeance and dignity on the part of religious and then revolutionary elites.[92] Religions and revolutions are accounted for by the 'psychism of losers', the deferred arrogance of those looking for apocalyptic retaliation under the guidance of astute managers of thymotic capital.[93] Leaving aside the clumsy, pamphleteering char-

---

91 Sloterdijk, *Zorn und Zeit*, 99.
92 See the perceptive synopsis of Sloterdijk's book in Žižek, *Violence*, 157–60.
93 The metaphoric use of the economic notion of capital to account for resentment and zeal is anticipated in another psychopathological tract on communism, Jules Monnerot's *Sociologie du communisme*, Paris: Gallimard, 1949, 308. I discuss Monnerot's work in Chapter 6.

acter of Sloterdijk's psycho-political verdicts on Marx, Lenin and Mao, *Rage and Time* belongs within the broader return to the political-religion approach to historical communism, and thus to the long philosophical Cold War I will explore later in this book. Above all, Sloterdijk's psycho-political essay is exemplary of the weakness of accounts that treat political affect as a kind of substance, of which different symbolic orders or formal organizations could then be the carriers or vehicles. The combination of a pseudo-naturalist psychology and a depoliticizing theory of secularization makes Sloterdijk's essays symptomatic of a broader trend. Indeed, his work can be seen as a kind of recapitulation of many of the themes of anti-fanatical rhetoric, both older and more recent, and it is in this spirit that I engage with it here, rather than for its limited conceptual contribution.

Underlying Sloterdijk's contemporary critique of fanaticism and his view of the twentieth century as 'a war-economy of *ressentiment*', as well as his proposals for a 'post-historical politics of de-dramatization', is, as with Fukuyama, a Nietzschean recourse to nature – which is to say hierarchy. *Isothymia*, the passion for equality, is always simultaneously driven by ambitions for megalothymic domination. It is also ontologically doomed, since in nature advantageous places are scarce and, as Sloterdijk puts it, the idea of a theatre made up solely of front rows is a fantasy. Inequality is destiny. Being a good liberal vitalist, Sloterdijk advocates the most painless, civilized mechanisms for the management of hierarchies and differences. His philosophical allegiances and political intuitions mean that he is unable to treat universalizing political abstractions as anything but vehicles for the supposedly deeper affective forces of *thymos* and *ressentiment*. His remedy against zeal and *ressentiment* as vectors of political subjectivation and social destabilization is explicitly modelled on Nietzsche: 'At the beginning of the twenty-first century, a time stirred up by new religious turbulence, his warning to remain faithful to the earth and send the tellers of otherworldly fairy tales to a doctor is even more relevant than it was at the end of the nineteenth.'[94] But how are we to 'neutralize the apocalyptic directors'?[95] It is here that

---

94 Sloterdijk, *God's Zeal*, 158.
95 Ibid., 159.

Sloterdijk, who as we have seen reproduces some of the key elements of the critique of fanaticism (secularization, political religion, political psychology, the suspicion towards radical universalism), connects with some of its customary diagnostic themes, namely medicalization and development.

Here as elsewhere, Sloterdijk's apparent originality is really an effect of his eclectic recombination of numerous elements from the tradition of anti-universalist thought. His post-historical politics of de-dramatization takes the form of practices of therapeutic pacification, but, tellingly, he notes the shortcomings of Nietzsche's own anti-Christian and affirmative remedies. These have little purchase on the current conjuncture, where – in language that seeks to provoke but merely succeeds in conjuring up a vague Spenglerian vibe – the 'vast majority of the many millions standing in line at the entrance to the final tunnel do not show any signs of pre-suicidal morbidity . . . but rather those of a faux-religiously channelled build-up of anger'.[96] Political and religious fanaticism are to be resolved by sprucing up the methods with which the liberal directors of capitalism, colonialism and imperialism always sought to deal with it: if our apocalypticism is merely a return of the 'social question' as a global bio-political question, then what needs to be done is to renew the old traditions of demography and developmentalism. On the one hand, following Gunnar Heinsohn – and mainstream Israeli conceptions of Palestinians as a 'demographic problem' – a muscular vigilance against the fanaticizing effects of the 'youth bulge' in Third-World, principally Middle Eastern, countries. On the other, invoking the spirit of the modernization theorist W. W. Rostow, an 'updated politics of development that also exports the secrets of the production and distribution of wealth to those countries previously inaccessible as a result of poverty, resentment and the machinations of perverse elites'.[97] That such confidence in the benevolent modernizing powers of the liberal West may pass as critical theory, or even as 'provocative', is dismaying. But it is also symptomatic of the way in which many of the tropes of the critique of fanaticism have embedded themselves into our philosophical

96   Ibid., 158–9.
97   Ibid., 159.

and public discourse, strangely amalgamating a hostility towards the abstract politics of universalist egalitarianism with a discourse in which politics becomes the global governance of post-history, whose principal aim is to convert unmanageable political rage into docile commercial desire, perhaps supplemented with a dose of self-help.

2

The Birth of Modern Politics Out of the Spirit of Millenarianism

Beware, I have put my words into thy mouth; I have lifted thee above the people and above the empires that thou mayest uproot, destroy, scatter and overthrow, and that thou mayest build and plant. A wall of iron against the kings, princes, priests, and for the people hath been erected. Let them fight, for victory is wondrous, and the strong and godless tyrants will perish.

Thomas Müntzer, *Sermon to the Princes*

Millenarianism – revolutionary class struggle speaking the language of religion for the last time – . . . is already a modern revolutionary tendency that as yet lacks *the consciousness that it is only historical.* The millenarians had to lose because they could not recognize the revolution as their own operation.

Guy Debord, *The Society of the Spectacle*

The revolutionary desire to realize the kingdom of God on earth is the elastic point of progressive civilization and the beginning of modern history.

Friedrich Schlegel, *Athenaeum Fragments*

It is common to cope with fanaticism by dismissing it as an atavism, a sign that cultural and political advance – under the banner of secularism, development or Enlightenment – is not yet complete. At the beginning of his intellectual history of the 'great separation' between politics and theology, Mark Lilla writes portentously: 'We assumed

that . . . fanaticism was dead. We were wrong.'[1] One of the paradoxes I
have outlined – that of fanaticism as both anti- and ultra-historical – is
present in this sentiment. Even for thinkers who do not assume any kind
of providential teleology that would lead us out of our religious, political and emotional immaturity, there is something about fanaticism that
goes against the proper grain of history, while at the same time denying the post-historical stability that would be the ultimate legacy and
completion of a Western history now understood as the emancipation of
our political sensibilities from the grip of partisanships and convictions.
Behind talk of a 'return of the religious' there is the sense that the hard-
won gains of a more or less linear journey, from fanaticism to tolerance,
from religious absolutism to civic secularism, are being eroded. In this
context, the uses of the idea of fanaticism are ambivalent: they signal
both the repudiation of a civilizing progress and the re-emergence of
a history of conflict that had been declared to be finished. Attending to
the discourse on fanaticism can tell us much about the temporal registers
in which we understand politics and, more precisely, about the way we
define the very distinction between what is deemed to be properly political and what is not, whether by excess of conviction or lack of a plausible
programme. In this chapter, I want to explore the time of fanaticism by
considering a series of historical and political reflections on a phenomenon which is itself defined by, and against, time: millenarianism.

ANACHRONISM AND SOCIALIST STRATEGY

Political movements mobilized by the expectation of the end of a profane
history of misery and oppression, and the establishment of an earthly
paradise of one sort or another (the 'millennium'), seem to be prime
candidates for the derogatory label of fanaticism. Not only does millenarianism generally reject politics as a horizon of institutional mediation
and deliberation, it also tends to designate the advocates of said order as
malignant enemies ('the Antichrist'). What's more, there is a distinctly
visionary element in millenarianism. It feverishly scans for signs of the
new heaven and the new earth, fanatically refusing to limit itself to finite

---

1   Mark Lilla, *The Stillborn God: Religion, Politics and the Modern West*, New York:
Vintage, 2008, 3.

perceptions, brandishing a declared insight into Being or God. Whether it takes the form of an anticipatory withdrawal from the world or an attempt to force its end, millenarianism is marked by its break with political time as a time of order – the repetitive order of cycles, the static order of stability or the cumulative order of development. But what if this seeming negation of the very coordinates for thinking the temporality of politics were not the last word on fanaticism and millenarianism? What if our own sense of political novelty and innovation were somehow entangled with these movements, magnetized and fascinated by the possibility of an ending? In order to explore these questions I will spend some of this chapter investigating the encounter between twentieth-century radical and Marxist thought, and the movement whose condemnation led to the initial crystallization of the discourse against fanaticism, the German Peasants' War of the early sixteenth century. But before delving into this *locus classicus* of the debate on fanaticism, it is important to look further into the question of political anachronism and the counter-intuitive idea that a modern politics of novelty could somehow be linked to apocalyptic and fanatical yearnings. To do so, I want to take a brief detour through an important debate in the social sciences which took place slightly more than half a century ago.

Far from being simply an obsession for mediaevalists, the study of millenarianism was charged with political urgency for a number of twentieth-century thinkers. A particularly fertile instance of the concern with the politics of the apocalypse can be registered in a 1956 seminar that took place at the University of Manchester, with the participation of Eric Hobsbawm, Peter Worsley and Norman Cohn. This was a moment of profound reflection on the social and political dimensions of millenarianism, cutting across anthropology, history, sociology and the study of religion, as testified by the books which these scholars would publish shortly thereafter: respectively, *Primitive Rebels: Studies in the Archaic Forms of Social Movement in the 19th and 20th Centuries* (1959); *The Trumpet Shall Sound: A Study of 'Cargo' Cults in Melanesia* (1957); and *The Pursuit of the Millennium: Revolutionary Messianism in the Middle Ages and its Bearing on Modern Totalitarian Movements* (1957). Bringing together two Marxist socialists (Hobsbawm and

Worsley) and an anti-communist liberal (Cohn), this was a discussion that remains vital for anyone wishing to come to grips with questions of time, history and fanaticism. Broadly speaking, we could say that Hobsbawm's text is preoccupied with the socio-historical relations between the archaic time of millenarianism and the transformative time of revolution; Worsley investigates the peculiar modernity instigated by the catastrophic impact of a mystifying capitalist economy on indigenous culture; Cohn sees in the apocalyptic movements of the Middle Ages the ideological and sociological precursors of twentieth-century totalitarianisms. The valuations of millenarianism follow political divisions: where Hobsbawm and Worsley discern in these risings the noble, if stunted, precursors of revolutionary realism, Cohn views millenarianism as the destructive product of an alliance between uprooted 'intellectuals' and a disparate rabble which, incapable of achieving real social progress, opts for a total negation of the political world, preferring conflagration to reform. Common to all three is a more or less explicit recognition of the modernity of millenarianism, associated with the shock of the encounter with capitalism. Millenarian anachronism – the reference to a vanished edenic compact or the wish to break out of time altogether – is ineluctably enmeshed in the now of economic development and its attendant political transformations (whether in the context of European state-formation or of imperial-colonial conquest), leading to unstable amalgams of nostalgias for a mythical past, encounters with a violently novel present, and aspirations for a redeemed future. The temporal indeterminacy of millenarianism as a social phenomenon can be encapsulated in the idea that it operates as a 'crisis cult',[2] that is, as a political-religious response by colonized, subaltern or 'backward' societies to 'a genuine social cataclysm that leaves them completely out of joint'.[3] Insofar as they react to this dislocating shock by something more than a mere defence of established culture and tradition, millenarian crisis cults always involve a measure of innovation, responding to

---

2   See Weston La Barre, 'Materials for a History of Studies of Crisis Cults: A Bibliographic Essay', *Current Anthropology*, 12: 1 (1971).
3   Michael Löwy, 'From Captain Swing to Pancho Villa. Instances of Peasant Resistance in the Historiography of Eric Hobsbawm', *Diogenes*, 48: 189 (2000), 3.

the imposition of a new temporality with temporal imaginaries of their own.[4]

The question of historical and political time is central to Hobsbawm's contribution to the Manchester seminar, later worked into his first book, *Primitive Rebels*. The temporality of the modern millenarianisms investigated by Hobsbawm is bound to sociological and geographical determinants. Hobsbawm's principal object is the peasantry in the impoverished and peripheral areas of European countries suffering the dispossessions and upheavals of capitalist modernization (Sicily in Italy, Andalusia in Spain). Millenarianism emerges as a reaction-formation whose primitive character is to be understood in political terms: the peasants who respond to the capitalist cataclysm by mobilizing on millenarian grounds are not yet capable of attaining the organizational solidity and political impact that qualify mature varieties of anti-capitalism – namely, the labour movement – which have grown in the belly of the capitalist beast. Noting that they still make up the numerical majority of the world's masses, Hobsbawm famously refers to the objects of his book as '*pre-political* people who have not yet found, or only begun to find, a specific language in which to express their aspirations about the world'.[5] The 'pre' is determined by a spatial exteriority or peripherality that translates on the temporal axis into backwardness, in terms of both political mentality and organizational capacity. Hobsbawm prefaces his study of modern millenarian movements with this instructive statement:

> The men and women with whom this book is concerned differ from Englishmen in that they have not been born into the world of capitalism as a Tyneside engineer, with four generations of trade unionism at his back, has been born into it. They come into it as first-generation immigrants, or what is even more catastrophic, it comes to them from outside, insidiously by the operation of economic forces which they do not understand and over which they have no control, or brazenly

4 See Vittorio Lanternari, *The Religions of the Oppressed: A Study of Modern Messianic Cults*, trans. L. Sergio, New York: Mentor, 1965, 253–4.
5 Eric J. Hobsbawm, *Primitive Rebels: Studies in Archaic Forms of Social Movement in the 19th and 20th Centuries*, New York: Norton, 1965, 2.

by conquest, revolutions and fundamental changes of law whose consequences they may not understand, even when they have helped to bring
them about. They do not as yet grow with or into modern society: they
are broken into it, or more rarely . . . they break into it. Their problem
is how to adapt themselves to its life and struggles, and the subject of
this book is the process of adaptation (or failure to adapt) as expressed in
their archaic social movements.[6]

Millenarian movements respond to this problem of adaptation in what is,
at least initially, a purely negative form. Insofar as they are driven by 'a
profound and total rejection of the present, evil world, and a passionate
longing for another and better one', failure to adapt seems to be their
raison d'être. Suffused with an apocalyptic ideology either drawn from
a pre-existing canon or syncretically fashioned, they are also, because
of their hostility to the political world as it stands, affected by a 'fundamental vagueness about the actual way in which the new society will be
brought about'.[7]

If politics entails an organization of means in view of calculable ends
then these movements are indeed pre-political – though perhaps this
should be understood in the sense of proto-political, of harbouring a radical potentiality to which alliances and struggles can accord a real political
valence. This is indeed the analytical, but also the prescriptive, purpose
of Hobsbawm's study, as it traces the amalgam of anarchism and peasant
radicalism in southern Spain and the absorption of the movement of the
Sicilian peasants and workers' leagues or *fasci* (not to be confused with
Mussolini's) into the socialist labour movement in Italy. But pre-political
can also mean something like ultra-political. The world-denial and hope
for radical transformation that is the 'archaic' response to capitalism as
cultural catastrophe and dispossession can also translate into an 'impracti-
cal and utopian' approach to politics, the resort to apocalyptic language
and bizarre behaviour (antinomianism, mass hysteria).

Hobsbawm's compelling thesis is that it is precisely the all-encompassing negativity and 'impossibilist' desire for a wholly new world of

6   Ibid., 3.
7   Ibid., 57–8.

millenarian movements which makes them – unlike other forms of pre-political mobilization, such as social banditry – politically moderniz-able. Paradoxically, the very fanaticism that makes it difficult to identify their 'rational political core' is, in the last instance, their rational political core. Millenarian utopianism is a *sui generis* political realism. It is 'prob-ably a necessary device for generating the superhuman efforts without which no major revolution is achieved'; what is more, these move-ments prove to both activists and observers that the world can indeed be utterly changed, to begin with by transforming previously depo-liticized masses into political subjects.[8] The 'revolutionism' integral to millenarian aspirations lends these movements a modern disposition not shared by types of contestation or rebellion that Hobsbawm character-izes as 'reformist'.[9] Conversely, revolutionism translates into doomed revolt if it is unable to find organizational forms that can actually gain traction on the very capitalist system that triggered the cultural crisis in the first place. Hobsbawm's own politics are manifest here, as he nega-tively compares Andalusia's conjunction of peasant millenarianism and anarchist agitation with the sublation of the Sicilian *fasci* into the labour movement, the former coded in terms of the recurrent defeat of heroic revolts, the latter as incorporation into a revolutionary politics capable of wresting real reforms from capitalism.[10]

The critique of Hobsbawm's political model of millenarianism played an important role in the genesis of subaltern studies in India. For Ranajit Guha, the very notion of the 'pre-political' occludes the logic of peas-ant revolts in the subcontinent, but more importantly it takes practical consciousness and political subjectivity away from those who time and again rose up against the rule of the British Empire. For Guha, this logic and this consciousness are based on a politics that systematically negates the radical distance and oppression that characterizes the subaltern's relation to the imperial authorities, as testified to in the types of violence employed by the peasant rebels. As Guha writes, 'once the glare of

---

8   Ibid., 60–1.
9   On the distinction between reformists and revolutionists, see ibid., 10–12, 63–4.
10   See Löwy, 'From Captain Swing to Pancho Villa', for some perspicuous criticism of Hobsbawm's evaluation of Spanish anarchism.

burning mansions died down and the eye got used to the facts of an uprising, one could see how far from haphazard it had been'.[11] For him, the idea of 'pre-political people' suggests forms of blind spontaneity or false consciousness which do not do justice to the distinctive features (the 'elementary aspects') that can be gleaned from peasant insurgencies. What's more, since economic exploitation took place in late eighteenth- and nineteenth-century India through the application of direct force, 'there was nothing in the militant movements of the rural masses that was not political'.[12] The point then is not to write the subaltern out of the progressive histories of labour and nation, to relegate them to the repetitious rhythm of futile rebellions, but to read through and against the distorting mirror of the colonial record the presence of a consciousness which, though defined by its (anti-colonial) negativity, is nonetheless political.[13]

More recently, Guha's collaborator in the *Subaltern Studies* journal, Dipesh Chakrabarty, has affirmed the legacy of this research programme by stressing its opposition to any 'historicism' that would seek to subordinate and align forms of political experience to the unity and continuity of a historical development, namely that of a totalizing, universal capitalism. Chakrabarty distinguishes between 'History 1' – the history of a capitalism that tries to unify and subsume all forms of behaviour and belief as its mere moments – and a non-denumerable plurality of 'History 2s', constantly interrupting, in myriad ways, the totalizing narrative of 'History 1'.[14] Just as he provides some comradely criticism of Guha's use of the categories of political subjectivity and agency (to the extent that it brackets the rebels' creedal claim to be mere conduits for divine anger, rather than autonomous actors), he also casts doubt on Guha's socio-historical claim that the negative consciousness of the peasant revolts is dialectically bound up with a

11   Ranajit Guha, *Elementary Aspects of Peasant Insurgency in Colonial India*, Durham, NC: Duke University Press, 1999, 20.
12   Guha, *Elementary Aspects*, 6.
13   Guha's analysis of the administrative uses of fanaticism, which I discuss in Chapter 1, is an instance of this method.
14   Dipesh Chakrabarty, *Provincializing Europe: Postcolonial Thought and Historical Difference*, Princeton: Princeton University Press, 2000, 3–23 and 47–71.

particular form or stage of political power (Imperial 'dominance without hegemony').

I have sketched only the barest outlines of this very important debate here. But it is already possible to see how our conception of politics is affected by the manner in which it is associated with broadly 'religious' mentalities, on the one hand, and figures of temporal advance and historical development, on the other. For partly different reasons and with different political vocabularies, the assorted 'posts' (post-colonialism, post-Marxism, post-structuralism, post-modernism, etc.) all dispute the concept of a history totalized by capitalism's real subsumption of external lifeworlds, just as they object to a politics concentrated by its orientation towards a single horizon of emancipation (whether in a liberal or socialist guise). The discussion over the political and the pre-political, over millenarianism and revolution, is an important prism for a much broader intellectual dispute: one concerned, as Guha's and Chakrabarty's criticisms of Hobsbawm reveal, with the fate of Marxism and its theory of history.

This is certainly not the place to address the complexities of Marx and Marxism's relation to what Chakrabarty calls historicism, or the accuracy of its characterization in *Provincializing Europe*. Teleologies of class or nation are clearly less persuasive nowadays than they might once have been, and have always been riven with aporias and contradictions. It is less evident that the totalizing embrace of capitalism can really permit us to assert the existence of so many exceptions to its rule. But perhaps the problem should be posed in a different guise, not so much as an epistemological problem about our knowledge of history and its alleged progress, or an ontological one about what may lie within or without the purview of accumulation. Rather, homing in on the crux of this debate, we should reconsider the issue in a political register.

Hobsbawm's adjective 'pre-political', though by no means entirely free from historical-materialist condescension towards 'primitive' forms of anti-capitalism, rests on an understanding of politics in terms of its efficacy, durability and capacity to generate a new and better world. The classical name that he gives to this capacity to effect change over time, and to distil the hopes, energies and experiences of the oppressed, is organization. The pre-political can indeed be the bearer of 'impossibilist' demands for radical change which make up the lifeblood and impetus of revolutionary politics; but it can also, because of the vagueness of its designs and the dispersion of its means, translate into defeat, or into a return to passivity. As Hobsbawm declares:

> without being imprinted with the right kinds of ideas about political organization, strategy and tactics and the right kind of programme, millenarianism inevitably collapses. . . . However, when harnessed to a modern movement, millenarianism can not only become politically effective, but it may do so without the loss of that zeal, that burning confidence in a new world, and that generosity of emotion which characterizes it even in its most primitive and perverse forms.[15]

Though Hobsbawm's understanding of organization might be vitiated by a communist exceptionalism that regards the Party as the only plausible motor and bearer of lasting and meaningful social change, it is the politics of emancipation rather than the philosophy of history that governs his take on millenarian or 'archaic' forms of political movement. Anachronism is not gauged here by a fixed standard of development, but by the ability of the exploited to find suitable ways, not merely to 'interrupt' the historical hegemony of capitalism but to shape it, and ultimately to undermine it.

Is it possible to take on the problem of anachronism, of modes of organization and belief out of joint with a politically and economically defined (and enforced) present, without resorting to the historicism and teleology rightly criticized by subaltern studies scholars? A positive reply might find an initial foothold in Ernst Bloch's dialectic of synchronicity and nonsynchronicity.[16] Writing as the Nazis were preparing their final assault on political power, and sensitive to the limitations of an 'enlightened' communism that disregarded the exploitation of the

---

15 Hobsbawm, *Primitive Rebels*, 106–7.
16 Chakrabarty does note Bloch's idea of the nonsynchronous among the moves against historicism from within the Marxist tradition, but as with the idea of 'uneven development', he finds it insufficient. As I hope to show, this judgment is rushed. See Chakrabarty, *Provincializing Europe*, 12 and 261, n. 38.

deep-seated and often unconscious resources of romantic anti-capitalism by Hitler and his shock-troops, Bloch sought to forge a theory of
fascism that would go beyond the restrictive idea according to which the
rise of Nazism represented nothing but a manipulative ploy on the part
of a rapacious and beleaguered bourgeoisie. Bloch thought it incumbent
upon the Left to confront head-on the affective purchase of distinctly
millenarian ideas, not least that of the 'Third Reich' itself – a perversion
of the anti-clerical and egalitarian heresies which find their source in the
writings of the twelfth-century Calabrian monk Joachim of Fiore, one
of Bloch's abiding reference-points. Simply to dismiss these out of hand
as cynical, obscurantist myths would have been to refuse oneself the
means not just to explain, but also to wrest from the Nazis the potentially
emancipatory dimensions of this 'heritage'. Bloch is also concerned with
the proliferation of occultism, a phenomenon in which the reactive and
apprehensive middle classes show a greater backwardness than peasants:

> The infringement of 'interest slavery' (*Zinsknechtschaft*) is believed in, as
> if this were the economy of 1500; superstructures that seemed long over-
> turned right themselves again and stand still in today's world as whole
> medieval city scenes. Here is the Tavern of the Nordic Blood, there the
> castle of the Hitler duke, yonder the Church of the German Reich, an
> earth church, in which even the city people can feel themselves to be
> fruits of the German earth and honor the earth as something holy, as the
> *confessio* of German heroes and German history. . . . Peasants sometimes
> still believe in witches and exorcists, but not nearly as frequently and
> as strongly as a large class of urbanites believe in ghostly Jews and the
> new Baldur. The peasants sometimes still read the so-called Sixth and
> Seventh Books of Moses, a sensational tract about diseases of animals
> and the forces and secrets of nature; but half the middle class believes in
> the Elders of Zion, in Jewish snares and the omnipresence of Freemason
> symbols and in the galvanic powers of German blood and the German
> land.[17]

---

17   Ernst Bloch, 'Nonsynchronism and the Obligation to Its Dialectics', trans. M.
Ritter, *New German Critique*, 11 (1977), 26 (this text is excerpted from Part II of Bloch's
Heritage of Our Times). Bloch notes that much of the bourgeoisie and petty bourgeoisie

As in many analyses of interwar fascism, Bloch homes in on those crucial intermediate groups that constitute the social penumbra around the class struggle between the proletariat and the bourgeoisie – the peasantry, the landowners, the petty bourgeoisie. Mindful that it would be wrong to view any of these as merely primitive in a country where social relations of production are never actually outside capitalism, Bloch wants to detect the ways in which, when it comes to their fears (of social demotion or anomie) and desires (of order or well-being), these groups are somehow out of sync with the rationalizing present of capitalism – the enlightened space occupied by the mainstream socialist and labour movements. For Bloch, the Germany of the 1930s is a country inhabited not just by disenchanted citizens, workers and exploiters.[18] Crisis has brought 'nonsynchronous people' to the fore: declining remnants of pasts whose hopes remain unquenched, easily rallied to the campaign of reaction.[19]

In a sense that is at once social and psychic, the political present is torn between the antagonistic and unfulfilled Now of capitalist conflict and the incomplete pasts that teem in its interstices. The collective emotional effect is a 'pent-up anger', which the Nazis and their capitalist boosters are able to mine and to exacerbate, while it remains off-limits to a communism whose enlightenmental rationalism risks becoming practically irrational. So it is that the 'monopoly capitalist upper class . . . utilizes gothic dreams against proletarian realities'.[20] The question of how to relate, intellectually and politically, to the nonsynchronous becomes central, since it is useless to console oneself with the evolutionist just-so story according to which the archaic will gradually be eroded by social and economic progress.

---

is often 'falsely synchronous', happy to revert to disenchantment once occultism is no longer expedient. Much the same could be said today for the supporters of Italy's Northern League, whose Padanian games and Longobard heritages are the kitsch ornament to bigotry and tax evasion.

18 Germany is the 'classical land of nonsynchronism, that is, of unsurmounted remnants of older economic being and consciousness'. Bloch, 'Nonsynchronism and the Obligation to Its Dialectics', 29.

19 'Anachronistic savagery and recollection are only discharged by the crisis, and answer to its objectively revolutionary contradiction with one that is subjectively as well as objectively reactionary, that is, nonsynchronous.' Ibid., 32.

20 Ibid., 27.

This is not to say that Bloch entertains a relativist solution, whereby all temporalities would be of equal worth, be they primitive or progressive. Indeed, he even resorts to some familiar orientalist explanations of irrational convictions: 'Living and newly revived nonsynchronisms, whose content is genuine, whose appearances bring along heathen crudity and panic nature. Revolutions against civilization in this demonic form were previously known only in the Orient, above all in the Mohammedan world. Their fanaticism still benefits only the White Guard in our country as well . . .' This echoes the habitual conjunction of fanaticism, archaism and reaction. But Bloch appends a crucial twist: ' . . . and will continue to do this as long as the revolution does not occupy and rebaptize the living Yesterday'.[21]

The threat of Nazism turns fanaticism into the terrain of a political struggle over fantasies and motivations: 'not the theory of the national socialists is serious, but its energy is, the fanatic-religious impact, which does not just come from despair and ignorance, but rather from the uniquely stirring power of belief'.[22] Though the political strategy of the proletariat must perforce be synchronous if it is to confront the capitalist Now, it is also required to recover and shape the kind of nonsynchronicity from where immemorial and invariant demands of justice stem. Bloch articulates this unfulfilled and 'unclaimed' task in terms of the relation between two forms of contradiction: on the one hand, the synchronous and determinate negativity of the organized proletariat, on the other, those 'subversively utopian' positivities that have 'never received fulfilment in any age'.[23]

---

21   Ibid., 27. Bloch's rather stereotypical link between Islam and fanaticism can also be found in *The Principle of Hope*, where he writes: 'Fanaticism as an element of faith is found only in the two religions which started out from Moses, in Christianity and Islam. Warlike intolerance (certainly not rejected by Jesus, who had come to start a fire in the world and wished that it was already burning) has as its paragon Moses, who smashed the golden calf.' This 'peculiar, passionate, typically Islamic submission primarily presupposed the union of God's will with the monomania of God's champion'. Ernst Bloch, *The Principle of Hope*, Vol. 3, trans. N. Plaice, S. Plaice and P. Knight, Oxford: Basil Blackwell, 1986, 1275.

22   Bloch, *Heritage of Our Times*, quoted in Anson Rabinbach, 'Unclaimed Heritage: Bloch's *Heritage of Our Times* and the Theory of Fascism', *New German Critique* 11 (1977), 13–14.

23   Bloch, 'Nonsynchronism and the Obligation to its Dialectics', 34.

To develop both practically and interpretively a multi-level dialectic capable of comprehending and crystallizing the multiple and contradictory temporalities at work within the capitalist present signifies for Bloch thinking how the nonsynchronous might already supplement the synchronous, and thus how its inchoate strivings for redemption may be wrenched away from their Nazi corruptions.[24] Unless a dialectical reclamation of nonsynchronicity is effected, at best the nonsynchronous will function as a kind of decoy, since 'capital uses that which is nonsynchronously contrary, if not indeed disparate, as a distraction from its own strictly present-day contradictions; it uses the antagonism of a still living past as a means of separation and struggle against the future that is dialectically giving birth to itself in the capitalist antagonisms'.[25] Against the kind of thinking that would merely contemplate the linear unfolding of the social totality, Bloch calls for a dialectic capable of grasping the powers of the nonsynchronous (the 'living Yesterday', the 'genuine nebulae' from the past) and launching them against both capitalism and obscurantism: 'The task is to extrapolate the elements of the nonsynchronous contradiction which are capable of antipathy and transformation, that is, those hostile to capitalism and homeless in it, and to refit them to function in a different context.'[26]

As in Hobsbawm, Bloch's reflection on the political ambivalence of movements and desires out of joint with the capitalist present revolves around questions of political hegemony and the prospects of alliances (between the proletariat and the immiserated nonsynchronous people of the middle classes and the peasantry) in which the organizational capacities of the synchronous are combined with the wishes and energies of the nonsynchronous. Bloch's 'refitting' – tragically a dead letter and perhaps a painfully impossible wish – is nonetheless more promising, since, while it shares the political standard of Hobsbawm's sympathetic survey of millenarianism, it eschews the evolutionist or

---

24   See Bloch, 'Nonsynchronism and the Obligation to Its Dialectics', 34–5.
25   Ibid., 32. On the limits of Bloch's theory of fascism, and the way in which it overlooks the specifically capitalist forms of organization and technology mobilized by the Nazis, see Rabinbach, 'Unclaimed Heritage', 14.
26   Bloch, 'Nonsynchronism and the Obligation to Its Dialectics', 36.

historicist premises for which the British historian was taken to task by Guha and Chakrabarty. Bloch's struggle with the open heritage and political consequences of the past-in-the-present, and with its unrealized futures, points, however sketchily, towards a sophisticated engagement with those anachronistic elements often branded as fanatical. This would be a thinking that neither relegates them to the archaic, nor celebrates them in the name of an irreducible anti-historicist difference. The problem of the nonsynchronous, of the profound ambivalence of those energies, aspirations and demands 'out of joint' with the capitalist Now, was a problem of profound political urgency for Bloch, not to be adjudicated on ontological or epistemological grounds. Similar principles dictated his critical exchange in the 1920s with Georg Lukács over Thomas Müntzer, the fanatic *par excellence*. But before delving into Müntzer and the German Peasants' War as the key *topos* for the political interrogation of millenarianism, I want to turn to the two other participants with Hobsbawm in the 1956 Manchester seminar – Peter Worsley and Norman Cohn – in order to delineate some of the sociological and anthropological dimensions of the problem of millenarian movements.

THE SOCIAL SCIENCE OF THE APOCALYPSE

Where Hobsbawm's studies of pre-political millenarian movements are preoccupied with an archaic peasantry and its adaptations to the shock of capitalism, and Guha's criticisms bear on the negative political consciousness of non-nationalist peasant rebellions, Peter Worsley's *Trumpet Shall Sound* investigates a more drastic and asymmetrical encounter: the twentieth-century impact of full-blown commodity culture on the indigenous populations of Melanesia. Worsley's feat is to take what appears to be the most ludicrously irrational of religious responses to political and economic modernity, the 'cargo' cults – with their simulated airplanes and landing strips, and their messianic conviction of the approach of a bountiful age in which new goods and commodities would no longer be prey to the whims of the White Man – and reconstruct its political rationality.[27] The crises these cults respond to are

---

27   Cargo cults were first recorded in the late nineteenth century (the Tuka Movement in Fiji was repressed by European authorities in 1885), and seemingly peaked in World

profound enough to warrant the term, coined by the Italian anthropologist Ernesto De Martino, of 'cultural apocalypses'. Not just the lifeworld and livelihoods, but the very cosmologies of the native populations are torn asunder by the arrival of an infinitely powerful and totally unfathomable social system.

The emergence of these cults can be seen, as Vittorio Lanternari argues, as a twin demand for 'freedom and salvation: freedom from subjection and servitude to foreign powers as well as from adversity, and salvation from the possibility of having the traditional culture destroyed and native society wiped out as a historical entity'.[28] Their valence is not just political, but epistemological: these new religions seek to bestow some kind of intelligibility on the otherwise wholly mysterious material culture of the whites, and especially onto the incomprehensible admixture of seemingly limitless resources and sudden shifts in the value and availability of commodities. Cargo cults can also be sympathetically conceived as ways to map cognitively this alien social form called capitalism. It's not just that the social and technical dimensions of the market were invisible to the islanders, who claimed a 'right' to the cargo in part because they could not conceive how the White Man had produced any of it.[29] The real blockage of intelligibility that the cult responds to concerns the constant, unpredictable and violent fluctuations that affect their world, the 'boom and slump, the closing of plantations, experimental stations and other government and private enterprise which appears to be flourishing, the pressure on natives to produce cash crops which realize progressively less from year to year'. Viewed as not only a response to the crisis born of imperialist impact

---

War Two and the years following. Distinct cargo-cult movements (the Taro Cult and Vailala Madness in Papua New Guinea, the John Frum cult in Vanuatu) are discussed by Worsley and in the ample literature on this phenomenon.

28   Vittorio Lanternari, *The Religions of the Oppressed: A Study of Modern Messianic Cults*, trans. L. Sergio, New York: Mentor, 1965, 239. See also, on redemption, religion and political power in the context of millenarian movements, Kenelm Burridge, *New Heaven, New Earth: A Study of Millenarian Activities*, Oxford: Basil Blackwell, 1971, 4–8.

29   'They believe European civilization has prevailed only because of its secret powers of magic and because of the greater amount of *mana* the white man is endowed with.' Lanternari, *The Religions of the Oppressed*, 251.

but as a way of coping with the crisis-prone nature of capitalism itself, the cargo cults – for all their easily derided pageantry – can be accorded a rationality of their own. As Worsley comments, 'it is clear that the labelling of cults as "irrational" begs the question. Indeed, a Melanesian might make out a good case for flinging the label of "madness" which has often been applied to these cults back at us, and asking whether his people, given the knowledge they possessed, have not made quite logical criticisms and interpretations of our own unpredictable and irrational society.'[30]

The rituals and expectations of these cults cannot be reduced to defensive formations, thrown up to insulate the indigenous culture from the brutal jolts of a capricious economic system. Their almost parodic assimilation of the signs and symbols of commerce – as well as of elements of the White Man's own crisis cult, Christianity – embodies the recognition that there is no going back. As the old rules are undone by a cultural apocalypse, the cults navigate the passage from 'no rules' to 'new rules': they are forced to innovate. In Hobsbawm's sense they are revolutionary, not reformist.[31] Their encounter with capitalism-as-crisis forces them into negating their own lifeworlds in order to prepare a response which, however excessive, is also an adaptation to new circumstances. Much as capitalism was said by Marx to have emerged in the *intermundia* of economic communities, by way of trade, so fanaticism comes into view at the frontier of political groupings, as both product and agent of conflict. In this respect the cargo cults seem to cut across the two types of critical encounters proposed by Toynbee, who, taking the Jewish responses to Roman imperialism in Palestine as his model, distinguished between 'herodianism' – denoting compromise, accommodation, and assimilation into the conquering culture – and 'zealotism', which is marked by identitarian closure and militant nationalism.[32] The Melanesian movements

---

30   Peter Worsley, *The Trumpet Shall Sound: A Study of 'Cargo' Cults in Melanesia*, 2nd ed, London: Paladin, 1970, 45–6.
31   See also Lanternari, *The Religions of the Oppressed*, 252–3.
32   Arnold J. Toynbee, *A Study of History: Abridgment of Volumes VII–X by D. C. Somervell*, Oxford: Oxford University Press, 1988, 231–5. I owe the reference to Domenico Losurdo, *Il linguaggio dell'impero. Lessico dell'ideologia americana*, Bari: Laterza, 2007, 47.

studied by Worsley seem to combine a conspicuous assimilation with a form of opposition that is not founded on a pre-existing identity, and in fact breaks with many of the habits and loyalties of the social arrangement that preceded the arrival of the white man.

Politically, these millenarian or messianic movements can be read as dismantling old boundaries between groups and established hierarchies within them, to create collectivities that are negatively bound by their shared experience of social cataclysm and by the hope for a reversal. This is what Worsley suggestively calls the 'integratory function' of cults which, in his study, emerge in 'stateless' societies where people exist in 'small, separate, narrow and isolated social units', which are consequently easily overrun by colonial powers.

> The main effect of the millenarian cult is to overcome these divisions and to weld previously hostile and separate groups together into a new unity. The social necessity which produces this drive toward integration is the subjection of all the separate units to a common authority – the Europeans. Since the people have developed new common political interests where previously they had none, so they must create new political forms of organization to give expression to this new-found unity. It is precisely this integratory function which is served by the millenarian cult.[33]

The cultural apocalypse visited upon the indigenous populations by the White Man is thus countered by something like a political apocalypse, if we understand by the latter the upsurge into the social of the 'undifferentiated',[34] of that which had been excluded by order and taboo; or if, with Sartre, we take Apocalypse to be the dialectical other to Alienation ('the suppression of the element of the Other'), the moment

---

33   Worsley, *The Trumpet Shall Sound*, 235–6.
34   See Malcolm Bull, *Seeing Things Hidden: Apocalypse, Vision and Totality*, London: Verso, 1999, 79. Bull suggests, partly relying on *The Trumpet Shall Sound*, that 'apocalyptic is dialectical and revolutionary. It is not the oppositions dissolved in the period of undifferentiation that are re-restablished, but a new set. The undifferentiated returns, that which was included is reincluded, and a new order is created, less exclusive than that which previously existed.'

when all relations of alterity are dissolved for the sake of 'subjective unity'.[35]

Once we take into account the response to imposed cultural collapse and the political function of integration, the apocalyptic dimension of certain anti-colonial movements suddenly becomes more intelligible. Tracing the correlations between eco-political catastrophes induced by imperialism and the emergence of what Norman Cohn aptly termed 'militant social chiliasm',[36] Mike Davis returns to the themes broached by Hobsbawm and Worsley, arguing for the political rationality of 'millenarian revolutions' against imperialism and its devastations. Looking into the origins of the Boxer Rebellion in China, Davis sees not simply an outburst of fanatical xenophobia, but a response to the traumatizing entanglement of geopolitical calculations, capitalist exploitation and ecological disaster. If we move past the stereotypes of fanaticism, it is possible to see how the 'esoteric doctrines of the Boxer movement were thus underlain by astute popular perceptions of imperialism'.[37] Davis also puts the famous late-nineteenth-century Canudos uprising in the backlands (*sertão*) of Brazil into the context of the ecological impact of capitalism. His interlocutor here is Euclides da Cunha, author of the classic 1902 chronicle of these events, *Rebellion in the Backlands* (*Os Sertões*), often hailed as the foundational text of Brazilian literature. Da Cunha, despite the arrogant liberalism for which Davis chides him, is also a precursor of sorts for his approach.

Os Sertões frames the account of the formation of the millenarian colony of Canudos and its brutal repression at the hands of the Brazilian army in terms of its ecological, not to say geological context.

---

35 Jean-Paul Sartre, *Cahiers pour une morale*, Paris: Gallimard, 1983, 430.

36 Norman Cohn, *The Pursuit of the Millennium*, 2nd ed, London: Mercury Books, 1962, xiv.

37 Mike Davis, *Late Victorian Holocausts*, London: Verso, 2001, 182. See also Davis's account of the 'neo-catastrophist epistemology' that underlay the Native American Ghost Dance and its instigation by the prophet Wovoka in the late nineteenth century in *Dead Cities*, New York: The New Press, 2003, 'White People Are Only a Bad Dream . . .', 23–31. Davis writes of how 'Every doomed people dreams of magical rebirth.'

A first-hand witness of the atrocities, having served as a kind of embedded reporter in the campaign, da Cunha begins with a lyrical-scientific
account of the territory and its formation. Geological violence seems
to presage and prepare the apocalyptic politics of the Canudos prophet
Antonio Conselheiro and his ragtag community. Long before its habitation, the land is both 'barbarously sterile' and 'marvelously exuberant',
an antithesis that da Cunha explicitly connects to Hegel's *Philosophy
of History*, declaring that a place for the backlands 'is lacking in the
German thinker's scheme'.[38] But what might appear as a kind of tellurian
determinism is soon inflected by human presence. Since nature 'does not
normally create deserts', the 'regressive evolution' of the arid backlands
demands that we take into account man as a 'geologic agent'. Da Cunha
is deeply sensitive to the catastrophic force of 'civilization'. 'The truth
is', he writes, 'man has not infrequently exerted a brutal reaction upon
the earth and, especially among us, has assumed throughout the long
course of our history, the role of a terrible maker-of-deserts' – deserts
that bear 'the suggestive appearance of enormous dead cities, crumbled
in ruins'.[39] Despite his avowed rationalism, and the attempt of *Os Sertões*
to steer Brazil towards progress between the regressions of millenarianism and the barbarism of its repression, da Cunha can also be a visionary
poet of the link between geological and social violence. His positivist
geographical determinism morphs into a frightening vision of the interaction of land and man: 'The martyrdom of man is here reflective of a
greater torture, more widespread, one embracing the general economy
of Life. It arises from the age-old martyrdom of the Earth.'[40] In a gesture
that radicalizes the customary link between millenarian fanaticism and
anachronism, da Cunha links political and geological regression.[41]

---

38   Euclides da Cunha, *Rebellion in the Backlands*, trans. S. Putnam, Chicago:
University of Chicago Press, 1944, 39–40. The section is entitled 'A geographical category that Hegel does not mention'.
39   Ibid., 43–4.
40   Ibid., 49.
41   Da Cunha's scheme of progression and regression occludes from him the practical, ecological dimension of the Canudos movement argued for by Davis, when he
writes that 'millenarianism in the *sertão* was also a practical social framework for coping
with environmental instability. . . . Canudos was a rational response to the relentless
chaos of drought and depression'. Davis, *Late Victorian Holocausts*, 189.

Joining geology and millenarianism is an anthropological reflection steeped in the sciences of the time. Though not entirely averse to racial stereotyping, da Cunha presents Brazil as a land where thinking of political development in terms of racial breeding, separation or purification is impossible. He mocks those who posit 'fanciful metachemistries' about the 'three races' ('Bantu Negro, Guarany Indian, and the white man'), projecting either a 'final victory of the white man' or a rise of the aboriginal base. For da Cunha – who in this sense might be said to share some kind of subterranean connection with the apocalyptic anti-racism of the millenarians at Canudos – there is no unity of race in Brazil, meaning that, even though he remains within the parameters of racial positivism, 'biological evolution' is premised on 'social evolution'. In a kind of positivist prophecy, he declares: 'We are pre-destined to form a historic race in the future.'[42]

The future, not that of a fully civilized modern republic but that of a chiliastic egalitarian kingdom, was also in the mind of Conselheiro, the backlands prophet whom da Cunha depicts as a 'striking example of atavism'. Political anatomy is inscribed into racial geography: 'It was natural that the deep-lying layers of our ethnic stratification should have cast up so extraordinary an anticlinal as Antonio Conselheiro.'[43] On this geo-biological bedrock, da Cunha erects a portrait of the 'racial messiah' of the backlands, an exemplary instance of what we could call charismatic fanaticism.[44] As a symptom of a nation struggling for unity and cohesion, Conselheiro is for da Cunha not just an individual, but a kind of synopsis of Brazil's social pathologies.

> In surveying the scene about him, this false apostle, whose excessive subjectivism predisposed him to a revolt against the natural order of things, was in a manner observing the formula of his own madness. He was not a misunderstood being. The multitude acclaimed him as the

---

42 Da Cunha, *Rebellion in the Backlands*, 54.
43 Ibid., 117. An anticline is a fold in the earth, with its oldest beds at the core, pushing up into the terrain and forming a crest. In keeping with the rest of da Cunha's account, the metaphor binds spiritual atavism to geological origins.
44 Ibid., 136.

natural representative of their highest aspirations. That was as far as it went with them: they were not concerned with his madness. As he continued to traverse a curve which would have led to the complete obscuration of reason, the milieu in its turn reacted upon him; it afforded him protection and corrected his aberrations to a degree, compelling him to establish some sort of unassailable logic even in his wildest imaginings, a certain show of order in his hallucinations, and a perduring consistency in everything he did. He manifested always a rare spirit of discipline in the control of his passions; and, as a consequence, the impressionable backlands could behold in his every word and deed the tranquillity, the moral elevation, and the sovereign resignation of an ancient apostle of faith. He was in reality a very sick man, to whom one could only apply Tanzi [and] Riva's concept of paranoia. In his ideational hallucinations the ethnic note was always prominent. He was a rare case of atavism. His morbid constitution led him to give a whimsical interpretation of objective conditions, thereby altering his relation to the external world; and this appeared as basically a retrogression to the mental state of the ancestral types of the species.[45]

Though such a figure may have been synchronous with a previous stage of social development, for instance that of early Christian monasticism, the logical intransigence and hallucinatory self-delusion of Conselheiro – albeit tempered by harmony with his sociological milieu – is for da Cunha an indicator of Brazil's incomplete civilization, signalled by the fact that it generates types that seem to belong to a phylogenetically and historically anterior moment. The prophet is a collective symptom; in the end, he is not really an agent. It is the desires of the rabble of the *sertão* that push him onwards, allowing him to 'externalize his insanity':

The multitude created him, refashioning him in its own image. It broadened his life immeasurably by impelling him into those errors

---

45   Ibid., 118–19. The reference is most likely to E. Tanzi and G. Riva, 'La paranoia. Contributo alla teoria delle degenerazioni psichiche', *Rivista Sperimentale di Freniatria*, published in several installments between 1884 and 1886.

which were common two thousand years ago. The people needed someone to translate for them their own vague idealizations, someone to guide them in the mysterious paths of heaven. And so the evangelist arose, a monstrous being, but an automaton. This man who swayed the masses was but a puppet. Passive as a shade, he moved them. When all is said, he was doing no more than to condense the obscurantism of three separate races. And he grew in stature until he was projected into History.[46]

Yet again, the idea of fanaticism as ahistorical serves as a warrant for trans-historical analogies. In da Cunha this familiar trope of anti-fanatical discourse is filtered by a positivist theory of progress and regression. At one point, he declares: 'History repeats itself. Antonio da Conselheiro was a crude gnostic.' Sameness through the ages is the cipher of fanaticism. Da Cunha is particularly adamant about the parallels with Montanism, the second-century Christian movement to which the theologian Tertullian belonged.[47] Like Montanism, Conselheiro's movement is an extravagant millenarianism convinced of the 'earth's epilogue': 'One could not desire a more complete reproduction of the same system of dogma, the same images, the same hyperbolical formulas, the very same words almost.' In a positivist vein, da Cunha adds that it is 'a splendid example of evolutionary stages among peoples. The retrograde type of the backlands reproduces the aspect presented by mystics of the past. Viewing him, one has a marvellous impression of a perspective down the centuries'.[48]

Analogies and identities can be reversed. In the work of Norman Cohn, millenarianism is not only a socio-political type recognizable through different epochs. It also contains a 'remote foreshadowing of present conditions', of those 'totalitarian' political movements which are alleged to have secularized the millennium.[49] I will return to this dimension of Cohn's work later, in the context of the debate over

---

46 Ibid., 129.
47 See Cohn, *The Pursuit of the Millennium*, 9.
48 Da Cunha, *Rebellion in the Backlands*, 134.
49 Cohn, *The Pursuit of the Millennium*, xiv, 307–19.

political religion. For the moment, I simply want to note the sociological aspect of his writing on North European millenarian movements of the Middle Ages. Distinguishing them from established forms of religious extremism or heresy, as well as from what we could call 'reformist' peasant struggles, Cohn wants to set revolutionary fanaticisms apart, underscoring the manner in which they bind millenarian prophecies and expectations with the attempt to transform the world, bringing heaven to earth.[50] Crucially, these movements don't arise in areas where misery and oppression might be naturalized by social stability or attenuated by custom. Their geography matches the geography of technological and economic change, rising production, social upheaval and the creation of new needs. If not capitalism proper, then at least commerce is what impels them into existence. Eschatology is no longer bound to conjunctures of political defeat, a 'future compensation for present affliction',[51] as it was in ancient Judaism. It is the bearer of dynamic claims born of the displacement and dispossession that invariably accompany the expanded horizons of a world whose customs and hierarchies have been unmoored by economic change. For Cohn, the mediaeval upsurge of 'subterranean revolutionary eschatology'[52] in these nexuses of transformation speaks not so much of defeat as of thwarted desire. Though many gained from commercial expansion, there were also 'many who merely acquired new wants without being able to satisfy them; and in them the spectacle of wealth undreamt-of in earlier centuries provoked a bitter sense of frustration'.[53] Who were these envious victims of progress? Deeming settled peasants to be revolutionary only in exceptional circumstances,[54] Cohn opts instead for a variant of the theory of the lumpenproletariat:

---

50   Ibid., 307.
51   Ibid., 3.
52   Ibid., xv.
53   Ibid., 28.
54   '[I]t was only very rarely that settled peasants could be induced to embark on the pursuit of the Millennium. And when they did so it was either because they were caught up in some vast movement which had originated in quite different social strata, or because their own traditional way of life was becoming impossible, or – which was the commonest case – for both these reasons together.' Ibid., 24.

Journeymen and unskilled workers, peasants without land or with too little to support them, beggars and vagabonds, the unemployed and those threatened with unemployment, the many who for one reason or another could find no assured and recognized place – such people, living in a state of chronic frustration and anxiety, formed the most impulsive and unstable elements in mediaeval society. Any disturbing, frightening or exciting event – any kind of revolt or revolution, a summons to a crusade, an interregnum, a plague or a famine, anything in fact which disrupted the normal routine of social life – acted on these people with peculiar sharpness and called forth reactions of peculiar violence. And the way in which they attempted to deal with their common plight was to form a salvationist group under the leadership of some man whom they regarded as extraordinarily holy.[55]

The affinities with da Cunha's account are substantial. Powerlessness, anxiety and desire goad a motley multitude, set adrift by the collapse of social order and differentiation, towards the millenarian solution. What in Cohn's Marxian turn of phrase is a 'surplus population',[56] in da Cunha's chronicle is a 'multifarious population', 'made up of the most disparate elements, from the fervent believer who had voluntarily given up all the conveniences of life elsewhere to the solitary bandit who arrived with his blunderbuss on his shoulder in search of a new field for his exploits'. What for Worsley was understood as the integrative function of millenarianism is here its horrifying massification and undifferentiation: 'under the spell of the place, all these elements were welded together into one uniform and homogeneous community, an unconscious brute mass, which, without organs and without specialized functions, continued to grow rather than evolve, through the mere mechanical juxtaposition of successive layers, in the manner of a human polyp'.[57] The same motif is present in da Cunha's horrified description of the 'monstrous *urbs*' or 'sinister *civitas*' which the followers of Conselheiro established after their 'hegira'. This is his account of millenarian urbanism:

---

55   Ibid., 30.
56   Ibid., 27. For the use of the term in Marx, see *Capital: Volume 1*, Chapter 25, Sections 3 and 4.
57   Da Cunha, *Rebellion in the Backlands*, 149.

The settlement, accordingly, grew in dizzying fashion, sprawling out over the hills. The dwellings which were thrown up being extremely rude ones, the homeless multitude was able to erect as many as a dozen a day; and, as this colossal weed patch took shape, it appeared to reflect in its physical characteristics, as if by a stereographic process, the moral attributes of the social strata which had found refuge there. It was the objectivization of a tremendous insanity. A living document whose implications were not to be evaded, a piece of direct corpus delicti evidence on the aberrations of the populace. It was all done wholly at random, with the fervor of the mad.[58]

The millenarian movement joins anomic difference with a horrifying homogeneity, and provides a doubly monstrous visage, binding the frenzied leader ('a buffoon maddened with a vision of the Apocalypse', writes da Cunha of Conselheiro) to his amorphous, fanatical retinue. In this respect da Cunha is following a template fashioned long before his time, in the foundational religious and polemical polemics triggered by the German Peasants' War, and focused on the figure of Thomas Müntzer, the itinerant preacher and political agitator whose short-lived, tumultuous ministry became a key testing ground for twentieth-century conceptions of the relation between politics, religion and historical change.

THE TIME OF THE SCHWÄRMER:
THOMAS MÜNTZER IN THE LIGHT OF REVOLUTION

'*Anno domini* 1525, at the beginning of the year, there was a great, unprecedented upheaval of the Common Man throughout the German lands' – thus wrote a contemporary of what is now known as the German Peasants' War.[59] More than three hundred years later, Marx referred to it as 'the most radical episode in German history'.[60] Fusing together

---

58   Ibid., 144.

59   Johannes Stumpf, *Reformationschronik*, quoted in Peter Blickle, *From the Communal Reformation to the Revolution of the Common Man*, trans. B. Kümin, Leiden: Brill, 1998, 94.

60   Karl Marx, 'On the Jewish Question', in *Early Writings*, trans. R. Livingstone and G. Benton, London: Penguin, 1992, 252.

theological radicalism with social conflicts stemming from profound economic transformations and the exactions of the German princes, the Peasants' War was not only the most notable popular revolt in Europe prior to the French Revolution (with around 100,000 peasants killed in its repression); it also became an important reference-point for any meditation on the bonds between religious activism and social upheaval, theology and politics.

Despite the presence of other eloquent leaders within this wide-spread and heterogeneous revolt, it is Thomas Müntzer who has been singled out as the emblematic figure in the Peasants' War, or, as Ernst Bloch would have it, 'the theologian of the revolution'. Attitudes to Müntzer have been divided, to say the least. In intellectual portraits and narratives almost invariably skewed by the politics of their authors, this 'servant of god against the godless' – as he signed some of his letters – has featured either as a dangerous fanatic, or as a heroic revolutionary precursor.

The idea of the *Schwärmer* or fanatic as the utmost threat to the orderly reproduction of society, bent on collapsing the city of God into the city of man in an apocalyptic conflagration, can indeed be traced back to the early responses to Müntzer by the Protestant monks of Wittenberg, and in particular by his erstwhile interlocutors Luther and Melanchthon. After their break around 1523, prompted by Müntzer's increasingly overt political agitation and his related repudiation of key tenets of Luther's preaching – above all the Pauline justification of obedience to earthly authorities – Luther, eager to demarcate his own project of reformation from Müntzer's subversive activities and to quell an anti-authoritarian and iconoclastic surge that could be laid at his door, lambasts 'the Satan of Allstedt' as fanatical, seditious and demagogical. In the *Letter to the Princes of Saxony concerning the rebellious spirit* (1524), the great reformer castigates Müntzer's doctrine of the primacy of the spirit over the letter and what he (correctly) perceives as its revolutionary implications: that it would lead the common people 'to overthrow civil authority and make themselves lords of the world', thereby besmirching a faith which fights against papal authority in order to purify itself *from* authority, not to overturn it. The 'villainous and bloodthirsty prophet', Müntzer, aims at imposing faith by the sword and drawing from the scriptures a principle of violence. The Gospels cannot justify this mutinous meddling in worldly things.

And yet the ban on political revolt as the greatest evil and impediment to salvation, joined with the legitimation of the authorities that rule over this fallen world, means that Luther, far from condemning violence as such, will extol it when it comes to the repression of the false prophet and his multitude of followers. In May 1525, in a screed written prior to, but published in the wake of, the rebel forces' bloody rout at Frankenhausen – *Against the Robbing and Murdering Hordes of Peasants* – Luther applied the great power of his pen to singing the praises of the princes' swords. In a text that could serve as the template for the many justifications of untrammelled violence against 'fanatics' in the centuries to come, he writes:

> Stab, smite, slay, whoever can. If you die in doing it, well for you! A more blessed death can never be yours, for you die obeying the divine Word and commandment in Romans 13, and in loving service of your neighbour, whom you are rescuing from the bonds of hell and of the devil. . . . If anyone thinks this too hard, let him remember that rebellion is intolerable and that the destruction of the world is to be expected every hour.[61]

Though none of Müntzer's many detractors through the ages reached the pitch of Luther's anathemas, the idea of Müntzer as a fanatic is widespread. Philipp Melanchthon, who had befriended Müntzer during the latter's early passage through Wittenberg, would later go on – in the anonymously published *History of Thomas Müntzer, the author of the Thuringian revolt, very profitable reading* – to justify the bloody repression meted out against the 'rabble' and its devil-possessed false prophet.[62] In his commentary on Aristotle's *Politics* (1529), he enshrined the notion of the fanatic in political theory, condemning as 'fanatical people'

61   E. G. Rupp and Benjamin Drewery (eds.), *Martin Luther*, *Documents of Modern History*, London: Edward Arnold, 1970, 126.
62   Hans-Jürgen Goertz, *Thomas Müntzer: Apocalyptic, Mystic and Revolutionary*, Edinburgh: T&T Clark, 1993, 11.

those who, like Müntzer and his comrades, would condemn private property on the basis of the Gospels and thus lay waste to the principles of 'civil society'.[63]

In opposition to the Augustinian separation of the two cities (the City of Man and the City of God), and to the Lutheran distinction between political and spiritual authority, Müntzer views the transformation of the inner or spiritual order of man, a mystical theme drawn from his reading of Christian mystics like Johannes Tauler, as inseparable from the transformation of the outer order. For Müntzer, the issue 'really was one of a transformation of relationships, namely those binding individuals to God, to themselves and to the church and temporal authorities respectively, and these authorities to God and people'. This is why the 'revolution in consciousness is a political and social revolution'.[64] As is manifest in Müntzer's crucial declaration of intent, the *Sermon to the Princes*, this revolution is inseparable in its very grammar from the thematic of apocalypse, of 'a full and final reformation'. Throughout, Müntzer rejects the very idea that any worldly authority, especially one implicated in the exploitation of the common people, should ever inspire fear or be immune from insurrection, if its rule is unjust. As Müntzer retorts to 'the unspiritual soft-living Flesh at Wittenberg' (i.e. Luther) in *Vindication and Refutation*, it is no idle desire for revolt that has spurred him to agitate among the miners of Mansfeld and other common men, but the belief that 'the power of the sword as well as the key to realise sins is in the hands of the whole community'. He adds: 'Anyone who wants to judge this matter fairly should neither love an insurrection nor, on the other hand, should he be averse to a justified uprising.'[65] In a passage that exemplifies the scriptural vitriol and political energy of his writing, this critique of the Lutheran justification of authority is combined with an attack on the kind of economic oppression facilitated by the princes' 'sword' (and Luther's theology):

---

63 Colas, *Civil Society and Fanaticism*, 8, 43.
64 Goertz, *Thomas Müntzer*, 204–5.
65 Peter Matheson (ed.), *The Collected Works of Thomas Müntzer*, Edinburgh: T&T Clark, 1988, 341.

What is the evil brew from which all usury, theft and robbery springs but the assumption of our lords and princes that all creatures are their property? The fish in the water, the birds in the air, the plants on the face of the earth – it all has to belong to them! To add insult to injury, they have God's commandment proclaimed to the poor: God has commanded that you should not steal. But it avails them nothing. For while they do violence to everyone, flay and fleece the poor farm worker, tradesman and everything that breathes, yet should any of the latter commit the pettiest crime, he must hang. And Doctor Liar [Luther] responds, Amen. It is the lords themselves who make the poor man their enemy. If they refuse to do away with the causes of insurrection how can trouble be avoided in the long run? If saying that makes me an inciter to insurrection, so be it![66]

Müntzer's fame as a *Schwärmer* is not just a product of his rabble-rousing. It also stems from his verve for unbridled vituperation, in rhetorical flights of arresting violence (which shouldn't blind us to the full range of his writing, from pastoral letters to scriptural exegesis, from dream interpretation to liturgy). As Engels noted: 'Incessantly he fanned the flame of hatred against the ruling classes. He spurred the wildest passions, using forceful terms of expression the like of which religious and nationalist delirium had put into the mouths of the Old Testament prophets.'[67] But the fury of his rhetoric refreshed the standard arsenal of apocalypticism. Take his letter to his arch-nemesis, Count Ernst von Mansfeld: 'Just tell us, you miserable, wretched sack of worms, who made you a prince over the people whom God redeemed with his dear blood?'[68] Or his warning to the common people that the priests 'will shit on you with a new logic, twisting the word of God'.[69] His exhortations range from the allegorical – 'The living God is sharpening his scythe in me, so that later I can cut down

66   Ibid., 335.
67   Friedrich Engels, *The Peasant War in Germany*, trans. M. J. Olgin, London: George Allen & Unwin, 1927, 137.
68   *The Collected Works of Thomas Müntzer*, 155.
69   Ibid., 340.

the red poppies and the blue cornflowers'[70] – to the frenzied, as in his letter to the people of Allstedt:

> Go to it, go to it, while the fire is hot! Don't let your sword grow cold, don't let it hang down limply! Hammer away ding-dong on the anvils of Nimrod, cast down their tower to the ground! As long as they live it is impossible for you to rid yourselves of the fear of men. One cannot say anything to you about God as long as they rule over you. Go to it, go to it, while it is day![71]

And his enemies – Luther, the 'godless', the priests and princes – find themselves the object of a rich panoply of insults: 'abandoned reprobates', 'thin-shitters', 'platelickers', 'clownish, testicled doctors', 'toad-spawn', 'whore-riders'.[72] As if Müntzer's authenticated writings were not enough, Melanchthon's *History* even puts the following declamation in his mouth, as if to seal the accusation of fanatical desecration and false prophecy: 'I shit on God if he does not do my bidding.' In the image and the reality of Müntzer, scatology and eschatology are never too far apart.

The image of Müntzer as the fanatic, transmitted in plays and chronicles as well as in his portraits – which, as Goertz's fine biography shows, were based not on observation but on a physiognomy of heresy – still exerted its fascination well into the twentieth century. Thus the historian G. R. Elton memorably introduces Müntzer as a 'youngish man full of violent hatred for all things other than they should have been, university trained, an idealist of the kind familiar in all revolutions'. Elton goes on to dub him 'the demonic genius of the early Reformation' and concludes, in terms wholly congruent with the tradition initiated by Luther and Melanchthon, that he was 'not so much a constructive revolutionary as an unrestrained fanatic, and in his preaching of violence a dangerous lunatic'.[73] But the most influential depiction of Müntzer as a fanatic is

---

70 Ibid., 54.
71 *The Collected Works of Thomas Müntzer*, 142.
72 Goertz, *Thomas Müntzer*, 79.
73 G. R. Elton, *Reformation Europe 1517–1559*, London: Collins, 1963, 91–4.

to be found in Cohn's *Pursuit of the Millennium*, a text that proposes a short-circuit between the distant past of the Peasants' War and the political exigencies of the present, lending its weight to the vastly influential idea of 'political religion'. For Cohn, 'Müntzer was a *propheta* obsessed by eschatological phantasies which he attempted to translate into reality by exploiting social discontent.'[74] His narrative of the theologian of the revolution, albeit driven by the need to condemn political fanaticism, often attains a quasi-cinematic effect, as when he writes: 'Obsessed as always by the impending destruction of the ungodly, he had a red crucifix and a naked sword carried in front of him when, at the head of an armed band, he patrolled the streets of the town.'[75]

This verdict represents the deliberate reversal of a communist and Marxist tradition that had adopted Müntzer as a heroic herald of egalitarian, revolutionary politics, precariously poised between a decaying mediaeval world of pre-capitalist communism, and the class struggle against the dispossessions and dislocations of an expanding capitalist economy. This tradition, which views Müntzer as the fiery precursor of contemporary revolutions, has generally downplayed the apocalyptic and mystical thrust of Müntzer's sermons and texts, as well as his theological and scriptural originality, focusing instead on his capacity to crystallize the discontent of the peasants and the common man and, eventually, to organize their revolt. The resurrections of Thomas Müntzer have frequently coincided with upsurges of revolutionary struggle. Thus the first proper biography of Müntzer, by Ströbel, was written in the wake of the French Revolution, while Zimmerman, author of the influential *General History of the Peasants' Revolt*, was a Young Hegelian who sought to read Müntzer through the radical democratic struggles of 1840s Germany. In his seminal *The Peasant War in Germany* (1850), arguably the first work of Marxist history, Engels turned to Müntzer in order to think through the defeat of the 1848 revolutions and to revive a fitting, if anachronistic, revolutionary emblem. Müntzer returned again with the defeated German revolution of

---

74   Cohn, *Pursuit of the Millennium*, 271. Cohn's polemical intent is obvious from the sentence immediately following: 'Perhaps after all it is a sound instinct that has led Marxists to claim him for their own.'
75   Ibid., 263–4.

1917–23, in Ernst Bloch's *Thomas Müntzer: Theologian of the Revolution*, but also in more popular modes, such as Berta Lask's agitprop play, staged in 1925 in Eisleben, for 'Red Müntzer Day'.[76] Mediated by Cohn's deeply unsympathetic work, even the Situationists in and around May '68 found in Müntzer and the heretical movements linked to his name a resource for the revolutionary present. All of these moments saw the revitalization of a 'fanatical' communist principle that was famously extorted from Müntzer under torture, shortly before his execution:

> All things are to be held in common (*omnia sunt communia*) and distribution should be to each according to his need, as occasion arises. Any prince, count, or gentleman who refused to do this should first be given a warning, but then one should cut off his head or hang him.[77]

The matrix for the recovery of Müntzer as a revolutionary icon – an icon of egalitarian iconoclasm, of the battle against what he called 'dead wooden things' – was and remains Engels's potent text, written after the defeat of 1848, as a way of reflecting on the objective and subjective obstacles to social transformation and of affirming a specifically German revolutionary heritage. The importance of Müntzer for Engels exceeds the simple evaluation of the Peasants' War, profoundly colouring the Marxist understanding of revolts that find their symbolism and legitimation in religious conceptions of the world. Engels's critical history rests on some key tenets: Müntzer is the representative of a class and of its political direction; apocalyptic theology is a historically necessary limitation of a political project ahead of its time; contrary to the image of him as a delirious demagogue, Müntzer is an astute revolutionary agitator and strategist. Engels presents a tripartite schema, in which three camps confront one another: 'the conservative Catholic camp' of the defenders of the status quo (imperial authorities, some princes, nobility, etc.), 'the camp of *burgher-like moderate Lutheran* reforms' (lesser nobility, burghers, some lay princes) and the '*revolutionary*' party' of plebeians

---

76 On the return of Müntzer, see Goertz, *Thomas Müntzer*, 12–19.
77 *The Collected Works of Thomas Müntzer*, 437.

and peasants, of which Müntzer is the most eloquent spokesperson. In a period when 'the dogmas of the church were at the same time political axioms',[78] theology functioned as the arena in which socio-political conflicts were both defined and intensified.

Despite what we might surmise from the name of the 'war' of 1525, for Engels it is the plebeians (the Mansfeld miners and poorer townspeople whom Müntzer strove to organize), rather than the peasants, who represent the crucial class, 'the only class that stood outside the existing official society'. In contrast to Cohn's later interpretation, which takes Engels as its polemical target, the sociology of the rebellion is not founded merely on the frustrated, heterogeneous and amorphous mass of the 'losers' of economic expansion, but on the idea of the making of a proto-proletariat of sorts, whose negative exteriority to the status quo can also be translated into a sustained political unity, rather than a purely apocalyptic aggregation. Müntzer's restless organizational activity – sermons, letters, constant peregrinations, flights and agitation, as well as his later armed endeavours – is in Engels's view aimed at fomenting the unity of this 'class', which is to say at building alliances among its disparate members, as well as between it and the peasantry in the broader 'party' of revolution. Political organizations, such as the 'League of the Elect' in Allstedt, or the 'Eternal Council' and revolutionary commune in Mühlhausen, have this as their purpose.[79]

When it comes to the theological dimension of Müntzer's preaching and of the peasants' demands, Engels writes of screens, flags or masks for an underlying class conflict.[80] Though this theme is a mainstay of Marxist theories of religion and ideology, the reasons adduced for it are significant. Behind religious consciousness, there lies a sociological compulsion. It is because Müntzer's own camp, the 'plebeians', were both the 'symptoms' of a decaying feudalism and the 'first precursors of modern bourgeois society' that they were compelled by this situation of transition into a forward-flight towards an apocalyptic

---

78   Engels, *The Peasant War in Germany*, 52.
79   The contribution of Karl Kautsky's treatment of Müntzer in his 1897 *Communism in Central Europe* lies in following the red thread of this organizational activity.
80   Engels, *The Peasant War in Germany*, 51.

ideology. For Engels, the fact that they were both symptoms and precursors explains

> why the plebeian opposition of that time could not be satisfied with fight-
> ing feudalism and the privileged middle-class alone; why, in fantasy, at
> least, it reached beyond modern bourgeois society then only in its incep-
> tion; why, being an absolutely propertyless faction, it questioned institu-
> tions, views and conceptions common to every society based on division
> of classes. The chiliastic dream-visions of ancient Christianity offered
> in this respect a very serviceable starting-point. On the other hand, this
> reaching out beyond not only the present but also the future, could not
> help being violently fantastic. At the first practical application, it natu-
> rally fell back into narrow limits set by prevailing conditions.[81]

In Engels's account, which laid the groundwork for the debate on the politics of millenarian movements, the question of fanaticism is closely entangled with that of time. From the vantage point of a secularized capitalism in which social relations and ideology are in some sense aligned with one another, sixteenth-century Germany appears as a world in which the vocabulary of theology and religious heresy was out of sync with the momentous development of productive forces and social relations. The Peasants' War was an anachronistic revolt, but not in the simple sense of an attempt to retain customs and relations doomed to obsolescence by primitive accumulation. The historical and sociological ambivalence of its partisans, both remnants and precursors, as well as the conflicting uses of a Christian discourse split between the justification of authority and the call to revolt, means that while the plebeians' heroic uprising was materially bound to fail, this is because of its prematurity rather than its backwardness. For Engels, there is a short-circuit between the primitive communist millenarianism of the peasants' rebellion – drawn from the ideational reservoir of early Christianity – and a realizable communist future. Contravening any rigid conception of the historical-materialist method, Engels takes the prophetic character

---

81 Ibid., 56.

of Müntzer seriously, seeing his preaching not just as the expression of
the demands of the oppressed, or as a compilation of their grievances,
but as 'a genius's anticipation of the conditions for the emancipation of
the proletarian element that had just begun to develop among the plebeians'.[82] Millenarianism is the form taken by this projection of a classless, stateless society, which could only become a real possibility many
centuries later.

But this nonsynchronism also means that Müntzer suffers the bitter fate
of leaders who are set tasks that present conditions make unrealizable: 'he
necessarily finds himself in a dilemma. What he *can* do is in contrast to
all his actions as hitherto practised, to all his principles and to the present
interests of his party; what he *ought* to do cannot be achieved.'[83] Either a
disastrous *fuite en avant* or a reformist retreat seem to be the only options
for an untimely revolutionary. In this gap between religious fantasy and
the real prospects of emancipation, the cunning of capitalist history meant
that the 'anticipation of communism by fantasy became in reality an anticipation of modern bourgeois conditions', as 'vague Christian equality'
turned into 'equality before the law'.[84] Writing of the short-lived experience of Müntzer's government in Mühlhausen, Engels comments that the
'social transformation that [Müntzer] pictured in his fantasy was so little
grounded in the then existing economic conditions that the latter were a
preparation for a social system diametrically opposed to that of which he
dreamt'; Müntzer's institutional experiments 'in reality never went beyond
a feeble and unconscious attempt prematurely to establish the bourgeois
society of a later period'.[85] Both a powerful heritage of unattained emancipation and a tragedy of inevitable failure, the Peasants' War, crystallized
in the figure of Müntzer, can only be redeemed by the concrete actualiza-
tion of what for the plebeian masses routed at Frankenhausen could only
be 'dream-visions'.

The positive, anticipatory dimension of Müntzer's communist millenarian anachronism is at the heart of the most significant re-evaluation

82   Ibid., 66.
83   Ibid., 135.
84   Ibid., 56.
85   Ibid., 136–7.

of the great *Schwärmer*, Bloch's *Thomas Müntzer: Theologian of the Revolution*, a book written in the midst of Germany's own thwarted revolution. In it, Bloch tries to do justice to the convergence of apocalyptic theology, mystical spirituality and revolutionary politics in the life and writings of the militant preacher. Insisting on the positive dimension of revolutionary nonsynchronism, Bloch does not see the theological impetus of the revolution of the common man of 1525 as the mere index of socio-economic immaturity. On the contrary, he depicts it as one of those situations that bear witness to the fact that a religious-political superstructure can be in advance of an economic base which will only later attain maturity. Bloch wishes to stress the anticipatory character of Müntzer's anachronism, without immediately relegating it to the scrapheap of necessary failures. With its emphasis on the primacy of the spirit and the necessity of suffering, its injunction that the believer make himself empty and detach himself from the world, but also its strong emphasis on the coming deification of man in the millennium, Müntzer's theology is for Bloch a driving force of his political agitation, not a mask for historical necessity.

Rather than accepting the disjunction between (premature) political content and (sterile) religious form, Bloch finds in Müntzer the paradoxical union of theology and revolution, without the one serving as an instrument for the other. Whereas Luther employed the prospect of the apocalypse in his justification of worldly authorities, for Müntzer – as demonstrated by his gripping and hallucinatory interpretation of the apocalyptic Book of Daniel in the *Sermon to the Princes* – it provides all the more reason to accelerate and intensify the struggle for a community of equals. In such a community, the fear of God would not be impeded by fear of the authorities; it would be possible for the poor and even the 'heathens' to embrace a Christian life without suffering the depredations of the 'godless'.[86]

Bloch's heretical Marxism, with its generous stance towards the religious drive and its subversion of some classic tenets of historical

---

86 Tommaso La Rocca argues that the 'godless' is a sociological and polemical category targeting those clerical and political authorities that stand in the way of a religion of the common man. See *Es Ist Zeit. Apocalisse e storia – studio su Thomas Müntzer (1490–1525)*, Bologna: Cappelli, 1988, 32–6.

materialism, could not but irk his political comrades. In his seminal 1923 essay 'Reification and the Consciousness of the Proletariat', which forms the theoretical core of *History and Class Consciousness*, Georg Lukács offered an incisive and intransigent critique of Bloch, centred on the place of pre-capitalist and religious forms of political subjectivity in the development of a proletarian politics.[87] In many respects, Lukács's critique of Bloch's 'anarcho-Bolshevik'[88] utopianism remains emblematic of dialectical arguments against transcendent, religious or messianic radicalisms. It also indicates how the debate about fanaticism can be read in part as a debate over what an effective anti-capitalist politics might mean.

Lukács's turn to Marxism had meant a drastic break with his earlier tragic and utopian leanings, and led him to make a claim for the proletariat's practical and epistemological uniqueness as a historical subject utterly unlike any previous class, however revolutionary.[89] For him, this necessitated a critique of any position that abided within the 'antinomies of bourgeois thought', those impasses that beset any thinking unable to critically grasp and practically terminate the pernicious effects of reification, understood as the transformation of social relations between people into calculable and abstract relations between things. The entirety of Lukács's essay can be regarded as an excavation of Marx's dictum from the 1843 *Introduction to the Critique of Hegel's Philosophy of Right*, which serves as its epigraph: 'To be radical is to go to the root of the matter. For man, however, the root is man himself.' For Lukács, any political and philosophical radicalism which remained tied to a generic notion of

---

87   On the close friendship and later polemics between Bloch and Lukács, see Michael Löwy, 'Interview with Ernst Bloch', *New German Critique* 9, 1976; *Georg Lukács: From Romanticism to Bolshevism*, trans. P. Camiller, London: NLB, 1979, 52–6.

88   Michael Löwy, *Redemption and Utopia: Jewish Libertarian Thought in Central Europe – A Study in Elective Affinity*, trans. H. Heaney, London: Athlone Press, 1992, 143.

89   'The self-understanding of the proletariat is therefore simultaneously the objective understanding of the nature of society.' Conversely, because of its objective social position, the proletariat is the bearer of a unique subjective possibility. As a human commodity, it is a subject-object, alone capable of dialectically transforming history. Georg Lukács, 'Reification and the Consciousness of the Proletariat', in *History and Class Consciousness*, trans. R. Livingstone, Cambridge, MA: The MIT Press, 1971, 149.

humanity and failed to comprehend Marx's analysis of the commodity could only be counter-productive.[90]

In this regard, Bloch's *Thomas Müntzer* is a natural target. Despite its fervent allegiance to the Bolshevik revolution, Bloch's book strives to identify a supra-historical, meta-political and meta-religious element, what he tellingly called an *Ubique*, an 'everywhere'. What Müntzer channels is a utopian impetus that cannot be exhausted or contained by socio-economic dialectic or political strategy. The critique of Bloch is situated in the midst of Lukács's treatment of the fate of humanism within Marxism, which is to say in the revolutionary theory that adopts and intensifies the political-epistemological 'standpoint of the proletariat'. Almost as if to correct what might have appeared as the prolongation of his own early romantic anti-capitalism – which protested against capitalism as an engine of dehumanization – Lukács tries to purge humanism of myth, which is to say of its debilitating compromise with reified bourgeois conceptuality. If humanism is really to dislocate the structures of reification, its non-dialectical immediacy must be overcome. Accordingly, 'If the attempt is made to attribute an immediate form of existence to class consciousness, it is not possible to avoid lapsing into mythology: the result will be a mysterious species-consciousness . . . whose relation to and impact upon the individual consciousness is wholly incomprehensible.'[91]

The picture that emerges is that of a battle between two humanisms. The first bases itself on what Lukács calls 'classical philosophy', and identifies a transcendental and trans-historical kernel of humanity to be ethically and cognitively rescued from its capitalist dehumanization. The second, a proletarian, revolutionary humanism, reinvents Protagoras's adage in order to argue that 'man has become the measure of all (societal) things', insofar as 'fetishistic objects' have been dissolved into 'processes that take place among men and are objectified in concrete relations between them'.[92] The

---

90 For Lukács, 'there is no solution that [cannot] be found in the solution to the riddle of commodity-*structure*'. Lukács, *History and Class Consciousness*, 83.

91 Ibid., 173.

92 Ibid., 185.

formulation of this revolutionary humanism constitutes Lukács's most unequivocal act of separation from his earlier ethical dualism, which posed an unbridgeable gap between the *ought* and the *is*, between the doomed radicalism of a romantic subjectivity and the impersonal mechanisms of a capitalist object-world. In *History and Class Consciousness*, capitalism can only be exploded from the inside, by an agent formed by the process of reification itself. Conversely, a revolutionary humanism can only emerge when social life is thoroughly subsumed under capitalist relations, when 'in this objectification, in this rationalisation and reification of all social forms . . . we see clearly for the first time how society is constructed from the relations of men with each other'.[93]

The harshness of Lukács's judgment on Bloch's *Müntzer* is of a piece with his attempt to define a revolutionary Marxian humanism. Bloch is the foremost communist exemplar of that utopian strand which Lukács depicts as the historical counterpart of a Christian dualism that left the City of Man unscathed, deporting human wishes to the City of God. For Lukács, Bloch is unable, as was Müntzer, to extricate himself from a theology that impotently juxtaposes a transcendent humanization to a dehumanized world, the utopian to the concrete. Within this utopian counterpart to a quietist and servile Christian ontology, Lukács isolates two strands (themselves forming a further antinomy, another blocked duality): on the one hand, a view of empirical reality for which the latter can only be transformed by an apocalypse; on the other, a radical interiorization, whereby humanity can only be attained in the figure of the saint. In either case, change is but a semblance.

Giving short shrift to the practical and strategic character of Müntzer's vision,[94] Lukács intensifies Engels's judgement on the role of theology in the German Peasants' War, not treating it merely as an anachronistic 'flag' and 'mask' for inarticulate social demands, but as an impediment and a diversion: 'Real actions then appear – precisely in their objective,

---

93   Ibid., 176.
94   See the critical comments on Lukács's treatment of Bloch's *Thomas Müntzer* in La Rocca, *Es Ist Zeit*, 191–5. This is to my knowledge the only text that specifically deals with these revealing passages in *History and Class Consciousness*.

revolutionary sense – wholly independent of the religious utopia: the latter can neither lead them in any real sense, nor can it offer concrete objectives or concrete proposals for their realisation.' Moreover, the duality between man's inner being and his empirical conditions – joined but not mediated by a theology of history (predestination, chiliasm, etc.) – is viewed by Lukács, in a variation on Weber's thesis, as 'the basic ideological structure of capitalism'. Thus it is 'no accident that it was the revolutionary religiosity of the sects that supplied the ideology for capitalism in its purest forms (in England and America)'. In sum, whether we look at Bloch's attempt to supplement the 'merely economic' dimension of historical materialism with a utopian spark, or at 'the way in which the religious and utopian premises of the theory concretely impinge upon Müntzer's actions',[95] we encounter the same symptom of the incapacity to overcome bourgeois thought, the same *hiatus irrationalis* between principle and practice, the spirit and the letter, the spiritual and the economic. For Lukács, only the proletariat, 'as the Archimedean point from which the whole of reality can be overthrown', is capable of suturing this hiatus and heralding a 'real social revolution' capable of 'restructuring . . . the real and concrete life of man', thus abolishing the reified duality between the utopian and the economic.[96]

In relating the theology of revolution to the antinomies of bourgeois thought – through its paroxystic transcendence of the world, which is powerless to unhinge the latter's material constitution – Lukács's criticism papers over the specificity of Bloch's treatment of a religious and utopian excess. Consider Bloch's reflections on Weber's sociology of religion. In a crucial passage of his *Thomas Müntzer*, which also relies on Marx's account of the historical masks of revolution in the 18th Brumaire, Bloch argues for the relative autonomy of 'moral and psychological complexes'. Without these it is not only impossible to comprehend the appearance of phenomena such as the German Peasants' War, but also to capture 'the deepest *contents* of this tumultuous human history, this

---

95   Lukács, *History and Class Consciousness*, 192.
96   Lukács, *History and Class Consciousness*, 193. 'Already the mechanical separation between economics and politics precludes any really effective action encompassing society in its totality' (195).

lucid dream of the anti-wolf, of a finally fraternal kingdom' – which is an indispensable stimulus to collective revolutionary action. To quote Jameson's perspicacious commentary on Bloch:

> what distinguishes the force of religion from the less binding, more contemplative play of art proper is the conjunction of absolute belief and collective participation which are united in the concept of the millenarian or the chiliastic. Through the second of these twin concepts, religion is distinguished from philosophy, where there can theoretically be such a thing as solitary truth: in Müntzer's theology, the very truth-coefficient of a theological doctrine is measured by collective need, by the belief and recognition of the multitudes themselves. Hence a theological idea, in contrast to a philosophical one, already implies in its very structure a church or group of believers around it, and exists therefore on a protopolitical, rather than a purely theoretical level.[97]

Recalling, after a fashion, Marx's own treatment of Germany's potentially revolutionary anachronism in the *Introduction to the Critique of Hegel's Philosophy of Right*,[98] Bloch – unlike Engels, Kautsky, and of course Lukács – does not see the theological impetus of the revolution of the common man of 1525 as the index of socio-economic immaturity. This is also evidenced in Bloch's review of *History and Class Consciousness*, 'Actuality and Utopia', where, though praising Lukács's towering achievement, he chastises him for carrying out 'an almost exclusively sociological homogenization' of the processes of revolution, transformation and humanization, which ignores the 'polyrhythmic' character of the totality and reproduces one of the products of reification, the rigid non-dialectical separation between domains (for instance, economics and religion).[99]

---

97   Fredric Jameson, *Marxism and Form*, Princeton: Princeton University Press, 1971, 156–7.
98   See my '*Ad Hominem*: Antinomies of Radical Philosophy', *Filosofski Vestnik* XXIX, 2 (2008).
99   Ernst Bloch, 'Aktualität und Utopie. Zu Lukács' "Geschichte und Klassenbewusstsein"', in *Philosophische Aufsätze*, Frankfurt: Suhrkamp Verlag, 1969.

Against the homogeneity of class and the synchronicity of revolution that he discerns in Lukács, for Bloch the Peasants' War bears witness to the fact that 'the superstructure is often in advance of an . . . economy that will only later attain its maturity'.[100] We see here how the nature of the relationship between social transformation and historical time is among the foremost sources of divergence in the understanding of millenarian movements and what heritage, if any, they bequeath to atheist anti-capitalism. The positive use of anachronism suggested by Marx, and given an extreme form by Bloch, as a recovery and repetition of Müntzer for a revolutionary present, is rejected by Lukács, for whom the revolutionary utopianism of the peasants' revolt was merely a by-product of a situation wherein a real restructuring of life was 'objectively impossible'.[101] As the tone of his references to the Russian Revolution suggests, Bloch saw the link between the theological-utopian impulse and a certain, socially determinate, backward and peripheral place within capitalism as a potential revolutionary advantage. Some of the comments on the social base of the Peasants' War likewise echo the critique of a linear and developmental philosophy of history that transpires from one of the drafts of Marx's famous letter on the Russian *mir*, in which he approvingly quotes the following line from the American anthropologist Lewis H. Morgan: 'The new system to which the modern society is tending will be a revival in superior form of an archaic social type.'[102]

Bloch rejects the purging of all non- or anti-social contents from the historical dialectic, its homogenization. This carries over into his

On Bloch's review, see also John Flores, 'Proletarian Meditations: Georg Lukács' Politics of Knowledge', *Diacritics*, 2: 3, 1972; Andrew Arato and Paul Breines, *The Young Lukács and the Origins of Western Marxism*, London: Pluto Press, 1979, 184–6, and Anson Rabinbach, 'Unclaimed Heritage: Bloch's *Heritage of Our Times* and the Theory of Fascism', 17–19. In his review, Bloch picks up on the theme of the Archimedean point, albeit in the mode of lament: 'Why don't we possess the Archimedean point that unhinges this world, as oppressive as it is unreal?'

100   Ernst Bloch, *Thomas Münzer, als Theologe der Revolution*, 2nd ed, Leipzig: Reclam, 1989 [1962], 51.
101   Lukács, *History and Class Consciousness*, 193. For Bloch, on the contrary, Müntzer's tragic defeat should never be hypostasized into a historical inevitability, and he should never be treated as a mere 'Don Quixote'.
102   Karl Marx, 'The "First" Draft', in Teodor Shanin (ed.), *Late Marx and the Russian Road*, New York: Monthly Review Press, 1983, 107.

treatment of the dualities of inner and outer, heavenly and worldly, theological and political, utopian and empirical – the very dualities that Lukács perceived as antinomies that reduced pre-proletarian politics to impotence. Rather than a historically determined contradiction or an irrational gap between theological semblance and political weakness, Bloch sees in Müntzer – the emblem of the tensions and potentialities of the peasants' revolt – the short-circuit or disjunctive synthesis between the poles of these supposed disjunctions. Joining the 'absolute natural right' of a millenarian Christianity (theocracy as equality)[103] to a strategic grasp of social forces and political forms (the alliance with the miners and the formation of the League of the Elect), Bloch's Müntzer combines 'the most efficacious at the real level and the most efficacious at the surreal level and puts them both at the summit of the same revolution'.[104] Perhaps more than any other, this formulation captures Bloch's ideal of a revolutionary (and therefore realist) inscription of utopian content into the course of history. It can also be illuminatingly contrasted to some of the more recent writing on the rebellions of 1524–26.

For Peter Blickle, one of the foremost historians of those events and the proponent of the appellation 'Revolution of the Common Man' rather than 'Peasants' War', theological and political efficacy certainly go hand in hand: 'concrete economic and social demands are arranged within a vindicatory nexus with "the Word of God" and "the Gospel"' – both of which were 'logograms of contemporary Reformation theology'.[105] Claims for redress based on reference to certain passages of scripture – for instance Acts 5:29, 'Because we do owe more allegiance to God than to any mortal' – were not just charged with legitimizing force; they managed to bring together the urban protests of guilds with the demands of peasant communities and assemblies into a collective form of 'positive

---

103 On the distinction between a Thomist and Lutheran relative natural right of fallen Christians bound to worldly authorities, and the subversive absolute natural right of the radical Reformation, see Ernst Bloch, *Natural Law and Human Dignity*, trans. D. J. Schmidt, Cambridge, MA: The MIT Press, 1987, 29–30.
104 Bloch, *Thomas Müntzer*, 93–4.
105 Peter Blickle, 'Social Protest and Reformation Theology', in *Religion, Politics, and Social Protest: Three Studies on Early Modern Germany*, K. von Greyerz (ed.), Boston: Allen & Unwin, 1984, 4.

protest'.[106] Recalling Worsley's remarks about the integratory function of millenarianism, the efficacy of this radical use of Christian doctrine is also that of a platform for cross-group alliances: 'It provides the basis for urban and rural anticlericalism, with its cutting-edge against the monasteries and orthodox clergy; it legitimises the demand for communal autonomy, exemplified in the call for the right to decide issues of correct religious doctrine, to elect the minister and to allocate tithes; and it is ultimately made the yardstick of social and political order.'[107] What's more, religious intransigence was a condition of political innovation: 'A few remarkable projects [in the Radical Reformation] – those of Michael Gaismair, Balthasar Hubmaier, Thomas Müntzer, and Hans Hergot – escaped the limits posed by previous experience only by displaying an absolute certainty about the demands of the gospel and the content of the godly law, and a total refusal to accommodate revolutionary goals to any existing social and political institutions.'[108]

This twin efficacy, utopian and realist, also governs Bloch's reading of Marx. Rather than the undertaker of utopian illusions, Marx is for Bloch the real heir to a subterranean lineage of chiliastic communism, whose pivotal contribution lies in providing a sober assessment of the immanent means for the realization of a supra-historical drive to 'mystical democracy'. 'His aim', writes Bloch, 'is to impose on the world through a hard-fought struggle, waged according to the wisdom of this very world, the edenic order required by rational socialism, which is profoundly millenarian, but which had been conceived hitherto in a far too arcadian manner, as a kind of beyond.'[109] Or, as Bloch puts it in a

---

106 'Positive protest ran via the Gospel from economic and social necessity towards a fairer and more just social and political order. Negative protest ran via the Gospel from social and political order and thus out of history.' Blickle, 'Social Protest and Reformation Theology', 4. Interpretations of Müntzer differ on whether he should belong to the first or to the second category.

107 Ibid., 8.

108 Peter Blickle, *The Revolution of 1525: The German Peasants' War from a New Perspective*, trans. T. A. Brady, Jr. and H. C. E. Midelfort, Baltimore: Johns Hopkins, 1985, 146.

109 Bloch, *Thomas Müntzer*, 89. See also 'Karl Marx, Death, and the Apocalypse: Or, the Ways in This World by Which the Inward Can Become Outward and the Outward Like the Inward', in *Spirit of Utopia*, trans. A. A. Nassar, Stanford: Stanford University

remarkable image in *Spirit of Utopia*, Marx is only homogeneous with capitalism in the same sense that the detective must somehow mimic the criminal. Bloch's view of socialist revolution and planning, which Lukács dismisses in *History and Class Consciousness* as a misunderstanding of the economy that separates it from the political, also originates in this attempt to think through a kind of rational millenarianism.

Sharing with Lukács an interest in the antinomic relationship between theological transcendence and political immanence, Bloch spends much of *Thomas Müntzer* dissecting and castigating Luther's capitulation to earthly powers and denial of mystical interiority. Luther's ultimate Manicheanism 'remains static, it does not entail any demand to suppress the tension, to re-establish, at least in the heavenly Kingdom, the very unity of this Kingdom'.[110] What Müntzer stands for, then, is not an overcoming of the antinomy of the empirical and utopian, which is perhaps irreducible, but another way of articulating it, one that would do justice both to social needs and spiritual drives. More strikingly, Bloch's Müntzer confronts the stringent demands and risks of collective revolutionary action in order to free the religious subject from the material burden and spiritual distraction imposed by an exploitative order. In a remarkable twist, rather than a humanist effort merely to alleviate suffering, Müntzer's theologically-driven revolt is aimed at relieving subjects from vulgar economic suffering, so that they may finally be free for Christian suffering (and redemption). As Bloch writes, when Müntzer 'straightens up the bent backs, it is in order to allow them to bear a real burden. If the people has fallen low enough so that, having itself become creature, it has more to fear from the creature than from God, it is entirely mistaken when it imagines that its masters are still established and commanded by God.'[111]

Press, 2000. Here Bloch writes that 'Marx thoroughly purified Socialist planning of every simple, false, disengaged and abstract enthusiasm, of mere Jacobinism' (236). For Bloch's provocative treatment of Marx's alleged 'secularization' of Christian and utopian contents, see 'Karl Marx and Humanity: Stuff of Hope', in *The Principle of Hope*, Vol. 3, trans. N. Plaice, S. Plaice and P. Knight, Oxford: Basil Blackwell, 1986.
110   Bloch, *Thomas Müntzer*, 136.
111   Ibid., 178.

This vision of communism as a freeing-up of radical and economically excessive utopian drives is also evident in Bloch's treatment of the state in the same period. In *Spirit of Utopia* he writes of the state as 'a great instrumental organization for the control of the *inessential*', armed with a 'purely administrative Esperanto', and whose only 'justification . . . is the simplifying, frictionless functioning of its organizational method, placed in the middle of illogical life, its only, entirely instrumental logic, the logic of a state of emergency'.[112] Thus, correcting Lukács's negative estimation, it is not the demarcation of politics from the economy that is at stake for Bloch, but the excess (though not the outright separation) of the utopian over the empirical. Radical political struggle and violence – the 'categorical imperative with a revolver in hand', as Bloch has it – are necessary not for their own sake, but as stepping-stones to an incommensurable and 'metapolitical' goal. Or, to borrow Bloch's effective allegory, 'the Messiah can only come when all the guests have sat down at the table'.[113] Contrary to what Lukács's objections might suggest, Bloch is not merely juxtaposing millenarian immediacy to economic mediation, but thinking of the utopian forms of immediate, non-alienated experience that could be produced by working through worldly relations (class struggles, planning, material needs, etc.).[114]

The confrontation between Bloch and Lukács shows the richness and complexity of the political and historiographic problem that Engels posed under the name 'Thomas Müntzer'. Anachronism and historical necessity, realism and utopianism, theology and economics are all at stake in trying to answer whether a political action motivated by religious conviction can be considered revolutionary, and whether

---

112   Bloch, *Spirit of Utopia*, 240.
113   Ibid., 246.
114   Adorno captured this aspect of Bloch's thinking well: 'For just as, in the words of Bloch's master, there is nothing immediate between heaven and earth which is not mediated, so too there can be nothing mediated without the concept of mediation involving a moment of the immediate. Bloch's pathos is indefatigably directed to that moment.' Theodor W. Adorno, 'The Handle, the Pot and Early Experience', in *Notes to Literature*, Vol. 2, R. Tiedemann (ed.), trans. S. Weber Nicholsen, New York: Columbia University Press, 1992, 219.

real social change needs to be aligned with the timing of capitalism, on pain of defeat or irrelevance. The questions raised by the Marxist treatment of millenarianism continue to have a bearing on the development of radical thought. Alain Badiou has recently sought to link his theory of the event-bound production of eternal truths to the idea or hypothesis of communism, understood as a trans-historical, regulative principle in accordance with which only a politics of uncompromising equality is compatible with genuine philosophical thought. For Badiou, communism as an ideal rather than a set of specified historical movements, parties or practices involves the idea that equality is a maxim of political action to be enacted immediately, not a distant social objective; the assertion that politics can exist without or beyond the state; the struggle against the immemorial distinction between intellectual and manual labour, and the production of a polyvalent worker.[115] Badiou's reassertion of the idea of communism ties back to a concept he first introduced in his co-authored book *De l'idéologie*, that of 'communist invariants'.

Badiou's initial formulation of this concept is made in the context of a reinterpretation of Engels's *Peasant War in Germany*. Badiou and Balmès invoke this text, and its treatment of Müntzer, in arguing against those who, in an elitist vein, would regard the Marxist notion of ideology as a warrant to condescend to masses supposedly mystified by capitalism into not realizing their own exploited status. On the contrary, the exploited have always known who exploits them and how.[116] Their problem rather is that their ideological struggles are forever taking place on the enemy's turf. As a demand for immediate, concrete equality, their revolt is therefore 'unrepresentable', a pure

---

115   See Alain Badiou, 'The Communist Hypothesis', *New Left Review*, 49 (2008), and the various pieces now collected in Alain Badiou, *L'hypothèse communiste*, Paris: Lignes, 2009.

116   Alain Badiou and François Balmès, *De l'idéologie*, Paris: Maspéro, 1976, 16. Despite their reliance on Engels, they criticize his class analysis of 'the plebeians'. For Badiou and Balmès, the struggle of Müntzer and his comrades 'does not reflect the residual persistence of millenarian communities, nor the stammerings of the proletariat . . . it is an ideology of the communist type reflecting and unifying a *peasant* revolt' (64).

'exception'.[117] Just as in Guha's reflections on anti-imperial insurgencies, resistance has to be approached negatively, through the distorting mirror of the dominant ideology. When it can make its voice heard, it is forced to borrow from its nemesis's vocabulary – that of theology, in the case of Müntzer. However, resistance has a positive autonomy that is not merely parasitic on the thinking and practice of exploiters. This autonomy is also a kind of spontaneous ideology of rebellion: 'All the successive great mass revolts of the exploited classes (slaves, peasants, proletarians)', write Badiou and Balmès, 'find their ideological expression in egalitarian, anti-property and anti-state formulations, which constitute the outlines of a communist programme. . . . It is the elements of this general position-taking of insurgent producers which we call *communist invariants*.'[118] What of the anachronism or nonsynchronicity that constitute the legacy of Engels's vision of Müntzer? Badiou and Balmès are also preoccupied with this problem, and they respond to it by analysing the revolt in terms of its form, content and history.

In its doctrinal form, which remains tethered to the dominant ideology, a revolt can at best be a heresy, which, however extreme, is always internal to the ruling representations. In its 'immediate popular content', however, every genuine revolt instantiates the communist invariants. It is at the level of history, the site of the contrast between Lukács and Bloch, that the invariants come to be affected by the temporalities of economic development and political strategy. Here Badiou and Balmès propose a kind of law, stating that in '*its historical reality* – its class efficacy – popular ideological resistance necessarily prepares the triumph and domination *of the ideas of the revolutionary class of the moment*'[119] – a gloss on Engels's melancholy recognition that Müntzer's millenarian egalitarianism paves the way for bourgeois legal equality. In affirming the autonomy and eternity of revolts under the banner of the communist invariants, Badiou and Balmès seem to resonate, albeit in a far less romantic mode, with Bloch's paeans to the

---

117   Ibid., 41.
118   Ibid., 66–7.
119   Ibid., 69–70.

Ubique of plebeian utopia. But they ultimately underwrite the classical thesis, present in Engels and recast by Lukács, that only the proletariat can permit the alignment or synchronization of form and content in a finally revolutionary, and not merely rebellious history. Only the proletariat, which they elsewhere call a 'logical power', 'is capable of making history in its own name' and thus of realizing those perennially thwarted, invariant ideas, turning the time of defeat into the time of victory.[120] Badiou jettisons this schema of realization in his later work, while retaining the idea of egalitarian invariants and the validity of what he calls the communist hypothesis, namely that a politics without and against domination is possible. In so doing, he seems to have abandoned the problems of ideology and synchronicity that he had earlier drawn from the predicament first outlined by Engels. One may wonder whether he has also abandoned a key dimension of the problem of millenarianism, and of fanaticism: the total opposition to existing society. It is to this question that I now turn.

MILLENNIAL MODERNITY

Testifying to the abiding fascination for social thought of Müntzer's theology of revolution, Bloch's millenarian Marxism stimulated another important reflection, by the Hungarian sociologist (and erstwhile friend of Lukács) Karl Mannheim. In *Ideology and Utopia*, his influential work on the sociology of knowledge, millenarian fanaticism or chiliasm – specifically modelled on Bloch's portrait of Müntzer – is presented as the paradigm or degree zero of utopia. Mannheim defines the latter as 'A state of mind [which is] incongruous with the state of reality within which it occurs', and, crucially, a state of mind which strives towards some kind of realization. For Mannheim, such utopias are 'situationally transcendent' ideas that have a transforming effect upon the existing historical-social order.[121]

Mannheim presents four types of utopia: chiliastic, liberal, conservative and socialist-communist. The first two are characterized by a kind of indeterminism or contingency (fanatical and decisionist in the first

---

120   Ibid., 74.
121   See Karl Mannheim, *Ideology and Utopia*, London: Routledge, 1936, 173, 185.

case, regulative and deliberating in the second);[122] the latter two by determinateness (inert in the first case, transformative in the second). Just as the question of the timeliness or synchronicity of political action and subjectivity was linked in the dispute between Bloch and Lukács to the necessity of capitalist development and the possibility of revolutionary change, with Lukács arguing for the inevitable defeat of Müntzer's rebels, here the varieties of utopia are coded in terms of the modalities of politics. Chiliasm, akin in this respect to pragmatic liberalism, but opposed to the determinist dimensions of conservatism and stagist socialism, is a doctrine of contingency. Utopias, for Mannheim, are qualified by different ways of experiencing social time, and the temporality of chiliasm is that of the *kairos*: of 'the moment of time invaded by eternity', but also of eternity dependent on decision.[123] Chiliasm is marked by a particular emotional and cognitive state that Mannheim calls 'absolute presentness',[124] where there is 'no inner articulation of time'. For chiliastic utopia, which Mannheim tellingly sees reincarnated in the figure of Bakunin, total revolution is 'the only creative principle of the immediate present'.[125]

Inasmuch as it is pitted against the old order in absolute and uncompromising fashion (to the point of pushing for a veritable exodus from the world), chiliasm is the purest form of utopia in Mannheim's schema. Its emergence and impact is nothing short of momentous:

> The decisive turning-point in modern history was, from the point of view of our problem, the moment in which 'Chiliasm' joined forces with the active demands of the oppressed strata of society. The very idea of the dawn of a millennial kingdom on earth always contained a revolutionizing tendency, and the church made every effort to paralyse this situationally transcendent idea with all the means at its command.[126]

---

122   On the antagonism between liberalism and chiliasm, see ibid., 203–4.
123   Michael Löwy, 'Utopie et chiliasme: Karl Mannheim (1890–1947) comme sociologue des religions', in Erwann Dianteill and Michael Löwy, *Sociologies et religion. Approches dissidentes*, Paris: PUF, 2005, 30.
124   Mannheim, *Ideology and Utopia*, 193.
125   Ibid., 196.
126   Ibid., 190.

This point of crystallization, in which 'chiliasm and the social revolution were structurally integrated',[127] signals for Mannheim the very birth of modern politics – 'if we understand by politics a more or less conscious participation of all strata of society in the achievement of some mundane purpose, as contrasted with the fatalistic acceptance of events as they are'.[128] The chiliasm of Müntzer and his epigones is the first properly anti-systemic movement.

> One of the features of modern revolution . . . is that it is no ordinary uprising against a certain oppressor but a striving for an upheaval against the whole existing social order in a thoroughgoing and systematic way.[129]

By allowing us to read chiliasm as a utopia rather than an ideology, dislocating the status quo rather than aiding in its reproduction, Mannheim also helps us to begin to move away from the view of fanaticism as a mere anachronism, or a social pathology of development whose signification is purely negative.

Utopias 'are not ideologies, i.e. they are not ideologies in the measure and in so far as they succeed through counteractivity in transforming the existing historical reality into one more in accord with their own conceptions'.[130] Moreover, chiliasm, with its determinate roots in a political movement of the oppressed – and with the particular temporality of decision, expectation and political action that it introduces into society – can in no way be reduced, as the detractors of millenarian movements so often do, to a kind of anti-representational frenzy. By contrast with the 'pejorative tradition' in the discussion of fanaticism,[131] we might welcome Mannheim's attention to the correlations between transformations in political mentalities and the social strata or groups that serve as their bearers, foreshadowing the interpretations of millenarianism by Hobsbawm and Worsley. In *Ideology and*

---

127   Ibid., 190.
128   Ibid., 191.
129   Ibid., 195, n. 2.
130   Ibid., 176.
131   See Olson, 'The Freshness of Fanaticism'.

Utopia, the 'object of sociological research is the correlation between different forms of utopia and the social strata aiming to transform the existing order'.[132] For Mannheim, though, these are transformations that do not simply occur at the level of ideas (what he condemns as the liberal-humanitarian prejudice). Rather, they engage energies, drives and affects which are non-representational without necessarily being anti-representational.

That said, Mannheim, in a sense exacerbating a problem already present in Bloch and to a lesser degree earlier in Engels, tends to connect the sociological and the ideational dimensions of sixteenth-century chiliasm – plebs, peasants and the millennium – without really delving into the political and organizational forms of these movements. This shortcoming is in part explained by the preference for the iconic, iconoclastic figure of Müntzer over any other leader – for instance, the Swiss revolutionary Michael Gaismair, whose 1526 *Territorial Constitution for the Tyrol* showed that the rebels, while maintaining their rhetorical assault on the 'godless', were not incapable of formulating detailed blueprints for agrarian reform and economic planning based on common ownership.[133] Though this pitfall is mostly avoided by the likes of Engels and Bloch, for whom Müntzer is a crystallization and a catalyst of a social demand for emancipation, the fascination with Müntzer's persona can lead to the insistent disavowal of the political and theoretical problems thrown up by any more thorough investigation of the war of 1525 and of peasant revolts in general. This is especially true in terms of the question of time. As Mannheim writes:

> It is the utopian element – i.e. the nature of the dominant wish – which determines the sequence, order, and evaluation of single experiences. This wish is the organizing principle which even moulds the way in which we experience time. The form in which events are ordered and the unconsciously emphatic rhythm, which the individual in his spontaneous observation of events imposes upon the flux of time, appears in the

---

132   Löwy, 'Utopie et chiliasme', 25.
133   See Tom Scott and Bob Scribner (eds), *The German Peasants' War: A History in Documents*, Amherst, NY: Humanity Books, 1991, 265–9.

utopia as an immediately perceptible picture, or at least a directly intelligible set of meanings.[134]

Political time, which social theories of millenarianism reveal to be a
complex conjunction of regression and anticipation, riven by nonsynchronism, is here subordinated to the static and visible time of
utopia. Neglect of the specific organizations, prescriptions and constituent processes undertaken by these putatively religious movements
means that the link between ideas, religion and social protest becomes
far too neatly aligned with the irreversible vector of a kind of historicism. In this vein, Mannheim argues that 'every age allows to arise (in
differently located social groups) those ideas and values in which are
contained in condensed form the unrealized and the unfulfilled tendencies which represent the needs of each age'.[135] There is something too
neat about this idea of a correlation between latent demands and their
social expression, which undermines and depoliticizes the link between
millenarianism and contingency. The question of politics is nonetheless
present in Mannheim's suggestion that the very distinction between the
utopia and ideology is a product of conflict:

> It is always the dominant group which is in full accord with the exist-
> ing order that determines what is to be regarded as utopian, while the
> ascendant group which is in conflict with things as they are is the one that
> determines what is regarded as ideological.[136]

Opting for an affective interpretation of millenarian politics, against a
narrower focus on its theological coordinates, Mannheim argues that
not ideas but 'ecstatic-orgiastic energies' were at stake in the spiritualization of politics during the Peasants' War, and that there is a positive
asymmetry between ideas and experiences in chiliasm, with the latter
taking centre stage. As he puts it, 'the essential feature of Chiliasm is its

---

134   Mannheim, *Ideology and Utopia*, 188.
135   Ibid., 179.
136   Ibid., 183.

tendency always to dissociate itself from its own images and symbols'.[137] Millenarian movements are defined not by their theological form but by their affective content, by the transformative collective energies that drive the situated negation and transcendence of the social status quo.

This negation and transcendence makes the most extreme of utopias – the one that seems to concentrate time into a molten instant and to pit itself against every feature of the reigning order – also the most modern. The paradoxes of fanaticism we encountered in the last chapter are here intensified: the theological negation of time by the instant heralds the political importance of time as revolution, modernity arrives in the guise of atavism, the rebellion of the dispossessed signals towards a world remade. Though its wish to turn the world upside down appears as an index of irrationalism – in what detractors see as an explosion of defeated *ressentiment*, an upsurge of pathological behaviour – for Mannheim there is a negative rationality in revolution: 'No ordinary uprising against a certain oppressor but a striving for an upheaval against the whole existing social order in a thoroughgoing and systematic way'.[138] In all of this, chiliasm has a primary and more recognizably modern antagonist, liberalism; it is also, as Bloch's work testifies, not easily disjoined from socialist and communist utopias which are never simply deterministic. A revolutionary utopia of uncompromising antagonism and transcendent conviction, borne by the dispossessed, faces off against the bourgeois utopia of gradual, calculable change. Both chiliasm and liberalism reject determinism. However, while for liberalism contingency is something pragmatically to be mastered, for chiliasm it is to be intensified as decision, and radical overturning – the *kairos*.

But, as we survey a golden age of liberal political thought in the next chapter, we shall see that when it comes to fanaticism and its close cousin, enthusiasm, the Enlightenment will find it remarkably difficult entirely to demarcate itself from ideas of unconditional conviction and revealed truth, and will often find itself branded as fanatical.

---

137   Ibid., 193.
138   Ibid., 195, n. 1.

3

Raving with Reason:
Fanaticism and Enlightenment

Immanuel Kant, the great destroyer in the realm of thought, far surpassed
Maximilien Robespierre in terrorism.

> Heinrich Heine, *On the History of*
> *Religion and Philosophy in Germany*

Each of us is the mystagogue and the *Aufklärer* of another.

> Jacques Derrida,
> 'Of a Newly Arisen Apocalyptic Tone in Philosophy'

Contemporary calls to revitalize the Enlightenment against the political depredations of religious unreason, varied as they are in their ideological origins and suggested therapies, seem to converge on the identification of fanaticism as a global threat to rationality and social peace. A
'folk Enlightenment',[1] rampant among pundits and politicians, demands
that 'we' consolidate the hard-won gains that make up 'Western values',
reason, liberalism, humanitarianism and so forth. Critical theorists concur
that 'the need remains for an unrelenting assault on religious fanaticism'.[2]
But as many critics of this 'Enlightenment reloaded' have already indicated,
there is much in these calls that is shallow, misdirected or hypocritical. The
Enlightenment they invoke is a curious construction: contrary to what
much recent historical scholarship suggests, it is presented as unified and
homogeneous, stripped of political tensions, geographical specificity and

---

1   Dan Hind, *The Threat to Reason*, London: Verso, 2007, 24–6, 51–5.
2   Stephen Eric Bronner, *Reclaiming the Enlightenment: Towards a Politics of
Radical Engagement*, New York: Columbia University Press, 2004, 14.

philosophical differences. Moreover, any disharmony between contemporary liberal-democratic beliefs and certain Enlightenment positions – such as defences of slavery and patriarchy, condemnations of atheism or apologies of natural hierarchy and authority – is papered over, or considered as merely extrinsic, a contingency of historical context which has been inexorably overtaken by the progress of mores and ideas.

DISEMBEDDING ENLIGHTENMENT

The character of this streamlined, ready-made Enlightenment is retroactively dictated by a set of parameters that already underlie the status quo ('our shared values', to quote a vapid and ubiquitous phrase), and which inner atavisms and external foes allegedly threaten. The peculiar tenor of current ideological campaigns against fanaticism derives from the smug conviction that 'we' are indeed enlightened, and the concomitant notion that the Enlightenment is something to be preserved rather than enacted, furthered or repeated. Especially prevalent is the idea that the Enlightenment is something like a cultural patrimony (a 'value', precisely) which defines our civilization. It would perhaps be otiose to point out the many ways in which emancipatory, rationalist visions originating in the French *Lumières* or German *Aufklärung* are systematically denied in the contemporary political panorama. If we can indeed speak of it as a project, much of the Enlightenment is not merely unfinished: it has been ignored, buried or traduced. What is more pertinent perhaps is that in identifying the Enlightenment with our hegemonic political and economic dispensation (or at least in treating the latter as the best approximation to the idea of a world founded on emancipated reason),[3]

---

3   The ideological gambit which consists in exculpating empirical liberalism by reference to its approximation to its transcendental ideal has been unsparingly dissected by Perry Anderson, 'Arms and Rights', in *Spectrum*, London: Verso, 2005. What Anderson says of the approach by the likes of Bobbio, Habermas and Rawls to the philosophical foundations of international law could also be said about the broader propagandistic uses of 'the Enlightenment': 'Against criticisms pointing to the disgraced reality . . . the ideal can be upheld as a normative standard untainted by such empirical shortcomings. Against charges that it is an empty utopia, the course of the world can be represented as an increasingly hopeful pilgrimage towards it. In this *va-et-vient* between ostensible justifications by universal morality and surreptitious appeals to a providential history, the upshot is never in doubt: a licence for the

contemporary commentators have engaged in two interrelated moves, both of which could be regarded as a betrayal of the radical or emancipatory potentials borne by various strands within what is viewed by many scholars today as a plural Enlightenment.[4] First, current invocations of the Enlightenment as a rhetorical gambit and an object of passionate attachment are complicit with the culturalization of rationality – that very identification of the emancipation of reason with 'the West' which so much critical scholarship has rightly, if at times undiscerningly, decried. Second, by pleading for the preservation of the Enlightenment, many of its current paladins end up draining it of its critical valence. It is as if we already knew what reason and emancipation entailed and simply needed to rearm ourselves for the immemorial struggle against ignorance. The daring, discipline and risk which represent the radical legacies of Enlightenment critique are thus evacuated for the sake of a picture of the Enlightenment as a precious possession, to be secured and defended.

Forgotten is the idea of a critical thought vigilant about its own prejudices and wary of colluding in the irrational perpetuation of authority. What we are left with is the ideological comfort of fighting on the side of the powerful while presenting oneself as a member of a beleaguered and courageous minority. In this dramaturgy, which pits the defenders of a more or less completed project against the spectres and regurgitations of its ancient enemies, the link between Enlightenment and the interrogation of what Foucault termed the 'ontology of the present' is obliterated. Where Foucault saw Kant's thinking on *Aufklärung* as inaugurating philosophy's own reflection on its problematic (and political) positioning in the present – with regard to a definite actuality, to certain specific authorities, to an 'us' that must be constantly questioned[5]

American empire as a placeholder for human progress' (165).

4   On the distinction between a radical and a moderate Enlightenment, see Jonathan I. Israel, *Enlightenment Contested: Philosophy, Modernity, and the Emancipation of Man 1670–1752*, Oxford: Oxford University Press, 2006, and 'Enlightenment! Which Enlightenment?', *Journal of the History of Ideas*, 67: 3 (2006). In a very different vein, see also J. G. A. Pocock, 'Enthusiasm: The Antiself of Enlightenment', in *Enthusiasm and Enlightenment in Europe, 1650–1850*.

5   Michel Foucault, 'What is Revolution?', in *The Politics of Truth*, Los Angeles: Semiotext(e), 2007, 85.

— the current vogue for a return to the Enlightenment that would act as a bulwark against the return of (political) religion takes place from a position alien to critique in any of its Kantian and post-Kantian acceptations. Enlightenment as a 'taste for thought and imagination as exercises in insubordination', as a perilous adventure rather than a 'mission' to combat enemies, vanishes when we are dealing with those rentiers of the Enlightenment who, empowered by the cheap heroism of simulated clashes between civilizations or belief-systems, think that their role is simply to defend a well-delimited possession, *the* Enlightenment, without risk or research of their own.[6] In this ideological pantomime, where many have gained an audience through mere stridency and posturing, it is arguably the idea of fanaticism that has served to support the widespread belief that we are experiencing the repetition or continuation of that struggle between reason and unreason, freedom and subjection, knowledge and ignorance which was first played out in the seventeenth and eighteenth centuries in Europe. Aside from obscuring the many vital legacies of those past movements for intellectual emancipation, this supposed ideological world war between the partisans of the Enlightenment and the fanatical forces of unreason creates a spurious form of political simplification, an ersatz intelligibility that leaves us none the wiser about religious politics and global conflicts.

DEFINING FANATICISM

I shall approach the Enlightenment (or Enlightenments, if we follow historians like Pocock or Israel) through the prism of what can readily be seen as its nemesis of choice, its foil or 'antiself'. As we are concerned with the polemical and conceptual vicissitudes of an idea, and not simply a term, I will be considering not just fanaticism but also enthusiasm, or exaltation – indicating as I proceed the linguistic and semantic context where the opposition between reason and its others is set in motion. Given the one-dimensional Enlightenment enlisted by much of today's political rhetoric, it is worth starting with what is regarded as an unequivocal emblem and monument of enlightened thought, Diderot

---

6   See Isabelle Stengers, *Au temps des catastrophes*, 139–51.

and D'Alembert's *Encyclopédie, ou dictionnaire raisonné des sciences, des arts et des métiers*. At first glance, the *Encyclopédie*'s entry on *fanatisme*, penned by a friend of Rousseau and future Girondin, Alexandre Deleyre,[7] is a compendium of views that our intellectual common sense would ascribe to *the* Enlightenment. Yet in its somewhat sprawling composition we also encounter a few surprises.

From the very start of the entry, an intriguing resonance is evident between Deleyre's prose style and the nature of his object. What dominates is the seemingly interminable list, a kind of parataxis. Fanaticism's core is not to be grasped through analysis or intuition, but by way of the dramatization – amalgamating history, hearsay and fiction – of its manifestations. Deleyre thus launches into the wilfully delirious scenography of an immense pantheon in which a boundless number of zealots and devotees perform patently absurd and mutually contradictory rituals of subjection to their particular absolutes (nudity and veiling, quaking and quietism, violence and passivity). As these fanatics come to be released into the wider world, Deleyre's narrative weaves together superstition and sectarianism, pseudo-religious ignorance and political conflict. The *Encyclopédie*'s project of toleration is conveyed by this narrative of monotony in difference, which also serves to forge the contrasting unity of reason, or of rational religion. Fanaticism is at once protean and univocal, engendering warring sects and driven by an essentially homogeneous logic, with its origins in that other crucial nemesis of enlightenment, superstition. Fanaticism is superstition in action. But the list, especially when it delights in exhibiting the many horrors and cruelties exercised by fanatics across the globe, also carries a plainly pedagogical function: the reader is edified by exhaustion and disgust, by the myriad ugly faces of unreason. The absurd and incompatible rituals in the pantheon of a thousand altars are invoked to bring home the idea that the workings of fanaticism are everywhere the same ('for all the nations and all the centuries'). Though Deleyre is not immune from Eurocentrism – evident in the repetition of ethnological stereotypes and the plea for a rational kernel to the Christian religion – the baleful universality of fanaticism

---

7   On Deleyre's life and works, see Franco Venturi, 'Un enciclopedista: Alexandre Deleyre', *Rivista Storica Italiana*, LXXVII: IV (1965).

introduces a principle of symmetry and generalized comparison into his account that not only casts light on the brutalities of the Inquisition or the crusades, but also introduces a vigorous critique of the fanaticism of imperialism, when 'the discovery of a new world hastened the ruin of our own' under the terrible exterminatory motto, 'go and force' (*allez et forcez*). As though by a boomerang-effect, the latter also leads – anticipating ideas that Arendt would popularize in the twentieth century – to inter-imperial struggles.[8] This, writes Deleyre, is where the *progress* of fanaticism has led. In the end, the ubiquity of fanaticism signifies that all history is the history of fanaticism – a phrase that Voltaire will make his own.

Deleyre's encyclopaedia entry is interestingly agnostic about causes. An anthropology of the passions underlies his narrative. Fear (*crainte*), as the 'first feeling of mankind', serves to inflame the fanatic, demonstrating that man 'is a monster composed of all the others'. But the drift of his approach is descriptive and prescriptive, not explanatory. Deleyre notes a multitude of incompatible causes (hunger or meanness, force or fear, politics or superstition) without deciding between them, concluding nevertheless that 'wherever the idea of satisfying the deity by the shedding of blood may come from, it is certain that once the blood starts flowing on the altars, it has not been possible to stop it'. Having said that, though precise triggers are not identified, certain prevalent traits are. Fanaticism is a 'madness of the people' linked to imitation, communication and demagogy, drawing the masses into a 'general vertigo'; it has 'consecrated war', such that 'the most detestable scourge is regarded as an act of religion'; it is the bearer of a literalist bent that would today be associated with fundamentalism;[9] it is a 'divinised injustice' seeking to 'appease the heavens with massacres'. When he does gesture towards a causal account, like many of his contemporaries it is to a theory of the faculties that Deleyre turns. After a gruesome list of self-flagellations

---

8   Deleyre posits a kind of typology of political fanaticisms: where politics is united with religion, as in Islam, fanaticism is externalized as a passion for conquest. Where some separation exists, as in Christianity, it turns into internecine warfare.

9   'We can call fanatics all these excessive (*outrés*) spirits who interpret the maxims of religion to the letter, and who follow this letter rigorously.'

and senseless cruelties, he writes that their only cause can be 'the extravagance of imagination pushed out of the natural boundaries of reason and life, by an inconceivable malady'.

'What then is fanaticism?' asks Deleyre. 'It is the effect of a false consciousness that abuses sacred things and enslaves religion to the whims of imagination and the unruliness of the passions.' Melancholy, a term that we will also meet below in Kant's account of fanaticism, is one of the foremost psychological indices of this politico-religious illness: 'The first and most common [symptom] is a dark melancholy caused by profound meditations. It is difficult to dream for a long time about certain principles, without drawing from them the most terrible consequences.'[10] If the imaginative ethnologies of cruel and absurd cults with which the entry opens identify the external enemies of a tolerant and reasonable polity, Deleyre's entry also points towards an immanent treatment of fanaticism. Perhaps fanaticism is not simply the absence of rationality, unreason, but reason unbound and unnatural. This much is also suggested by Deleyre when he notes that it is fanaticism's proximity to justified conviction, like superstition's proximity to true religion, which makes it such a dangerous force: 'note that fanaticism only reigns among those whose heart is righteous but whose mind is false, mistaken in their principles but right [*justes*] in their consequences'. Fanaticism orbits around truth, mixes with it, infusing it with a power of persuasion that the simple absence of verisimilitude and rationality would lack. Whence Deleyre's suggestion that the 'mixture of false and true is more nefarious than an absolute ignorance'. Indeed, though the initial grotesque pageant of fanaticism might suggest that it is a product of particularism and partisanship, Deleyre joins many commentators in seeing fanaticism as also an effect of an *excess* of universality, as legislators try to extend their laws to areas and peoples for which they were not designed. Though he initially defines it as 'superstition in practice', Deleyre, echoing Hume's distinction between superstition and

---

10   Though the 'symptoms of fanaticism are as different as the characters it affects', Deleyre suggests a paradigmatic distinction, borrowed from the history of Jewish movements (as recounted, for instance, in Josephus's *Jewish War*), between phlegmatic obstinate zealots and frenetic bilious *sicari*.

enthusiasm, notes that superstition subjugates and degrades men, while its child fanaticism, for all its horrors, lifts them up.

But the pragmatic bent of the *Encyclopédie* means that Deleyre cannot restrict himself to narrative, description and phenomenology. Fanaticism requires 'remedies'. Given the references to maladies and madness it is not surprising that a medical response is suggested for the more egregious specimens: cold baths, bloodletting and clinical imprisonment. Since like the proverbial hydra they regenerate with every attack, and mere banishment is futile, the worst fanatics simply need to be locked up where, as Deleyre puts it, they'll go out like burning embers. Ridicule, as in Shaftesbury's influential *Letter on Enthusiasm*, is also considered. But for Deleyre, possibly anticipating his later revolutionary participation, the real remedies are to be found in politics. In the shadow of the wars of religion, the enlightened project for a social homeopathy is primarily concerned with peace and order – which is why Deleyre is even willing to consider the possibility (though he quickly dismisses it) that an inquisitorial political order could stabilize the polity and prevent internecine violence. Ultimately, the authorities need to be gentle and pacific, since 'persecution engenders revolt, and revolt enhances persecution'. States are to be improved by the philosophical spirit. But just as the entry is drawing to a close – after a long prayer to an anti-fanatical God, that He may excommunicate those who fatuously call on His authority to justify their depredations – Deleyre gives the link between politics and fanaticism a significant twist. Having described and diagnosed the cruel excesses of fanatical conviction, he pleads for a 'fanaticism of the patriot', a 'cult of the hearths' that alone can lend energy and substance to a society or polity. In words that we'll see echoed by Kant, the French encyclopaedist affirms that nothing great can be produced without this excessive zeal, this secular, and we might say nationalist, form of passionate belonging.

Some of the rifts and strains in the *Encyclopédie* project can be registered in this apparent inconsistency in the estimation of fanaticism's qualities. Though much of Deleyre's tack is reproduced by Voltaire – who simply summarizes the *Encyclopédie* entry in the first section of the article on 'Fanaticism' in his own *Philosophical Dictionary* – the approbation of a form of political fanaticism, alien to the author of *Candide*, can be traced to Deleyre's sympathy for Rousseau's plea for a 'civic fanaticism', and the latter's ambiguous defence of this 'great passion' in the 'Profession of Faith of a Savoyard Vicar' in Book IV of his pedagogical *Bildungsroman*, *Émile*. Where something in fanaticism seems to be recuperable for both Deleyre and Rousseau, Voltaire will have none of it. For him, the very notion of a manageable political fanaticism is anathema, whence his harsh controversies with Rousseau. Indeed, to the extent that he perceives all passionate political conviction as noxious to peace and stability, his thinking can be characterized as broadly anti-political. Voltaire pins his hopes on the disappearance of *'l'affreuse politique'*, appalling politics.[11] The opposition between fanaticism and tolerance so crucial to Voltaire's entire oeuvre, from the early ode *Sur le fanatisme* (1732) to his play *Fanaticism, or Mahomet the Prophet* (1741) and the *Treatise on Tolerance* (1765), is also structured as an opposition between pathological militancy and the virtues of indifference. Preventing the emergence of violent sects and the contagion of irrational convictions, while maintaining the social peace: this is Voltaire's aim when faced with fanaticism, whose 'history' is defined by the way that it 'violates all divine and human conventions in the spirit of religion'. Though not an enemy of religion *per se* (atheists too are enemies of political stability), it is the volatility of religion that concerns Voltaire: the manner in which it can so easily abet destructive frenzies, or mutate into *l'infâme*, that contemptible mixture of superstition and fanaticism, the religious passion of crowds and partisan spirit, persecution and blind dogmatism. In *La Henriade*, he will write of fanaticism as the denatured child of religion, armed to defend it but intent on destroying it from within. In the play on Mohammed, the tragic protagonist Séide, awakening from his fanaticization by the prophet, will stress the closeness between religious and social duty, on the one hand, and the violence of fanaticism, on the other: 'The love of my duty and my

11   Quoted in Raymond Trousson, 'Tolérance et fanatisme selon Voltaire et Rousseau', in *Rousseau and l'Infâme: Religion, Toleration, and Fanaticism in the Age of Enlightenment*, J. T. Scott and O. Mostefai (eds), Amsterdam: Rodopi, 2008, 33.

nation, / My respect and my religion, / Everything in humans most respectable / Inspired in me deeds the most abominable'.[12]

Even worse in Voltaire's opinion, beneath the warring parties of zealots and sectarians there is only one shared element: their hatred for the tolerant *philosophe*. Hence his barbed vignette at the end of the 'Fanaticism' entry in the *Philosophical Dictionary*:

> A report is publicly spread abroad by some person, that there exists a giant seventy feet high; the learned soon after begin to discuss and dispute about the color of his hair, the thickness of his thumb, the measurement of his nails; they exclaim, cabal, and even fight upon the subject. Those who maintain that the little finger of the giant is only fifteen lines in diameter burn those who assert that it is a foot thick. 'But, gentlemen,' modestly observes a stranger passing by, 'does the giant you are disputing about really exist?' 'What a horrible doubt!' all the disputants cry out together. 'What blasphemy! What absurdity!' A short truce is then brought about to give time for stoning the poor stranger; and, after having duly performed that murderous ceremony, they resume fighting upon the everlasting subject of the nails and little finger.[13]

As in Deleyre, this is a supremely monotonous history, since all sects 'have the same bandage over their eyes'.[14] It is also a viral history: 'Today we understand by fanaticism a religious madness, dark and cruel. It is a mental illness which is caught like the pox. Books communicate it far less than assemblies and speeches.' But Voltaire's view of remedies is ultimately more pessimistic. Laws and a de-fanaticized religion cannot prevent the 'plague of souls', especially when they are confronted with

---

12   Voltaire, *Le Fanatisme, ou Mahomet le prophète*, Paris: Flammarion, 2004, 200.
13   Voltaire, *Philosophical Dictionary* (1764), in *The Works of Voltaire: A Contemporary Version*, Vol. 5, including a critique and biography by J. Morley, notes by T. Smollett, trans. William F. Fleming, New York: E. R. DuMont, 1901, 30. The more readily available version of the *Philosophical Dictionary* is based on the 'pocket' or *portatif* version.
14   This underlying homogeneity is given a scatological turn in one of Voltaire's letters to D'Alembert, from December 1757, where he writes: 'Papist fanatics, Calvinist fanatics, all moulded out of the same shit soaked in corrupted blood.' Quoted in Trousson, 'Tolérance et fanatisme selon Voltaire et Rousseau', 35–6.

'fanatics of cold blood'. In despair, Voltaire exclaims: 'What can you answer to a man who says he would rather obey God than men, and who consequently is certain to deserve heaven by cutting your throat?' Once fanaticism has gangrened a brain, it is pretty much incurable. And when even the likes of Newton are prone to believe in the apocalypse, humankind must appear as a poor species.[15] Only the gradual spread of philosophy might offset the epidemical effects of fanaticism. As the *Treatise on Tolerance* affirms: 'Philosophy, philosophy alone, this sister of religion, has disarmed the hands that superstition had for so long bloodied; and the human mind, as it awakens from its drunkenness, was shocked at the excesses to which it had been carried by fanaticism.'[16] But the gradual illumination of minds does not preclude the possibility of properly political remedies, of the enforcement of tolerance and the suppression of fanaticism by means military and violent. If 'to deserve tolerance men must cease being fanatical',[17] what happens if they refuse? Writing to D'Alembert in 1767, Voltaire rejoices that Catherine II has sent 'forty thousand Russians [to Poland] to preach tolerance with bayonets at the ends of their rifles'.[18]

Such disabused lines point us in the direction of a more political reckoning with the eighteenth-century philosophical discourse on fanaticism, which cannot be so easily reinterpreted as the struggle between emancipation and backwardness, equality and subjection. On Voltaire's side, it is evident that along with the horror at the cruel and idiotic character of religious persecution, there is an underlying concern with social peace, with order and stability – which sometimes, as in the lines on the Russian troops above, trumps other considerations of justice. This much is made clear not only by his support for 'enlightened despots', but in his sympathetic depiction of authoritarian arrangements in the Ottoman Caliphate and the Chinese Empire as models of toleration. The abhorrence of politics, of metaphysical abstraction, and indeed of atheism – the philosophy of powerful men operating in 'this circle of crimes that

---

15   Voltaire, *Philosophical Dictionary*, 29.
16   Voltaire, *Traité sur la Tolérance*, Paris: Gallimard, 1975, 31.
17   Ibid., 98.
18   Quoted in Trousson, 'Tolérance et fanatisme selon Voltaire et Rousseau'.

imbeciles call *politics, coup d'état, art of governing*'[19] – is grounded on this same desire to suppress the causes of social scission and violence. It is in this light that we can also consider Voltaire's praise for pluralism, along the lines of his quip that in England a single religion would be despotism; two mean civil war; but thirty make for peace. This pluralism can also take the form of religious (and political) indifference, to be cultivated as the balm against internecine or sectarian violence.

It is this indifference that revolts Rousseau, who like Deleyre accommodates fanaticism to the extent that it might prove necessary to vitalize and unify a polity.[20] Indeed, the contrast between Rousseau and Voltaire on the issue of fanaticism demonstrates to what extent this is a problem best tackled in terms of the character of the social bond. Where Voltaire imagines a peaceable, philosophical disengagement from violent conflict over beliefs, Rousseau fears the emasculating and politically debilitating effects of a doctrine that dissipates the passions only in order the better to expand the reign of interests. But Rousseau's focus on the passions also means that he at times treats fanaticism as so intractable that it warrants only retaliation on its own violent terms.[21] Shifting the focus onto this political dimension of the debates around fanaticism allows for a complexity that the simple trope of fanaticism as anti-Enlightenment, and of Enlightenment as anti-fanaticism, does not permit. Furthermore, it makes it possible to reflect on why being common foes of (a certain type of) fanaticism did not preclude violent disagreements between the likes of Rousseau and Voltaire on the remedies for aggressive religious

---

19   Quoted in Trousson, 'Tolérance et fanatisme selon Voltaire et Rousseau', 39, n. 69.

20   See Zev Trachtenberg, 'Civic Fanaticism and the Dynamics of Pity', in *Rousseau and l'Infâme*, which is especially concerned with the relationship between pity, identification and a civic fanaticism that can take a rather xenophobic bent. Trachtenberg writes of Rousseau's '(unstated) belief that in order to make men into citizens, they must be made into civic fanatics' (205), and traces the manner in which Rousseau struggles with the negative repercussions of such a fanaticism, redacting the term from his earlier variants of the *Social Contract*.

21   Trousson, 'Tolérance et fanatisme selon Voltaire et Rousseau', 49. For a discussion of Rousseau's objections to the idea of fanaticism as an epistemological problem, linked to superstition and manipulation, see Christopher Kelly, 'Pious Cruelty: Rousseau on Voltaire's *Mahomet*', in *Rousseau and l'Infâme*.

ideologies, on the place of philosophy, on the role of the passions and, last but not least, on what kind of politics could put an end to the blight of religious warfare, ignorance and superstition.

Important differences can also be registered in their respective treatments of the figure of Mohammed as politician and 'fanatic'. In Voltaire's 1741 play *Fanaticism, or Mahomet the Prophet*, he is portrayed principally in the guise of the manipulator, driven by the lust for conquest and by plain lust ('an armed Tartuffe', as Voltaire writes to Frederick II)[22] to 'fanaticize' his young, zealous followers. In the tragedy the fanatic is Séide, driven by Mahomet and his deputy Omar into inadvertently murdering his true father Zophir, sheikh of Mecca, and into committing near-incest with his real sister Palmira, the object of the prophet's attentions. Enlightenment demystification here takes the form of revealing the base motivations behind the psychic and political use of fanaticism, the disenchanted power behind murderous piety. But alongside this classic theme, Voltaire's (anti-)political thought is also present. It is not another, better political order for which the tragedy pleads; rather, the victim of Mahomet's designs, the sheikh Zophir, stands for the defence of a stable order built on custom and observance ('my gods, my laws, my country') against the upheaval of a seditious innovator. As dramatized in Voltaire's play, the opposition against fanaticism is the opposition against an unsettling, inflammatory novelty that is in turn shown to be founded on the basest of motives. The alternative is not emancipation, however, but the calm of custom. Deleyre too repeats the trope of Mahomet as a figure of fanaticism, but he adjudicates between those who see him as a fanatic and those who, like Voltaire, see him as a hypocritical 'fanaticizer' by answering that he is both: a fanatic in youth, when fanaticism naturally flourishes, and an impostor in his older age, when hypocrisy and colder, Machiavellian designs set in. Mahomet, in this view, was once the young Séide.

Rousseau's challenge to Voltaire is more severe. For Rousseau, 'anyone who misses the emotional basis of fanaticism is bound to underestimate its

---

22   As Christopher Kelly points out in 'Pious Cruelty', Voltaire's role in editing Frederick the Great's treatise *Anti-Machiavel* can be closely linked to the critique of the manipulation of fanaticism in the play on Mohammed.

potential force and resistance to reason'.[23] The likes of Voltaire are also incapable of grasping the role of passion in politics, including the kind of politics that may be linked to equality and emancipation. What's more, the political and religious conviction of Mohammed also shows him in a different light to Voltaire's schematic villain. While for Voltaire Mohammed is cast as a devious realist and hypocrite, a 'Machiavellian armed prophet who makes use of religion for his purely political purposes',[24] cynically enlisting 'pious cruelty and holy homicide' for his earthly ends, Rousseau – dissenting from Voltaire more at the normative than the descriptive level – depicts him as a founder, giving strength and solidity to his political community through the establishment of a civic religion: 'while proud philosophy or the blind partisan spirit see in [Mohammed or Moses] only lucky impostors, the true politician admires in their institutions this great and powerful genius which oversees lasting arrangements'.[25] This contrast between Rousseau and Voltaire is thus not only an anthropological or methodological one, pitting civic passion against civilizing indifference; it also reveals, beneath divergent estimations of fanaticism, different understandings of politics and its relationship to religion. Fanaticism is here not simply a social and spiritual pathology, but something that affects the very nature of the social compact. Among the dilemmas that haunt the Enlightenment is whether fanaticism is to be fought as an external foe, or whether one should inoculate oneself against it by means of unconditional and passionate attachments – without which even the most rational polity would seem to rest on shaky affective foundations. The political and philosophical debate around enthusiasm, which we'll consider in the next section, revolves around this question.

THE AMBIVALENCE OF ENTHUSIASM

While fanaticism has met with almost universal opprobrium in philosophy and politics, the notion of enthusiasm (*enthousiasme, Enthusiasmus, Begeisterung*), whose fortunes are profoundly entangled with those of fanaticism, has a far less univocal history – witness the manner in which

---

23 Ibid., 181.
24 Ibid., 178.
25 See *The Social Contract*, Book IV, Chapter 8.

it now pervades the language of marketing, management and everyday life ('could you please show more enthusiasm?'). Where fanaticism harkened back to the bloody rituals around the goddess Bellona and her *fanum* (temple), the Greek *Enthousiasmos* denotes the in-pouring or in-breathing of the divine, as performed by the 'inspired pythonness at Delphi'.[26] Plato's theory of poetic inspiration, expounded in the *Phaedrus* and the *Ion*, and revisited by the thinkers of the Renaissance, established a deep and wide-ranging tradition in which enthusiasm stands for a kind of creative derangement. In the fifteenth century, the Platonist commentator Marsilio Ficino forged a potent interpretation of Platonic enthusiasm: 'The soul, which tries to grasp through the senses as much as possible of divine beauty and harmony, is enraptured by divine frenzy. Plato calls celestial love the unutterable desire, which drives us to recognize divine beauty. To see a beautiful body arouses the burning desire after divine beauty and, therefore, those who are inspired are transported into a state of divine madness.'[27] Even in those situations where it became a term of abuse, enthusiasm never seems entirely to lose the trace of a noble transcendence, of a transport – however irregular or dangerous – towards the Good, the True or the Beautiful. As we shall see with regard to Kant, it will also become a term with an explicitly positive political valence.

Enthusiasm, though, also has a history of censure. In the seventeenth and eighteenth centuries, especially in England, there developed a wide-ranging and heterogeneous critique of enthusiasm, one that has been expertly explored by a host of recent intellectual historians.[28] Especially in the early Enlightenment period of the seventeenth

---

26   J. G. A. Pocock, 'Enthusiasm: The Antiself of Enlightenment', in *Enthusiasm and Enlightenment in Europe*, 9.

27   Margot and Rudolf Wittkower, *Born Under Saturn*, 98. On the later shift in the paradigm of enthusiasm in the *Encyclopédie*, away from divine frenzy towards reason, see Mary D. Sheriff, 'Passionate Spectators: On Enthusiasm, Nymphomania, and the Imagined Tableau', in *Enthusiasm and Enlightenment in Europe*, 53–5.

28   See the essays in the already mentioned *Enthusiasm and Enlightenment in Europe, 1650–1850*; Michael Heyd, *'Be Sober and Reasonable': The Critique of Enthusiasm in the Seventeenth and Early Eighteenth Centuries*, Leiden: Brill, 1995; Frederick C. Beiser, *The Sovereignty of Reason: The Defense of Rationality in the Early English Enlightenment*, Princeton: Princeton University Press, 1996.

and early eighteenth centuries – which emerges from this literature as a complex force-field comprising philosophical systematization, religious sectarianism, the questioning of theology, political struggle and scientific development – enthusiasm is a protean and polemical term through which deep-seated and momentous ideological conflicts were played out. To survey this fascinating history would take us too far afield, but it is worth dwelling on some aspects of the critique of enthusiasm that resonate with our own inquiry into the shifting political significance of debates around fanaticism.

One way to conceive of the development of Enlightenment polemics against enthusiasm in England is in terms of the passage from an intra-theological accusation – levied at those heretics who presume to speak directly to God, without the mediation of religious authorities and institutions – to a critique of the (political) theology of revelation, and then to a fully secularized diagnosis of disruptive political forms, culminating in the backlash against the French Revolution. As the discussion of Müntzer has already intimated, a relatively linear narrative is offset by the already political nature of the religious upheavals that affected Germany and England in the sixteenth and seventeenth centuries. In effect, the fear of enthusiasts (and fanatics) as foes of religious-political order gave rise to much literature for which the radical Reformation and the rebellious German Anabaptists served as the very emblem of dangerous convictions. So, for example, in the informatively named 1646 text *Englands Warning by Germanies Woe: or An Historicall Narration, of the Originall, Progresse, Tenets, Names and severall Sects of the Anabaptists, in Germany and the Low Countries*, by Friedrich Spanheim, we get the following rogues' gallery of politicized religious groups, threatening to upset the stability of the commonwealth and the uprightness of Christianity:

[I]t is not manifest by what names these Sectaries are called, and for what cause they are given them: and they are either generall or speciall: The generall are *Anabaptists, Catabaptists, Enthusiasts, Fanaticks* and *Libertines*. . . . It appears likewise that they are called *Enthusiasts*, for the *Enthusiasms, raptures* and other such like things, which they give out for *secret* and *divine inspirations*; and for which, they will not onely have place given to their owne dreames, either in exposition of the Scripture, or determining points of faith, or in direction of the especiall actions of a mans life, but (at leastwise divers of them) ascribe thereunto uncontrollable authority; for which cause also the name of *Fanaticks* [*fanaticorum*] was given them.[29]

Anabaptists, enthusiasts, 'fanaticks' – all threaten order with their pretensions to access an 'uncontrollable authority' that transcends established political and religious institutions. Following the path traced out in the sixteenth century by Luther and Melanchthon in their polemics against Müntzer and the peasant *Schwärmer*, these intra-Protestant attacks against divisive and antinomian sects combine the repudiation of a heresy with the urgent warning against a political threat. Such attacks tended to give way from the mid-seventeenth century onwards to accounts of enthusiasm as a delusion whose causes or unvarying essence may be sought in a malfunctioning physiology or an over-excited imagination, in texts such as Meric Casaubon's *Treatise Concerning Enthusiasm*, Henry More's *Enthusiasmus Triumphatus*, and later in Shaftesbury's *Letter on Enthusiasm*.[30] But though the aetiology changes with the passage from

---

29   Quoted in Heyd, *"Be Sober and Reasonable"*, 20 (see also Heyd, 40). Heyd argues that the derogatory use of enthusiasm emerged in fact out of late polemics against Anabaptists, referred to by one of their detractors as '*Enthusiastae Extatici* and *Verzückten Bruder*' (12). Another instance of the reference to Anabaptism to smear seventeenth-century radical religious movements is Richard Blome's 1660 *The Fanatick History, or, An Exact Relation and Account of the Old Anabaptists and New Quakers*.

30   This clinical perspective on enthusiastic and fanatical behaviours, as fundamentally ahistorical and monotonous, was also prominent in the later German Enlightenment: 'the clinician posited a psycho-physiological essentialism. As different as they might at first seem, sixteenth-century Anabaptists and the Parisian mobs of the early 1790s – or the Neoplatonists of the ancient world and the Mesmerists of the 1780s – were manifestations of the same elementary force. Each new outbreak of the disease confirmed that human nature had its ineradicable dark side, its irrational urge to pervert a natural synergy of cognitive and affective energies. From this point of view, there was no need to sort out essential differences among the phenomena lumped together under *Schwärmerei*, or to ask whether those differences ought to be explained by reference to specific historical contexts.' Anthony J. La Vopa, 'The Philosopher and the *Schwärmer*: On the Career of a German Epithet from Luther to Kant', in *Enthusiasm and Enlightenment in Europe*, 89.

a theological denunciation to an enlightened diagnosis of enthusiasm, the concern over the impact on authority of claims to revelation remain. With the passage from a purely religious concern to an epistemological and political use of the category, we also witness an almost limitless extension of the term, to which many commentators have called attention. In Pocock's insightful formulation:

> enthusiasm begins its journey toward applicability to any system that presents the mind as of the same substance, spiritual or material, as the universe that it interprets, so that the mind becomes the universe thinking and obtains an authority derived from its identity with its subject matter ... [enthusiasm denotes] the mind's identification with the ideas in it, these in turn defined as correspondent or identical with the substance of reality.

Hume spoke of this phenomenon as the 'self-deification of the auto-intoxicated mind'.[31] The political usages of this expanded variant are patent. It is not just claims to revelation or personal inspiration that fall under the rubric of enthusiasm, but also philosophies founded on a fundamental identity between the thinker and the thought (materialism, pantheism, etc.). The accusation could thus be levied not just at sects in the Anabaptist mould but at those forms of 'popular rationalism' that suffused traditions of anti-authoritarian radical thought in the period of the English Civil War.[32] The theological condemnation of unregulated claims to personal revelation could be recast as a critique of any claim to a direct knowledge of reality, of the kind put forward by thinkers whose pantheist or natural right doctrines came into direct conflict with the religious, political and epistemic monopolies of state authorities.

---

31 Pocock, 'Enthusiasm: The Antiself of Enlightenment', 14, 26. This is a position that could in turn lead to a 'rationalist messianism' (26), of the kind that Burke, a *sui generis* defender of the Enlightenment according to Pocock, sought to counter.

32 Christopher Hill, *The World Turned Upside Down: Radical Ideas During the English Revolution*, London: Penguin, 1975, 209, 229. The critique of enthusiasm also targeted forms of popular science which tried to remove the monopoly of science and medicine from state institutions and professional classes. Unofficial practitioners of the sciences were dismissed as 'fanatics in physic' (295).

Viewed from this angle, the critique of enthusiasm becomes far more complex than a narrative of Enlightenment reason against religious revelation might suggest.

Interestingly, historians diverge precisely on this point. Frederick Beiser, for instance, regards the question of enthusiasm as primarily epistemological (rather than religious or political), and its critique as an intrinsic dimension of the advance of Enlightenment rationality. For him, it is a product of the *via moderna* and 'a consistent development of the nominalist critique of rationalist theology'.[33] All 'the enthusiasts rejected a *natural* and *discursive* reason as a rule of faith',[34] while their opponents turned to criteria of natural causality and legitimate evidence. A paragon of such a critique of enthusiasm may be found in Locke's 1690 *Essay Concerning Human Understanding*, which contends that genuine lovers of truth do not entertain 'any proposition with greater assurance, than the proofs it is built upon will warrant'.[35] What lies beyond evidence is merely 'surplussage', originating in pathological interests and inclinations, not true *philia*. The claim to revelation is incapable of advancing any criteria to prove that divine inspiration has indeed taken place. Moreover, 'he that takes away reason, to make way for revelation, puts out the light of both, and does much-what the same, as if he would persuade a man to put out his eyes, the better to receive the remote light of an invisible star by a telescope'.[36] The combination of the force of inner inclination and its projection onto an exalted external source makes enthusiasm a potent motor in human affairs, but its structure is ultimately circular – we could even say narcissistic. Enthusiasm is 'an *ignis fatuus* that leads [men] constantly round in this circle; it is a revelation, because they firmly believe it, and they believe it, because it is a revelation'.[37] It is also a form of laziness, since it exempts us from the labour of seeking and presenting

---

33   Beiser, *The Sovereignty of Reason*, 187.
34   Ibid., 194.
35   John Locke, *An Essay Concerning Human Understanding*, in *The Works of John Locke in Nine Volumes*, Vol. 2, London: Rivington, 1824, 272.
36   Ibid., 273.
37   Ibid., 277.

evidence for our supposed truths.[38] In Locke's treatment, enthusiasm attains a generic status and a malleable extension – capable of covering political and religious sectarianism, theology, rationalist metaphysics, and any form of thought that does not subject itself to stringent standards of sensory evidence.[39]

This neat image of an empirically grounded reason against the illegitimate claims of enthusiasm becomes complicated once we consider it in its cultural and political context. Behind the myriad behaviours stigmatized as enthusiastic, we can make out the question of (political, religious, philosophical) authority. It is this that brings together 'zealous sectarians, millenarians, prophesiers, and other radical groups and individuals who opposed the existing Church order', but also Platonists, experimental philosophers, or even rationalists like Descartes, guilty of 'philosophical' or 'contemplative' enthusiasm.[40] For Michael Heyd, rather than a simple battle between an emerging enlightenment and regressive forms of religious inspiration and rationalist theology, the critique of enthusiasm needs to be understood as the product of the crisis of an order founded on Scripture, humanistic learning, Aristotelian scholasticism and Galenic medicine; the institutional and symbolic crisis of the transcendental legitimation of the political order. The new

---

38   This theme of work against revelation will also appear in Kant, for whom shirking cognitive labour marks out the 'superior tone' of the lazy, vain and antisocial *Schwärmer*. See Immanuel Kant, 'On a Newly Arisen Superior Tone in Philosophy' (1796), in *Raising the Tone of Philosophy: Late Essays by Immanuel Kant, Transformative Critique by Jacques Derrida*, P. Fenves (ed.), Baltimore: Johns Hopkins, 1993, 53. See also La Vopa, 'The Philosopher and the *Schwärmer*', for perspicuous comments on the 'application of a distinctly modern discourse of labor and consumption' to *Schwärmerei* in the 1790s, linked to the expansion of leisure and print culture.

39   Locke is emblematic of Pocock's treatment of the enlightened assault on enthusiasm: 'the marriage of Athens and Jerusalem, philosophy and monotheism, for which the Enlightened desired to substitute an empirical philosophy, a morality of sociability, and a God who could be inferred rather than known'. Pocock, 'Enthusiasm: The Antiself of Enlightenment', 23.

40   Heyd, *"Be Sober and Reasonable"*, 4. Voetius (Martin Schoock), in his *Admiranda Methoda*, claimed that Descartes' philosophical method 'leads straight not only to scepticism, but also to enthusiasm, atheism and frenzy' (113). Casaubon also viewed Descartes as an enthusiast, because of the manner in which the French philosopher bypassed the evidence of the senses. In his 1696 *The Method to Science*, Sergeant identified Descartes' Inward Light with 'the method of Fanaticks in religion' (129).

physiological, scientific and philosophical idioms that were thrown up by this crisis and relied so widely on the disparagement of enthusiasm 'were all allied with defenses of the social and political order',[41] inasmuch as they sought to preserve it against the excessive and unregulated claims of those who trumpeted an access to truth without mediation, be it religious or political – those who, to use a Weberian formulation, staked their standing on charisma rather than institutions.

The critique of enthusiasm is also far more unified than its targets, so that it might be seen as 'a misguided historical exercise to search for a clear definition of enthusiasm, let alone to look for a well-defined movement'.[42] Any retrospective view whereby the anti-enthusiasts are firmly on the side of an emancipated and emancipatory rationality, and their nemeses on that of a regressive reliance on revelation, is difficult to maintain. While we tend to think of claims to revelation as excuses for the illegitimate prerogatives of absolutist despots and theocratic clerics, and their critique as inherently anti-authoritarian, things are not so straightforward. As studies of seventeenth-century radical thought indicate, claims to revelation, or to a kind of plebeian and pantheist rationalism, could bolster potent challenges to political and religious authorities. Indeed, as the editors of an excellent collection on enlightenment and enthusiasm tell us: 'The critique of enthusiasm was launched in the name of multiple and divergent projects. It was considered a threat to authority and order, not only in various forms of religious excess, but also in more secular guises of hyper-rationality, isolated introspection, mass conformity, and so on.'[43] If the process of Enlightenment involved the shaping of a (cognitively) rule-following and (politically) law-abiding circumscribed self, autonomously giving itself the very laws it was externally compelled to respect, then its enthusiastic 'antiself' was a menace precisely to the extent that it was 'unbounded, self-devouring, heteronomic'.[44]

---

41   Lawrence E. Klein and Anthony J. La Vopa, 'Introduction', in *Enthusiasm and Enlightenment in Europe*, 2.
42   Heyd, *Be Sober and Reasonable*, 5.
43   Klein and La Vopa, 'Introduction', 1.
44   Ibid., 4.

Over the seventeenth and eighteenth centuries, a certain idea of modernity and rationality constituted itself with a mutable 'enthusiasm' as its counterpart. But much as the repudiation of revealed truth may seem, in retrospect, one of the foremost conquests of secular reason,[45] its role in the intellectual and political crises of authority of that time is not at all univocal. 'The discourse of enthusiasm was repeatedly used to marginalize and thereby silence, according to class or gender or cognitive mode or religious affiliation. It was used to constitute authority against forms of power that were perceived as threatening.'[46] The reliance on the supernatural, or on a rationalist-pantheist cognition of the structure of nature, could be a potent boon to egalitarian and subversive movements, while the policing of truths through sensory evidence could work in the service of established authorities. Similarly, enthusiasm could drive processes of secularization, or reinstate the transcendent authority of religion.[47] Cartesian and Spinozist rationalism, and the mathematized sciences they promoted, could be derided as enthusiastic, while the opposition to enthusiasm might be based on Aristotelian psychologies or theories of the humours which we would be hard pressed to link to 'Enlightenment'.

As the earlier attacks on religious sectarianism and metaphysical rationalism morphed into the repudiation of egalitarian politics,[48]

---

45 This is the basic thesis in Mark Lilla's *The Stillborn God*.

46 Klein and La Vopa, 'Introduction', 5. See also, in the same volume, Jan Goldstein, 'Enthusiasm or Imagination? Eighteenth-Century Smear Words in Comparative National Context', 29, and Heyd, *"Be Sober and Reasonable"*, 26 (on enthusiasm against the mediation of Christian authority) and 170 (on the attacks on the 'levelling Principle' of the enthusiastic French prophets).

47 'These were crosscurrents to the stream of secularization . . . for sometimes the enthusiasts constituted the radical front line, shattering the grip of inherited religious ideas, but at other times, and perhaps more typically, these enthusiasts were caught up in the most uninhibited of the very kinds of "spirituality" that rational religion aimed to purge.' John H. Zammito, *Kant, Herder and the Birth of Anthropology*, Chicago: University of Chicago Press, 2002, 191. This ambivalence unsettles the tidy image of the Enlightenment as a process of rationalization and secularization.

48 'The attacks on "democrats" and other political radicals in the revolutionary era echoed two earlier rhetorical campaigns: the one against sectarian dissent and the one against philosophical system-builders,' Klein and La Vopa, 'Introduction', 5. Though it should be noted that the attacks on sectarian dissent (for instance that of Müntzer in Germany or the Ranters in England) were *already* attacks on political radicalism.

enthusiasm in effect proved to be a 'foil that was difficult to control', since advocates of Enlightenment could themselves be accused of claiming unmediated access to reality. This is why the 'modernity constituted in one way or another as the obverse of enthusiasm was neither stable nor unified'.[49] Enlightenment thought entertained fraught and ambivalent relations with its apparent counterparts. It relied on the thought-forms it tried to exorcise, and often found itself locating its very nemesis within reason itself. As Pocock has argued, 'the Enlightenments from their outset recognized the possibility of an intellectual fanaticism arising within as well as without the enterprises in which they were engaged'.[50] It is this fanaticism of reason that Kant mined with relentless rigour.

KANT THE FANATIC

If the Enlightenment may be characterized, from a certain vantage point, as the assertion of the this-worldly rights of immanence against the religious and political prerogatives of transcendent sources of authority, then Kant's philosophy – grasped in the complex unity of its epistemological, cosmological, moral and political moments – is a delimiting of immanence, dominated by a critical vigilance against the transgression of those limits without which critique slips back into hubris or superstition. Kant inherits from the Enlightenment the preoccupation with fanaticism understood as a pathology of transcendence, the delusion that reason may legislate upon that about which it has no experience. For Kant too there is no knowledge of a realm beyond worldly experience. But his solution to the problems of supersensible cognition is profoundly ambivalent. On the one hand, he continues the struggle of the radical Enlightenment against superstition, dogmatism and the socially divisive effects of religious allegiance; on the other, given the link between the limits of reason and Kant's practical defence of faith, he exercises great caution when it comes to the reductive aims of a materialist Enlightenment that would seek to excise religion altogether. Furthermore, there is in Kant, certainly if viewed with Nietzschean lenses, something like a 'ruse of transcendence': the return, in the guise

49   Klein and La Vopa, 'Introduction', 3.
50   Pocock, 'Enthusiasm: The Antiself of Enlightenment', 7.

of practical reason, that is to say of universally binding abstract moral precepts, of authorities which in some sense lie beyond the domain of human and natural relations.

The particular distribution of immanence and transcendence within Kantian thought – so rife with repercussions for European philosophy as a whole – can orient our inquiry into his approach to the question of fanaticism. In effect, contrary to the strand within the Enlightenment that took fanaticism to denote forms of action and belief which were extrinsic to reason (religious sectarianism, cultural atavisms, political partisanship and so on), for Kant fanaticism is immanent to human rationality itself. Vigilance against unreason is no longer simply a matter of proper political arrangements or social therapies, of establishing secularism or policing madness; it is intrinsic to reason's own operations and capacities, requiring reason's immanent, legitimate uses to be separated from its transcendent or illegitimate ones. But this introjection of fanaticism, so to speak, also means that Kant is compelled to confront the ambivalence of fanaticism: its disturbing proximity, as an abstract passion, to those forms of action he deems to be politically and morally noble because they are universalizable. This is especially evident in his efforts to distinguish between enthusiasm (*Enthusiasmus*) and fanaticism (*Schwärmerei*),[51] a conceptual pair that's particularly significant in terms of his own allegiance to the event which, more than any other, lies at the source of contemporary anti-fanatical discourse: the French Revolution. Fanaticism is in a sense at the heart of the genesis of Kant's critical philosophy, as he assumes and transforms the heritage of Enlightenment discourse through what we could call fanaticism's 'incorporation' into reason, or reason's inoculation by and from fanaticism. But with the

---

51   The attempt to clean up philosophical German to distinguish clearly between *Enthusiasmus* and *Schwärmerei* is not the monopoly of Kant. In 1775 Christoph Martin Wieland sought to provide these terms with 'fixed meaning' and stop them from becoming mere 'curse words'. He was followed in this by *Popularphilosoph* Christian Garve, who wished to distinguish between delusional *Schwärmerei*, itself divided into religious and political variants, and *Enthusiasmus* as creative inspiration. On the 'semantic crisis' around enthusiasm/fanaticism and attempts at resolution, see La Vopa, 'The Philosopher and the *Schwärmer*: On the Career of a German Epithet from Luther to Kant', 86.

dramatic politicization of the Enlightenment heralded by the French Revolution, Kant's thought comes into contact with the disparaging of egalitarian and universalist politics as fanatical.[52] Whether implicitly, in the 'theory-practice debate' of 1793, or explicitly, in Nietzsche's polemics almost a century later, Kantianism is branded as a 'moral fanaticism', a subjection of life to abstract and transcendent principles of right. Thus, though Kant's philosophy represents a sustained struggle against fanaticism, locating fanaticism where even its Enlightened arch-enemies did not suspect its presence, it is also true, as Nietzsche himself acerbically noted, that Kant was 'the true son of his century, which before any other can be called the century of enthusiasm'.[53]

When the question of fanaticism, of *Schwärmerei*, emerges in Kant's thinking in the mid-1760s, it is not primarily in the politico-religious register that preoccupied the likes of Deleyre and Voltaire in France, or More and then Shaftesbury in England. It is with mediums, madness and melancholia that Kant initially grapples. But a fundamental concern, which he later explicitly translates into moral and political arguments, is already present: how can an indispensable enthusiasm be separated from a pernicious fanaticism? And more broadly: how can affect be enlisted in a project of enlightenment? At the junction of a theory of humours and modern mental pathology, Kant's *Essay on the Illnesses of the Head* poses this problem precisely in terms of the distinction between *Enthusiasmus* and *Schwärmerei*, a constant through both his so-called pre-critical and critical periods, the two phases of Kant's work that have the 1781 *Critique of Pure Reason* as their watershed. As Kant writes, with reference to his much-admired Rousseau:

---

52   For an attempt to disentangle an Enlightenment compatible with religious authority from an extreme, fanatical and revolutionary Enlightenment, see Friedrich Karl von Moser's 1792 essay 'True and False Political Enlightenment', in *What is Enlightenment? Eighteenth-Century Answers and Twentieth-Century Questions*, J. Schmidt (ed.), Berkeley: University of California Press, 1996. Fanaticism is here not a product of obscurantism, but of an excess of light. Moser reminds his readers that 'all good police regulations prevent and prohibit bringing an open flame into flammable places' (213).

53   Friedrich Nietzsche, *Daybreak: Thoughts on the Prejudices of Morality*, trans. R. J. Hollingdale, Cambridge: Cambridge University Press, 1982, 'Preface (1886)', 3.

This ambiguous appearance of phantasy [*Phantasterei*] in moral sentiments that are in themselves good is enthusiasm [*Enthusiasmus*], and
nothing great in the world has been done without it. Things are altogether different with the fanatic (visionary, *Schwärmer*). The latter is
actually a lunatic with a supposed immediate inspiration and great inti-
macy with the powers of heaven. Human nature knows no more dangerous delusion.

In a note from *Observations on the Feeling of the Beautiful and the Sublime*,
published in the same year as the *Essay*, Kant declares that:

Fanaticism must always be distinguished from *enthusiasm*. The former
believes itself to feel an immediate and extraordinary communion with
a higher nature; the latter means the state of the mind in which it has
become inflamed by any principle above the proper degree, whether it
might be by maxims of patriotic virtue, or of friendship, or of religion,
without the illusion of a supernatural communion having anything to do
with it.[54]

Claims to revelation and inspiration had of course been the object of critical and polemical scrutiny from the first stirrings of the Enlightenment.
In the English case, this was often in terms of enthusiasm, in the etymo-
logically precise sense of being visited or inspired by God. Kant relies
instead on a non-theological term, albeit one polemically adopted by

---

54   Immanuel Kant, *Observations on the Feeling of the Beautiful and the Sublime*,
trans. J. T. Goldthwait, Berkeley: University of California Press, 2003, 108. On the
difference between an enthusiasm grounded in freedom and a pathological *Schwärmerei*,
see also Peter Fenves, *A Peculiar Fate: Metaphysics and World-History in Kant*, Ithaca:
Cornell University Press, 1991, 243, n. 42 (Fenves also notes the very early discussion of enthusiasm in climactic-geographical terms in the 1754 essay 'The Question
Whether the Earth is Aging, Considered Physically'). Kant also distinguishes between
fanaticism and superstition, and seems to concur with Hume's suggestion, mentioned
in Chapter 1, that of the two superstition is more threatening to reason. For Kant,
fanaticism, which among the Germans and the French is but 'an unnatural outgrowth
of the noble feeling that belongs to the character of these peoples . . . is on the whole far
less pernicious than the superstitious inclination even though it is violent at the outset',
since it later 'cools' and becomes 'orderly', while superstition traps its victim in delusion and immaturity (108–9).

Luther himself, *Schwärmer*, to designate those who delude themselves into thinking that they have a sensual experience of the transcendent, and who promise nothing but swarming confusion. However, although Kant will outline different ways of showing how the enthusiast, inflamed by principle, is 'altogether different' from the fanatic, policing the border between these two positions proves to be extremely difficult. For Kant, both enthusiasm and fanaticism are propensities that impinge on human thought in its most admirable aesthetic, cognitive and practical activities, and his denunciation of their dangers is also a recognition of their perverted nobility. It is in this sense that we should consider Kant's preoccupation with melancholy as an 'ambiguous passion'.

As Monique David-Ménard has noted in her study of the 'madness in pure reason': 'Because he depreciates reality, the melancholic who is enthused can become the champion of morality.'[55] In exploring the aesthetic sublimity of a life lived according to principles, Kant writes in the *Observations* of how in the deterioration of the moral man's character, 'earnestness inclines towards dejection, devotion toward fanaticism, love of freedom to enthusiasm'.[56] In these lines we already have an inkling of the link between fanaticism and a misplaced inwardness, as well as an intimation of the affinity between enthusiasm and politics. Kant's critical vigilance is thus largely turned inwards, in a bid to prevent sublime feelings from mutating imperceptibly into mental illnesses. Vigilance, however, does not translate into self-observation. As he notes in his courses on anthropology, compiling inner perceptions into 'a diary of an *observer of oneself*' can 'easily lead to enthusiasm [*Schwärmerei*] and madness [*Wahnsinn*]'. Such an 'eavesdropping' on oneself is for Kant particularly dangerous, because it subordinates the principles of thought and the reflexivity of our faculty of representation to the unruly flux of inner sense, and neglects the only experiences which we can really rationally observe: external experiences. In sum, such fanatical self-observation is for Kant 'the most direct path to illuminism or even terrorism, by way of a confusion in the mind of

---

55   Monique David-Ménard, *La folie dans la raison pure. Kant lecteur de Swedenborg*, Paris: Vrin, 1990, 119.
56   Kant, *Observations on the Feeling of the Beautiful and the Sublime*, 66.

supposed higher inspirations and powers flowing into us, without our help, who knows from where'.[57] Such excessive attention lavished on oneself should be offset by the detour through experience and, most significantly, by the use of abstraction, which demonstrates a 'freedom of the faculty of thought and the authority of the mind, *in having the object of one's representations under one's control*'.[58]

This question of critical monitoring, and of the character of abstraction, is present in one of the most remarkable of Kant's writings, in which we see the question of fanaticism span the seemingly separate terrains of mental pathology, occult phenomena and metaphysics. In the 1766 *Dreams of a Spirit-Seer Elucidated by Dreams of Metaphysics* – a text uncharacteristically replete with satire, confession and anecdote, but whose philosophical significance should not be underestimated – Kant, allegedly at the instigation of friends and acquaintances, tackles the unsettling proximities between the claims (or dreams) of a rationalist, Leibnizian metaphysics and the speculative hucksterism of Emmanuel Swedenborg, who had just published his eight-volume *Arcana Coelestia*.

Though Kant mentions religious authorities at the outset – acerbically referring to Holy Rome's 'exploitation-right to [the] spirit-realm' – what is actually at stake is the undecidability between forms of reasoning which Kant had hitherto championed and the phenomenon of spiritualism, which he confesses to being tempted by – a temptation that will better allow him to vanquish it. 'The frontiers between folly and understanding', we read in *Dreams*, 'are so poorly marked that one can scarcely proceed for long in one region without occasionally making a little sally into the other.'[59] The details of Kant's argument – combining

---

57   Immanuel Kant, *Anthropology from a Pragmatic Point of View*, R. B. Louden (ed.), Cambridge: Cambridge University Press, 2006, 21–2. See also Immanuel Kant, 'Some Remarks on Ludwig Heinrich Jakob's *Examination of Mendelssohn's Morning Hours*', in *Anthropology, History and Education*, R. B. Louden (ed.), Cambridge: Cambridge University Press, 2007, 190.

58   Kant, *Anthropology*, 20.

59   Immanuel Kant, 'Dreams of a Spirit-Seer Elucidated by Dreams of Metaphysics', in *Theoretical Philosophy 1755–1770*, trans. and ed. D. Walford with R. Meerbote, Cambridge: Cambridge University Press, 1992, 343. See also *Anthropology*, 85, where Kant argues that Swedenborg's *Schwärmerei* (rendered by the translator as 'enthusiasm') stems from taking 'the real appearances of the world present to the senses' as a

linguistic analysis, physiology and metaphysics – will not detain us here. What matters for our examination of Kant's conflicted critique of fanaticism are the reasons he adduces for taking such interest in Swedenborg's disreputable fancies. Of course, the Swedish seer is an exemplary *Schwärmer*, transgressing the very principles that order our experience of the external world. His is not just a delusion of reason [*Wahnwitz*] but a 'systematic delusion of the senses [*Wahnsinn*] in general'.[60] Sensory delusion involves the mistaken projection of inner sense onto the outer world. Kant speaks here, in both a perceptual and a more broadly cognitive sense, of the point of convergence, the *focus imaginarius* of our representations, which is placed in the object when we're dealing with external experiences and in ourselves when we're dealing with 'the images of imagination'. The victim of *Wahnsinn* is one who 'places mere objects of his own imagination outside himself, taking them to be things which are actually present before him'.[61]

But Swedenborg's sensory delusion is systematic and, despite Kant's claim that it is the famous medium's hallucinations rather than his speculations which interest him, it is evident that the 1766 text is preoccupied with *Schwärmerei* as 'the intellectual construction of a universe', not just with the 'fanatical intuition' of a contact with spirits. The rationally undecidable character of the 'difference between metaphysical idealism and delirium' will lead Kant to the *Critique of Pure Reason*, in which the inquiry into the subjective constitution of experience – Kant's 'Copernican revolution' – will place the struggle against 'the dogmatic-fanatical will to knowledge' on a new footing. But already in the *Dreams*, the response to fanaticism is not simply physiological and diagnostic – a study of illnesses of the head. It is a question of 'the *limits of human reason*', of recognizing that we are not endowed with 'the wings which would enable [human reason] to fly so high as to cleave clouds which

---

mere symbol of the intelligible. Kant contrasts this with the enlightened use of symbolism, which consists in maintaining its difference from the rational or intellectual, as when we distinguish between the 'shell' of public worship and the universal content of religion.

60   Kant, 'Dreams of a Spirit-Seer', 347.
61   Ibid., 333.

veil from our eyes the mysteries of the other world'.[62] This limitation of reason can only be understood in terms of an overarching interest that is both moral and cosmopolitical. Though his verdict is that we may hold opinions on, but never gain knowledge of, spirits, Kant detects in the attraction of Swedenborg's otherwise nonsensical system of spirits the index of a 'hope for the future'. This hope is a defect, but it is also a rational inclination, and one that Kant refuses to relinquish.

But the engagement with Swedenborg also has a more meta-political dimension. What draws us to the very idea of a community of spirits is our 'dependency on the *universal human understanding*', on the 'will of others outside ourselves', which gives rise to a moral 'obligation'. In explicitly Rousseauian terms, Kant writes that 'in our most secret motives, we are dependent on the general will'. How could we not be charmed by the idea of an 'immediate community of spirits' that would dispel 'the anomalies . . . which are normally so embarrassingly conspicuous in the contradiction between the moral and the physical circumstances of man here on earth'?[63] The *Schwärmer* is not operating simply at the level of sensory delusions. The dreams of the spirit-seer, like the dreams of the metaphysician, are predicated on our – moral and political – dreams. The turn to immaterial substances or principles as grounding our action in the world and our forecasts about the future is not merely the result of 'lazy philosophy';[64] it is an effect of our reason's need to communicate with others, living and dead, in 'one great republic'.[65]

The guiding themes of Kant's critical philosophy – the limits of human reason, the curtailment of speculation, the grounding of moral faith – emerge alongside the motif of fanaticism, understood as a sensory, cognitive and moral-political phenomenon. The three Critiques will prolong this project, if anything dignifying the tendency to excessive speculation by treating it as an immanent disposition of reason, rather than a more or less accidental pathology, or illness of the head. With the study of transcendental illusions in the 'Transcendental Dialectic', we

62   Ibid., 354, 359.
63   Ibid., 322–3.
64   Ibid., 318.
65   Ibid., 328.

pass, to follow David-Ménard's useful characterization, from madness properly so-called to the 'madness of reason'. This madness is in a sense incurable, since it concerns reason's antinomic drive to cognize the totality, to think the unconditioned. Kant's strategy is to harness this drive for the sake of practical reason.

Kant's engagement with the question of fanaticism plays out, in closely interrelated ways, in the philosophical, aesthetic and political registers. In 1786, spurred by a heated debate over Spinoza's pantheism and its potentially irreligious consequences,[66] Kant wrote the essay 'What Does it Mean to Orient Oneself in Thinking?' There, he sought to present his philosophy as one that rejected as fanatical the idea, associated with Spinoza, of a possible intuition of being and necessity. He also wished to demarcate himself from the anti-Spinozist position, identified with the philosopher Jacobi, which tried to drive a wedge between faith and reason. Instead Kant argued that his masterwork, the *Critique of Pure Reason*, by determining the limits of our understanding, 'completely clips dogmatism's wings', that is, it fatally undermines Spinoza's brand of rationalism which, claiming an insight into being without any recourse to sensibility, 'leads directly to fanaticism'.[67]

For Kant, reason can immunize itself against the threat of dogmatic, ontological fanaticism. This is one of the chief purposes of critique as a method of inquiry. But the fight against reason's own propensity to fanaticism also has a political side, overtly if elliptically addressed by Kant. Indicating the context of censorship under which he himself laboured, he portrays the self-legislation of reason as the only way to pre-empt state repression of the subversive or atheistic effects of the fanatical position.[68]

---

66   On the so-called *Pantheismusstreit* or *Spinozismusstreit*, see Frederick C. Beiser, *The Fate of Reason: German Philosophy from Kant to Fichte*, Cambridge, MA: Harvard University Press, 1987, 44–126.

67   Immanuel Kant, 'What Does it Mean to Orient Oneself in Thinking?', *Religion and Rational Theology*, trans. and ed. A. W. Wood and G. Di Giovanni, Cambridge: Cambridge University Press, 1996, 15. I have modified the translation to render *Schwärmerei* as 'fanaticism', rather than Wood and Di Giovanni's 'enthusiasm'.

68   On Kant's struggles over his writings on religion, and especially the pressures he was put under by Frederick William II's minister for ecclesiastical affairs, the Rosicrucian Johann Christoph Wöllner, see Allan W. Wood's introduction to *Religion and Rational Theology*.

Autonomy emerges as an *antidote* to authority and heteronomy. 'Freedom in thinking', writes Kant,

> signifies the subjection of reason to no laws *except those which it gives itself*; and its opposite is the maxim of a lawless use of reason (in order, as genius supposes, to see further than one can under the limitation of laws). The natural consequence is that if reason will not subject itself to the laws it gives itself, it has to bow under the yoke of laws given by another; for without any law, nothing – not even nonsense – can play its game for long.[69]

Unbelief is what characterizes a reason that refuses to legislate over itself, which seeks to be independent from its own need. This is ultimately an orienting need to presuppose the existence of an unlimited supreme being, for the sake of morality. Autonomy is thus as much self-rule as self-monitoring. The 'unbelief of reason' ultimately leads to 'libertinism, i.e. the principle of recognizing no authority at all'. And, as Kant writes, 'at this point the authorities get mixed up in the game'. So, 'freedom in thinking finally destroys itself if it tries to proceed in independence of the laws of reason'. Invocation of the laws of reason points us to the dialectical bond that Kant perceives between the dogmatic or ontological thinking of substance (Spinozism) and an atheist or libertine attack on the compass of rational faith. Furthermore, those who wish to undermine Spinozism with a *credo quia absurdum*, an irrational belief in the face of ontological rationalism, are equally portrayed as harbingers of unruliness.[70]

In the 1790s Kant returned to the question of *Schwärmerei*, recasting the difference between fanaticism and enthusiasm and singling

---

69 Kant, 'What Does it Mean to Orient Oneself in Thinking?', 16.
70 On the *Schwärmerisch* character of Spinozism, see also Kant, 'Some Remarks on Ludwig Heinrich Jakob's *Examination of Mendelssohn's Morning Hours*', in *Religion and Rational Theology*, 178, and the hand-written *Reflexionen* translated by Peter Fenves as 'On Philosophical Exaltation', in *Raising the Tone of Philosophy*, 103 (where 'exaltation' derives from the removal of 'the separate existence of all things') and 105 (Spinozism as the 'highest level of exaltation'). Both texts are from the period of the 'Orientation' essay. The term 'exaltation' is Fenves's rendering of *Schwärmerei*, for reasons outlined in the translator's note to *Raising the Tone of Philosophy*, x–xii.

out the affect of enthusiasm. Kant distinguishes affect from passion
by its 'impetuous and unpremeditated' character, whereas passion
is 'persistent and deliberate'; thus resentment is an affect, hatred a
passion.[71] Though he favours a kind of righteous apathy (which for
detractors such as Herder would still amount to fanaticism, albeit of
a cold variety), Kant defines affect as a pathological but purposeful
supplement, providentially bestowed on us by nature 'until reason
has achieved the necessary strength'. Enthusiasm may be elicited by
linking moral and political principles to examples that 'enliven' the
will. In other words, in order to avoid becoming pathological affect
must be referred to reason as its cause.[72] Affect must remain an effect,
and not a cause.

The distinction between fanaticism and enthusiasm also surfaces in
the *Critique of Judgment*, where the transcendental inquiry into the feelings of the beautiful and the sublime also involves a treatment of unruly
excitations that may nevertheless serve to further universal principles.
Affect is like a sudden, unintentional transport which, though inimical
to reason's self-mastery, can nevertheless betoken a sublime experience of moral (and political) principles that lie beyond the sensible, and
which we negatively encounter in the painful failures of our cognition.
Kant here defines enthusiasm as follows:

> If the idea of the good is accompanied by affect [as its effect], this
> [affect] is called *enthusiasm*. This mental state seems to be sublime, so
> much so that it is commonly alleged that nothing great can be accom-
> plished without it. But in fact any affect is blind. . . . For an affect is an
> agitation of the mind that makes it unable to engage in free deliberation
> about principles with the aim of determining itself according to them.
> Hence there is no way it can deserve to be liked by reason. Yet enthu-
> siasm is sublime aesthetically, because it is a straining of our forces by
> ideas that impart to the mind a momentum whose effects are mightier

71   Immanuel Kant, *Critique of Judgment*, trans. W. S. Pluhar, New York: Hackett,
1987, 132, n. 39. See also Kant, *Anthropology*, 149, and the very insightful entry on
'Affect' in Howard Caygill, *A Kant Dictionary*, Oxford: Blackwell, 1995, 56–9.
72   Kant, *Anthropology*, 152.

and more permanent than are those of an impulse produced by presentations of sense.[73]

It is this aesthetic-affective character of enthusiasm to which Kant will accord political significance in the *Conflict of the Faculties*. In that text, it is not the action that brings about the French Revolution, but the affect it elicits in remote and disinterested spectators, which acts as a sign that humanity may indeed be the agent of its own improvement, that there is such a thing as human progress in history. The public character and universality of the enthusiasm of the revolution's sympathisers 'demonstrates a character of the human race at large and all at once; owing to its disinterestedness, a moral character of humanity, at least in its predisposition, a character which not only permits people to hope for progress toward the better, but is already itself progress insofar as its capacity is sufficient for the present'.[74]

The difference between enthusiasm and fanaticism is here figured in terms of distance and disinterest, whereas in the *Critique of Judgment* it is the character of sight or insight that is at stake. Famously, Kant considers enthusiasm in light of (Hebraic) iconoclasm, which in banning graven images permits a negative exhibition of the infinite. This does not transgress into a sensible vision of the infinite, but is instead sublime precisely because its reference is to our way of thinking, to the supremacy of (invisible) ideas over sensation. As in the earlier reflections on Swedenborg and the essay on orientation in thinking, for Kant fanaticism mistakes inner imagination for outer sense, or subjective conviction for objective knowledge. Not merely a physiological derangement, it involves the marriage of the needs of reason with the fantasy that these needs could be immediately satisfied in experience. Kant argues that enthusiasm as a 'pure, elevating, and merely negative exhibition of morality involves no danger of *fanaticism*, which is the *delusion* [*Wahn*] of wanting to SEE something beyond all bounds of sensibility, i.e.

---

73   Kant, *Critique of Judgment*, 132. Note how Kant is returning to his pre-critical remarks on the 'greatness' of enthusiasm.
74   Immanuel Kant, 'An old question: Is the human race constantly progressing?', in *The Conflict of the Faculties*, in *Religion and Rational Theology*, 302.

of dreaming according to principles (raving with reason). The exhibition avoids fanaticism precisely because it is merely negative. For *the idea of freedom is inscrutable* and thereby precludes all positive exhibition whatever.'[75]

It is precisely with regard to the idea of freedom that Kant again touches on the question of fanaticism in his 1793 text, 'On the Common Saying: "This May Be True in Theory, But It Does not Apply in Practice"'. Like the 'Orientation' essay, 'On the Common Saying' emerges out of a polemic. It intervenes in the debate triggered by the translation into German by Friedrich von Gentz of Burke's *Reflections on the Revolution in France*.[76] For our purposes what matters is not so much the detail of Kant's argument, as the very gesture that the essay embodies. Against the counter-revolutionary position, which views the subjection of politics and custom to abstract principle as the very essence of fanaticism, or even terrorism, Kant engages in a dogged if cautious defence of the rights of theory. Having fought off the sensory delusions and speculative superstitions of *Schwärmerei*, he now finds himself implicitly denounced as a fanatic.[77] Though it might appear shrouded in prudence, Kant's response is a powerful one. In the 1793 essay, to quote Domenico Losurdo, Kant 'unmasks the call to "practice" or "happiness" as the call to the maintenance of the status quo. . . . The refusal of theory is the refusal of any project of radical transformation, a project which is either judged empty and abstract because of its transcendence vis-à-vis the existing social-political system, or is ruinous and appalling because of its pretence to realise concretely, even through harsh struggles, a new social-political order.'[78]

---

75   Kant, *Critique of Judgment*, 135.
76   La Vopa, 'The Philosopher and the *Schwärmer*', 103; Domenico Losurdo, *Autocensura e compromesso nel pensiero politico di Kant*, Naples: Bibliopolis, 2007, 152–65. See also Hannah Arendt, 'Friedrich von Gentz' (1932), in *Essays in Understanding 1930–1954: Formation, Exile and Totalitarianism*, New York: Schocken, 1994, 50–56. On the relationship between counter-revolutionary thought and the transformations in the uses of the idea of fanaticism, see Conze and Reinhart, 'Fanatismus'.
77   'Kant's Critical Philosophy offered the discourse of *Schwärmerei* a new kind of clinical precision; but it also confirmed a growing suspicion that philosophical antidotes were really new forms of disease.' La Vopa, 'The Philosopher and the *Schwärmer*', 91.
78   Losurdo, *Autocensura e compromesso*, 161.

Seen in the context of the reaction to the 'epidemical' and 'atheistical' fanaticism of the French Revolution, and especially to the part played in it by abstraction and metaphysics, the image of Kant as a political moderate, so common today, becomes harder to sustain. To get a sense of how Kant could be viewed as a revolutionary and an extremist of sorts, it suffices to turn to Nietzsche's famous attacks on what he scornfully termed 'Königsbergian Chinadom'.[79] Much of Nietzsche's genealogical war on the view of the True and the Good as disincarnate principles immune from conflict and contest is in effect founded on a *sui generis* continuation of the Enlightenment's, and especially Voltaire's, condemnation of *le fanatisme*. For Nietzsche, however, fanaticism is not primarily to be understood in terms of religious sectarianism or superstition, but as a fanaticism of reason – one that is already detectable in Socrates and Plato.[80] As he had noted in his lectures on Plato, speaking of philosophy's tyrannical bent, 'the conviction that one possesses the truth makes one fanatic'.[81] Characteristically eliding moral, political and epistemological certainties – all of which he regards as founded on the same nihilistic belief in a true world behind the illusory, apparent one – Nietzsche juxtaposes two forms of intellectual life: 'men of conviction' versus vigorous, free-thinking sceptics.

'Convictions are prisons', he writes. Those who live in dutiful fidelity to an idea, who require 'some unconditional Yes and No', abdicate their sovereignty to become mere instruments, weak slaves of a higher will. The man of conviction is prey to a performative contradiction: 'Conviction is the backbone of the man of conviction. *Not* to see many things, not to be impartial in anything, to be party through and through, to view all values from a strict and necessary perspective – this alone is the condition under which such a man exists at all. But he is

---

79   Friedrich Nietzsche, *The Antichrist*, trans. R. J. Hollingdale, London: Penguin, 1990, § 11, 134.
80   See Domenico Losurdo, *Nietzsche, il ribelle aristocratico. Biografia intellettuale e bilancio critico*, Torino: Bollati Boringhieri, 2002, 82.
81   Quoted in M. Brown (ed.) *Plato's Meno*, New York: Bobbs-Merrill, 1971, 102. See also Losurdo, *Nietzsche*, 83. On the 'tyrannical tendency' of philosophy, see Friedrich Nietzsche, *Human, All Too Human, I*, Stanford: Stanford University Press, 1995 [1878], § 261, 'The tyrants of the spirit', 176–9.

thereby the antithesis, the *antagonist* of the truthful man – of truth . . .'.
Recognizing such a contradiction would mean 'immediate destruction'.
For Nietzsche, truly great intellects are driven not by belief but by a
grand passion that expresses itself as the freedom to posit and destroy
values, unconstrained by allegiance to any one given truth. For them,
conviction is merely a means.

What we have here is a contrast between two articulations of affect
and truth: while the Nietzschean free spirit takes pride in his capacity to
adopt and discard truths at will, the passions of the man of conviction –
who is also, as the above quote suggests, a *partisan* man – are inextricable from his beliefs. This is why he is for Nietzsche a fanatic. The historical exemplars he selects signal that for Nietzsche, too, fanaticism is a
politico-religious phenomenon: 'The pathological conditionality of his
perspective makes of the convinced man a fanatic – Savonarola, Luther,
Rousseau, Robespierre, Saint-Simon – the antithetical type of the
strong, emancipated spirit. But the larger than life attitudes of these *sick*
spirits, these conceptual epileptics, impresses the great masses – fanatics are picturesque, mankind would rather see gestures than listen to
reasons. . .'.[82] Such polemical (and psycho-pathological) deployments of
the idea of fanaticism are revealing of Nietzsche's tactical stance towards
the Enlightenment, reiterating its criticisms of irrational convictions and
otherworldly attachments while disputing any univocal claim to truth or
universality.

The political intent of Nietzsche's handling of fanaticism as a term
of opprobrium is especially evident in his criticisms of Kant. Unlike
many contemporary commentators – but like Marx, who saw in Kant's
philosophy 'the *German theory* of the French revolution'[83] – he regards
Kant as an unalloyed supporter of the overturning of the *ancien régime*.
Nietzsche depicts the disembodied, life-denying moral doctrine of
the transcendental philosopher as inseparable from the universalizing
impetus of the French Revolution – 'the daughter and continuation of

---

82   Nietzsche, *The Antichrist*, § 54, 185.
83   Karl Marx, 'The Philosophical Manifesto of the Historical School of Law'
(1842), cited in François Furet, *Marx and the French Revolution*, trans. D. Kan Furet,
Chicago: University of Chicago Press, 1988, 100.

Christianity', with its levelling 'superstition of "equal men"', and the first act of the 'last great slave rebellion'.[84] For Nietzsche, both Christianity and the revolution of the Rights of Man rest on notions of duty and virtue abstracted from the concrete differences between peoples, groups and individuals, between different wills and affirmations.

The raising of universal standards is 'mortally dangerous', since it cannot but ultimately lead to an exhaustion of life, a quashing of that very instinctual and natural joy which is the precondition for any affirmation. Though his ends and motivations differ markedly, Nietzsche here follows quite closely in the footsteps of the counter-revolutionary, anti-fanatical tradition that has its principal source in Burke's *Reflections*. The target remains the role of abstraction in politics and morality, understood as the artificial denial of some kind of nature, where the latter is synonymous with hierarchy, difference and domination. The differential affirmation of life, as an embodied activity of valuation, a struggle between wills to power, is neutralized, which is to say equalized, at the political level by the ascendancy of 'French fanaticism'.[85] Likewise, the centrepiece of Kant's moral thought, the idea of a universalizable categorical imperative, constitutes a 'sacrifice to the Moloch of abstraction'.[86]

Allegiance to the French Revolution is proof of the dangers inhering in Kantian morality:

Did Kant not see in the French Revolution the transition from the inorganic form of the state to the *organic*? Did he not ask himself whether

---

84   Friedrich Nietzsche, *The Will to Power*, W. Kaufmann (ed.), trans. W. Kaufmann and R. J. Hollingdale, New York: Vintage, 1968, § 864, 461; *The Will to Power*, § 184, 111; *Beyond Good and Evil*, trans. W. Kaufmann, New York: Vintage, 1989, § 46, 61. The analogies, resonances and parallels – as well as the lags and disjunctions – between France's political revolution and Germany's philosophical revolution, were a mainstay of German intellectual debate in the first half of the nineteenth century. Heine, for instance, addressed the French public in the 1830s as follows: 'We have uprisings in the world of ideas just as you do in the material world, and tearing down the old dogmatisms makes us as hot as storming the Bastille makes you.' Heinrich Heine, *On the History of Religion and Philosophy in Germany*, T. Pinkard (ed.), trans. H. Pollack-Milgate, 2007, 88. The key source on this question is Stathis Kouvelakis, *Philosophy and Revolution: From Kant to Marx*, trans. G. M. Goshgarian, London: Verso, 2003.
85   Nietzsche, *Daybreak*, 3.
86   Nietzsche, *The Antichrist*, § 11, 134.

there was an event which could be explained in no other way than by a moral predisposition on the part of mankind, so that with it the 'tendency of man to seek the good' would be *proved* once and for all? Kant's answer: 'The Revolution is that.' The erring instinct in all and everything, *anti-naturalness* as instinct, German *decadence* as philosophy – *that is Kant!*[87]

Elsewhere, Nietzsche sketches a criticism of the notion of enthusiasm, so central to the Kantian approach to the Revolution: 'that gruesome farce', he writes, 'which, considered closely, was quite superfluous, though noble and enthusiastic [*schwärmerischen*] spectators from all over Europe contemplated it from a distance and interpreted it according to their own indignations and enthusiasms [*Begeisterungen*] for so long, and so passionately, that *the text finally disappeared under the interpretation*'. A central Nietzschean category, interpretation, is enlisted to strip Kant's account of enthusiasm of its universality, questioning not just its fidelity to the 'text', to factual historical truth, but turning it into a pathologically perspectival phenomenon ('their *own* indignations and enthusiasms'), as also signified by Nietzsche's avoidance of Kant's own term, *Enthusiasmus*.

To the extent that, like Robespierre, he was 'bitten by the moral tarantula Rousseau' and 'harboured in the depths of his soul the idea of . . . moral fanaticism', Kant's profound sympathy and affinity for the French Revolution comes as no surprise to Nietzsche, who also notes that Kant inevitably had to translate his revolutionary enthusiasm in a peculiarly German way, namely by projecting an 'undemonstrable world, a logical "Beyond"'.[88] The French fanatics of equality were thus greeted at a distance by a fanatic of the ought, of the 'thou shalt'.[89] Though Nietzsche condescends to recognizing Kant's merit in making 'the epistemological scepticism of the English possible for Germans', his portrait is unforgiving:

---

87   Ibid., § 11, 134. The allusions to specific passages in the *Critique of Judgment* and the *Conflict of the Faculties* are unmistakable.
88   Nietzsche, *Daybreak*, 3.
89   Nietzsche, *The Will to Power*, § 888, 474; § 940, 495.

Kant: inferior in his psychology and knowledge of human nature; way off when it comes to great historical values (French Revolution); a moral fanatic [*Moral-Fanatiker*] à la Rousseau; a subterranean Christianity in his values; a dogmatist through and through but ponderously sick of this inclination, to such an extent that he wished to tyrannize it, but also weary right away of scepticism; not yet touched by the slightest breath of cosmopolitan taste and the beauty of antiquity.[90]

The sworn enemy of fanaticism, Kant, has the epithet turned against him – a testament to the remarkable plasticity of fanaticism as a term of disparagement and diagnosis. Unlike in Kant's own formulation of fanaticism, it is not an unwarranted claim to divine inspiration or communion with spirits that Nietzsche charges Kant with; nor is Kant guilty of an undue extension of the claims of reason beyond its proper domain (as Kant claimed of Spinoza). Rather, Nietzsche attacks Kant on two fronts, both intimately connected with his broader response to political philosophies of egalitarianism, viewed as Christian in their origin and nihilist in their consequences.

Kant's moral fanaticism stems from two operations of dissimulation. On the one hand, a particular valuation is hypostasized through abstraction as transcendent, thereby crushing the joyful and affirmative difference of life; on the other, Kant's commitment to truth is undermined when viewed as an episode in the 'psychology of conviction'. In Nietzsche's eyes, the categorical imperative is merely the persuasion of a 'party man', which Kant mendaciously disavows by linking morality to supreme motives and ultimately to God.[91] Nietzsche employs against Kant a term, 'moral fanaticism', that the latter had introduced into the *Critique of Practical Reason*, where it denotes behaviour undertaken not from duty alone but because of spontaneous inclination, in the self-conceit that deems certain actions to be commendable for their merit or nobility.[92] In a sense, Nietzsche is not wide of the mark. The vocabulary Kant uses to distinguish dutiful from fanatical action is

---

90   Ibid., § 101, 64. See also § 382, 206.
91   Nietzsche, *The Antichrist*, § 55, 185–7.
92   Immanuel Kant, *Critique of Practical Reason*, trans. W. S. Pluhar, 2002, 110.

one of partisanship: 'the moral state in which [the subject] can be each time is *virtue*, i.e. the moral attitude in the *struggle*, and not *holiness* in the supposed *possession* of a complete *purity* of the will's attitudes'.[93] Militant virtue, in the subjection to the abstract and universal law, and not ennobling sanctity or valour (indulging in 'dreams of imaginary moral perfections') – this is Kant's Robespierrean recommendation, which, like the life of the French revolutionary, alerts us to 'the uneasy coincidence of democracy and fanaticism present at the birth of modern European politics'.[94]

LEGACIES OF LIMITATION

An examination of the backlash against Kant as a moral fanatic for the revolutionary politics of virtue can serve as a corrective of sorts to his current moderate image as a patron figure for an ethical liberal cosmopolitanism. Kant's own 'self-censorship and compromise', along with the neglect of the historical contexts that gave their urgency and radicality to his interventions,[95] mean that today we find it difficult to understand how in the 1830s Heine could write of Kant's 'destructive, world-crushing thought', or remind his French readers of the 'social importance' of the *Critique of Pure Reason*.[96]

Readers of Kant tend to take on board his diagnosis of fanaticism, understood as the delusion of seeing the infinite, or acting directly on the supersensible (what Kant identified as the chimera of 'intellectual intuition'). But they often fail to confront his 'fanatical' defence of the ethico-political rights of abstraction, or his related account of revolutionary enthusiasm. This allows Kant to be enlisted in the elaboration of an ethics of finitude, aimed at neutralizing the Promethean hubris that stems from presuming that politics can proceed from theoretical knowledge of the ways of the world. The risk to be averted is that of 'a politics of abstraction . . . overly attached to an idea at the expense of a frontal

---

93   Ibid., 109.
94   Ruth Scurr, *Fatal Purity: Robespierre and the French Revolution*, London: Vintage, 2007, 5.
95   See Losurdo, *Autocensura e compromesso*, 5–29.
96   *On the History of Religion and Philosophy in Germany*.

denial of reality'.[97] In this view, the 'Kantian revolution in philosophy is a lesson in limitation'.[98] On one level, this is unexceptionable. As we have seen, Kant's philosophy is indeed aimed at clipping the wings of speculative reason. But this seeming curtailment of thought, which binds knowledge to the restrictive parameters of human sensory experience, is accompanied by claims for the universality of moral (and in a sense, political) principle that are anything but limited or finite. The centrality of the human species as a subject of moral and historical development in Kant's political writings is a case in point.

The enthusiasm which greets the French Revolution among its Prussian spectators is important for Kant precisely because of what it indicates about the progressive tendencies of humanity. The affect that accompanies the revolutionary good is itself a sign that warrants the formulation of what Kant, casting limitation to the wind, calls a 'prophetic history'. Genuine enthusiasm, which is enthusiasm for an ideal – that is, an abstraction – does not produce knowledge. However, it makes it possible to grasp and to further a truth about humanity as a whole. The revolution is an unpredictable event, but one with a properly transcendental significance. As Kant writes in *The Conflict of the Faculties*, 'such a phenomenon in human history *will not be forgotten*, because it has revealed a tendency and faculty in human nature for improvement such that no politician, affecting wisdom, might have conjured out of the course of things hitherto existing, and one which nature and freedom alone, united in the human race in conformity with inner principles, could have promised'.[99]

The place of the idea of humanity in the semantic force-field that encompasses fanaticism and enthusiasm is revealing. A clue is provided in one of Kant's hand-written annotations from the 1780s: 'Superstitious religion bases itself on a principle of subjecting reason to the delusion of perceptions. In fanaticism human beings raise themselves above

---

97 Simon Critchley, 'Mystical Anarchism', *Critical Horizons*, 10: 2 (2009), 300.
98 Critchley, *Infinitely Demanding*, 1. I have criticized Critchley's instantiation of a politics of finitude in 'A Plea for Prometheus', *Critical Horizons*, 10: 2 (2009).
99 Kant, *The Conflict of the Faculties*, 304.

humanity.'[100] In claiming direct personal access to the supersensible, whether through spirit-seeing or intellectual intuition, the *Schwärmer* effectively forsake the universality of the species, which can only ever be indirectly presented – for instance in revolutionary 'prophecies' – but never simply known. In affirming access to the All, the human vanishes. The negative exhibition of humanity, which makes for the sublimity of enthusiasm, is thus predicated on the systematic critique of fanaticism. But, as we saw, this repudiation of the sensory delusion of knowledge of the immaterial is the prelude to the affirmation of the truth of the abstract and the defence of the rights of theory – precisely the gesture that led detractors of the French Revolution, from Gentz to Nietzsche, to regard Kant as a moral fanatic.

The fanatical humanist that emerges from Nietzsche's various excoriations of Kant sheds an interesting light on contemporary efforts to use the latter's idea of enthusiasm to renew political thought. Hannah Arendt's much-praised posthumously published lectures on Kant's political philosophy have played a considerable role in this move. Arendt turned to Kant to hone her theory of public judgment as a cornerstone of politics, emphasizing the role of the spectator, and of a political aesthetics, in what she presented as Kant's 'unwritten' political doctrine. Though fanaticism does not explicitly feature in her treatment, the juxtaposition between the disinterested, enthusiastic judgments of the distant onlookers engaging in a public use of reason and the possibly criminal upheavals that actually make up the messy reality of the overturning of an old regime and the foundation of a new one might suggest an alignment of fanaticism with revolution. Or perhaps, more in keeping with the overall tenor of Arendt's thinking, fanaticism would lie – in a manner not entirely alien from Nietzsche's statements on the matter – in the affirmation that there can be a politics of humanity per se.[101]

---

100 'On Philosophical Exaltation', in *Raising the Tone of Philosophy*, 105. I have modified the translation, to render *Schwärmerei* as fanaticism, instead of exaltation.
101   See Hannah Arendt, *The Human Condition*, Chicago: University of Chicago Press, 1958, 116, 176. Arendt is especially critical of Marx's attempt to turn the species (or species-being, *Gattungswesen*) into a subject of history, regarding it as an obfuscation of plurality, one of the basic conditions of political life.

Arendt stresses that Kant's aesthetic and political doctrine of judgment is not one of universality, but rather – to the extent that it is based on cases, examples and occasions that cannot be subsumed under pre-given criteria – one that links singularity to generality. Furthermore, she sees the notion of species in Kant as indicating that what is at stake is the plurality of men, not humanity or Man as such. The political question of judgment would thus be: 'Why are there men rather than Man?'[102] Now, though it is clear that the notion of the species is not simply reducible to that of humanity – since in Kant it is meant to indicate the point of contact, in prophetic history, between the causality of nature and the principles of freedom – Arendt's turn to plurality occludes Kant's defence of abstraction in politics. That judgment in politics cannot be deduced from knowable and fixed criteria does not turn it into a matter of trial and error, or of personal sensibility. The impersonal dimension of judgment – which Arendt perspicuously grasps when she speaks of 'something nonsubjective in what seems to be the most private and subjective sense'[103] – and the impersonality of the feeling that greets the sudden event of emancipation in a distant land, signal that the abstract dimension of humanity, over and above 'men in the plural', is indispensable for Kant. As opposed to the fanaticism and superstition that compel individual human beings to adopt a 'superior tone' on the grounds of their privileged access to the supersensible, the enthusiasm that is humanity's sign to itself that it indeed exists – at least as a tendency or disposition – goes beyond plurality. Kant's species is not just a population, or even a multitude. Kant cannot so easily be enlisted for a project in which political plurality would be pitted against abstract universals in order to ground a politics of finitude and forestall the totalitarian transgressions of abstract politics.

What of the trope of the spectator, which plays such a crucial role in Arendt's account? Leaving aside the specific political reasons that might have suggested to Kant, as an accommodation to Prussian political conditions, the institution of an 'insurmountable *distance* between

---

102 Hannah Arendt, *Lectures on Kant's Political Philosophy*, R. Beiner (ed.), Chicago: University of Chicago Press, 1992, 40.
103 Ibid., 67.

[the] revolution and anyone who merely contemplates it from a specta-tor's position',[104] can we see the spectator as a safeguard against political *Schwärmerei*? Arendt, who defines politics as concerted and unpredicta-ble action in a public space of appearance, notes in her lectures that Kant 'does not know either a faculty or a need for *action*'.[105] This is true to a certain extent: the capacity for collective historical action, the experi-ence of oneself as a member of a species with a disposition to progressive development, can only be experienced indirectly in Kant, not through the activity of a political militant, but only by way of what Arendt calls, linking it to Kant's notion of a world citizen or cosmopolitan, a world spectator.[106] The limitations and contradictions of the spectator's stance, which externalizes and in a sense naturalizes the very event it is enthusi-astic about, stripping it of its subjective dimension, are evident. Stathis Kouvelakis has captured them well:

> A position '*à la Kant*' is illusory not because it presents itself as subjec-tive but, in a certain sense, because it is not subjective enough: because it holds that an 'objective' upheaval can take place in the world on a level that is indifferent and, as it were, external to the deliberations of a subject confined to his enthusiasms for the 'spectacle' of a remote battle. This observing consciousness does not take into account the 'always-already' of a network of day-to-day decisions in which subjective activ-ity is entangled. By dissociating the form of the event from its content, this consciousness condemns itself to oscillating between enthusiasm at a distance and aestheticized indifference to worldly affairs.[107]

From another, related angle, what Arendt referred to as the 'clash between the spectator and the actor'[108] appears as a 'fetishistic disa-vowal', which immunizes one's own immaculate and transcendental

---

104   Kouvelakis, *Philosophy and Revolution*, 10. See also Losurdo, *Autocensura e compromesso*.
105   Arendt, *Lectures*, 19. She also argues that 'Kant could conceive of action only as acts of the powers-that-be' (60).
106   Ibid., 58.
107   Kouvelakis, *Philosophy and Revolution*, 10.
108   Arendt, *Lectures*, 58.

enthusiasm from contagion by the bloody empirical deeds on which it nevertheless relies.[109] Although there is considerable truth in these and other criticisms of Kant's politics of the spectator, many of them rely, as does Arendt, on the notion of this spectator as impartial. In her gloss on Kant's politics of judgment, via a parable by Pythagoras, she argues that 'only the spectator occupies a position that enables him to see the whole; the actor, because he is a part of the play, must enact his part – he is partial by definition. The spectator is impartial by definition – no part is assigned to him.'[110] But this 'distribution of the sensible', which puts partial actors on one side and impartial, that is to say universal, spectators on the other, overlooks an important element in Kant's argument.[111] For what allows these spectators' 'affective participation in the good' to serve as a sign of human progress is not their impartiality, but the very fact that, at the risk of persecution, they are taking sides for the revolution.[112] It is not impartiality but partisanship that defines the universal import of political judgment. The public risk and absence of any potential personal gains from the revolutionary events are indeed gauges of universality for Kant. These are not disincarnate, objective spectators, judging in terms of a dispassionate vision of the whole; instead they embody a passionate yet disinterested partisanship.

To complicate matters further, the enthusiasm of the spectator is an enthusiasm at his own species' capacity to act. As *The Conflict of the Faculties* states: 'There must be some experience in the human race which, as an event, points to the disposition and capacity of the human

---

109   Slavoj Žižek, *In Defense of Lost Causes*, London: Verso, 2008, 15, where Žižek sees Kant's attitude replicated in the support of certain Soviet observers for a revolution of whose violence they were clearly aware.

110   Arendt, *Lectures*, 55.

111   For some interesting reflections on the aesthetic and political limitations of the distinction between actors and spectators, which gives to one group the capacities that it strips from the other, see Jacques Rancière, *Le spectateur émancipé*, Paris: La Fabrique, 2008, 7–29.

112   See Jeffrey Lomonaco, 'Kant's Unselfish Partisans as Democratic Citizens', *Public Culture*, 17, 3 (2005). Lomonaco, from whom I take this translation of Kant's expression *Theilnehmung am Guten mit Affect*, rightly underscores the centrality of partisan judgment in *The Conflict of the Faculties*. His attempt to enlist Kant in revitalizing the spectating character of democratic citizenship is less persuasive.

race to be the cause of its own advance toward the better, and (since this should be the act of a being endowed with freedom), toward the human race as being the author of this advance.'[113] For reasons that likely derive from both political caution and philosophical principle, Kant, as Arendt notes, indeed lacks a theory of political action. As evinced by his wrestling with the right of resistance and his contortions to prove the legitimacy of the French Revolution (which he presents not as an uprising but as a legislative act), political action proper seems to vanish in the very gap between freedom and nature, when it is not relegated to states of exceptions and civil wars. But we can also say that the spectator 'acts' through the risky choice of public partisanship, and that what his enthusiasm signals towards is the very capacity of the human being to be a collective historical political agent.

There is some irony therefore in the fact that Kant's treatment of judgment and enthusiasm has been enlisted precisely to undermine the all-too-abstract grand narrative of human progress for which the French Revolution served as a sign. In the wake of the critique of totalitarianism and in the context of a crisis of Marxism, the attempt to formulate a finite politics for contemporary democracies – one shorn of the totalizing hubris of both socialism and capitalism – has adopted Kant as its tutelary figure. In the early 1980s Jean-François Lyotard, in dialogue with Jean-Luc Nancy and Philippe Lacoue-Labarthe – who in 1980 had set up their *Centre de recherches philosophiques sur le politique* to forward a research programme in which finitude played a crucial role – turned to the Kant of the third *Critique* and *The Conflict of the Faculties* to rethink politics in a postmodern situation devoid of a unified, universal horizon, and especially of the historical directionality and moral-political orientation sought by Kant. Explicitly returning to Kant in terms of what Foucault had called the 'sagittal' relationship to the present, to 'our time', Lyotard tries to maintain the link between enthusiasm and the event while doing away with the abstract universality of humanity.

Where the tension between registers of cognition and intelligibility (freedom and history, knowledge and truth, acting and spectating,

---

113   Kant, *The Conflict of the Faculties*, 301.

reason and sensibility, etc.) was dramatized by Kant as the site of the negative exhibition of a moral and practical universality made all the purer by its demarcation from the delusions of fanaticism, Lyotard, who reads Kant through the Wittgensteinian lens of incommensurable 'phrases' and 'language games', regards the link between affect and history in terms of a radical heterogeneity; of the failure, impossibility or 'wrong' of subsuming one regime of discourse of experience into another. Politics would instead concern the precarious transition between different regimes. Rather than bearers of a fragile and indirect universality, Lyotard's events are such because they thwart the total and the universal. Auschwitz destroys the subsuming of the real by the rational; Budapest '56, the subsuming of proletarian revolts by communism; May '68, that of liberation by liberalism; the crisis of '73, that of the market mechanism by post-Keynesian economics. While the spirit of some of Lyotard's manoeuvre – his attempt to think events as not being submerged by 'Capital's phrase' – is commendable, in light of our own exploration of fanaticism it is difficult not to see the transmutation of Kant into a 'prologue of postmodernity' as the attempt to strip him of the last vestiges of his own fanaticism, of those very humanist abstractions that led Nietzsche to see him as a *Fanatiker*.

Is faithfulness to Kant's project to be found in the critical inheritance of his universalist enthusiasm for revolution – along a lineage that includes Hegel, Heine and Marx[114] – or are we instead enjoined to prolong his cognitive critique of *Schwärmerei*, to engender an anti-fanatical politics of finitude and heterogeneity, in which humanity as such is emphatically not a historical actor? Lyotard's painstaking reading of Kant's aesthetic thought is set on negating the universality inherent in enthusiasm as negative exhibition, stressing instead both its failure and its broadly physiological dimension, as when he writes of 'an agitation on the spot, in the blind alley of incommensurability'.[115] Something similar can be said of his characterization of the Kantian spectator. Whereas for Arendt the spectator carried an impartial view of the whole, for Lyotard Kant's

---

114 See Kouvelakis, *Philosophy and Revolution*.
115 Jean-François Lyotard, 'The Sign of History' (1982), in *The Lyotard Reader*, Andrew Benjamin (ed.), Oxford: Basil Blackwell, 1989, 403.

account of the response to the French Revolution reveals 'the paradox of feeling (of feeling publicly) in common a formlessness for which there is no image or sensory intuition'.[116] But, aside from an excessive stress on visuality and the question of presentation, what this account misses – in its accentuation of the heterogeneous and the formless – is the sameness that underlies the experience of enthusiasm as an experience of the historical capacities of the species. The partisan affect is itself a sign of humanity's capacity to be the cause of its own advance; it is the negative exhibition of collective freedom.

The manner in which Lyotard strains the event's opposition to the universal, motivated by the attempt to dislocate Kant's moral destination into a postmodern heterogeneity of purposes, is too bound up with the anti-totalitarian commonplace that treating principles in terms of their universality, and history in terms of its totalization, is somehow causative of, or at best complicit with, horrific wrongs and oppressions.

ENTHUSIASM AFTER *ENTUSIAZM* (CODA)

Enthusiasm is a frequent term in the writings of Lenin, and remained an important signifier for the Russian Revolution. Witness Dziga Vertov's film *Entusiazm*, an epic paean to Stalinist industrialization, in which the strictures of propaganda mingle with genuine enthusiasm. In most cases, the term is used in a conventional manner to designate the energy, passion and motivation that should accompany the building of socialism. But there is a rather obscure and perhaps uncharacteristic text of Lenin from 1913, only published posthumously, which we cannot but read as a commentary on Kant's *Conflict of the Faculties*. Entitled 'Conversation', it consists of exchanges between two 'bystanders' of revolution. In short, two spectators – a position that Lenin himself was forced to assume at different stages in his political career. The first bystander is scolding the revolutionaries for their factional fighting, and attacking political organization as ultimately harmful of the proletariat's interests. The second retorts with a striking update of Kant's reflections on enthusiasm:

---

116   Ibid., 407.

We are both outsiders, that is, neither of us is a direct participant in the struggle. But bystanders who are trying to understand what is happening before their eyes may react to the struggle in two ways. Looking on from the outside, one may see only what one might call the outward aspect of the struggle; speaking figuratively, one may see only clenched fists, distorted faces and ugly scenes; one may condemn it all, one may weep and wail on account of it. But one can also, looking on from the outside, understand the *meaning* of the struggle that is going on, which is slightly, if you will excuse my saying so, more interesting and historically more significant than the scenes and pictures of the so-called excesses or extremes of the struggle. There can be no struggle without enthusiasm and no enthusiasm without extremes; and as far as I'm concerned I hate most of all people who focus their attention on 'extremes' in the struggle of classes, parties and factions. . . . And this is about something big, historically big. A work-ing-class party is being built up. Workers' independence, the influence of the workers on *their own* parliamentary group, decisions by the workers themselves on questions of their own party – such is the great historical significance of what is going on; the mere wish is becoming *fact* before our very eyes. You are afraid of 'extremes' and you regret them, but I watch in admiration a struggle that is actually making the working class of Russia more mature and adult, and I am mad about one thing only – that I am a bystander, that I cannot plunge into the midst of that struggle . . .[117]

An empiricist spectator, who simply registers the violence, factionalism and setbacks of the movement, is juxtaposed to one whose own enthusi-asm or admiration knows how to accept the possibly excessive enthusi-asm of the participants, because it can refer to the principles that underlie it, to the wish becoming fact. Lenin's spectator is also only a relative one, biding his time before he can participate. But this does not mean that he ignores the specificity of spectatorship. In effect, the second bystand-er's arguments for enthusiasm are based on an explicit defence of the principle of publicity. To the first bystander's argument that factional

---

117 Vladimir Ilyich Lenin, *Collected Works*, Vol. 17, Moscow: Progress Publishers, 1977, 44.

fighting will engender public falsehoods, the second replies that publicity is 'a sword that itself heals the wounds it makes' – an expression that wouldn't be out of place in Kant's writing.

Bound as it is to universality, enthusiasm cannot be dispersed in heterogeneity. Nor should it be accorded to spectators while stripped from the political agents. To traverse the critique of fanaticism in its multifarious guises can also allow us to hone a theory of political affect, of affective participation in the good – something not so easily pigeonholed by those sceptical or deflationary doctrines that see in unconditional political commitments and abstract passions only preludes to violence and disaster.

4

The Revolution of the East:
Islam, Hegel, Psychoanalysis

What is it to cure a culture, to diagnose a religion? What kinds of explanation, identification and prescription are involved in questions like 'What went wrong with Islam?' Inquiries such as these are not innocent ones, and the ideological reasons for their pervasiveness in the recent period are not difficult to fathom. But what are the stakes when the person asking such a question is not an Orientalist historian, or an imperial consultant, but a psychoanalyst – or, at least, someone drawing analytical insight and speculative authority from Freud or Lacan? I want to explore what lies behind psychoanalytic diagnoses of the putative maladies, impasses or discontents of Islam, and of religion 'in general'. Though hardly a major force in the vast intellectual industry that has tried to present governments and publics in the capitalist core with serviceable images of Islamic politics, culture and mentality, psychoanalysis is of particular interest here for the manner in which it inquires into the relation between the cultural and the psychic. To the extent that 'Islamic' terrorism or fundamentalism is a privileged target of contemporary uses of the idea of fanaticism, attention to how it is handled in a psychoanalytic register can be instructive, especially in terms of one of the concerns of this book: the culturalization and psychologization of politics under the aegis of fanaticism, and the concomitant definition of a liberal political norm. Examining the encounter between psychoanalysis and Islam brings to the surface something like the political unconscious of psychoanalysis itself as a secular science and a secular clinic, as well as the broader reliance of some psychoanalytic thought on the equation of political conviction with fanaticism. I want to inquire how and why a certain normative political notion of the secular (not to be taken as a synonym for atheism) has found its way into psychoanalytically inspired treatments of Islam, the Arab world, or the Middle East. In other words, how a certain dislocated, maladaptive, voided subject – the subject of psychoanalysis – has been rendered normative and congruent with the institutions and ideals of the liberal-democratic (or, to use Alain Badiou's term, capitalo-parliamentarian) state.

My starting point lies in the trope of psychic submission, of subjection to the One, which psychologically marks out the subject of Islam as a bellicose fanatic or a helpless fatalist. The most important formulation of this idea of a fanatical religion of absorption into unity, and a significant precursor for contemporary psychoanalytic reflections, is, as I will show, Hegel's account of Islam in his philosophies of history and religion. In both philosophy and psychoanalysis, it is by contrast to something like a fanatical submission to the One, an excessive monotheism, that a form of 'Judeo-Christian' subjectivity might be regarded as normative. In this light, the 'Islamic subject' is perceived as having failed in its secularization: failed to broach the attenuation of the One, effected by specifically cultic mediations (the Trinity, the neighbour, etc.) which, once secularized, carry over a dissipated religious content into a disenchanted social sphere. It is worth asking how concepts of civilization, culture and religion – so central to the formation of a discourse on fanaticism – are interrogated within psychoanalysis. This allows us to reflect on the anti-political timelessness that is ascribed to that which is marked out as non- or pre-secular. Finally, I want to consider under what terms psychoanalytic and philosophical discourses are capable of articulating the relation between politics, religion and subjectivity without merely replicating or underwriting the very fantasies that perniciously structure our political and ideological space.

A FANATICISM OF THE ONE

Gil Anidjar has provocatively declared that, just as Montesquieu invented Oriental Despotism, so Hegel invented the Muslims.[1] Whereas

---

1   Gil Anidjar, *The Jew, The Arab: A History of the Enemy*, Stanford: Stanford University Press, 2003, 133.

Kant's remarks on religious iconoclasm and the sublime in the *Critique of Judgment* had asymmetrically brought together 'the Jews' and 'Islam', Hegel's conceptual placement of 'Mahometans' in *The Philosophy of History* and *Philosophy of Religion* can be seen to inaugurate the perception of Islam as a politicized religion characterized by a particular type of subjectivity, the subjectivity of fanaticism (*Fanatismus*). But didn't the *Lumières* – specifically Voltaire, author of the play *Le fanatisme, ou Mahomet le prophète* – give the modern figure of the fanatic its shape? If we take fanaticism as the antithesis of religious toleration, as the subject's habitation by a violent and monomaniacal theological unreason, this is true. But the concept of fanaticism forged by Voltaire is not religiously specified in anything like an unequivocal fashion. That is why Mohammed – who is not himself a fanatic in the play, but a sexualized impostor and lucid manipulator of the human proclivity to fanaticism and superstition – can serve as the avatar for Voltaire's Catholic enemies closer to home (a function Islam served in more than one tract from the period).[2] The claim that Hegel philosophically invented Muslims as the bearers of a distinct type of 'fanatical' subjectivity can thus be articulated with the idea that Hegel's conception of *Fanatismus* is in many respects discontinuous with Voltaire's *fanatisme* – and, we could add, Kant's *Schwärmerei*.

It is possible to identify a significant shift in the idea of fanaticism, from its Enlightenment figure as violently intolerant religious consciousness to its Hegelian formulation. Though in this transition some key features are retained – for instance, the secular circumscription of the religious as a limited sphere – in Hegel fanaticism is articulated, not just as the irrational and arbitrary imposition of a particular set of beliefs and practices, but in terms of a mode, albeit a destructive one, of universality. Islamic religion and Muslim subjectivity appear in Hegel's writings as the carriers of a universal claim having important analogies with the forms of political subjectivity that characterize the historical and political phenomenology of European Spirit. Tellingly, in *The Philosophy of History*, Hegel refers to Islam as 'the *Revolution of*

---

2 See Juan Goytisolo, 'Voltaire y el Islam', *El País*, 4 May 2006. English translation available at: http://www.monthlyreview.org.

the East'. The content of this revolution is depicted in fiercely universalist terms:

> [Islam] destroyed all particularity and dependence, and perfectly cleared up and purified the soul and disposition; making the abstract One the absolute object of attention and devotion, and to the same extent, pure subjective consciousness – the Knowledge of this One alone – the only aim of reality; making the *Unconditioned* the *condition* of *existence*.[3]

In such passages, which could of course also be regarded as apotheoses of the Orientalist treatment of Islam as a doctrinal and cultural monolith, Hegel is rare among European philosophers in according to Islam a spiritual and conceptual dignity. Instead of burying it in the lascivious ornamentation of oriental despotism, Hegel, in what may be termed a meta-religious register, depicts it as a high point of abstract thought. The 'Oriental principle', as he calls it, commands the destruction of worldly particularity and its spiritual elevation to the One, 'the one infinite Power beyond all the multiplicity of the world' – whence Hegel's characterization of Islam, in the wake of Kant's reflections on its iconoclasm, as 'the religion of sublimity'. In terms of the philosophical typology of religions – a practice that, as we shall see, is significant for evaluating the psychoanalytic approach to Islam – it is of interest that the Hegel of *The Philosophy of History* presents the move from Judaism to Islam as dialectical, even though, by promoting an abstract worship of the One, it ends up generating a sterile impasse. Why would Spirit (*Geist*) reach this dead end?

The dislocation of God from being the exclusive possession of a people is depicted by Hegel as engendering a universalizing personality, freed from ethno-national particularity.[4] But for Hegel, Islam, if one may put it this way, takes universalism too far. In Islam,

---

3   G. W. F. Hegel, *The Philosophy of History*, New York: Dover, 1956, 356.
4   The ascription of particularity to Judaism, and the concomitant view of Christianity as the differentiated universality that sublates Jewish particularism and Islamic fanaticism, would of course deserve a discussion in its own right. For one treatment of these themes, see Andrew Benjamin, 'Particularity and Exceptions: On Jews and Animals', *South Atlantic Quarterly*, 107: 1 (2008).

subjectivity has ... worship for the sole occupation of its activity, combined with the design to subjugate secular existence to the One. ... Subjectivity is here living and unlimited – an energy which enters into secular life with a purely negative purpose, and busies itself and interferes with the world, only in such a way as shall promote pure adoration of the One.[5]

The One, juxtaposed to all particularity, absorbs (and absolves) a purely negative subjectivity. This God knows no limitations, and overtakes the whole of human experience and language. To use a Lacanian formulation, the unrepresentable Real comes to colonize and to undermine the Symbolic order. The subject of Islam, in this Hegelian image, is a subject without qualities or predicates. Rather than permitting a mediation of freedom within a differentiated social bond, Islam's politics of the One – its 'passion for the real' – means that its only way to hold the faithful together is through the abstract tie of divine unity, which enjoins a constant expansion driven by a generic 'energy'.[6] This depiction of Islam as a religion of the One permits Hegel to rearticulate, rather than to repeat, the standard tropes of European Orientalism: it is because of its purely abstract universality that Islam is basically expansionist (and that its belligerent subjects can express such heroism); and it is the insubstantial, 'inorganic' character of its social compact which so easily tips it over into stagnation or degeneration (and explains why its subjects can sink into such dissolute sensuality and corporeality when the passion for the One inevitably flags).

In this way, Hegel labels Islam with the idea of fanaticism:

Abstraction swayed the minds of the Mahometans. Their object was, to establish an abstract worship, and they struggled for its accomplishment with the greatest enthusiasm. This enthusiasm was *Fanaticism*, that is,

---

5 Hegel, *The Philosophy of History*, 356–7.
6 Ibid. This trope is present, in vulgarized form, in the Ur-text of the 'clash of civilizations' thesis: Bernard Lewis's 1990 article from *The New Atlantic*, 'The Roots of Muslim Rage'. Here he singles out Islam as the only religion that can rival Christianity for 'its worldwide distribution, its continuing vitality, its universalist aspirations'.

an enthusiasm for something abstract – for an abstract thought which sustains a negative position towards the established order of things. It is the essence of fanaticism to bear only a desolating destructive relation to the concrete.[7]

Islam is depicted as an inherently 'fanatical' religion because the singular or concrete form of subjectivity, understood as freedom, is absent. Such political and moral freedom is paradigmatically identified with the 'consummate religion' of Christianity and its integration and overcoming in the modern state-form. This might well be regarded as an 'insensitive schematization' based on the idea of a uniform Islam, understood through the prism of an 'absolute and systematic difference' with the Christian West.[8] As noted, the German Idealist philosopher does indeed bear an interesting, if complex, affinity with these Orientalist themes. But Hegel's philosophical capture of Islam is not based simply on the idea of the opposition between the 'rational, humane, superior' Christian West and the 'aberrant, undeveloped, inferior' Islamic Orient.[9] Rather, the Oriental fanaticism of the Revolution of the East in many respects parallels the fanaticism of the Revolution in and of the West.

If we turn to the 1824 *Lectures on the Philosophy of Religion*, this view of Islam as the dead-end of an excessive universality, as a fanatical religion of destruction for and by the One, is complicated by crossing over, in terms of the crucial notion of abstraction, from the dialectic of religions to the political field. In a significant passage, we are presented with the abstractive fanaticism of Islam as isomorphic to the abstract egalitarianism of the French Terror:

In the Islamic doctrine there is merely the fear of God: God is to be venerated as the One, and one cannot advance beyond this abstraction. Islam is therefore the religion of formalism, a perfect formalism that allows nothing to take shape in opposition to it. Or again in the French

---

7 Hegel, *The Philosophy of History*, 358.
8 Edward W. Said, *Orientalism*, New York: Vintage, 1994, 68, 300.
9 Ibid., 300.

Revolution, liberty and equality were affirmed in such a way that all spirituality, all laws, all talents, all living relations had to disappear before this abstraction, and the public order and constitution had to come from elsewhere and be forcibly asserted against this abstraction. For those who hold fast to the abstraction cannot allow anything determinate to emerge, since this would be the emergence of something particular and distinct in contrast with this abstraction.[10]

These lines could, of course, be taken as the matrix for the normatively liberal tradition of thought which, under the umbrella of the concept of political religion, casts a dark light on the seemingly de-differentiating universalism that affects all projects seeking to subject social mediations to the unity of an abstract principle (God or Equality). Unsurprisingly, Hegel cannot be so easily enlisted.

IN DEFIANCE OF THE STATE

From the standpoint of Hegel's philosophy of history, his understanding of the French Revolution in particular, it is possible to speak of a 'necessary and legitimate fanaticism', whose destructive and abstractive powers may qualify it as a 'modernizing agent'.[11] But what of fanaticism grasped synchronically, in the context of the modern state? In the *Philosophy of Right*, fanaticism no longer appears as a necessary if truculent moment in the historical adventures of Spirit. Now – arguably much closer to the thematic of toleration which motivated Voltaire's handling of the concept – it features as the pathological retention of a right over absolute truth and rationality that would trump that of the state. Though religion and the state share the same content, and religion can accordingly serve as the factor that integrates citizens into the state, their form

---

10   G. W. F. Hegel, *Lectures on the Philosophy of Religion, Vol. 3: The Consummate Religion*, Berkeley: University of California Press, 1985, 218. In *The Philosophy of History* we already find a link between Robespierre's *la liberté et la terreur* and what Hegel sees as *la religion et la terreur* (358).

11   Renzo Llorente, 'Hegel's Conception of Fanaticism', *Auslegung*, 20: 2 (1995). I have relied on Llorente's insightful article throughout this section. On Hegel's relationship to the French Revolution, see Domenico Losurdo, 'Liberalism, Conservatism, the French Revolution, and Classic German Philosophy', in *Hegel and the Freedom of the Moderns*, Durham, NC Duke University Press, 2004.

differs. Where the state provides knowledge founded on a determinate
and differentiated form of rationality, embodying the Absolute in a
concrete universality that articulates rather than suppresses particularities in their freedom and (relative) autonomy, the content of religious
consciousness appears 'in the form of feeling, representational thought,
and faith'.[12]

It is when the inwardness of religious doctrine trespasses into the
domain of objective law and the state's monopoly over it; when 'the
communities whose doctrine remains at the level of representational
thought assume a negative attitude towards the state',[13] and their
'polemical piety' (Hegel's term) brings them into confrontation with
the state, that the problem of fanaticism rears its head. Fanaticism here
denotes the attempt by a religious community to 'impart objectivity to
their (representationally conceived) doctrine in defiance of the state'.[14]
In holding fast to religious consciousness against the objectivity of the
state, fanaticism 'repudiates all political institutions and legal order as
restrictive limitations on the inner emotions and as incommensurate
with the infinity of these'. It is a 'hatred of *law*, of *legally* determined
right'.[15] Religion opposes law and the state to the extent that, in its
fanatical form, it seeks to impose – that is, to lend objectivity to – the
self-sufficiency of a merely representational thought. As Renzo Llorente
notes, this kind of fanaticism 'necessarily wills abstract representations,
all particularizations proving incompatible with the essential indeterminacy of representational thought'.[16]

Fanaticism here signals the repudiation of the state and its determinate articulation of society through the law – that is, through a rational
cognition or knowledge of differences that does not subordinate individuality to an abstract Absolute. In imposing the 'formalism' of its
'unconditional subjectivity' it directly contravenes the precondition of

---

12 G. W. F. Hegel, *Elements of the Philosophy of Right*, trans. H. B. Nisbet, Allen
W. Wood (ed.), Cambridge: Cambridge University Press, 1991, 293. Quoted in
Llorente, 'Hegel's Conception of Fanaticism', 85.
13 Llorente, 'Hegel's Conception of Fanaticism', 87.
14 Ibid., 88.
15 *Elements of the Philosophy of Right*, 293 and 279. Quoted in ibid.
16 Ibid., 92.

the modern state, which declares the latter's superiority over particular religious doctrines and communities. In other words, it contravenes Hegel's unique understanding of secular modernity. What is unique about Hegel's juxtaposition of fanaticism and the secular foundation of the modern state is the fact that this is not simply a question of immunizing society against the strife created by religious particularisms (as in Voltaire's *Treatise on Tolerance*, for example); what is at stake is a philosophical conflict between universalities which enter into rivalry once religious consciousness refuses its proper, subordinate, place.

A number of elements from Hegel's formulation of fanaticism are of broader interest. To begin with, fanaticism identifies a politics of the One as an undifferentiated principle of action, which makes it at once abstractive and destructive. Its subjective and affective dimension is that of an 'enthusiasm for the abstract'. A certain dialectical dignity may be ascribed to fanaticism as a moment in the development of Spirit (as in the French Terror). But in the modern state, where the objectivity of law and the differentiation of society surpass and subsume religious consciousness in a secular polity, fanaticism, in the guise of 'polemical piety', appears as a pathology – both of the fanatical subject and of the fanatical religious community. To the extent that this kind of fanaticism is a challenge to the state, '*religious* fanaticism is necessarily *political* in nature – indeed, is by definition a kind of *political fanaticism*'.[17] Mobilizing the notion of Islam as a thoroughly political, and consequently expansionist, religion, Hegel's discussion of fanaticism in the philosophies of history and religion suggests that a religion of the One cannot but be a politics of the One. Such fanaticism is a negation of the modern politics of a differentiated state based on the subsumption of religious doctrine and subjectivity to a law that allows for concrete unity-in-difference. The task of the state is thus also to educate religious subjects and communities into the rational cognition and recognition of the objectivity of the law and the limits of faith.

---

17   Ibid., 96.

OF TERRORISTS, PERVERTS AND PSYCHOTICS

Though by no means deriving directly from Hegel's positioning of Islam and fanaticism in the context of the adventures of Spirit and the apparatus of the state, contemporary attempts to delve into Islamic political subjectivities (and, symptomatically, political psychologies) can be usefully related to the complex of ideas that Hegel delineates under the rubric of fanaticism. To take a particularly pertinent case, Bruno Étienne's writings on the suicidal and apocalyptic strains of Islamism focus on fanaticism as the key subjective determinant of new and aberrant figures of militant politics. Relying on previous explorations of the concept by Norman Cohn and Dominique Colas, Étienne too regards fanaticism as the transgression of the proper boundary between religion and politics, 'a slippage from the religious to the political field'.[18] The fanatic, subject to a transcendent and otherworldly demand, is the chief antagonist of civil society. As a paranoiac, he repudiates all otherness, and can only affirm his own unconditional belief in a seemingly unattainable transcendence through profanation (a pathologically enjoyable form of iconoclasm which undermines the notion of a 'religion of sublimity').[19] As Étienne writes: 'To exclude alterity by carrying out purifying murders nevertheless implies that one feels attacked from all sides. This paranoiac closure stems from the fact that every ideal of the ego is confused with an ideal imaginary Islamic "we" in absolute Unity, the *Tawhîd*: the Oneness of God induces the oneness of the *Umma*, and thus the fusion into the One.'[20] It is this fusional ideal which for Étienne characterizes contemporary political modalities of fanaticism in the Muslim world. As he argues, invoking an Arabic term with a serendipitous homophony with our topic:

> *Fanā* . . . means extinction in the One. . . . Fanatics are thus all those who constitute the house (*Mîthl Bayt*), the temple of Unicity. . . . The

---

18 Bruno Étienne, *Les combattants suicidaires* suivi de *Les amants de l'apocalypse*, Paris: L'Aube, 2005, 87.
19 'The passage to the act is [for the fanatic] the enjoyment of an iconoclastic violation.' Ibid., 96.
20 Ibid., 22.

fanatic *is* truth and this truth is one: it animates, agitates and arms him. He doesn't have to search for it in doubt, to construct it, to discover the true, to travel. He enjoys without delay or relay an immediate certainty, which inhabits and possesses him entirely, propelling him forward. Violently. Gathered together, fanatics believe that they are the only organized servants of the All-True, of the One whose instruments they are; they hate those who ignore this and they want the world to bend to the law of the One who bends the universe to His necessity.[21]

This abstract fury for the One seems to echo Hegel's phenomenology of the (Islamic) fanatic. But Étienne is not content with reproducing the classical image of fanaticism as the political religion of the One. He thinks that a psychoanalytic explanation is in order, and enlists to this end the concept of the death-drive as the clinical translation and explanation of the theological concept of *Fanā*, but more specifically of the passage of fanaticism to the (terrorist) act: 'The death-drive results from a surfeit of energies freed by the failure of the containing capacities of representations. The surfeit of excitations leads to a rupture: the actor or agent is emptied of his own desires. He is then the object of a movement of unbinding whose outlet is a war neurosis.'[22] There are interesting affinities between the overall schema underlying this point and Fethi Benslama's view – in the context of a far richer and analytically more serious work – that psychoanalysis should perceive the emergence of radical Islamism in terms of the 'caesura of the subject of tradition and the unleashing of forces of destruction of civilization that directly follow from it'.[23]

Though Étienne's recruitment of the notion of death-drive is too cursory to call for much scrutiny, it should be noted that he places it at the crossroads between a speculative energetics (the 'surfeit of excitations')

21   Ibid., 95. According to the *Encyclopaedia Britannica*, 'Fanā' ('to pass away' or 'to cease to exist')' is 'the complete denial of self and the realization of God is one of the steps taken by the Muslim Sufi (mystic) toward the achievement of union with God.'
22   Ibid., 85. See the perspicacious critique of this approach in Talal Asad, *On Suicide Bombing*, New York: Columbia University Press, 2007, 51–3.
23   Fethi Benslama, *La psychanalyse à l'épreuve de l'Islam*, Paris: Aubier, 2002, 12.

and an idea of 'representation' that symptomatically oscillates between the imaginary and the symbolic. The theme that representations (or mediation *tout court*) function as a form of civilizing containment that the fanatic undermines is a staple of those discourses that regard fanaticism as the simultaneously anti- and hyper-political counterpart of the modern subject.[24] It is worth recalling that the religious fanaticism diagnosed by Hegel in the *Philosophy of Right* was upbraided precisely for being a form of representational thought – or, we could hazard, an imaginary politics of devotion at odds with the integration of politics and religion within the objective rationality of the state (so that mediation and representation are, for Hegel, not synonymous).

By juxtaposing energetic excess and representational containment, Étienne grounds the analysis of political-religious insurgency, violence and terrorism in the classic figure of the fanatic – a figure characterized by a destructive homogenizing passion, to be understood by its negations (of the difference between religious dogma and civil society, the sacred and the secular, the self and the other, etc.) rather than by any *sui generis* relationship to a certain symbolic and imaginary repertoire. By way of contrast, Slavoj Žižek's treatment of religious politics in terms of perversion can serve as an antidote to the school of thought that regards political-religious extremism simply in the mode of its destructive anti-representational drive. In his recent *How to Read Lacan*, Žižek offers a commentary on Lacan's remark in *Four Fundamental Concepts* about 'the subject who determines himself as an object, in his encounter with the division of subjectivity', in light of the letter to Ayaan Hirsi Ali by Mohammad Bouyeri, killer of the polemical Dutch film director Theo van Gogh. Behind the ultra-fanatical declaration by Bouyeri – 'No discussions, no demonstrations, no petitions: only Death will separate the Truth from the Lies' – Žižek sees at work the pervert's tactic of displacing division upon the Other: 'The pervert claims direct access to some figure of the big Other (from God or history to the desire of his partner), so that, dispelling all the ambiguity of language, he is able

---

24   It dominates, for example, Colas's *Civil Society and Fanaticism*, where fanaticism is portrayed as a profaning refusal of symbolization, an 'acting out' against symbolization, as well as a form of paranoia and psychosis.

to act directly as the instrument of the big Other's will.'[25] This is to be taken in two asymmetrical senses: Bouyeri becomes an undivided subject (an agent of God's wrath) by displacing division onto his nemesis Hirsi Ali, 'inconsistent with herself, lacking the courage of her own beliefs', and onto God, who sanctions the absolute separation between the True and the False. This is why Žižek can use this grim vignette to lend credence to the suggestion that the 'fundamentalist' (along with the 'liberal cynic') is on the side of knowledge, while the militant atheist stands on the side of belief.

The virtue of Žižek's Lacanian suggestion is that it does not treat the violent repudiation of secular standards of justification as the result of a pure negation of limits and constraints, as a wish to be absorbed and annihilated by the One. Rather than the abyss of interiority, Bouyeri presents the unsettling case of an exteriorized zealotry. The division or splitting of the subject is not overcome by some kind of psychotic fusion, but through the stigmatization of a divided other (Bouyeri's target is 'inconsistent with herself') and the submission to a divisive Other (a God of wrath). The pervert's presupposition that his acts directly implement the divine will also means that he need not be troubled by the kind of psychosis that is so often and so easily ascribed to the fanatic. That the denial of division is in its own way mediated by the Other militates against the hypothesis of fusional fanaticism; the externalization of the pervert's knowledge also means that the common view of the fanatic as absorbed by their conviction – causing such perplexity when we learn of their everyday banality – is untenable.

THE CHRISTIAN STANDARD

Though the paradigm of fanaticism and of the psychic forms that allegedly accompany it ('enthusiasm for something abstract') is entangled with the history of the philosophical and Orientalist reception of Islam

---

25 Slavoj Žižek, *How to Read Lacan*, London: Granta Books, 2006, 116. This might also prove a more fruitful avenue for the consideration of the question of authority, both psychic and political, in psychoanalytically-informed treatments of Islam. Étienne, for instance, predicates the upsurge of fanaticized energies on a withdrawal of paternal authority ('*Sans pères ni repères, les groupes de pairs créent des repaires,*' 100).

– let's not forget that Hegel christened Arabia *das Reich des Fanatismus* – it is also, despite its recent geopolitical fortunes, rather generic in its application. Indeed, in the *philosophes'* campaigns against fanaticism, the Islamic world served at times as the tolerant foil for a denunciation of Europe's internecine religious strife. More recently, however, Atlantic discourse on Islam has yoked a long-term concern with the Arab and Muslim 'mind' to the constant reiteration of secularism as the key stake of the current religious and political crisis. It is this hard-won result of the history of Christendom which can allegedly explain both the civilizational subalternity of the Islamic world and its supposed collective 'rage'. In Bernard Lewis's by now notorious terms: 'This is no less than a clash of civilizations – the perhaps irrational but surely historic reaction of an ancient rival against our Judeo-Christian heritage, our secular present, and the worldwide expansion of both.'[26]

The projected continuity between 'our' Judeo-Christian heritage and 'our' secular present plays a significant part in the entanglement of historical-cum-civilizational narratives, disquisitions on theology and accounts of political subjectivation which pertain to the discussion of psychoanalysis and Islam. The question, to borrow the terms from a recent heated debate about the extension, depth and coherence of the thesis of a Judeo-Christian (or 'Western') secular heritage, could be posed as follows: is there a psychic *Sonderweg* (special path) which accompanies the secular *Sonderweg* of the Christian West, such that psychoanalysis would be compelled both to recognize its interiority to such a path and its differential (or even normative) relationship to the 'Islamic subject'?[27] If so, psychoanalysis could find itself as a midwife of secularism – in other words, as an institution that takes the parameters of acculturation (and of pathology, anomaly and dislocation) provided by Western Christendom and its secular inheritance as somehow normative. What are the pitfalls of 'secularizing' the psychoanalytic subject,

---

26   See 'The Roots of Muslim Rage'.

27   See Gil Anidjar, '*The Stillborn God*: A review in three parts', *The Immanent Frame*, available at: <http://www.ssrc.org/blogs/immanent_frame/2007/12/26/a-review-in-three-parts/>, and the reply by Mark Lilla, 'Our Historical *Sonderweg*', *The Immanent Frame*, available at: <http://www.ssrc.org/blogs/immanent_frame/2008/01/04/our-historical-sonderweg/>.

and of turning psychoanalysis into a secular clinic, a move whose political payoff would be to welcome recalcitrant cultures into a disenchanted West? Can we differentiate between Freud's original commitment to a profane atheism and this secular agenda? To answer such questions we need to reflect on how secularism, besides functioning as a political ideal, as well as 'an ontology and an epistemology',[28] might also make certain claims on the psyche.

Žižek's recent essay on Benslama's *La psychanalyse à l'épreuve de l'Islam*, 'A Glance into the Archives of Islam', is good place to start.[29] In his several forays into materialist theology and Pauline militancy, Žižek, far more than the likes of Badiou for instance, mounts a trenchant rearticulation and defence of what, following Bloch, we may call the atheism in Christianity and the Christianity in atheism.[30] In his polemical excavations of the non-perverse core of Christianity – Christianity as the cipher for an ethico-political subjectivity founded on the inexistence of the Other – Žižek has strived to produce a theory of the political subject couched in terms of a singular universality. In a number of texts, above all *The Puppet and the Dwarf*, this has taken the form of investigating the intricate dialectic between Christianity and Judaism, Love and Law, and extracting of a materialist, acosmic kernel from theology and subjectivation. But where, if anywhere, does 'Islam' fit into all this?[31]

---

28   Talal Asad, *Formations of the Secular: Christianity, Islam, Modernity*, Stanford: Stanford University Press, 2003, 21.

29   A different application of psychoanalysis to the politics of the Middle East which focuses on the structure of Arab despotism rather than Islamic subjectivity and links secularism to writing and authority rather than faith, can be found in Moustapha Safouan, *Why Are the Arabs Not Free? – The Politics of Writing*, Oxford: Blackwell, 2007.

30   For a more sustained engagement and critique of this position, see Lorenzo Chiesa and Alberto Toscano, 'Agape and the Anonymous Religion of Atheism', *Angelaki: Journal of the Theoretical Humanities*, 12: 1 (2007).

31   For a brief critical account of the (Hegelian) image of Islam in Žižek, see Ian Almond, *The New Orientalists: Postmodern Representations of Islam from Foucault to Baudrillard*, London: I.B.Tauris, 2007. For Žižek's own retort to accusations of Christian Eurocentrism, see the pointedly titled 'I Plead Guilty – But Where's the Judgment?', his reply to William David Hart, 'Slavoj Žižek and the Imperial/Colonial Model of Religion' – both in *Nephantla*, 3: 3 (2002). Also Hart's rejoinder, 'Can a Judgment be Read?', *Nephantla*, 4:1 (2003).

As Žižek himself notes, Islam poses a problem for the teleologically-inclined historian of religions due to its bothersome anachronism – it emerged after Christianity, the 'religion to end all religions' – but also due to its 'misplaced' character. As Lévi-Strauss wistfully noted, by occupying the geographical area between the Christian West and the Orient, Islam impedes the happy fusion of the two 'halves' of human civilization. Žižek follows Benslama's excavation of the 'archive' or the 'obscene secret mythical support' of Islam, which locates it – rather predictably – in the symbolic and epistemological role allotted to the veiled Muslim woman (such that 'the ultimate function of the veil is precisely to sustain that there *is* something, the substantial Thing, behind the veil'). As yet, Žižek has been unable or unwilling to articulate the kind of philosophical (as opposed to merely ideological or sociological) encounter with Islam that he has repeatedly staged with Judaism and Christianity. As it stands, what we have here is not a dialectical confrontation between Islam and the acosmic, psychoanalytic materialism advocated by Žižek, but rather a mere antithesis that gives rise to formal comparisons, failing to affect our picture of universality in any lasting manner. Typically, where Islam is called upon, it is as a politicizing ethos or concrete form of antagonism, and not as a template for potentially emancipatory forms of subjectivation.

This mere antithesis – whereby Islam is not the precursor of the (Christian) matrix of (singular) universality, but another universality (which notoriously turns both Judaism and Christianity into its unknowing precursors as the subordinate 'religions of the Book') – stems from the anachronism that Žižek himself indicates in his essay on Benslama. As we already saw with Hegel, Islam is held to be out of sequence: an anomalous, excessive universalism which ignores the ability of Trinitarian Christianity and its state to integrate – i.e. to differentiate into appropriate spheres – the political and the religious, and thus closes off the path for the secularization of political authority and social power.

In Hegel, as in Žižek, this absence of secularization (or conversely, this fanaticism of the One) is related to the suggestion that the singular or concrete form of subjectivity, that is, freedom, is absent from Islam.

This vision of Islam as the abstract universalism of the One turns it into the non-dialectical counterpart of a Christian atheism of singular universality, whose features, duly inventoried by Žižek for the sake of an ethics and politics of the act and the exception (sacrifice, incarnation, a split and impotent God, the theology of the Trinity), seem absent from the ideational repertoire of Islam. At this point, Žižek might indeed agree with the Italian judge who, faced with the protest of a Finnish mother wishing to have the crucifix removed from public classrooms, described it as a 'symbol of secularism'. The legacy, in Žižek, of Hegel's treatment of Islam as the religion of fanatical universalism serves to confuse the methodological atheism of psychoanalysis with the normative narrative of secularization, which stipulates that without passing through a set of specifically Christian theological, historical and psychic figures (Trinity, incarnation, absurd faith, etc.), the subject cannot attain modernity.

For all of psychoanalysis's avowed atheist aims, not properly distinguishing a refusal of transcendent agency and cosmic holism from the historico-philosophical epic of a self-overcoming Christianity risks consigning psychoanalytic discourse on religion to a parochial, culturalist defence of 'our' Western legacy, and eventually into obtuse demands that 'Muslims' go through their own Reformation or the like. The result of such a secular strategy and teleology is almost invariably 'to enclose the Other in religion all the better to expel him from politics'[32] – turning social struggles and geopolitical strategies into matters of a prejudicially-defined culture, and even more vaguely defined mentalities, which no quantity of psychoanalytic sophistication can really sunder from the colonial tradition of inquiry into the native 'mind'. The idea of transforming psychoanalysis into a secular clinic aimed at diagnosing the phantasmatic impasses that prevent 'Arabs' or 'Muslims' from becoming the properly pathological subjects of modernity (rather than fanatics stuck between crumbling tradition and fear of 'Westoxification')[33] leaves itself open to the accusation that psychoanalysis might constitute

32 François Burgat, *L'islamisme à l'heure d'Al-Qaida*, Paris: La Découverte, 2005, 191.

33 A temptation which is present, for instance, in Benslama's otherwise rich and probing book.

yet another stage in that cunning of Christianity which has often taken
the name of 'secularism'. As Anidjar has written:

> Christianity . . . actively disenchanted its own world by dividing itself
> into private and public, politics and economics, indeed, religious and
> secular. And Christianity turned against itself in a complex and ambiv-
> alent series of parallel movements, continuous gestures and rituals,
> reformist and counterreformist, or revolutionary and not-so-revolution-
> ary upheavals and reversals while slowly coming to name that to which
> it ultimately claimed to oppose itself: 'religion'. Munchausen-like, it
> attempted to liberate itself, to extricate itself from its own conditions:
> it *judged* itself no longer Christian, no longer 'religious'. Christianity
> (that is, to clarify this one last time, Western Christendom) judged and
> named itself, *reincarnated* itself, as 'secular'. . . . Christianity invented the
> distinction between religious and secular, and this it *made* religion. It
> made religion the problem – rather than itself. And it made it into an
> object of criticism that needed to be no less than *transcended*.[34]

BACK TO FREUD

Taking Christian secularism as both historically and psychically
normative hampers psychoanalytic thinking about politics and culture
in a number of ways. It ethnicizes and culturalizes the unconscious by
presuming that one can gain insight into the psychic disturbances and
political difficulties of individual 'Muslims' by postulating fantasies
that take place at the level of the religious text itself. This 'textual-
ism', which supposes that something pertinent can be directly gleaned
from a religious scripture about social practices and individual trou-
bles, is of course one of the principal operations of the Orientalism
dissected by Edward Said. But it neglects the fact that – aside from
being intensely variable for biographical, political and conjunctural
reasons – the relation between individual and group psychology is
never a question of expression or emanation. As Mladen Dolar has
indicated, in Freud

---

34   Gil Anidjar, *Semites*, Stanford: Stanford University Press, 2008, 45, 47.

the unconscious is neither individual nor collective – an individual unconscious depends on a social structure, whereas the collective unconscious would demand a defined collectivity, a community to which it would pertain, but no such pre-given community exists. The unconscious 'takes place' precisely between the two, in the very establishment of the ties between an individual (becoming a subject) and a group to which s/he would belong. Strictly speaking there is no individual or collective unconscious; it intervenes at the link between the two.[35]

But neither 'Islam' nor 'Christianity' constitute monolithic social structures or vocabularies of motive, especially not in today's uneven and conflicted capitalist world; it would be spurious to fancy that one can draw political lessons from treating them as such. That they still provide copious fantasmatic material is not in doubt. The fact that militants and ideologues may present the religions on behalf of which they allegedly act as theologically unified, textually consistent entities should not lead critics and scholars to do the same. Treating political subjectivities as expressive of a cultural and religious essence can only add to the politically instrumental and analytically barren civilizational discourses whose resurgence has accompanied recent geopolitical conflicts. In this historical-political context, it would be far more useful, rather than viewing theological narratives as immediately present in the personal-political unconscious, to consider the power and impact of specifically political psychic forms. This is the great value of Alain Grosrichard's *The Sultan's Court*, a book which demonstrates that psychoanalysis, instead of prolonging the fallacies of civilizational or culturalist thought, can enact a profoundly dialectical and historically astute critique of the fantasies that structure our political thinking. In Grosrichard's work, the relation between texts and fantasy, as well as the inscription of 'cultural' alterity within the unconscious, never takes a fallacious expressive form

---

35   Mladen Dolar, 'Freud and the Political', *Unbound*, 4: 15 (2008), 25. For a contrasting position, which sees in Freud's group psychology 'a colonial historiography of the emergence of the modern individualized man out of organicism (the primitive tribalist)', see Wendy Brown, *Regulating Aversion: Tolerance in the Age of Identity and Empire*, Princeton: Princeton University Press, 2006, 168.

– of the kind that would justify turning to the Quran to grasp the fantasies of contemporary Muslims, or to speculate about the problems of authority in the contemporary Muslim world on the basis of ideas of paternity in Islamic theology. In Grosrichard, the object of a psychoanalytically-informed critique of ideology is the manner in which the fantasy of the Other's (anti-)politics structures our own, in which the belief in their beliefs allows us to believe that we don't believe. Fantasies set cultural contradictions to work, rather than revealing the essential features of a religion or culture. As Dolar has argued, fantasies tell us little about their objects (in Grosrichard's case, the seraglio and Oriental despotism) but a lot about their producers and advocates. By projecting our own impotence and inconsistencies onto the distant Other, we can pawn off our own disavowed belief in authority and subjugation to power onto third parties. The fantasy lets the European subject believe that 'somewhere, in some distant Asian land, there are some people naïve enough to believe'. This unburdens the secular, disenchanted subject of the psychic weight of his own less than limpid relations with political authority. The Orientalist fantasy of the seraglio thus allows the European subject to delegate belief in despotic power, and in the Other's enjoyment, to 'subjects supposed to believe'. His self-image as autonomous, sceptical and free is thus reliant on a distant scene of superstition, fanaticism and absolute subjection.[36]

When it attempts to delve into the tangled web of politics, culture and religion, a psychoanalytic critique operating with the category of fantasy must work on the principle that a (political or religious) fantasy is always a fantasy of the other's beliefs, and indeed about the other's fantasies. What's more, as the adventures of Oriental despotism reveal, the very idea of the other's unified culture or religion is itself a fantasy that allows us to entertain the belief that our own position is consistent and unified – in the case explored by Grosrichard, the position of a liberal polity entirely purged of slavery and blind subjection. The study of political fantasies reveals the way that relations with others (and their

---

36 Mladen Dolar, 'Introduction: The Subject Supposed to Enjoy', in Alain Grosrichard, *The Sultan's Court: European Fantasies of the East*, trans. L. Heron, London: Verso, 1998, xiv, xxiii–iv.

absence) structure our own fragile identifications. It is the fantasy of the other's self-enclosed civilization that allows 'us' (and them) the false security of feeling that we ourselves belong to a coherent, unified civilization – especially when this civilization is the one which regards itself, as in the recent fad for Judeo-Christian atheism or secularism, as having uniquely transcended the organicist constraints of 'traditional' civilizations, cultures or religions; as truly being the culture that one *has* rather than the culture whereby one *is had*.[37] A relational-political approach to fantasy, of the kind proposed by Grosrichard and Dolar, can serve a potent critical function, whereas an expressive-civilizational model, which would entertain the delusion that we can have insight into the other's collective political unconscious through a study of theological texts or myths, does not – indeed, it risks generating further myths which merely give succour to self-satisfied political fantasies of autonomy and liberality. It is such a relational-political model that Said hints at in *Freud and the Non-European*, where he writes of 'Freud's profound exemplification of the insight that even for the most definable, the most identifiable, the most stubborn communal identity – for him, this was the Jewish identity – there are inherent limits that prevent it from being fully incorporated into one, and only one, Identity'.[38]

Said proposed a defence of humanist secularism which did not leave it open to the possessive, secularizing philosophies of history which are so prone to pontificate about 'our' (Christian) legacy of atheism, toleration, liberalism and so on. Said referred to Vico's *verum factum* principle, 'the secular notion that the historical world is made by men and women, and not by God, and that it can be understood rationally according the principle formulated by Vico in *New Science*, that we can really know only what we make or, to put it differently, we can know things according to the way they were made'.[39] Against Anidjar's suggestion that secularism translates into the cunning of a 'Christian imperialism',[40] it is important

---

37 See Brown, *Regulating Aversion*, 150–1.
38 Edward W. Said, *Freud and the Non-European*, London: Verso, 2003, 53–4.
39 Edward W. Said, *Humanism and Democratic Criticism*, Basingstoke: Palgrave, 2004, 11.
40 Anidjar, *Semites*, 52.

to defend the idea, crucial to Freudian psychoanalysis, of secularism as a kind of methodological atheism – a praxis-centred, materialist and naturalist inquiry into transindividual behaviour and psychic structure which, to paraphrase Althusser, would strive 'not to tell itself stories'. Against the comforts of culturalist discourse, which would more or less surreptitiously advocate the superiority of one set of fantasies or myths over another, Freud's depiction of the religious illusions that respond to human helplessness and constitute the process of human civilization takes a salutary distance from the Christian concept of religion attacked by Anidjar, and from the apologetic narrative of Christian secularization that undergirds it. Unlike much of the discourse about secularism, which focuses on the appropriate distance or differentiation between the political and the religious – often raising liberalism to the status of an unalloyed truth and exalting its current territories as 'lands of freedom' – Freud's radical and disenchanted Enlightenment perspective centres on the possibility of emancipating humanity from illusion. For him it is not a matter of giving religion its proper place within society, let alone of denouncing the illusions of others the better to justify our own.

Whatever other problems it may raise, Freud's generic use of the category of religion (quite distinct from the one which allows Lacan to acerbically designate Christianity as the 'true religion' in *Le Triomphe de la religion*) has the great value of breaking with the parochialism of the culturalist discourse about religion, which always implies a choice about which religion is better, more emancipated, more civilized – or, to use Hegel's expression for Christianity, more 'consummate'.[41] Freud's unreverent approach also manifests a salutary indifference to the specific forms that religion (or indeed illusion more broadly) takes. When in 1907 he writes that 'one might venture to regard obsessional neurosis as a pathological counterpart of the formation of a religion, and to describe that neurosis as an individual religiosity and religion as a universal obsessional neurosis',[42] Freud, showing his fidelity to a radical and

---

41   See Chiesa and Toscano, 'Agape and the Anonymous Religion of Atheism', 118.
42   Sigmund Freud, 'Obsessive Actions and Religious Practices' (1907), in *The Complete Psychological Works of Sigmund Freud*, Vol. 9, J. Strachey (ed.), London: The Hogarth Press, 1959, 126.

materialist Enlightenment, is shifting the register to an anthropological discourse about the structures of belief. Such a methodological atheism is not devoid of a certain meta-political discourse, embodied in Freud's sympathy for a 'dictatorship of reason', for the slow 'geological' progress of the (scientific) intellect as a social force.[43] But more importantly for our purposes, unlike a psychoanalytically-inflected theory of secularism or 'Christian atheism', this methodological atheism is not generative of further political fantasies, illusions of autonomy or cultural superiority.

The slow, patient struggle against 'universal obsessional neurosis' is free of the dubious religious and cultural partisanship of those who believe that certain illusions have an emancipatory potential that makes them superior to others. When it comes to matters of religion, the turn to Kantianism and German Idealism run the risk of wedding psychoanalysis to a constricting narrative that turns every one of its concepts into merely a secularized variant of Christian theology. Freud's greater closeness to the intransigent reductivism of eighteenth-century materialism, his allegiance to the Radical Enlightenment, makes him a far surer and less biased guide in tackling the relation between psychic and religious life without propping up myths and fantasies, or smuggling the consolation of religion under the guise of unbelief. If the methodology of psychoanalysis is atheistic and scientific, it cannot allow itself to serve as the vehicle for the interminable 'secularizing' of Christianity, or for the depoliticizing study of cultural-religious fantasies supposedly expressed by individuals in distant lands. Believing by proxy – believing in the other's belief, in his fanaticism – is no substitute for the laborious struggle against our illusions.

---

43   On the dictatorship of reason, see Dolar, 'Freud and the Political', 20. On the geological progress of the intellect against illusion, see Freud, *The Future of an Illusion*, New York: Anchor Books, 1964, 90: 'Are we not all at fault, in basing our judgments in periods of time that are too short? We should make the geologists our pattern.'

5

The Clash of Abstractions:
Revisiting Marx on Religion

The only service which may still be rendered to God today, is that of declaring atheism an article of faith to be enforced.

Friedrich Engels

The 'truth of religion' – what religion really is – is discovered in philosophy.... The truth of philosophy – what philosophy really is – is discovered in politics.... The truth of politics, and hence of the state ... is to be found in society: social relationships account for political forms.

Henri Lefebvre, *The Sociology of Marx*

In a biography he later repudiated, the British historian E. H. Carr painted an unforgiving portrait of Karl Marx as an intellectual fanatic. For Carr, Marx believed in the correctness of his doctrine and the righteousness of his cause, as well as in its world-transforming future, 'with the faith of a fanatic in things not seen'. His was an intellectual rather than an emotional fanaticism, in which the logic of the system led to a kind of madness. The outcome was a 'fanatical intolerance ... so catholic in the choice of its victims that it is not altogether easy to discover the laws of its incidence'.[1]

Though virulent polemic and intellectual intransigence are mainstays of Marx's work, the portrait of Marx the fanatic does not stand up to scrutiny, neglectful as it is of the constant inquiry, political curiosity and sceptical intelligence that mark the German thinker's procedure. The

---

1   Edward Hallett Carr, *Karl Marx: a Study in Fanaticism*, London: Dent, 1934, 61–2.

disparaging view of Marxism as a fanatical dogma or political religion is, as we shall see, more resilient. Two dimensions of the idea of fanaticism are frequently employed in criticisms of Marx and Marxism. First, Marx's thought is reproached for its covert revitalization of a millenarian or prophetic vision of historical change, with communism as the secular counterpart of heaven and the revolution as the site of the Last Judgment. Second, both the Marxist theory of capitalism and the Marxist practice of politics are taxed with wishing violently to impose cold abstractions upon the plurality and complexity of the real world. Instead of looking in Marx for a theory or a use of fanaticism, I want to explore how in working through, and moving beyond, the critique of religion, he formulates a position which can, contrary to such charges, make a vital contribution to rethinking the contemporary relationship between politics and religion. With Marx, we can move beyond the poverty of contemporary debates and gain some traction on fanaticism as a phenomenon that is intimately caught up with the political and social dynamics of universality and abstraction.

MARX AND THE RE-ENCHANTMENT OF CATASTROPHIC MODERNITY

In the contemporary study of religion as a factor of social change and political mobilization, Marx is treated at best as a marginal reference, at worst – as he himself noted of the treatment of Hegel in his time – as a 'dead dog'.[2] A number of trends seem to speak against Marx: the global impasse, or even reversal, of a secularization process that he appears to have taken for granted; the turbulent rise of explicitly religious forms of political subjectivity; the persistence or resurgence of religion, both as a principle of political authority and as a structuring presence in everyday

---

2   For Engels's own thinking on religion, over and above *The Peasant War in Germany*, see Michèle Bertrand, *Le statut de la religion chez Marx et Engels*, Paris: Éditions Sociales, 1979, 176–85. For a rather uncharitable but useful survey of Engels's writings on religion see David McLellan, *Marxism and Religion*, London: Macmillan, 1987, 35–57; for a more sympathetic take, see Michael Löwy, 'Marxism and Religion: Opiate of the People', *New Socialist*, 51 (2005). Roland Boer's five-volume series on Marxist engagements with religion and theology, *Criticism of Heaven and Earth*, will be an indispensable reference for any future debate on these issues (the first two volumes, *Criticism of Heaven* and *Criticism of Religion*, have been published by the Historical Materialism Book Series).

life. Such trends seem to militate for relegating Marx to a historical
moment (the European nineteenth century), a political subject (the
workers' movement) and a notion of temporality (as progress, development and revolution) that, for better or worse, lie behind us. Whether we
grasp the present scenario through the differential lens of post-colonial
critiques, the hegemonic and homogeneous prism of neo-liberalism, or
the bellicose culturalism of the infamous 'clash of civilizations', Marx's
relevance is in severe doubt. To compound this state of affairs, which
could also be read in terms of a revenge of the sociology of religions
against a Marxian 'master narrative', we cannot ignore the significance
of the religious question within the so-called crisis of Marxism of the
1970s and onwards. When Michel Foucault, in his enduringly controver-
sial reports on the Iranian revolution, stressed the irrelevance of Marx's
dictum on religion as the 'opium of the people' in accounting for the
role of Islamic politics in the overthrow of the Shah,[3] he was expressing
a commonly-held rejection of the supposed secular reductivism characteristic of Marxism. Alongside Iran, the complex entanglement of popular rebellion and religion in the Polish Solidarność movement and Latin
American liberation theology[4] wrong-footed a theory of revolutionary
praxis which took the 'practical atheism' of the proletariat as a sociological given.[5] This situation has been exacerbated today in a context
where the ebb of projects of human emancipation is accompanied by
the pauperization and brutalization of a surplus humanity inhabiting a
planet of slums, the catalyst for a twenty-first-century 're-enchantment
of a catastrophic modernity'[6] in which 'populist Islam and Pentecostal

---

3   Michel Foucault, quoted in Afary and Anderson, *Foucault and the Iranian
Revolution*, 186. Michèle Bertrand argues that its common use as an analgesic at the time
indicates that opium would have been a less pejorative comparator than it is today, and
points out that its use with reference to religion originates in Kant. Bertrand, *Le statut
de la religion chez Marx et Engels*, 48. Löwy cites its use as a simile by the likes of Heine
and Hess before Marx, in 'Marxism and Religion: Opiate of the People'.
4   For an important Marxist engagement with the question of liberation theology, see Michael Löwy, *The War of the Gods: Religion and Politics in Latin America*,
London: Verso, 1996.
5   Friedrich Engels, *The Condition of the Working Class in England*, London:
Penguin, 1987, 143.
6   Mike Davis, *Planet of Slums*, London: Verso, 2006, 195.

Christianity (and in Bombay, the cult of Shivaji) occupy a social space analogous to that of early twentieth-century socialism and anarchism'.[7]

Can Marx's thinking on religion survive the challenge posed by what appear to be the dramatic reversals in the secularizing tendencies and revolutionary opportunities that he identified in the European nineteenth century? And can a Marxian social theory withstand its 'expatriation' into a political scenario in which explicitly Marxist actors, whether states or movements, are weak or non-existent?[8] The most economical response, though perhaps the most facile, would be to indicate the continuing vitality of historical materialism in the study of the socioeconomic dynamics behind the current religious resurgence, whether in the context of rampant planetary urbanization, or through the analysis of the role of neo-liberalism and 'accumulation by dispossession' in fostering the conditions for religious militancy.[9] However, rather than restating the virtues of Marxism for a systemic and systematic understanding of the conditions for today's refulgent religiosity, it is worth taking the aforementioned dismissals of Marx seriously and tackling what we might call the subjective element of religious-political conviction – its mobilizing force – alongside questions regarding the explanation of religious phenomena and the supposed secularization of capitalist societies. This might allow us to restore some of the richness of the problems raised by Marx, and even to treat his seeming anachronism as a resource in displacing some of the numerous commonplaces about religion, society and politics that have come to dominate our public and academic discourse. While endowed with their own complex reality and efficacy, appearances – including that of the contemporary centrality of religion to political life – are rarely the whole story. As Marx puts it, in a mordant description of his method: 'the philistine's and vulgar

7 Mike Davis, 'Planet of Slums', *New Left Review*, 26 (2004), 30.
8 See Alberto Toscano, 'Marxism Expatriated: Alain Badiou's Turn', in *Critical Companion to Contemporary Marxism*, Jacques Bidet and Stathis Kouvelakis (eds), Leiden: Brill, 2008.
9 David Harvey, *A Brief History of Neoliberalism*, Oxford: Oxford University Press, 2005, 171–2, 186. For a criticism of the limits of theories of imperialism for a 'geosociology' of religious-political militancy, see Chetan Bhatt, 'Frontlines and Interstices in the War on Terror', *Development and Change Forum 2007*, 38: 6 (2007).

economist's way of looking at things stems from . . . the fact that it is only the direct form of manifestation of relations that is reflected in their brains and not their inner connection. Incidentally, if the latter were the case what need would there be of science?'[10]

We could add that it is this philistine myopia for the inner connections that has dominated much recent writing seeking to explain and to counter the political return to religion by reaffirming the philosophical legacies of naturalism and atheism. What is striking about invocations of a besieged Enlightenment project against the depredations of religious fanaticism is their blindness to the consequences of the transformation and radicalization of Enlightenment ideals in the political and intellectual turmoil of the nineteenth century. The impression given by much of the popular literature in defence of secularism and atheism is that at an intellectual level – to put it in a nutshell – the 1840s still lie ahead of us. It is indeed to the early 1840s, the only period of sustained writing on the link between politics and religion in Marx's work, that we now turn. Understanding Marx's intellectual intervention into this critical moment in German and European history provides a necessary orientation for examining the way in which the problem of religion, in its various guises, is both addressed and transformed in the further development of Marx's work.

THE CRITICISM OF EARTH

Glossing over the formidable flowering of radical theory and intellectual activism in the context of which Marx makes his first interventions,[11] and emphasizing what is 'living' in it today, it is possible to summarize Marx's stance as a critique of the critique of religion. This might seem a very peculiar formulation to define a thinker who was both a combative atheist,[12] armed with an awesome arsenal of anti-religious invective, and

---

10   Marx to Engels, 27 June 1867, quoted in Karl Marx, *Capital: Volume 1*, London: Penguin, 1990, 19, n. 11.
11   For insightful and detailed accounts of this crucial moment, see Kouvelakis, *Philosophy and Revolution*, and Warren Breckman, *Marx, the Young Hegelians, and the Origins of Radical Social Theory*, Cambridge: Cambridge University Press, 1999.
12   'The Curtain Raised', interview with Marx in the *World*, 18 July 1871, in Karl Marx, *The First International and After: Political Writings*, Vol. 3, London: Penguin, 1974, 399.

a theorist who unequivocally subscribed to the Enlightenment conviction that 'man makes religion'.[13] But, as we shall see, everything hinges on how this 'makes' is to be understood.

Marx's intervention into the politics of religion initially takes place in the ambit of his 'philosophical journalism'.[14] In his 1842 'The Leading Article in No. 179 of the *Kölnische Zeitung*', Marx, impelled by a republican and democratic *élan*, confronts the 'German newspapers [which] have been drumming against, calumniating, distorting and bowdlerising the religious trend in philosophy.'[15] This trend, which comprises the works of 'Hegel and Schelling, Feuerbach and Bauer', is under attack in the press for the way it rationally responds to the politicization of religion in the form of the Christian state. As Marx judiciously notes, it is the very attempt by agencies of the state to religiously legitimate politics in a non-theocratic vein which secularizes religion and opens it to philosophical disputation: 'When religion becomes a political factor, a subject-matter of politics, it hardly needs to be said that the newspapers not only may, but must discuss political questions. . . . If you make religion into a theory of constitutional law, then you are making religion itself into a kind of philosophy.'[16]

Marx confronts the anti-philosophical and conformist opinion of his day with the fact that the moment one begins to speak of a Christian state, it becomes impossible to forestall a logic of complete secularization. For

---

13 Marx never reneges on the rationalist credo set out in his doctoral dissertation: 'That which a particular country is for particular alien gods, the country of reason is for God in general, a region in which he ceases to exist.' Karl Marx, 'Fragment from the Appendix' in *The Difference Between the Democritean and Epicurean Philosophy of Nature*, in *Collected Works*, Vol. 1, London: Lawrence and Wishart, 1975, 104.

14 Breckman, *Marx, the Young Hegelians, and the Origins of Radical Social Theory*, 272.

15 Marx, 'The Leading Article in No. 179 of the *Kölnische Zeitung*' in *Collected Works*, Vol. 1, 196. I am grateful to Roland Boer for pointing out to me the importance of this article.

16 Marx, 'The Leading Article', 198. This brief, early phase of Marx's intellectual career has been portrayed by Breckman in terms of 'Marx's campaign against the transcendental personalism of the Christian state', a campaign which, picking up on arguments formulated by the Young Hegelians, focuses on the solidarity between the principle of sovereignty, on the one hand, and the atomization and privatization through law and property of the state's subjects, on the other. See Breckman, *Marx, the Young Hegelians, and the Origins of Radical Social Theory*, 277.

either such a state is equivalent to the reasonable state, in which case its Christianity is redundant and philosophy is fully adequate to thinking through the state-form; or rational freedom cannot be developed out of Christianity, and consequently religion is simply external to the state: 'You may solve this dilemma in whatever way you like, you will have to admit that the state must be built on the basis of free reason, and not on religion.'[17] Though this radical democratic secularism can be registered, in a mutated form, in later pronouncements by Marx, it does not exhaust Marx's position.

Ludwig Feuerbach's materialist reappropriation for humankind of those fundamental sensuous and intellectual capacities (or species-being) that religion had projected or 'alienated' into the Godhead, played a fundamental role in the inception of Marx's thought. Feuerbach had in fact connected this expropriation of the human by the divine to an unsparing criticism of religion's violent unreason, returning to themes broached in the *Lumières* in terms of his own philosophical anthropology. As he wrote in *The Essence of Christianity*, where he also upbraided the Christian religion for its intolerant partisanship:

> Religion is the relation of man to his own nature, – therein lies its truth and its power of moral amelioration; – but to his nature not recognized as his own, but regarded as another nature, separate, nay, contradistinguished from his own: herein lies its untruth, its limitation, its contradiction to reason and morality; herein lies the noxious source of religious fanaticism, the chief metaphysical principle of human sacrifices, in a word, the *prima materia* of all the atrocities, all the horrible scenes, in the tragedy of religious history.[18]

Marx initially also drew inspiration from Bruno Bauer's unsparing anti-theistic criticism of the baleful effect of religious belief on universality and self-consciousness. That said, Marx's early writings can be understood in terms of his progressive, rapid realization that the attack on

---

17   Marx, 'The Leading Article', 200.
18   Ludwig Feuerbach, *The Essence of Christianity*, trans. G. Eliot, New York: Harper & Row, 1956, 197.

religion – while a vital spur to undermining the Christian legitimation of state power – is always insufficient, or even a downright diversion, in attaining its own avowed ends, namely the emancipation of human reason. Atheistic criticism overestimates the centrality of Christianity to the state and treats the state's secularization as an end in itself. The slogan encapsulating Marx's intervention into the fraught 1840s debate over religion and politics is 'from the criticism of Heaven to the criticism of Earth'. The outcome of Marx's philosophical operation is to separate political and economic critique from the Left Hegelians' absorbing concern with Christianity, giving critique autonomy as a secular discourse no longer parasitic on the religious ideology and authority it sought to criticize.[19] The clearest form of this redirection in the aims of 'irreligious criticism' is to be found in the letter to Arnold Ruge of 30 November 1842, where Marx declares that 'religion should be criticised in the framework of political conditions [instead of criticizing] political conditions . . . in the framework of religion . . .; for religion in itself is without content, it owes its being not to heaven but to the earth, and with the abolition of distorted reality, of which it is the *theory*, it will collapse of itself'.[20]

This provocative and problematic declaration that religion is 'without content' of its own in turn introduces Marx's belief in the 'withering away' of religion as a corollary of social revolution. However, against the image of religion in a certain Enlightenment materialism as a mere delusion or conspiracy, Marx, while never reneging on his militant atheism, affirms what we might term the social necessity of religion as a form of consciousness and an ordering principle of collective life. When Marx writes of religion as a theory of the world, he is making a properly dialectical point: religion provides an inverted picture of reality because reality itself is inverted. Though there's a case to be made for the idea that Marx draws this 'transformative method', (involving the 'inversion of subject and predicate and exposure of the hypostasized form of both')[21] from Feuerbach, he also explicitly refers to the limits of a mate-

---

19   Breckman, *Marx, the Young Hegelians, and the Origins of Radical Social Theory*, 293.
20   Quoted in ibid., 278.
21   Ibid..

rialist humanism vis-à-vis religion in order to specify his own position. As he sets out in the fourth of the 'Theses on Feuerbach':

> Feuerbach starts off from the fact of religious self-estrangement, of the duplication of the world into a religious, imaginary world, and a secular one. His work consists in resolving the religious world into its secular basis. He overlooks the fact that after completing this work, the chief thing still remains to be done. For the fact that the secular basis lifts off from itself and establishes itself in the clouds as an independent realm can only be explained by the inner strife and intrinsic contradictoriness of this secular basis. The latter must itself be understood in its contradiction and then, by the removal of the contradiction, revolutionised. Thus, for instance, once the earthly family is discovered to be the secret of the holy family, the former must itself be annihilated theoretically and practically.[22]

To bring religious abstraction 'down to earth' by revealing it to be a distorted projection of human essence is thus insufficient. For Marx, religion possesses a social logic of separation and autonomization (its establishment as an apparently 'independent realm'),[23] whose bases in a really inverted world must be the object of theoretical and practical criticism. Marx's critique of the Young Hegelians' critique of religion – and *a fortiori* his views on the insufficiency of the attack on religious delusion in French materialism and the Enlightenment – will persistently take this twofold form: an elaboration of the social logic of abstraction (as a result of the 'inner strife and intrinsic contradictoriness of [the] secular basis') and an elucidation of the necessity for revolution ('the removal

---

22 Karl Marx (with Friedrich Engels), *The German Ideology*, New York: Prometheus, 1998, 570. See the commentary in Bertrand, *Le statut de la religion chez Marx et Engels*, 29.

23 As Derrida notes: 'Marx advances that belief in the religious spectre, thus in the ghost in general, consists in autonomising a representation (*Vorstellung*) and in forgetting its genesis as well as its real grounding (*reale Grundlage*). To dissipate the factitious autonomy thus engendered in history, one must again take into account the modes of production and techno-economic exchange.' Jacques Derrida, *Specters of Marx: The State of the Debt, the Work of Mourning and the New International*, trans. P. Kamuf, London: Routledge, 2006, 214–15.

of the contradiction') if the real grounds of abstract domination are to be removed.[24] In order to tackle the endurance of religious abstractions it is imperative to investigate the social dynamics into which they are inscribed, and the dependence of these abstractions on given modes of production and social intercourse. As Marx writes in *The German Ideology*:

> In religion people make their empirical world into an entity that is only conceived, imagined, that confronts them as something foreign. This again is by no means to be explained from other concepts, from 'self-consciousness' and similar nonsense, but from the entire hitherto existing mode of production and intercourse, which is just as independent of the pure concept as the invention of the self-acting mule and the use of railways are independent of Hegelian philosophy. If he wants to speak of an 'essence' of religion, i.e., of a material basis of this inessentiality, then he should look for it neither in the 'essence of man', nor in the predicate of God, but in the material world which each stage of religious development finds in existence.[25]

In the 1844 Introduction to the 'Contribution to the Critique of Hegel's Philosophy of Right', Marx had noted that the 'abolition of religion as the *illusory* happiness of the people is the demand for their *real* happiness. To call on them to give up their illusions about their condition is to call on them to give up a condition that requires illusions. The criticism of religion is, therefore, in embryo, the criticism of that vale of tears of which religion is the halo.' We might say that the early conviction whereby the struggle against religion is the 'embryo' of true revolutionary transformation gives way, through Marx's deepening study of the system of exploitation and his own political engagement, to a belief that such an anti-religious struggle might even serve as a detour or a cloak for real political struggle. That is, Marx comes to the idea that the aims

---

24   In this regard, it is useful to keep the following assertion from the *Grundrisse* in mind: 'individuals are now ruled by *abstractions*, whereas earlier they depended on one another'. Karl Marx, *Grundrisse*, trans. M. Nicolaus, London: Penguin, 1973, 164.
25   Marx, *The German Ideology*, 172.

of atheism and Enlightenment cannot be accomplished through a bald affirmation of Godlessness and Reason as matters of consciousness or mere pedagogy. His criticisms of Max Stirner and Bruno Bauer in *The German Ideology* and *The Holy Family* elaborate on this conviction that it is necessary to step outside an obsessive confrontation with 'religious representations', precisely in order to examine and transform the very conditions of possibility for these representations, for their seemingly autonomous, 'spectral' existence.

Thus, it is in the broadly Kantian sense of 'critique' – not as mere criticism but as an excavation of the conditions of possibility of a form of thought – that Marx provides us with a potent critique of the critique of religion, pointing out the latter's mode of operation and its limitations. It would be difficult to underestimate the relevance of this gesture today, as we are confronted with anti-religious arguments which, whatever the sincerity or nobility of their motivations, often rely on the idealist, asocial view that the sway of religious representations and ideologies over human affairs can be terminated by a mere change of consciousness. Marx indicates that consciousness always takes social forms, and that these forms are in turn marked by a certain necessity. His critique of the Young Hegelians asks what the conditions of production of religious representations are, in order then to ask how these conditions themselves might be transformed. The anti-theism of his contemporaries is an obstacle to a consequent political atheism, inasmuch as it remains within the ambit of theological reasoning. Stirner in particular 'shares the belief of all critical speculative philosophers of modern times that thoughts, which have become independent, objectified thoughts – ghosts – have ruled the world and continue to rule it, and that all history up to now was the history of theology, [so] nothing could be easier for him than to transform history into a history of ghosts'.[26]

The vision of the struggle against religious domination as a 'fight against [the] thoughts and ideas of the ideologist', where hierarchy is reduced to the 'domination of thought' and the political structure of rule

---

26   Ibid., 173.

in modern times can be equated with a 'clericalism' that even includes the likes of Robespierre and Saint-Just, is for Marx emblematic of the dead end of a supposedly radical thought which not only takes religion on its own terms, but succumbs to a generic fight against transcendence, unable to grasp the real conditions for the production of (and domination by) abstraction.[27]

Alongside this methodological prescription, which in one form or another will accompany Marx throughout his work, there is also something to be learned from Marx's attention to the importance of political conjuncture, as well as historical and geographical specificity, in the criticism of religion. Behind the attack on the Young Hegelians' tendency to remain at the level of theology, to fight ghosts with ghosts, lies Marx's estimation that anti-religious mobilization was – despite the necessity of the demand for radical secularization – if not a rearguard action, at least an insufficient programme. Confident of a secularizing trend which, spurred by revolutionary politics between 1793 and 1848, 'sufficiently announced the direction of the popular mind in Europe', Marx remarked, in an 1854 article for the *New York Tribune* tellingly entitled 'The Decay of Religious Authority': 'We are still witnesses of this epoch, which may be characterized as the era of democratic revolt against ecclesiastical authority.' But he also indicated the tendency to an ever more opportunistic use of religious legitimation for state violence, in a period such as his own, when religion was no longer an actual *casus belli*.[28]

Some years thereafter, in the 1867 Preface to *Capital*, he had occasion to note – while making one of his characteristic jabs at craven clerical authorities – that atheism itself was no longer in the vanguard even in terms of its capacity to provoke the authorities: 'The Established Church . . . will more readily pardon an attack on thirty-eight of its thirty-nine articles than on one thirty-ninth of its income. Now atheism

---

27   Ibid., 186–91. Likewise, in his criticism of Bauer in *The Holy Family*, Marx will declare that 'when we come to the *political* part of the Jewish question we shall see that in politics, too, Herr Bauer the theologian is not concerned with politics but with theology'. Marx and Engels, *The Holy Family*, in *Collected Works*, Vol. 4, 108.

28   Marx, 'The Decay of Religious Authority' (1854), in *Marx on Religion*, J. Raines (ed.), Philadelphia: Temple University Press, 2002, 188–9.

itself is a *culpa levis* [a venial or minor sin], as compared with the criticism of existing property relations.'[29] Some might argue that new forms
of reactionary or fundamentalist religious politics have reversed this
verdict, that Marx remains rooted in a historical moment that is not trans-
posable to our own. Here it is worth considering the place of reflection
on religious phenomena within the wider sweep of his thought, including his mature critique of political economy. Three aspects of Marx's
thought speak to contemporary debates on the politics and sociology
of religion: the social explanation of religion; the nature of religious-
political subjectivity; the process of secularization and the politics of
secularism. I will treat these in order, before considering the somewhat
unorthodox proposition that capitalism itself may constitute a kind of
religion.

THE HISTORY OF A THING WITHOUT HISTORY

The error of anti-theistic critique – which remains within the ambit of
theology, unable to grasp the real social processes that condition the
necessity and 'objective illusion' characteristic of religious phenomena – is part and parcel of what Marx regards as the shortcoming of
the Enlightenment tradition of which he is, in many respects, a proud
heir. Whether we are dealing with money or with religion, the crucial
error is to treat real abstractions as mere 'arbitrary product[s] of human
reflection. This was the kind of explanation favoured by the eighteenth
century: in this way the Enlightenment endeavoured, at least tempo-
rarily, to remove the appearance of strangeness from the mysterious
shapes assumed by human relations whose origins they were unable to
decipher.'[30] The strangeness of religion cannot be dispelled by ascribing
it to clerical conspiracies or psychological delusions, to be cured through

---

29 Marx, *Capital: Volume 1*, 92.
30 Marx, *Capital: Volume 1*, 186. Marx's move beyond the generic and mental
abstractions of Feuerbach is discussed in Jacques Rancière, 'The Concept of
"Critique" and the "Critique of Political Economy"', in *Ideology, Method and Marx*,
A. Rattansi (ed.), London: Routledge, 1989; and Roberto Finelli, *Astrazione e dialet-
tica dal romanticismo al capitalismo (saggio su Marx)*, Roma: Bulzoni Editore, 1987.
I have explored this question in 'The Open Secret of Real Abstraction', *Rethinking
Marxism* 20: 2, (2008).

mere pedagogy. But does Marx bend the stick too far the other way? After all, there is good reason to feel that the early Marx's position on religious phenomena takes the guise, to borrow a term from contemporary cognitive science, of a kind of 'eliminativist materialism' – a denial of any autonomy or indeed reality to religion. Already in the 'Leading Article' of 1842, Marx had stripped religion of any causal efficacy: 'It was not the downfall of the old religions that caused the downfall of the ancient states, but the downfall of the ancient states that caused the downfall of the old religions.'[31]

In *The German Ideology*, religion, alongside 'morality . . . metaphysics and all the rest of ideology as well as the forms of consciousness corresponding to these' is stripped of any 'semblance of independence'.[32] Marx even adumbrates a sketch of naturalist psychology whose echoes one could find today in the likes of Richard Dawkins and Daniel Dennett: 'The phantoms formed in the brains of men are also, necessarily, sublimates of the material life-process, which is empirically verifiable and bound to material premises.'[33] The notion of religion as a kind of non-being, an 'inessentiality', in the language of the 1844 Introduction, is also in evidence in 'On the Jewish Question', his 1843 rejoinder to Bauer: 'since the existence of religion is the existence of a defect, the source of this defect must be looked for in the *nature* of the state itself. We no longer see religion as the *basis* but simply as a *phenomenon* of secular narrowness.'[34]

But as Marx moves beyond this political reduction to the secular basis of the state, into the historical-materialist accounting with real abstractions heralded by the fourth thesis on Feuerbach, a crucial factor is added to his understanding of religion – one that allows him to propose means of explaining, rather than merely explaining away, religious phenomena. It is not enough to derive 'the religious restriction on the free citizens from the secular restriction they experience', to 'turn theological questions into secular questions' and 'resolv[e] superstition into history', as

---

31 Marx, 'The Leading Article'.
32 Marx, *The German Ideology*, 42.
33 Ibid. Michèle Bertrand tries to develop these insights in a more psychoanalytic direction in Bertrand, *Le statut de la religion chez Marx et Engels*, 65.
34 Marx, *Early Writings*, 217.

Marx enjoins us to do in 'On the Jewish Question'. [35] Rather, we are to look to 'the inner strife and intrinsic contradictoriness' of a 'secular basis',[36] to be conceived not in terms of the state but rather in those of 'the entire hitherto existing mode of production and intercourse'.[37]

By the time of his mature work on the critique of political economy, we can say that Marx has moved beyond the 'eliminativist' programme, which he polemically counterposed to the theological foibles of the Young Hegelians, to an incorporation of the religious phenomenon into a theory of the social emergence of different modes of 'real abstraction'. Thus, in an important long footnote to *Capital*, Marx suggests – as a corollary to a discussion of a 'critical history of technology' that would be mindful of 'the mode of formation of [man's] social relations' – the possibility of a similarly critical 'history of religion'. His methodological reflections are immensely suggestive for coming to grips with a histori-cal-materialist understanding of religion:

> It is, in reality, much easier to discover by analysis the earthly core of the misty creations of religion, than, conversely, it is to develop from the actual relations of life the corresponding celestialised forms of those rela-tions. The latter method is the only materialistic, and therefore the only scientific one. The weak points in the abstract materialism of natural science, a materialism that excludes history and its process, are at once evident from the abstract and ideological conceptions of its spokesmen, whenever they venture beyond the bounds of their own speciality.[38]

This passage demonstrates the vitality and endurance of Marx's critique of the critique of religion, his opposition to a complacent reduction of religious phenomena to their secular basis (whether this is understood in terms of species-being, the state, or even a static notion of economic intercourse). His analysis opens up in a much more forthright manner the possibility of a study of religion as a real abstraction, developing

---

35   Karl Marx, *Early Writings*, 217.
36   Marx, *The German Ideology*, 570.
37   Ibid., 172.
38   Marx, *Capital: Volume 1*, 493–4, n. 4.

'from the actual relations of life the corresponding celestialised forms of those relations'.[39] In *The German Ideology*, Marx had made the following lapidary declaration:

> 'Christianity' has no history whatever and . . . all the different forms in which it was visualised at various times were not 'self-determinations' and 'further developments' 'of the religious spirit', but were brought about by wholly empirical causes in no way dependent on any influence of the religious spirit.[40]

Notwithstanding the continuity in the denial of independence to the religious phenomenon, *Capital*, which leaves behind the polemical targets of *The German Ideology* (Feuerbach, Bauer, Stirner), opens up the possibility of a materialist history of religion. While denying religion any causal autonomy, it allows us to think the conditions for its 'real-apparent' autonomization. In her fine study on the status of religion in Marx and Engels, Michèle Bertrand has elaborated on this methodological suggestion by distinguishing in their work between a path of demystification and one of constitution. Commenting on Marx and Engels's exchange on the historical-materialist explanation of the implantation of Islam in the Middle East, she writes: 'Instead of referring religious representations back to the real world that underlies them, it's a matter of understanding why the history of real mutations has taken a religious form.'[41] Or, in the words of *Capital*, 'the Middle Ages could not live on

---

39   In this regard, the footnote in *Capital* suggests the possibility of applying to religious phenomena the 'scientific method' famously outlined in *A Contribution to the Critique of Political Economy*. See Karl Marx, *A Contribution to the Critique of Political Economy*, New York: International Publishers, 1970, 206.

40   Marx, *The German Ideology*, 166.

41   Bertrand, *Le statut de la religion chez Marx et Engels*, 82. On Marx and Engels's views on Islam see Gilbert Achcar, 'Religion and Politics Today from a Marxian Perspective', *Socialist Register 2008*, London: Merlin, 2007, 67–72. In his letter to Marx of 18 May 1853, Engels writes: 'Mohammed's religious revolution, like every religious movement, was *formally a reaction*, a would-be return to what was old and simple.' On this text, see G. H. Bousquet, 'Marx et Engels se sont-ils intéréssés aux questions islamiques?', *Studia Islamica*, 30 (1969); and Nicholas S. Hopkins, 'Engels and Ibn Khaldun', *Alif: Journal of Comparative Poetics*, 10 (1990).

Catholicism, nor could the ancient world on politics. On the contrary, it is the manner in which they gained their livelihood which explains why in the one case politics, in the other case Catholicism, played the chief part.'[42] It is not simply a matter of referring the illusory autonomy and separation of religious representations to a material basis, but of showing the socio-historical necessity and rootedness of the 'phantoms' and 'sublimates' of a specific religious form. This point is ably captured by Jacques Derrida, who notes how in Marx, 'only the reference to the religious world allows one to explain the autonomy of the ideological, and thus its proper efficacy, its incorporation in apparatuses that are endowed not only with an apparent autonomy but a sort of automaticity . . . as soon as there is production, there is fetishism: idealisation, autonomisation and automatisation, dematerialisation and spectral incorporation'.[43]

But if the full development of a historical-materialist critique of abstractions, moving beyond demystification to constitution, allows us to think of a critical history of religion that would surpass the eliminativist position asserted in *The German Ideology*, we are still faced with the problem of the plurality of religions. Indeed, as Bertrand rightly notes, is it even possible to speak of 'religion in general'? Considered as theory, religion might answer to a relatively invariant human need to render the world intelligible, and as practice, to master it; but this still does not tell us why '*this*' religion has found a receptive terrain, why men have been sensitive to its message. A religion only exists to the extent that a social group declares its adherence to it, drawing from it certain practices, and so on. How is a religion born? Why does it gain followers? How does its audience grow?'[44] Needless to say, these are questions that the mature Marx, who viewed religion as a waning force, was not preoccupied with answering (unlike the Engels of *On the History of Early Christianity*). However, we may find in Marx an embryonic theory of the correlation between certain religious forms and institutions, on the one hand, and

42   Marx, *Capital: Volume 1*, 176, n. 35. In his contribution to *Reading Capital* (1965), Balibar linked this passage to a defence of the concept of 'determination in the last instance'. Louis Althusser and Étienne Balibar, *Reading Capital*, London: Verso, 1997, 217–18.
43   Derrida, *Specters of Marx*, 207–9.
44   Bertrand, *Le statut de la religion chez Marx et Engels*, 83.

certain social systems (and more specifically types of alienation), on the other. The outlines of such a theory are drawn in the chapter on the commodity in *Capital*, where Marx writes:

> For a society of commodity producers, whose general social relation of production consists in the fact that they treat their products as commodities, hence as values, and in this material form bring their individual, private labours into relation with each other as homogeneous human labour, Christianity with its religious cult of man in the abstract, more particularly in its bourgeois development, i.e. in Protestantism, Deism, etc., is the most fitting form of religion.[45]

This 'fit' suggests that, rather than being the offspring of a clerical conspiracy, Christianity is regarded by Marx as bound to capitalism by a certain mode and intensity of abstraction.

Christianity is the superstructural correlate of the autonomization of material production from the communal and the concrete to the extent that it presents itself as the religion of autonomy. In *The German Ideology*, Christianity is indeed defined by the manner in which it fights against determination by 'heteronomy as opposed to autonomy of the spirit'.[46] Hints in Marx's work suggest that the apparent autonomy and abstraction attained by the value-form under commodity-production is especially well suited by the Christian religion.[47] Indeed, inasmuch as religion is both a hypostasis of, and a manner of coping with, natural and social forces, we could say, paraphrasing Marx's 1844 Introduction to the 'Critique of Hegel's Philosophy of Right', that Christianity is in this sense a theory (or logic) of capitalism. In Marx, this insight regarding the affinity of Christianity and capitalism also takes on a

---

45   Marx, *Capital: Volume 1*, 172.
46   Marx, *The German Ideology*, 272. These reflections are indebted to some precious suggestions by James Furner. Needless to say, he is exempted from any responsibility for my argument and its possible flaws.
47   The widespread idea of an elective affinity between Christianity and capitalism has come under important criticism. See, among others, Maxime Rodinson, *Islam and Capitalism*, London: Penguin, 1977; and Jack Goody, *The Theft of History*, Cambridge: Cambridge University Press, 2007.

more overtly historical and sociological tint. In the *Grundrisse*, Marx forwards an argument which, as Michael Löwy notes, parallels Weber's thesis in *The Protestant Ethic*, to wit, that: 'The cult of money has its asceticism, its self-denial, its self-sacrifice-economy and frugality, contempt for mundane, temporal and fleeting pleasures; the chase after the eternal treasure. Hence the connection between English Puritanism or Dutch Protestantism and money-making.'[48] But these brief sociological aperçus must be thought of in the context of Marx's methodological revolution, his formulation of a historical-materialist study of social, cultural and intellectual abstractions on the basis of the real abstractions of the value-form, money and abstract labour. Marx's critique can now return to the attack on the personalism, atomism and false equality of the Christian state on a far firmer footing, while losing none of its dialectical bite:

> The development of capitalist production creates an average level of bourgeois society and therefore an average level of temperament and disposition amongst the most varied peoples. It is as truly cosmopolitan as Christianity. This is why Christianity is likewise the special religion of capital. In both it is only man in the abstract who counts. One man in the abstract is worth just as much or as little as the next man. In the one case, all depends on whether or not he has faith, in the other, on whether or not he has credit. In addition, however, in the one case, predestination has to be added, and in the other case, the accident of whether or not a man is born with a silver spoon in his mouth.[49]

---

48 Quoted in Löwy, 'Marxism and Religion: Opiate of the People'. In the *Contribution*, Marx repeats the same insight in an even more 'Weberian' vein when he writes that 'in so far as the hoarder of money combines asceticism with assiduous diligence he is intrinsically a Protestant by religion and still more a Puritan'. Marx also defines the credit system as Protestant, because of its faith 'in money value as the immanent spirit of commodities, faith in the mode of production and its predestined order, faith in the individual agents of production as mere personifications of self-valorizing capital'. Karl Marx, *Capital: Volume 3*, trans. D. Fernbach, London: Penguin, 1991, 727.
49 Karl Marx, *Theories of Surplus Value*, Vol. 3, Moscow: Progress, 1971, 448. See also Marx, *Grundrisse*, 839.

And if Christianity is the 'special religion of capital', it can never be just a fantasy or a conspiracy.[50] To the extent that the society of commodity producers it 'fits' is stamped with a certain necessity – indeed, to the very extent that the forms of abstraction and alienation such a society implies prepare the communist socialization of the means of production – it is an integral, if contingent and transitory, component of world capitalism. Marx's early intuition that only human emancipation – rather than secularism or Enlightenment pedagogy alone – can snuff out the 'illusory sun' of religion can thus be restated: 'The religious reflections of the real world can, in any case, vanish only when the practical relations of everyday life between man and man, and man and nature, generally present themselves to him in a transparent and rational form.'[51]

PROTEST, SUFFERING AND THE LIMITS OF THE SECULAR

Clearly then, Marx holds on to the perspective, evident at the very least since *The German Ideology* and the 'Theses on Feuerbach', whereby only revolutionary praxis can provide the real 'criticism of that vale of tears of which religion is the halo'. In light of the recent theoretical preoccupation with religious matrices of militant political subjectivity (in the writings of Badiou, Negri and Žižek, among others) what can Marx tell us – beyond the historical-materialist explanation of organized religions and institutions – about the political resources of religious subjectivity? More generally, how can we link a 'structural' study of the material bases of religion[52] with issues of belief, passion and agency?[53]

---

50   Although Marx is particularly caustic regarding the hypocrisy and brutality that frequently accompany religious allegiance. See Marx, *Capital: Volume 1*, 375, n. 72 and 917.
51   Ibid., 173.
52   It belongs to the peculiarity of Marx's materialism that these 'bases' comprise realities that we may regard as abstract, notional or indeed ideal: the value-form, the commodity-form, abstract labour, etc.
53   One crucial question which this chapter does not tackle is the Marxian response to the idea of an ineliminable anthropological basis to religious phenomena, which no amount of social transformation will ever dissipate. Important indications in this regard can be found in Bertrand, *Le statut de la religion chez Marx et Engels*, 161–85 (on the future of religion); Ernesto De Martino, *La fine del mondo. Contributo all'analisi delle apocalissi culturali*, C. Gallini (ed.), Turin: Einaudi, 2002, 446–62 (on the anthropological deficit in Marxist theories of religion); and Paolo Virno, *Scienze sociali e 'natura umana'*, Soveria Mannelli: Rubbettino, 2003.

These questions are of particular significance because, as already noted, criticism or repudiation of Marx's work has often involved depicting it as the source for a fundamentally religious subjectivity, if not an outright fanaticism. This political-religion approach to Marxism relies on the idea that Marxism is somehow the (degenerate) secularization of fundamentally Christian visions of salvation.[54] Such an approach is pre-emptively and categorically repudiated by Marx and Engels themselves, when they condemn any attempt to fashion a 'new religion' to motivate and crystallize social struggles:

> It is clear that with every great historical upheaval of social conditions the outlooks and ideas of men, and consequently their religious ideas, are revolutionised. The difference between the present upheaval and all earlier ones lies in the very fact that man has at last found out the secret of this process of historical upheaval and hence, instead of once again exalting this practical, 'external', process in the rapturous form of a new religion, divests himself of all religion.[55]

In his own lifetime as a political organizer, Marx was of course faced with various attempts to infuse religion into the socialist politics of the workers' movement. A view of religion as a politically ambivalent phenomenon can be gleaned from his work. Famously, he speaks of religion as both 'the *expression* of real suffering and a protest against real suffering'; not just the religion of the state, but 'the sigh of the oppressed creature, the heart of a heartless world, and the soul of soulless conditions'. This view is poetically summarized in the prescription according to which criticism should not merely aim at plucking 'the imaginary flowers on the chain' of social domination (i.e. religion), it should

---

54   See Jacob Stevens, 'Exorcizing the Manifesto', *New Left Review*, 28 (2004). His sharp critique of Gareth Stedman Jones's reading of the *Manifesto* also provides a useful introduction to the political religion thesis and its contemporary uses. A positive account of Marxism as the 'historical successor of Christianity', can be found in Alasdair MacIntyre, *Marxism and Christianity*, Harmondsworth: Pelican, 1971.
55   Marx and Engels, review of G. Fr. Daumer's *Die Religion des Neuen Weltalters*, in *Neue Rheinische Zeitung, Politisch-ökonomische Revue* (1850), in *Collected Works*, Vol. 10, 244.

'throw off the chain and pluck the living flower'.[56] Marx's views on the progressive politicization of religion are bleak to say the least, and not based merely on his 'specific . . . aversion for Christianity'.[57] To begin with, he offers a sociological judgment about the 'practical atheism' of the working-class, to which must be added the desacralizing effects of the epic narrated in *The Communist Manifesto*, in which the bourgeoisie has 'drowned the most heavenly ecstasies of religious fervour . . . in the icy waters of egotistical calculation' and 'stripped of its halo every occupation [and] converted . . . the priest . . . into its paid wage labourer'.[58] On the grounds of these facts and tendencies, the attempt by many of his political contemporaries at generating a Christian socialism is showered with scorn.

Even when he had yet to sunder his philosophical allegiance to Feuerbach, Marx already rejected 'the possibility of translating Christian love into a love of humanity'.[59] In his political interventions, the historical affinity between Christianity and capitalism is not accompanied by any faith in the affinity between Christianity and capitalism's transcendence. Though a 'fitting' superstructural correlate of abstract-value and the exchange of commodities between 'equals', Christianity is depicted as a feeble weapon against capitalism at best, and a fig leaf at worst. As Marx and Engels write in *The Communist Manifesto*:

---

56 Marx, 'A Contribution to Hegel's Philosophy of Right. Introduction', in *Early Writings*, 244. It is interesting to note that in his sympathetic account of the 'spiritualization of politics' during the Iranian revolution, Foucault tries to play off the idea of a religion of protest qua 'spirit of a world without spirit' *against* that of religion as the 'opium of the people'. Foucault, quoted in Afary and Anderson, *Foucault and the Iranian Revolution*, 255.

57 Marx to Lasalle, 16 June 1862, *Collected Works*, Volume 41, 377. This aversion might also explain why, unlike Engels, Marx does not produce any accounts of conjunctures in which religion may play the role of a flag, a mask or a screen (to use some of Engels's own metaphors) for forms of emancipatory or communist politics. Marx is also unconcerned for the most part with what Gilbert Achcar calls 'the *incitement dimension* of religion'. Achcar, 'Religion and Politics Today from a Marxian Perspective', 58.

58 Karl Marx and Friedrich Engels, *The Communist Manifesto*, London: Penguin, 2002, 222.

59 Breckman, *Marx, the Young Hegelians, and the Origins of Radical Social Theory*, 282.

Nothing is easier than to give Christian asceticism a Socialist tinge. Has
not Christianity declaimed against private property, against marriage,
against the State? Has it not preached in the place of these, charity and
poverty, celibacy and mortification of the flesh, monastic life and Mother
Church? Christian Socialism is but the holy water with which the priest
consecrates the heart-burnings of the aristocrat.[60]

In his scathing piece on 'The Communism of the *Rheinischer Beobachter*',
Marx produces the following tirade on the idea of 'social principles of
Christianity' as substitutes for communist revolution, again proving
that, when the conjuncture demands it, and notwithstanding the subtlety
of his critique of the critique of religion, he is a coruscating foe of religious hypocrisy:

The social principles of Christianity preach the necessity of a ruling
and an oppressed class, and for the latter all they have to offer is the
pious wish that the former may be charitable. . . . The social principles
of Christianity preach cowardice, self-contempt, abasement, submis-
siveness and humbleness, in short, all the qualities of the rabble, and the
proletariat, which will not permit itself to be treated as rabble, needs its
courage, its self-confidence, its pride and its sense of independence even
more than its bread. The social principles of Christianity are sneaking
and hypocritical, and the proletariat is revolutionary. So much for the
social principles of Christianity.[61]

In passages such as this Marx seems unequivocal in effecting a separation between politics and religion, developing his own communist political practice on stringently irreligious grounds. What does Marx have to
say, then, about the question of the secular – understood both in terms
of political secularism and a historical process of secularization – which
so preoccupies contemporary thinkers?

---

60   Marx and Engels, *The Communist Manifesto*, 246–7.
61   Karl Marx, 'The Communism of the *Rheinischer Beobachter*' (1847), in Karl Marx
and Friedrich Engels, *Collected Works*, Vol. 6, London: Lawrence & Wishart, 1976,
231.

In his early writings as a radical democrat, Marx strongly advocated a secular 'state of human nature', ingeniously arguing on the basis of Christianity's supposed pioneering of secularism itself. He asks rhetorically: 'Was it not Christianity before anything else that separated church and state?' And he proceeds to chastise Christians who appeal to a 'Christian state', thus thoroughly undermining the mission of the Church: 'does not every moment of your practical life brand your theory as a lie? Do you consider it wrong to appeal to the courts if you have been cheated? But the apostle writes that it is wrong.' Marx proceeds, in a manner relevant to contemporary invocations of how the spirit of religion should animate political laws, to dismantle the idea of a non-theocratic state that would somehow express the religious idea. Against the advocates of a Christian politics, he writes: 'It is the greatest irreligion, it is the arrogance of secular reason, to divorce the general spirit of religion from the actually existing religion; this separation of religion from its dogmas and institutions is tantamount to asserting that the general spirit of the law ought to prevail in the state irrespective of particular laws and positive legal institutions.'[62]

In Marx's later political career, however, the idea of a secular state voided of its religious character and not interfering in the religious lives of its subjects is no longer to be seen as the goal of criticism and emancipation, but merely as a necessary but insufficient 'transitional demand' on the way to overcoming the political limits of capitalism, and *a fortiori* of liberalism. This much is evident in the 1875 *Critique of the Gotha Programme*, where Marx upbraids the intellectuals of the Socialist Workers' Party of Germany for their timid remarks on 'freedom of conscience':

> If one should want, in this era of the *Kulturkampf*, to remind the liberals of their old catchwords, then surely it should only have been done in this form: Everyone should be free to relieve himself religiously as well as physically without the police sticking their noses in. But at this point the workers' party ought to have expressed its awareness that bourgeois

---

62 Marx, 'The Leading Article', 199–200.

'freedom of conscience' only means the toleration of every possible kind of *religious freedom of conscience*, while its own goal is rather the libera-tion of the conscience from all religious spookery. But it chooses not to go further than the 'bourgeois' level.[63]

The theoretical bases of this political stance were laid more than thirty years before, in Marx's critique of Bauer. Bauer chastises those Jews who wish to be emancipated as Jews for remaining at the level of religious priv-ilege (the demand for specific religious rights) and religious prejudice (the attempt to maintain what Bauer calls 'the powers of excommunication' consubstantial with the being of religion). But Bauer, in order to elimi-nate the 'religious opposition' between Jew and Christian, predicates the political emancipation of the Jew (and the Christian) on the emancipation from religion, on abolishing religion in the sense of radically 'privatizing' all religious privileges. It is at this point that Marx intervenes: 'Bauer asks the Jews: Do you from your standpoint have the right to demand *politi-cal emancipation?* We pose the question the other way around: Does the standpoint of *political* emancipation have the right to demand from the Jews the abolition of Judaism and from man the abolition of religion?'[64]

Marx's negative response, and his unique understanding of secular-ism, involves turning to the example of the 'free states of North America' as the testing ground for investigating what happens when 'the Jewish question lose[s] its *theological* significance and become[s] a truly *secular* question'. Where the state is no longer Christian and religious privilege is not inscribed in legislation, it becomes possible to confront Bauer's theses with a situation that supposedly presents their institutional reali-zation. It is only with reference to the American situation that we can ask, as Marx does: 'What is the relationship between *complete* political emancipation and religion?' The peculiar answer, still cause of much debate and investigation today, is that the politically emancipated North American free states are ones in which not only does religion exist but 'it exists in a *fresh* and *vigorous* form'. Consistently with Marx's overall

---

63   Karl Marx, 'Critique of the Gotha Programme', in *The First International and After: Political Writings*, Vol. 3, D. Fernbach (ed.), London: Penguin, 1974, 357–8.
64   Marx, *Early Writings*, 216.

methodology, the American case allows us to see how the persistence of religion, far from being the 'basis' of 'secular narrowness', is its 'phenomenon': 'We therefore explain religious restriction on the free citizens from the secular restriction they experience.'[65] The persistence of religion is for Marx a symptom which, in order to be elucidated, requires his distinction between political and human emancipation, between the secularization of the state and social liberation. Thus, 'religious weaknesses' are not to be criticized on their own ground but through a 'criticism of the political state'. It is this step which, according to Marx, Bauer is unable to take, being bound, like his post-Hegelian contemporaries, to a fundamentally theological framework.

In political emancipation, according to Marx's dialectical presentation, religion can persist, and indeed flourish (as it does in the American case), because it is ultimately the state which is 'emancipating itself from the *state religion*', and by the same token separating itself from the very civil society in which it tolerates, or indeed fosters, the continuation of private religion and private interests. '*Political* emancipation from religion is not complete and consistent emancipation from religion, because political emancipation is not the complete and consistent form of *human* emancipation.' A 'state can be a *free state* without man himself being a *free man*', not just because religion continues to be practised in private but also because freedom through the state is itself religious in form: 'Religion is precisely that: the devious acknowledgment of man, through an intermediary.'[66] This is the crux of Marx's argument against Bauer: the state, though it might transcend religious *content* by separating itself from any confessional determination, retains religious *form* by embodying the alienated freedom of man in something external to him. As he puts it: 'The perfected political state is by its nature the *species-life* of man in *opposition* to his material life. . . . Where the political state has attained its full degree of development man leads a double life, a life in heaven and a life on earth, not only in his mind, in his consciousness, but *in reality*.'[67] The private spirituality of atomized

---

65   Marx, *Early Writings*, 217. As noted above, in Marx's early writings this 'secular basis' is still understood in primarily political rather than socio-economic terms.
66   Ibid., 218.
67   Ibid., 220.

individuals in civil society is thus accompanied and compounded by the objective spirituality or transcendence (the real abstraction) of the secular state-form itself. Political emancipation 'neither abolishes nor tries to abolish man's *real* religiosity', because it both perpetuates religion at the level of private law (where it becomes 'the essence of *difference*') and spiritualizes human nature, estranging it into the transcendent domain of state sovereignty. Whence Marx's deeply counter-intuitive dialectical affirmation that true secularization – meaning emancipation from alien abstractions – can only be achieved through an unsparing practical criticism and overcoming of the liberal secular state, which, through a cunning of reason, turns out to be the formal realization of religious content:

> Indeed, the perfected Christian state is not the so-called *Christian* state which recognises Christianity as its foundation, as the state religion, and which therefore excludes other religions. The perfected Christian state is rather the *atheist* state, the *democratic* state, the state which relegates religion to the level of the other elements of civil society. The state which is still theological, which still officially professes the Christian faith, which still does not dare to declare itself a *state*, has not yet succeeded in expressing in *secular, human* form, in its *reality* as a state, the *human* basis of which Christianity is the exaggerated expression.[68]

Marx, in quasi-Hegelian vein, recognizes the momentous importance of the emergence of the democratic secular state, while simultaneously taking the opportunity to advocate the shift from the criticism of political theologies to a political criticism of the state-form itself. Is this to succumb to a dubious 'metaphoric identification of secular and theological phenomena',[69] to portray liberalism as the bearer of a fundamentally religious form of abstraction, whose apotheosis is to be found in the separation of state and civil society?

---

68   Ibid., 222.
69   Contrary to Breckman, I think that attention to Marx's theory of real abstractions allows us to see in his critique of the transcendent or 'religious' dimensions of liberalism and capitalism something more than 'metaphoric identification'. See Breckman, *Marx, the Young Hegelians, and the Origins of Radical Social Theory*, 294–5.

THE RELIGION OF EVERYDAY LIFE

While the form of Marx's critique of the Young Hegelians' critique of religion feeds into his mature critique of political economy, it is also true that the 'secular basis' will increasingly come to signify the mode of production and social intercourse, and only secondarily the state-form itself. Nonetheless, it is important to confront the charge that the link between the theological and the political-economic in Marx is merely metaphorical. As I've suggested, the correlation between seemingly secular and theological phenomena understood as instances of abstraction is not just pertinent to the state-form, it is in many respects determinant for Marx's overall understanding of capitalism. When Marx inquires into the elusive ontology of commodities, 'sensuous things which are at the same time suprasensible or social', he is forced to say that in order 'to find an analogy we must take flight into the misty realm of religion. There the products of the human brain appear as autonomous figures endowed with a life of their own, which enter into relations with each other and with the human race.'[70]

This autonomy, as Marx's analysis of commodity-fetishism demonstrates, goes much deeper than (and also conditions) the autonomy of the state that 'On the Jewish Question' had laid bare. Marx leaves behind the critique of the religious form taken by the modern state, in which man contemplates and is dominated by his own alienated species-being, to tackle the more insidious and intangible 'religion of everyday life'.[71] In this respect, and in spite of Marx's draining of real autonomy and real history from religion in *The German Ideology*, there is considerable truth to Derrida's comment about 'the absolute privilege that Marx always grants to religion, to ideology as religion, mysticism, or theology, in his analysis of ideology in general'[72] – if by privilege we understand the necessity of the religious analogy for grasping the process of autonomization that characterizes a society, that of capitalism, in which men are dominated by abstractions. This domination needs to move beyond the state-form and into the everyday realm of production, consumption and

---

70   Marx, *Capital: Volume 1*, 165.
71   This expression appears in Marx, *Capital: Volume 3*, 969.
72   Derrida, *Specters of Marx*, 185.

circulation, where men 'have already acted . . . before thinking'.[73] It is only thus – by tracking the emergence of real abstractions out of social relations – that the tradition of anti-theological criticism from which Marx emerged may be truly surpassed. This criticism was trapped by a fantasy of omnipotence; it thought that the mental critique of illusory ideas was sufficient to dispel them. As Marx wrote of Stirner: 'He forgets that he has only destroyed the fantastic and spectral form assumed by the idea of "Fatherland", etc., in the brain . . . but that he has still *not touched* these ideas, insofar as they express *actual* relations.'[74]

It is in terms of the domination of social life and its actual relations by seemingly autonomous abstractions that in *Capital* Marx employs the idea of fanaticism, to denote the subjectivity of a capitalist possessed by a drive to accumulate which eludes ordinary psychological under-standing: 'in so far as he is capital personified, his motivating force is not the acquisition and enjoyment of use-values, but the acquisition and augmentation of exchange-values. He is fanatically intent on the valorization of value; consequently he ruthlessly forces the human race to produce for production's sake.' Such fanaticism is for Marx 'respect-able', to the extent that it creates the conditions for its own overcom-ing. But it is also a fundamentally systemic fanaticism, a fanaticism that results from the abstract but compelling imperative to accumulate. Capitalist fanaticism lies beyond the individual psyche, in the 'imma-nent laws of capitalist production'.[75] To the extent that it is a matter of compulsive ritual rather than moral choice, it can be characterized as a quasi-religious fanaticism.[76]

This is why the project of moving from the criticism of Heaven to the criticism of Earth requires overcoming the liberal juxtaposition between the secular life of civil society and the fanatical propensity of religious belief, in order to attend to the religion of everyday life. Is this to say that a process of historical secularization of abstractions has

---

73   Marx, *Capital: Volume 1*, 181.
74   Marx, *The German Ideology*, 139.
75   Marx, *Capital: Volume 1*, 739.
76   On the capitalist as fanatic, see Marshall Berman, 'Freedom and Fetishism' [1963], in *Adventures in Marxism*, London: Verso, 1999, 42.

allowed capital to replace religion in its function, to transubstantiate religion into commodity-relations? This is the perspective wonderfully conveyed in *The Religion of Capital*, the 1887 satirical dramatization by Paul Lafargue, Marx's son-in-law, of an imaginary London Congress where the ruling classes of Europe meet to debate which forms of belief can best pacify labour unrest. The emblematic declaration is voiced by the 'great English statistician, Giffen':

> Now, then, the only religion that answers the needs of the moment is the religion of Capital. . . . Capital is the true, only and omnipotent God. He manifests Himself in all forms and guises. He is found in glittering gold and in stinking guano; in a herd of cattle and in a cargo of coffee; in brilliant stores that offer sacred literature for sale and bundles of porno-graphic etchings; in gigantic machines, made of hardest steel, and in elegant rubber goods. Capital is the God whom the whole world knows, sees, smells, tastes. He exists for all our senses. He is the only God that has yet to run into an atheist.[77]

This very insight was the object of a brilliant and beguiling fragment by Walter Benjamin, entitled 'Capitalism as Religion'.[78] In contem-porary theory, the idea of capitalism as a religion of everyday life has been consistently advocated by Slavoj Žižek. He has revisited, through a psychoanalytic prism, Marx's theory of commodity-fetishism, now conceived as the ground for a theory of the 'secular' endurance of belief, for instance in the 'faith in money-value' of which Marx speaks in Volume 3 of *Capital*. Žižek reads the predicament of Western capitalist societies as follows:

> Commodity fetishism (our belief that commodities are magical objects, endowed with an inherent metaphysical power) is not located in our mind, in the way we (mis)perceive reality, but in our social reality

---

77   Paul Lafargue, *La religion du Capital*, Paris: L'Aube, 2006, 13.
78   See the excellent discussion of Benjamin's text, alongside Weber, in Michael Löwy, 'Capitalism as Religion: Walter Benjamin and Max Weber', *Historical Materialism*, 17: 1 (2009).

itself. . . . If, once upon a time, we publicly pretended to believe, while deep inside us we were sceptics or even engaged in obscene mocking of our public beliefs, today we tend publicly to profess our sceptical/ hedonist/relaxed attitude, while inside us we remain haunted by beliefs and severe prohibitions.[79]

This position dovetails quite nicely with Benjamin's conviction that capitalism is a 'purely cultic religion' (the rituals of this 'utilitarian' cult include sale and purchase, investment, stock speculation, financial operations, and so on). Combined with his treatment of fundamentalism as a kind of perversion based on the ascription of objective truth to texts, freeing the adept from the tragic burden of faith, and with Marx's vision of the capitalist fanatic, Žižek's account of belief under capitalism suggests a peculiarly dialectical inversion in the relationship between the secular and the spiritual. The capitalist subject is the personification of an impersonal drive whose unconditional character can readily be regarded as fanatical; conversely, the fundamentalist subject demonstrates, in his most fanatical actions, a form of conviction whose reliance on 'objective' truth is modelled more on the certainties of science than on the tribulations of faith. This suggests that far from being the last and most extreme remnant of ideology in a post-ideological and post-historical age, fanaticism also exists in a complex ideological force-field within which the difference between the secular and the religious provides only limited, if at times significant, orientation.

---

79 Slavoj Žižek, *How to Read Lacan*, 93–4. Derrida defends the ineliminability of faith in 'Marx & Sons', 255.

6

The Cold War and the Messiah: On Political Religion

Meditating on the infinite may be a religious activity, so may writing a cheque, eating corpses, copulating, listening to a thumping sermon on hell fire, examining one's conscience, painting a picture, growing a beard, licking leprous sores, tying the body into knots, a dogged faith in human rationality – there is no human activity which cannot assume religious significance.

Kenelm Burridge, *New Heaven, New Earth*

Paul is a fanatic! Paul is a zealot, a Jewish zealot, and for him this step is a tremendous one. The spiritual costs that he must bear he doesn't take upon himself for the sake of some blather in the spirit of this great *nomos* liberalism. He is totally illiberal; of that I am certain. . . . Sure, Paul is also universal, but by virtue of the 'eye of the needle' of the crucified one, which means: transvaluation of all the values of this world.

Jacob Taubes, *The Political Theology of Paul*

The faith is not political and politics is not a religion.

Benedict XVI

The secular critic will level the charge of fanaticism at any political behaviour infused by the absolute unconditionality and unmediated abstraction which he ascribes to religious (and therefore irrational) forms of behaviour. The religious commentator will find the sources of fanaticism in the perilous secularization of the modern world, in a nihilism that unleashes hubristic claims allegedly alien from true faith.

But what happens when these otherwise incompatible forms of anti-fanaticism come together, united by common enemies? A particularly instructive instance of both the cross-purposes and the strange alliances elicited by the problem of fanaticism is to be found in the tendency to treat twentieth-century 'totalitarian' movements (Italian Fascism, German Nazism, Soviet Communism) as secular or political religions – an appellation designed, among other things, to identify the fanatical mindset of their adherents. Where Marx had enjoined us to think of religion within the broader purview of ideology, this trend demands that we consider extreme or illiberal political ideologies as types or perversions of religion.

THE ISLAM OF THE TWENTIETH CENTURY

From the 1920s, it became common for opponents of totalitarianism to account for its radical novelty in terms of the introduction, into an otherwise secularized, deliberative or liberal political realm, of forms of conviction and behaviour of a religious sort.[1] Whether their absolute claims were deemed to trespass onto the spiritual territory of the churches, or to destroy the limits constitutive of liberal democracy, these new political religions seemed at once to advance lethal threats to established faiths, and to revoke a process of secularization that had shunted the totalizing claims of unconditional conviction beyond the pale of politics. The Machiavellian or Hobbesian breaks that had signalled the birth of the modern science of politics through the expulsion of faith and sacred authority were threatened with reversal. The 'religious' element in these new movements could be understood in terms of the passions they elicited, their types of organization, or their ultimate aims.

---

1   As Emilio Gentile notes, the notion of political religion had been in circulation since the French Revolution. He records its use by Condorcet, and later by Lincoln. Emilio Gentile, *Le religioni della politica. Fra democrazie e totalitarismi*, 2nd ed, Bari: Laterza, 2007, 5. An important precursor here is Vilfredo Pareto, who in *Les systèmes socialistes* (1901) referred to socialism as 'the great religion of modern times', and in his seminal theory of elites reflected on the organizational parallels between socialism and militant ecclesiastical movements, its affinity with the temporality of millenarianism, and its similar emergence from moments of crisis. See Vilfredo Pareto, *The Rise and Fall of Elites*, New Brunswick, NJ: Transaction, 2006, 53–4, as well as his discussion of the importance of religious sentiment in the lower classes during revolutions (40).

For Christian critics it was the trespass into spiritual interiority carried out by these ersatz political faiths that was most threatening. It nullified the separation between the spiritual and the temporal that made compromises with authoritarian but pro-religious regimes possible, and at times attractive. In addition to concrete anti-religious measures (considerably less present under fascism), politics as faith threatened to displace religion. Nikolai Berdyaev, expelled from the USSR in the famous 'philosophy steamer', wrote of the 'switching over of religious energies' effected by Russian communism, whose spiritual taproots he located in the nihilist and apocalyptic strains of Russian spirituality. Like many advocates of the political religion thesis, Berdyaev relied on an anthropological presupposition, namely that man is a 'religious animal' whose propensity to devotion can consequently be exploited for non-religious ends.[2] Focusing on the object of faith rather than its affective character, the Italian Christian-Democrat priest and politician Don Luigi Sturzo spoke in this respect of *statolatria*, the idolatry of the state, reviving the traditional Catholic opposition to heathen cults and false prophets, while 1930s papal encyclicals castigated 'neo-paganism'.[3]

Such protestations were frequently based on the notion that behind the emergence of these totalizing anti-religious religions of politics lay the neglect of organized spirituality (sometimes referred to as *theophobia*) and the deification of Man, as well as a kind of dialectic of Enlightenment in which the undermining of Christian transcendence had opened the door to an unprecedented immanent irrationality. The total politicization of existence was, such critics felt, tantamount to soul-death. Secular

---

2   Nikolai Berdyaev, *The Origin of Russian Communism*, trans. R. M. French, Ann Arbor: University of Michigan Press, 1960, 171, 160.

3   Sturzo's contention that political religions are 'the abusive exploitation of human religious sentiment' plays an important role in a recent cantankerous and bullishly Catholic popular history of the relation between politics and religion in the twentieth century: Michael Burleigh, *Sacred Causes: Religion and Politics from the European Dictators to Al-Qaida*, London: Harper Collins, 2006, xi. Burleigh, who dwells on the organizational analogy (calling Russian revolutionaries 'a counter-community of the estranged' and quoting Semyon Frank's estimation of the Bolsheviks as 'militant monks of the nihilistic religion of earthly contentment'), pointedly refers to Soviet communism as 'the first illegitimate brother of religion to assume political power and to demonstrate the horrors of applied rationality' (37).

critiques of the total movements of the interwar period, not preoccupied with the defence of a proper domain of the spirit, were more likely to revive the traditional arsenal of the Enlightenment critique of fanaticism, in which 'religion' stands in for a combination of iron discipline, intolerance and unreason. In a different register than Christian critics, they focused on the fusion of two strands of human experience that the secular West was supposed to have kept separate. One of the more striking dimensions of this analysis and attack on the political religions was the recurrence of the figure of Islam as a cipher for the totalizing fusion of the political and the religious.

In a variation on the parallel explored by Hegel and others, Bertrand Russell wrote of Bolshevism in 1920 that it combined, in a radically new admixture, 'the characteristics of the French Revolution with those of the rise of Islam'. He linked these two political religions, contrasting them with the 'personal religions' of Christianity and Buddhism, in the following manner: 'Mohammedanism and Bolshevism are practical, social, unspiritual, concerned to win the empire of this world.'[4] The stress here is on religion as a worldly motivational, organizational and martial force, along the lines of Élie Halévy's observation that the 'age of tyrannies' was dominated by the '*étatisation* of thought' and the 'organization of enthusiasm'.[5] Emphasizing manipulation over organization, Keynes would also regard Leninism as a new religion, marked by 'zeal and intolerance', and, reviving Voltaire's link between fanaticism and hypocrisy, conviction and suggestion, declared that 'Lenin is a Mohammed and not a Bismarck'.[6] In his sprawling 1949 treatment of social and speculative sources of the Soviet secular religion, *Sociologie du communisme*, Jules Monnerot called communism the 'Islam of the

---

4   Bertrand Russell, *The Practice and Theory of Bolshevism*, London: George Allen & Unwin, 1920, 5, 114. Russell's definition of Bolshevism as a religion is firmly in the lineage of Enlightenment anti-fanaticism.

5   Élie Halévy, *L'Ère des tyrannies. Études sur le socialisme et la guerre*, Paris: Gallimard, 1990. It was in his 1939 review of Halévy's book, now published in this volume, that Raymond Aron first discussed political religions (270).

6   Quoted in Gentile, *Le religioni della politica*, 63. Catholic critics also weighed in. Sturzo, in his *Politica e morale* (1938), commenting on the Lenin mausoleum, wrote that 'for the Russians he has become a secular Mohammed'. Quoted in Gentile, 151.

twentieth century' – since, like its Oriental precursor, it too tried to join a universal state with a universal doctrine, while their shared overcoming of nationality meant that both were movements unchecked by borders, and thus globally threatening. Accordingly, 'the communist is a religious fanatic serving an expanding Empire which tends toward world domination'; the difference between totalitarianism and tyranny is the former's 'sacralization of the political; it presents itself as a secular and conquering religion of the "Islamic" type: lack of distinction between the political, religious and economic, concentrated and, above all, undefined power'.[7] This peculiarly anti-historical analogy, which had the advantage of presenting the Russian Revolution as a more Oriental than European phenomenon, was sufficiently plastic to be applied to Nazi Germany as well as to Asiatic communism. Thus, the Protestant theologian Karl Barth declared that it was 'impossible to understand National Socialism unless we see it in fact as a *new Islam*, its myth as a new Allah, and Hitler as this new Allah's Prophet'.[8] Carl Jung echoed him: 'We do not know whether Hitler is going to found a new Islam. He is already on the way; he is like Mohammed. The emotion in Germany is Islamic, warlike and Islamic. They are all drunk with a wild man.'[9] In today's popular discourse, the resurgence of the political religion thesis, alongside disarmingly sterile 'debates' on God and atheism, seems difficult to disentangle from a historical moment that has led anxious right-wing commentators to invert Monnerot's line and speak of Islam as 'the communism of the twenty-first century'.[10]

Whatever the cogency and limitations of the political religion thesis (a discussion which is part of a broader, 'post-Marxist' re-legitimation of the concept of totalitarianism in the wake of a return to cultural and

---

7 Jules Monnerot, *Sociologie du communisme*, Paris: Gallimard, 1949, 21, 380.

8 Karl Barth, *The Church and the Political Problem of Our Day*, New York: Scribner, 1939, 43.

9 Quoted in Richard Stiegmann-Gall, 'Nazism and the Revival of Political Religion Theory', *Totalitarian Movements and Political Religions*, 5, 3 (2004), 378. He writes of 'a strong orientalising tendency in contemporary [to Nazism] Christian apologia'.

10 See Christopher Caldwell, *Reflections on the Revolution in Europe: Immigration, Islam and the West*, London: Allen Lane, 2009, 217.

ideal explanations as against political-economic ones) its resilience
testifies to our continued preoccupation with the menace of fanaticism,
understood as a form of political conviction that is radically incompatible with reasonable norms of action and deliberation. Though atheists
and Christians, liberals and conservatives can all be found pejoratively
referring to secular or political religion, the basic features of this concept
resonate with the long tradition of anti-fanatical discourse. Like fanaticism broadly construed, political religions are marked by an enthusiasm for abstraction, by some drive to unfettered totality (in the guise
of expansion, but in the case of communism also of borderless universality), and by forms of radical organizational unity (in the form of
parties, movements, states) that make them into *ecclesiae militans*, militant churches.[11] Like theories of totalitarianism, the political religion
approach latches onto these formal dimensions while neglecting actual
content, social composition and explicit doctrine, and at the expense of
of detailed causal and conjunctural analysis.[12] Formal likenesses are
privileged over political trajectories and contexts.

Theorists of political religion tend to assume a vision of human nature
which includes some kind of disposition to the religious as a basic feature of
being human. They also rely to varying degrees on philosophies of history
in which the idea of secularization plays a prominent role – though some
advocates of this approach view psychological attunement to the sacred
as pathological, others as a blessing, while secularization is perceived by
some as a baleful dynamic, by others as a conquest to be defended. I want
to explore this entanglement of anthropology and history by looking at
different perspectives on the religions of the political, and specifically at
the manner in which, in continuity with previous discourses on fanaticism,
the very idea of political religion serves to disqualify any kind of politics of
conviction as the ersatz effect of fanatical religiosity.

---

11   The organizational analogy was explicitly employed by Hitler himself, who
declared that 'It was with Himmler that the SS became this extraordinary militia,
devoted to an idea, faithful unto death. In Himmler I see our Ignatius of Loyola.' Quoted
in Domenico Losurdo, 'Towards a Critique of the Category of Totalitarianism',
Historical Materialism, 12: 2 (2004), 46.
12   For this criticism, with specific reference to Nazi Germany, see Stiegmann-Gall,
'Nazism and the Revival of Political Religion Theory'.

Returning to these questions today is warranted by the resurgence of those views of politics as religion that emerged in Europe during the interwar period and then established themselves, with more or less exclusive focus on communism and the Soviet Union, with the full ideological flowering of the Cold War shortly after the end of World War Two. John Gray begins his *Black Mass*, instructively subtitled *Apocalyptic Religion and the Death of Utopia* – a book that brackets together as 'political religions' neo-liberalism and Bolshevism, Islamist terrorism and neo-conservative democratic warmongering – with the following statement: 'Modern politics is a chapter in the history of religion.' His is a history in which the utopian projects whose 'debris' we observe today, 'though they were framed in secular terms that denied the truth of religion were in fact vehicles for religious myths'.[13]

This theory of secular form as a vehicle for religious content derives from Cohn's *Pursuit of the Millennium*.[14] Writing in the midst of the Cold War, and in contrast to the sympathetic treatment of millenarianism by the likes of Hobsbawm, Cohn sought to unearth the atavism at the core of modern totalitarian movements, identifying the mediaeval marriage of surplus populations and apocalyptic prophets as the dark precursor of both Soviet Communism and National Socialism. The result was a trans-historical concept of revolutionary fanaticism, covering violent mass movements that sought a salvation both 'terrestrial and collective', movements whose politics were boundless and beyond reform.[15] For Cohn, this apocalyptic politics is marked by a refusal of representation and mediation; it aims at a total, unanimous community, devoid of internal strife.[16] Key to this bold short-circuit across the ages,

---

13 John Gray, *Black Mass: Apocalyptic Religion and the Death of Utopia*, London: Allen Lane, 2007, 1. The notion of vehicle allows Gray to ride roughshod over historical difference, such as when he argues that Zoroaster is 'the ultimate source of faith-based violence that has broken out again and again throughout Western history' (10).
14 On Gray's reliance on Cohn, see Critchley, 'Mystical Anarchism', 277–85.
15 Cohn, *The Pursuit of the Millennium*, 308.
16 Showing the resilience and sometimes subterranean effects of the idea of political religion and the discourse on fanaticism, this historical critique of a politics of total transparency is incorporated into Ernesto Laclau's post-Marxist deconstruction of the idea of communism. See Ernesto Laclau, *New Reflections on the Revolution of Our Time*, London: Verso, 1990, 3–85.

with its symptomatic use of analogies impervious to massive historical discrepancies, is the idea of a basic continuity in the structure of feeling of apocalyptic militancy, whether in explicitly religious or deceptively modern and technocratic guise. A 'subterranean current' links all these movements which strive to purify the world by destroying the agents of corruption. In organizational terms, the modern specificity of party and bureaucratic organization is ignored in order to seize and reveal the fanatical kernel, turning the likes of Müntzer's League of the Elect into the secret prologue of the SS or the NKVD. For Cohn, regardless of historical context or institutional structure, the pattern is the same. Prophetic visions lead to the formation a group of adepts, 'a true proto-type of a modern totalitarian party: a restlessly dynamic and utterly ruthless group which, obsessed by the apocalyptic phantasy and filled with the conviction of its own infallibility, set itself infinitely above the rest of humanity and recognized no claims save that of its own supposed mission'. A millennial promise uttered by a prophet to a marginalized and heterogeneous mass – this remains the 'source of the giant fanaticisms which in our day have convulsed the world'.[17]

Though Gray reproduces Cohn's link between mediaeval and modern millenarianism, he ratchets up the claims for the continuity between the absolutist and apocalyptic claims of religion and the utopian designs of politics. In order for his narrative to include everyone from Trotsky to Dick Cheney, Hitler to Bin Laden, Gray must generate an unstable amalgam between the religious critique of political religion – which depicts Enlightenment rationalism as a hubristic attempt to supplant true faith – and the secular critique of political religion, for which the mere fact of belonging to the category of religion is already a mark of irrationality. Scepticism, fallibilism and realism are here the opponents of both apocalyptic religion and any kind of secular utopianism that presumes to transform human nature or remake society. The claim that the historical break signalled by the Enlightenment is already infused with Christian messianism makes it possible to conclude that the whole revolutionary tradition, from

---

17   Cohn, *The Pursuit of the Millennium*, 319.

Jacobinism to the Bolsheviks and onwards, is merely 'a secular reincarnation of early Christian beliefs'.

When Gray writes that 'modern revolutionary movements are a continuation of religion by other means', his grounding assumption is clear. There exists a basic affective and anthropological drive or function known as 'religion', characterized by absolute certainty, invariant across wildly different, genealogically distant and geographically unconnected phenomena of militancy. In this respect, an argument like Gray's hearkens back to the generic definition of religiosity that underlay Gustave Le Bon's theory of crowds. There, Le Bon discussed religion in the following terms:

> A person is not religious solely when he worships a divinity, but when he puts all the resources of his mind, the complete submission of his will, and the whole-souled ardour of fanaticism at the service of a cause or an individual who becomes the goal and guide of his thoughts and actions. Intolerance and fanaticism are the necessary accompaniments of the religious sentiment. They are inevitably displayed by those who believe themselves in the possession of the secret of earthly or eternal happiness. These two characteristics are to be found in all men grouped together when they are inspired by a conviction of any kind. The Jacobins of the Reign of Terror were at bottom as religious as the Catholics of the Inquisition, and their cruel ardour proceeded from the same source.[18]

This univocity of fanaticism in secular utopias and apocalyptic religions allows Gray, who views philosophies of history as theodicies in disguise, to depict the irreligious political extremism of the twentieth century and the recent rise of religious fundamentalism as two modalities of what is basically the same pathology – the millenarian conviction that human nature may be transformed and the Good brought to earth.

More than with Cohn, whose account did not impugn the Enlightenment, Gray resonates with another influential purveyor of a variant of the political religion thesis, J. L. Talmon. Talmon, for whom

---

18   Gustave Le Bon, *The Crowd: A Study of the Popular Mind*, New York: Macmillan, 1896, 64.

Rousseau rather than Müntzer is the villain, traces the origins of what he calls modern 'totalitarian democracy' to the 'political messianism' of eighteenth-century philosophy, and its belief in the worldly realization of an egalitarian society founded on the idea of a rationally accessible natural order. The continuous arc that he traces is shorter than Gray's, having its intellectual origins in the lead-up to the French Revolution.[19] The ideological urgency of the book, like Cohn's both a scholarly study and a Cold War screed, is explicit. Not visionary hallucinations or divine intoxication, but confidence in the intelligibility and feasibility of a rational society, is what for Talmon marks out a democratic and totalitarian messianism. Tapping into the tradition of conservative condemnation of the French Revolution, which he shares with Gray, Talmon juxtaposes the two strands of eighteenth-century thought: an 'empirical' liberalism founded on notions of trial and error, open to the wisdom of custom and habit, and respectful of durable institutions, versus the totalitarianism implicit in any politics of human emancipation that neglects concrete differences and disdains pragmatic obstacles. Accordingly, if 'empiricism is the ally of freedom and the doctrinaire spirit is the friend of totalitarianism, the idea of man as an abstraction, independent of the historic groups to which he belongs, is likely to become a powerful vehicle of totalitarianism'.[20] In Talmon's case, however, the continuity is not quite total. The persistence of a transcendent dimension in properly religious messianic movements means that they don't attain the extremes of violence proper to 'secular messianic monism', whose vocation is to scorn every boundary, transgress every limit. What's more, the social conditions of modernity mean that political messianism does not just attract volatile and heterogeneous groups of followers; it is animated by 'popular enthusiasm'. Revolutionary and totalitarian democracy carry a threat that mediaeval millenarianism did not.

But the lesson drawn remains the same as Gray's, and more importantly, the same as that of their forebear Burke: that the study of political

---

19   As he writes, 'the modern secular religion of totalitarian democracy has had unbroken continuity as a sociological force for over a hundred and fifty years'. J. L. Talmon, *The Origins of Totalitarian Democracy*, London: Sphere Books, 1970, 8.
20   Ibid., 4.

religion as the modern incarnation of fanaticism teaches us the importance of limits in politics. Whether apocalyptic or rationalist in origin, the very idea that the world can be changed through human action, and that abstractions such as equality can be forced into social being, is a recipe for disaster. As Gray summarizes: 'The use of inhumane methods to achieve impossible ends is the essence of revolutionary utopianism.'[21] Against neo-conservative exhortations to export American freedom, Gray prefers the counsel of the 'Old Right', to affirm human frailty, political conventions and customs, and to abjure any 'apocalyptic', unrealistic attempt to realize the Good and enforce 'progress' in the face of inevitably finite and fallible circumstances. The latter represents, in his words, 'Enlightenment fundamentalism'.

On this reading, political religion, understood as the reciprocal corruption of belief by political instrumentality and of political realism by apocalyptic expectations, is anchored by what has been rightly termed an 'implausibly abstract' understanding of history, 'inexorably linked to a version of intellectual cause and political effect whereby the unyielding abstractions of Enlightenment rationalism become the ideological cause of revolutionary violence and terror'.[22] Accounts such as Cohn's, Talmon's and Gray's offer meta-historical narratives, broadly linked to theories of secularization, which ultimately evacuate history and politics of specificity, while analogies and metaphors are passed

---

21   Gray, *Black Mass*, 18.

22   These expressions are taken from two compelling, panoramic treatments of the current state of the political religion debate by Richard Shorten, which have influenced my own account: 'The Status of Ideology in the Return of Political Religion Theory', *Journal of Political Ideologies*, 12: 2 (2007), 183; 'The Enlightenment, Communism and Political Religion: Reflections on a Misleading Trajectory', *Journal of Political Ideologies*, 8: 1 (2003), 23. Shorten discusses Gray, briefly but pungently, alongside Tzvetan Todorov in 'The Status of Ideology', 168–9. He enumerates the shortcomings of the Enlightenment-as-secular-religion thesis – advocated before Gray by Carl Becker (in *The Heavenly City of the Eighteenth-Century Philosophers*), Talmon and Simon Schama (in *Citizens*), as well as by Michael Oakeshott (who opposed the politics of scepticism to the politics of faith) and Isaiah Berlin – in 'The Enlightenment, Communism and Political Religion', 24–7. On Becker's influence on Gray, see Malcolm Bull's review of *Black Mass*, 'The Catastrophist', *London Review of Books*, 29: 21 (2007).

off as explanations.[23] Their object of criticism is a political enthusiasm both abstract and absolute. Ironically, for all of their suspicion towards the radical Enlightenment, the terminology of religion – millennium, apocalypse, messianism – is used to disqualify, rather than to explore the structures of belief and ritual that may underlie political practice. Such positions, which often accuse the Enlightenment of a perverse sacralization of politics, symptomatically oscillate between finding the source of twentieth-century evils in excesses of faith or in excesses of reason, and mostly come to rest in that familiar Burkean motif whereby it is faith in reason, or rational fanaticism, which is the principal culprit.

Whether we seek its origins in political disorientation, ideological immaturity or the anxiety generated by contemporary forms of violence and conflict, there is something quite remarkable about the return of Cold War nostrums, essentially unchanged, into the contemporary public arena, at a time when – whatever one's views of the original critiques of totalitarianism – rigid blinkers are required to treat the present as a mere repetition of the struggle of the 'free world against Totalitarianism', or, more grandiosely, of scepticism versus absolute conviction, or reasonable faith versus idolatrous fanaticism.[24] Much of the recent resurgence of the notion of political religion has been dismayingly derivative, especially when it comes to popularizing treatments aiming to draw lessons for present predicaments from the interwar and Cold War literature on totalitarian movements. This is all the more reason to revisit the original polemical context of the political religion debate and to consider the uses of fanaticism within it.

---

23   Shorten, 'The Status of Ideology', 171. Given Shorten's rather devastating treatment of the return of political religion theory, and the latter's passing off of similes for causalities, I'm less than sympathetic to his attempt to revise that same theory, turning it into a dimension of ideological analysis specifically concerned with the practice of treating certain entities or concepts as sacred, immune from criticism or amendment (what he terms 'decontestation'). This still seems to leave the history out, generating merely formalistic or functionalist typologies.

24   We also can't disregard the institutional and generational continuity that ties ideological Cold Warriors to present propagandists for the 'war on terror'. I owe this point to Benjamin Noys. That said, attention to these sociological factors does not exhaust the question of how and why the language of the Cold War still has such purchase in public and academic spheres.

ARENDT'S RETORT

Given the close relation between the idea of totalitarianism and theories of political religion, with their frequently shared tendency to emphasize formal, ideal-typical analogies over specific historical and material trajectories, one might superficially expect Hannah Arendt – the most respected philosophical advocate of the idea of totalitarianism, and herself a critic of the zealous drift of the French Revolution – to have had some sympathy for the political religion thesis. On the contrary, her opposition to the idea of political religion was vehement, never more so than in her lecture 'Religion and Politics'.[25] Testifying to the ideological force-field into which Arendt was stepping, it was originally delivered at a Harvard University conference entitled 'Is the Struggle Between the Free World and Communism Basically Religious?', held in 1953, at the very end of the Korean war. The call for papers had originated from the French liberal philosopher Raymond Aron, whose emphasis ever since the late 1930s on communism as a 'secular religion' – displacing transcendent faiths and promising earthly salvation – had done much to shape the debate. The essay was then published in the journal *Confluence*, edited at that time by none other than Henry Kissinger.

The political motivation of Arendt's repudiation of the political religion approach is clear. Prolonging a critical line that she had employed in numerous texts – chiding other Cold Warriors for their ideological attachment to anti-Stalinism and not sparing those 'ex-Communists' who, armed with the dubious authority of conversion, now sought to defend the Free World with the same zeal that they had previously reserved for Stalin – Arendt stressed the need to maintain a fundamental asymmetry in the Cold War. To congeal freedom into an entity to be defended, like a kind of civic if Christianized counter-religion opposed to the secular religion of communism, was for her a recipe for disaster. 'Confronted with a full-fledged ideology', she admonished, 'our

---

25   Some of the themes of this essay were anticipated in 1950 in a brief response to a *Partisan Review* questionnaire, asking important thinkers and writers for their view on 'the new turn toward religion among intellectuals and the growing disfavor with which secular attitudes and perspectives are now regarded'. See Hannah Arendt, 'Religion and the Intellectuals', in *Essays in Understanding*, 228–31.

greatest danger is to counter it with an ideology of our own. If we try to inspire public-political life once more with "religious passion" or to use religion as a means of political distinctions, the result may very well be the transformation and perversion of religion into an ideology and the corruption of our fight against totalitarianism by a fanaticism which is utterly alien to the very essence of freedom.'[26]

For Arendt, who was understandably if problematically attached to the idea that the American political tradition was innocent of fanaticism,[27] the notion of political freedom, which she deemed alien to religious thought, was closely bound up with a world devoid of religious sanction and dogmatic certainty; the creation of an ideology of freedom, and, even worse, a religious ideology of freedom, could not but trouble her. Her ambivalence in this regard is instructive, for in many ways her attempt to identify a radical core within the American constitutional and revolutionary tradition, especially when it operated with threadbare anti-Jacobin stereotypes, lent succour to this same (Cold War) ideology. Despite Arendt's intriguing turn to the 'lost tradition' of revolutionary and workers' councils, her fidelity to American republicanism and her polemic against the French Revolution led to philosophical apologetics for a 'free world' whose actual practice was, for many of those on the receiving end, synonymous with cruelty and dispossession.[28]

The targets of Arendt's criticism were anti-communist comrades in arms. Her friend Waldemar Gurian had long been an advocate of the notion of communism as a 'social and political secular religion'. He had even coined the term 'ideocracy' (later employed by conservative historians of the USSR like Malia and Besançon) to designate the manner in which doctrinal laws of historical change, monopolized by

---

26 Hannah Arendt, 'Religion and Politics', in *Essays in Understanding*, 384.
27 In a letter to Jaspers from January 1946, she refers the political atmosphere of the US as 'immune from fanaticism'. Quoted in Enzo Traverso, *Il totalitarismo*, Milano: Bruno Mondadori, 2002, 90.
28 It is striking to see a thinker who made such an important contribution to the study of imperialism with the second part of *Origins*, ignore the historical record so wantonly when it comes to American expansionism and power politics: for instance when she speaks of the US as a polity that 'has withstood all temptations, despite strong and ugly racial prejudices in its society, to play the game of nationalist and imperialist politics'. Hannah Arendt, 'Rand School Lecture', in *Essays in Understanding*, 224.

the Party, took the place of God in Christianity.[29] For Arendt, who emphasized the need to take ideologies at their word, such claims ignored the fact that communism 'never tries to answer religious questions specifically', and that, unlike the tragic atheism explored by Kierkegaard and Dostoevsky, it had left behind the secular condition of doubt which lent modern faith its specific tonality.[30] Her two main targets were the German émigré and conservative political philosopher, Eric Voegelin, and the French social theorist Jules Monnerot. They represented for Arendt the two main strands of the political religion debate: the first explained the emergence of ersatz religions through a conservative narrative of secularization; the second relied on a social anthropology of the sacred to present totalitarian movements as usurpers of deep-rooted religious functions.[31]

Voegelin had been a pioneer in this debate, with his 1938 essay *The Political Religions*. Citing the example of the Egyptian pharaohs, he had brought attention to the religious, even mystical, dimension of the state prior to the unstable Christian separation between the City of God and the City of Man, Christ and Caesar, the holy and the temporal. Religion consisted in ascribing to an entity the status of *realissimum*, an uncontestable core around which all beings and behaviours pivoted.[32]

---

29   Berdyaev also speaks of 'ideocracy' when he accuses Russian communism of being 'one of the transformations of the Platonic utopia'. Berdyaev, *The Origin of Russian Communism*, 168. For a critique of Malia's interpretation of Soviet communism as ideocratic from within the camp of theorists of totalitarianism, see Claude Lefort, *Complications: Communism and the Dilemmas of Democracy*, trans. J. Bourg, New York: Columbia University Press, 2007.

30   The aim of this was of course not to defend communism, but rather to exacerbate its difference: 'To call this totalitarian ideology a religion is not only an entirely undeserved compliment; it also makes us overlook that Bolshevism, though it grew out of Western history, no longer belongs in the same tradition of doubt and secularity, and that its doctrine as well as its actions have opened a veritable abyss between the free world and the totalitarian parts of the globe.' Arendt, 'Religion and Politics', 371. These arguments are rehearsed in her review of Gurian's book: 'Understanding Communism', in *Essays in Understanding*, 363–7.

31   These broadly match the two approaches singled out by Shorten in 'The Status of Ideology in the Return of Political Religion Theory'.

32   Eric Voegelin, *The Political Religions*, in *The Collected Works of Eric Voegelin*, *Volume 5: Modernity Without Restraint*, Columbia and London: University of Missouri Press, 2000, 30–3.

The 'inner-worldly religions' decapitated the system of transcendence and displaced this eminently real status onto earthly entities, 'sacralizing' them – to use an expression from Emilio Gentile. What remained was the political structure already inhering in the religious symbolism of emanation, hierarchy, unity, evil, apocalypse and domination, as well as in notions such as *corpus mysticum* and *sacrum imperium*. As 'the Western ecclesia dissolves into political subentities', religiosity is at one and the same time censored and displaced, re-emerging, most clearly, in the mystical body of the *Volk* and the sacred empire of the *Reich*. In Voegelin's early work, as Arendt summarized, 'all political authority has a religious origin, and . . . politics itself is necessarily religious'.[33]

In his later series of lectures, *The New Science of Politics*, Voegelin returned to this theme but inscribed it within a much bolder theory of history. Now, the struggle against the totalitarian political religions was coded as the millennial battle between an order based on faith and transcendence and a Gnosticism which sought to 'immanentize the eschaton', that is, to politicize the idea of revelation and apocalypse – a theme we've already encountered in the likes of Cohn and Gray. This is not a simple tale of secularization understood as the fading of religious belief from the social and political world. With 'the end of political theology in Orthodox Christianity' – in other words, the theological retreat from the idea that spirituality could be directly represented by political powers, fusing Church and Empire – the temporal sphere was for Voegelin de-divinized, in a kind of intra-Christian secularism. It was not until the social turmoil of the twelfth century, in the apocalyptic narratives of Joachim of Fiore (an important if subterranean influence on Müntzer), that, Voegelin argues, the social and political world was again infused with religious meaning, drawing on the millenarian resources of Christian heresy, which, by way of shorthand, he calls Gnosticism.[34] Political religion is thus

---

33 Arendt, 'Religion and Politics', 387, n. 10.
34 Aron echoed this notion of Gnosticism in an essay originally written in a Festschrift for Voegelin. See Raymond Aron, 'Remarques sur la gnose léniniste', in *Machiavel et les tyrannies modernes*, Paris: Éditions de Fallois, 1993.

placed within a historical narrative that sees the 'resurgence of the eschatology of the realm'[35] – with its proto-political symbols of the three ages, its leader or prophet, and its brotherhood – as a crucial element in a fundamentally malevolent modernity.

Voegelin, for whom the liberal opponents of the political religions of Nazism and Communism are merely suffering from a milder strain of Gnosticism, thinks that the very structure of modern politics is inseparable from this 'new eschatology'. We must, he writes, 'recognize the essence of modernity as the growth of Gnosticism'.[36] Even more peremptory is his link between liberalism and totalitarianism under the aegis of progress: 'Totalitarianism, defined as the existential rule of Gnostic activists, is the end form of progressive civilization . . . [the] journey's end of the Gnostic search for a civil theology'.[37] Voegelin's epochal polemic repeats many of the enduring themes of the critique of fanaticism. Above all it targets the idea that history itself is intelligible, and therefore an object of calculated, progressive action, along with the related idea that human nature can be changed. Echoing Burke, resistance to re-divinization is understood as both a defence of transcendent faith and a call for political realism, under which human history cannot be the object of novelty or truth. When the fulfilment that Christianity relegated to the end-time becomes inner-worldly, in an 'immanent hypostasis of the eschaton', we are confronted by a 'theoretical fallacy': 'Things are not things, nor do they have essences, by arbitrary declaration. The course of history as a whole is not an object of experience; history has no eidos [overarching ideal unity] because the course of history extends into the unknown future. The meaning of history, thus, is an illusion; and this illusionary eidos is created by treating a symbol of faith as if it were a proposition concerning an object of immanent experience.'[38] In one sense, this is a classic, even somewhat Kantian, epistemological

---

35   Eric Voegelin, *The New Science of Politics*, Chicago: The University of Chicago Press, 1952, 110.
36   Ibid., 126.
37   Ibid., 132, 163.
38   Ibid., 120.

critique of fanaticism as the mistaking of the empirical for the transcendental. And yet it is precisely pitted against the dialectic of political action, social causality and historical teleology that Kant tried to defend, and which he bequeathed to Hegel and then Marx. We can also note the paradoxical predicament of enemies of historical understandings of emancipation like Voegelin, who must themselves create philosophies of history against the philosophy of history.

In Arendt's view, any such account is itself based on a mistaken understanding of secularization, and specifically on the illegitimate passage from the recognition that authority was historically bound up with religion to the idea that 'the concept of authority is itself of a religious nature'. Though Arendt doesn't explore Voegelin's anti-liberal and anti-totalitarian theory of Gnosticism, it is clear that she is not willing to draw any epochal or civilizational lessons from the bare fact, as she puts it, that 'religious creeds and institutions have no publicly binding authority and that, conversely, political life has no religious sanction'. To suppose that this absence of sanction must turn into a disastrous hubris, into the divinization of History and Man, is a presumption she can't accept, precisely because – and this is where metahistorical and anthropological theories of political religion converge – it would imply that political life must in some sense or another be subordinated to a religious function.

It is this idea which is Arendt's main target. With a characteristic suspicion of the social sciences, she takes to task an understanding of communism that would ignore its historical and political substance, its specific conditions of emergence, in order to view it in functional terms, as an instance of, or substitute for, the generic category of religion. 'The confusion', she writes, 'arises partly from the particular viewpoint of sociologists who – methodically ignoring chronological order, location of facts, impact and uniqueness of events, substantial content of sources, and historical reality in general – concentrate on "functional roles" in and by themselves.'[39]

This list of accusations could very well be applied to much of the literature on political religion and fanaticism. It could also be levied at

---

39   Arendt, 'Religion and Politics', 385. The quote is taken from Arendt's reply to Jules Monnerot's criticisms of her original piece.

much writing on totalitarianism: something that Arendt herself became aware of in the 1950s, as her *Origins of Totalitarianism* was enlisted in a Cold War vision of social science, to which, despite her commitment to the 'free world', she could not subscribe. In Arendt's reply to Voegelin's review of her book, she stressed that what she had offered was 'a historical account of the elements which crystallised into totalitarianism'.[40] The key, if slippery term here is 'elements', which signals Arendt's attempt to combine a theoretical grasp of the structure of totalitarianism with the historical contingency of its emergence.

In 'Religion and Politics', the main representative of the functionalist approach criticized by Arendt is Jules Monnerot. Though Arendt doesn't quote it, his claim that communism was the Islam of the twentieth century is emblematic of the evacuation of history she so strenuously objected to. Monnerot had been a founding member, alongside Georges Bataille and Roger Caillois, of the *Collège de Sociologie*, a short-lived but deeply influential intellectual venture (1937–39) whose objective, in the wake of Durkheim and Mauss, and in response to the cultic and zealous dimensions of fascism and Hitlerism, had been the reinvention of 'sociology' as a discipline capable of grasping the political force of the sacred, considered as a dimension 'heterologous' to rational calculation but uneliminable from the social.[41]

Shortly before the exoteric, para-academic experience of the *Collège*, Bataille had participated in an esoteric attempt to found a sacred and sacrificial community, *Acéphale*. Violently opposed to the dictatorship of utility, self-interest and work which it regarded as the bane of contemporary life, *Acéphale* sought to break through politics as normally understood (and through the limitations of the avant-garde, surrealism in particular) into a dimension of community, expenditure and loss of self that Bataille termed 'the sacred' – a dimension liberated by the death

---

40   Arendt, 'A Reply to Eric Voegelin', in *Essays in Understanding*, 403.
41   On Monnerot's fraught relations with the Collège, which he abandoned almost immediately, and his long political drift to the far right, see Jean-Michel Heimonet's intellectual biography *Jules Monnerot ou la démission critique – 1932–1990. Trajet d'un intellectuel vers le fascisme*, Paris: Kimé, 1993. For the work of the Collège, see the collection edited by Denis Hollier, *The College of Sociology (1937–1939)*, Minneapolis: University of Minnesota Press, 1988.

of God and the erosion of institutional religion. The 'programmatic' text for *Acéphale*, written in 1936, is tellingly prefaced by an epigraph from Kierkegaard which reads: 'What looks like politics, and imagines itself to be political, will one day unmask itself as a religious movement.' Pleading for ecstasy against conformity, for abandonment against conservation, Bataille will declare that: 'Existence is not only an agitated void, it is a dance that forces one to dance with fanaticism.'[42]

The basic thesis of Monnerot's *Sociologie du communisme* – translated into English as *The Sociology and Psychology of Communism*, more likely to pre-empt confusion in the United States about Monnerot's *sui generis* idea of sociology – is that Marxist communism is at one and the same time the censorship of the religious and its disavowed projection onto the political. In this sense, Monnerot regards communism as the continuation of the failed exorcism and displacement of the sacred by the Enlightenment.[43] The critique of myth, belief and religion would thus be guilty of opening a breach for new, and more dangerous, mythologies.

The key concept in Monnerot's account is affectivity, placing him in the camp of those thinkers of political religion who, like Talmon and Voegelin, stress its experiential dimension. However, Monnerot goes further in this regard, to the extent of positing something like a hydraulic model where there would be a given quantum of affective energy of a 'sacred' type, a kind of religious intensity, which would then have to discharge itself through one formal conduit or another; he also stresses the role of the 'lower' psychological drives. Behind the rationalist illusion of the disappearance of religion, an age-old collective passion play would be at work, with novel political forms functioning as the bearers for affective responses in an essentially invariant repertoire of emotions and dispositions. The energies and fervours once attached to explicitly religious rituals and symbolisms would be available for other libidinal investments. Whence the notion that new myths celebrating the Nation,

---

42   Georges Bataille, 'The Sacred Conspiracy', in *Visions of Excess: Selected Writings, 1927–1939*, A. Stoekl (ed.), Minneapolis: University of Minnesota Press, 1985, 178–81. See also 'The Sacred', 240–5. I thank Benjamin Noys for drawing my attention to these pieces.
43   Heimonet, *Jules Monnerot*, 128–9.

the Race, the Individual, come to fulfil the functions hitherto accorded to the divine. The new political religions are thus the purveyors of 'substitutory satisfactions'.[44] And perhaps the greatest satisfaction of all is the one provided by communism, which harnesses base affective forces into the deification of Man, and the thanatological prospect of the de-differentiated, homogeneous, inert 'paradise' that for Monnerot is the classless society.

In terms familiar from sundry anti-fanatical polemics, especially those against the French Revolution, Monnerot sees the sacred as displaced into a 'messianism of the human species'.[45] But the roots of his analysis in sacred sociology, the anthropology of totemism and a psychoanalytic energetics means that this displacement is not thought in merely formal terms, by way of analogies between party and church, devotion and militancy, but rather as the repetition of an archaic, cultic practice. Writing of the role of the species in communism, Monnerot declares: 'By hypostasising this abstraction, one creates a transcendent and voracious entity, and when one declares that present individuals are to be sacrificed for future ones – or to the Species . . . – one nourishes this entity with human sacrifices.'[46] In a reactionary variation of a theme dear to the *Collège de Sociologie*, Monnerot's attack on communism as a secular religion is based on the idea that it is precisely the (ultimately impossible) expulsion of the sacred from the social, what he calls nihilism, which prepares the dominion of a degraded form of the sacred in the guise of communism. Monnerot's idea of nihilism, like Voegelin's account of Gnosticism, with its reliance on a grounding notion of religious experience, shows how the two strands of political religion that Arendt distinguishes as the historical and the functional are almost invariably entwined. An anthropological understanding of sacred functions is joined to the metahistorical narrative of Christianity's displacement by the secular religion of communism. The power of these negative philosophies of history is such that even Arendt, who wants to liberate politics and freedom from the embrace of a religiously inflected history,

---

44   Monnerot, *Sociologie du communisme*, 434.
45   Ibid., 433.
46   Ibid., 447.

partly succumbs to their dubious charm when she treats the reduction of political ideologies to religious functions, the 'desubstantializing functionalization of our categories', as the symptom of a broader process, 'the growing functionalization of society'. In a markedly 'deductivist'[47] approach which seems to ignore her own doctrine of historical elements, she links this to her condemnation of Marx's 'dangerous socialization of man'. An even stronger statement can be found in her reply to Voegelin, where she declares that the introduction of 'semi-theological arguments' in the discussion of totalitarianism is the symptom of a functionalization that she views as 'in many respects the last and perhaps the most dangerous stage of atheism'. In his own reply to Arendt's 'Religion and Politics', Monnerot chided her for the suggestion that the secular religion thesis is blasphemous in its dependence on a notion of religion without God. To Monnerot's assertion of the scientific validity of this stance in the anthropology of religion, and of the presence of sundry religions which do indeed dispense with God, Arendt has no particularly convincing reply – her characteristically Eurocentric reference to 'the worshiper of the kangaroo, whom I could easily take into account' does not improve matters.[48]

Contemporary approaches to the question of politics and religion continue to rely, perhaps inevitably, on philosophies of history articulated in some sense around notions of secularization – whether they're analysing a supposed 'return' of a religiosity that history had doomed to obsolescence, or viewing unconditional political commitments or 'fanaticisms' as atavistic resurgences, in secular garb, of affective structures of a fundamentally religious kind. Even when the object is not the condemnation of religious political subjectivities, but rather a broader reflection on theological elements in the forms of modern power, the

---

47 On this aspect of Arendt's thinking (which follows the Cold War tendency of *deducing* Stalinism from the ideas of Marx) and its tension with the richness of Arendt's study of the elements of totalitarianism, see Losurdo, 'Towards a Critique of the Category of Totalitarianism', especially useful for its attention to the impact of the Cold War on Arendt's ideas. For Losurdo, the 'main flaw of the category of totalitarianism is that it transforms an empirical description tied to specific characteristics into a general logical deduction' (50).

48 Arendt, 'Religion and Politics', 379, 406–7, 385.

reliance on narratives of secularization is strong, occluding the more complex temporalities that emerge, for example, in the analyses of mille-narian politics we encountered earlier. It is to a recent instance of these narratives that I now turn, in order to explore the broader effects of the idea of political religion on our thinking of historical time and political action.

ECONOMIES OF DOMINATION AND SALVATION

'Modernity, having removed God from the world, not only has not exited theology, but it has only, in a certain sense, brought to comple-tion the project of providential *oikonomia*.'[49] With these lines, Giorgio Agamben closes his latest, and longest, addition to the *Homo Sacer* project begun in 1995, *The Kingdom and the Glory*. This declaration synthesizes two key tenets of Agamben's study. First, the claim that the Church Fathers, in developing Trinitarian theology, Christology and angelol-ogy, lay the groundwork for an economic theology of government that remains operative in the current dispensation of Western modernity. Second, the idea that the atheism or secularism which nominally char-acterize contemporary political philosophy – be it liberal, conservative or Marxist – are surface-effects beneath which lie the compulsions of a theological matrix, a 'governmental machine' with its roots sunk deep in the Christian past. In other words, the limits and impasses of today's political thought are to be understood in terms of a cunning of secu-larization: the apparent disappearance of Christian theology from the commanding heights of politics is simply the determinate form taken by the ultimate origination of contemporary political action in the twin apparatus composed of a political theology of sovereignty and an economic theology of governmental administration. What's more, in a line of questioning that takes him, via a long Heideggerian detour, to views about the sacralization of politics that resonate with the recent resurgence of the political religion approach, Agamben sees the contem-porary dominion of the spectacle in matters political and economic as a prolongation of the theology of 'glory', the alienated celebration of

---

49 Giorgio Agamben, *Il Regno e la Gloria. Per una genealogia teologica dell'economia e del governo*, Vicenza: Neri Pozza, 2007, 314.

man's potentiality in the image, first of God, today of Capital.

Though in this book Agamben is not primarily preoccupied with the vicissitudes of religious and political subjectivity that have given rise to the problem of fanaticism, his claim to have produced a genealogy linking modern structures of power to a theological matrix makes him a significant interlocutor for a reflection on contemporary fanaticism, especially in terms of the connection between the idea of secularization and the analysis of the radical politics of conviction. In particular, it is striking that an author overtly hostile to facile historicism should be so drawn to arguments for continuity that end up belittling the contingency and specificity of politics and its contexts of emergence. Rather than a precarious force-field catalysed and constrained by social and economic compulsions, modern politics is seen as merely bringing to completion the Christian 'economy' of providence. Critical theory also succumbs to the affirmation of a continuity between the theological and the political: Marx's notion of praxis 'basically is only the secularization of the theological conception of the being of creatures as divine operation'.[50] Lines such as these echo one of the more influential attempts to think the theological undercurrents in the philosophy of history, Karl Löwith's 1949 *Meaning in History*. This study, referred to repeatedly in Voegelin's own account of the Gnostic deification of History, popularized the idea of Marxism as a secularized providential narrative seeking a unified principle of historical meaning in the dialectic of modes of production and the redemptive horizon of the classless society. Löwith's interpretation of Marx is rather one-dimensional, insensitive to the anticipations and nonsynchronicities which draw the historical-materialist account of the temporalities of accumulation and political action away from the holism and linearity of a philosophy of history. Also, prefiguring the millenarian verdict put forward by the likes of Cohn, Löwith produces a starkly reductive account of historical materialism as 'essentially, though secretly, a history of fulfilment and salvation in terms of social economy'[51] – a secret which is difficult to countenance if we consider the critical engagement of both Marx and Engels with the question of religion

---

50   Ibid., 106.
51   Karl Löwith, *Meaning in History*, Chicago: University of Chicago Press, 1949, 45.

in general, and of millenarianism in particular. Löwith even opts for an ethno-religious pseudo-explanation to account for the persistence of a horizon of redemption in Marx:

> He was a Jew of Old Testament stature, though an emancipated Jew of the nineteenth century who felt strongly anti-religious and even anti-semitic. It is the old Jewish messianism and prophetism – unaltered by two thousand years of economic history from handicraft to large-scale industry – and Jewish insistence on absolute righteousness which explained the idealistic basis of Marx's materialism. Though perverted into secular prognostication, the *Communist Manifesto* still retains the basic features of a messianic faith: 'the assurance of things to be hoped for'.[52]

Though he would probably baulk at such a philologically and methodologically blunt narrative, Agamben's own statements on Marx's secularization of Christian themes suggest a certain affinity with Löwith. In particular, it is difficult to see how the invocation of genealogy really exempts Agamben from the de-historicizing and de-politicizing effects of asserting a fundamental political-theological continuity behind the explicit categories and self-understanding of more or less all forms of contemporary social and political thought, which would find themselves the unwitting vehicles of the mortifying structures of theological authority. His attempt to generate a 'theological genealogy' of the economy is driven by the wish to prolong Foucauldian insights into 'biopolitics', according to which the primacy of sovereign power is both supplanted by, and recombined with, a government of life, wherein

---

52   Ibid., 44. Arendt made a reference to Marx's Jewish heritage in one of her rare moments of unguarded praise for the German thinker: 'In the country which made Disraeli its Prime Minister, the Jew Karl Marx wrote *Das Kapital*, a book which in its fanatical zeal for justice, carried on the Jewish tradition much more efficaciously than all the successes of the "chosen man of the chosen race".' Hannah Arendt, 'The Moral of History' (1946), quoted in Losurdo, 'Towards a Critique of the Category of Totalitarianism', 32. The link between Judaism and a 'fanaticism of justice' was also made, pejoratively, by Werner Sombart. See Domenico Losurdo, *Il revisionismo storico*, Bari: Laterza, 1990, 221.

power is not primarily aimed at sheer violent domination, but at a productive management of individuals and populations. Significantly, in a characteristic methodological short-circuit which he pioneered in *Homo Sacer*'s treatment of bare life and sovereignty, Agamben turns for help to a debate between Carl Schmitt and the theologian Erik Peterson. He takes his distance from Schmitt's allegiance to the idea of political theology, and shows that Peterson himself steps back from admitting the significance to the early Christian theologians of the notion of *oikonomia*. Defined by Aristotle as the 'administration of the house', in contradistinction with the form of collective or public power exercised in the *polis*, in Xenophon '*oikonomia* is presented as a functional organization, an activity of management which is not bound to rules other than that of the orderly functioning of the house (or of the undertaking in question). It is this "managerial" paradigm that defines the semantic sphere of the term *oikonomia* (as of the verb *oikonomein* and of the noun *oikonomos*) and determines its progressive analogical broadening outside of its original limits.'[53] As Agamben details, the *oikonomia* is modelled by Xenophon on the organization that reigns over an army or within a seafaring vessel. But if the semantic core of the idea of economy is already implanted in Ancient Greek philosophy, why engage in a *theological* genealogy?

Where Foucault had located, beginning in the mid-eighteenth century, the emergence of 'governmental reason' in the early discourse of political economy and the concurrent practice of administering the health and productivity of populations, Agamben turns the clock back two millennia: to the writings of Aristotle and Xenophon on the economy, then to the fate of this notion within the theology of the Church fathers, beginning with Paul. In the process he abandons Foucault's commitment to discontinuity, as well as his related nominalist disdain for the assumption that substances, essences or universals can be registered across different historical domains. Where Agamben decodes a hidden theological machine behind the operations of the secular world, for Foucault 'the secret [is] that [things] have no essence or that their

---

53   Agamben, *Il Regno e la Gloria*, 32–3.

essence was fabricated in a piecemeal fashion from alien forms'.[54]

The stakes become clearer when Agamben comes to the discussion of the place of *oikonomia* in what he calls the providential paradigm and the 'ontology of acts of government' that underlies it. As he writes: 'Providence (government) is that through which theology and philosophy try to deal with the splitting of classical ontology into two separate realities: being and praxis, transcendent good and immanent good, theology and *oikonomia*. It presents itself as a machine aimed at rearticulating together the two fragments in the *gubernatio dei*, in the divine government of the world.'[55] A theorem from a Heideggerian history of being – the sundering of being and praxis – is adduced to account for the determining significance of Christian theology in shaping the political and metaphysical horizon of 'the West' (a term that Agamben seems to employ without much qualification or reflection) up to 'our' very own modernity. In this regard, it is the specifically Christian fate of *oikonomia*, as the anarchic immanence of a divine government tenuously articulated, via providence, with a transcendent God who 'reigns but does not govern', which justifies the theological character of this genealogical investigation.

For Agamben, the 'providential *dispositif* (which is itself nothing but a reformulation and development of theological *oikonomia*) harbours something like the epistemological paradigm of modern government'. In the guise of separation between 'legislative or sovereign power and executive or governmental power', the modern state inherits 'the theological machine of the government of the world'.[56] Where Voegelin's *New Science of Politics* perceived modernity as the surfacing of a virulent Gnosticism, in a conservative apology of Christianity's de-devinization of politics, Agamben instead paints political modernity as trapped in mechanisms fabricated by Christian theology.

But by what right does Agamben pass from the insistence on certain

---

54 Michel Foucault, 'Nietzsche, Genealogy, History', in *Language, Counter-Memory, Practice: Selected Essays and Interviews*, Daniel F. Bouchard (ed.), Ithaca, NY: Cornell University Press, 1977, 139, 142.
55 Agamben, *Il Regno e la Gloria*, 157.
56 Ibid., 158.

conceptual constellations and semantic kernels – across different epochs and discursive formations – to the overarching conviction that such an archaeological inquiry is of urgent political significance? In what way is the religious framework still at work in a putatively godless politics? Unlike a historian of ideas or concepts who might wish to track the secret endurance and operative impact of certain thought-patterns across periods and conjunctures, Agamben – in this respect the kin of Voegelin – is unconcerned with forms of transmission beyond textual ones. When, for instance, he states that Malebranchian occasionalism is still present within Rousseau's conceptions of political economy and popular sovereignty, or that a theological notion of order subtends Smith's 'invisible hand', he does not attend to the possibility that ideas may be generated outside the closed history of Western metaphysics, that political and economic concepts may exceed or escape a pernicious theological inheritance. Nor does Agamben consider that the resilience of certain thought-forms – such as the idea of providence – might be less relevant than their redeployment to radically different ends, within incommensurable contexts. Nor, finally, is there a serious consideration given to the possibility – supported, for instance, by the derivation, which Agamben himself shows, of the theological *dispositif* of bureaucracy from the empirical history of empires – that it is not so much the continuity of the theological, but the persistence of certain social relations and their imaginaries which explains the endurance of certain concepts of government and forms of organization across such a *longue durée*.

It is symptomatic in this respect that Agamben dismisses the theoretical significance of the secularization debate that pitted the likes of Hans Blumenberg, Carl Schmitt and Karl Löwith against one another in the 1960s. For Agamben, secularization is a strategic gambit, not a strictly historiographic thesis. As a discursive strategy, secularization involves the polemical reference of political terms to their theological origin.[57] Secularization is 'a strategic operator, which marks political

---

57 It is here that Agamben introduces a rather mystifying 'methodological' term, that of the *segnatura* (signature). Secularization functions as an element within a science of signatures, that is, a study of 'something that, in a sign or a concept, marks it

concepts to refer them back to their theological origin'.[58] Rather than a philosophy of history per se, Agamben bases this strategy on the idea of indices or 'signatures' that allow us to pass from a supposedly desacralized phenomenon to its sacralized precursor. Hence the rather mystical postulation that only some may 'possess the capacity to perceive signatures and to follow the dislocations and displacements that they operate in the tradition of ideas'.[59] There is no need to actually gauge the mechanisms that allow for the transition from one discursive field to another, since the very presence of the signature immanently refers us back to an origin in the theological field, which accordingly – in a move critically dissected in Blumenberg's work – delegitimates the political concepts themselves. Political economy, for example, is reduced to a 'social rationalization of providential *oikonomia*'.[60] The 'theory' of signatures, like so many attempts to link the religious to the political, thus seems to engage in what we could call a reductivist idealism, a mirror-image of sorts of the much-maligned Marxian reduction of ideal structures to social relations. The historical materialist reduction is in fact one that certain passages of Agamben's book would make rather more plausible than the search for theo-economic signatures. For instance, in referring to the pseudo-Aristotelian treatise *De Mundus*, Agamben shows how the perception of the governmental apparatus of the Persian king would influence the later image of divine hierarchies, as 'the administrative apparatus through which the sovereigns of the other conserve their kingdom becomes the paradigm of the divine government of the world.'[61]

But something more problematic is at stake than Agamben's reference

---

and exceeds it to refer it back to a determinate interpretation or a determinate domain, without thereby departing from the semiotic to constitute a new signification or a new concept'. Agamben, *Il Regno e la Gloria*, 16. See also Agamben's recent tract on method, Giorgio Agamben, *Signatura rerum. Sul metodo*, Turin: Bollati Boringhieri, 2008. For an earlier use of the notion of secularization, see his comments on Weber in Giorgio Agamben, *The Time That Remains: A Commentary on the Letter to the Romans*, trans. P. Dailey, Stanford: Stanford University Press, 2005, 19–23.

58   Agamben, *Signatura rerum*, 68.
59   Agamben, *Il Regno e la Gloria*, 16.
60   Ibid., 310.
61   Ibid., 96.

to a mode of research, the search for signatures, which so heavily depends on putative personal insight and analogical thinking. This has to do with the idea of a theological origin. Behind this reference lies not only Agamben's sympathy towards the Schmittian variety of secularization, but the conviction of a historical-ontological continuity that allows one to assert that our political horizon is still determined – and worse, unconsciously determined – by semantic and ideational structures forged within a Christian theological discourse. It is also this idea of origin, so alien to Foucault's Nietzschean genealogy, which permits Agamben to claim that his archaeological endeavour to unearth the theological matrix of modern domination is also an ethical and political gesture. Since all the categories of radical politics are *de jure* steeped in the same metaphysical mire as the apparatuses of the administration and the taking of life; since all of our politics is religion (to the extent that theology itself was already steeped in the symbolism of authority), only a root-and-branch transformation, a messianic change, is adequate to our predicament: 'This is why it is senseless to oppose secularism [*laicismo*] and the general will to theology and its providential paradigm; only an archaeological operation, which goes back before the split that produced them as rival but inseparable brethren, can dismantle and render inoperative the whole economic-theological apparatus.'[62]

Thus, though Agamben does not subscribe to the apologetic Christian purposes that Hans Blumenberg, in his *Legitimacy of the Modern Age* (written against both Löwith and Schmitt), registered in the discourse on secularization – the idea that the conceptual patrimony of the Church had been expropriated and misused – he does manifest one of the key aspects of that discourse, the idea of a substantial continuity. As Blumenberg writes: 'Only where the category of substance dominates the understanding of history are there repetitions, superimpositions and dissociations – and also, for that matter, disguises and unmaskings.' Despite his inevitable Heideggerian protestations to the contrary, it is only the idea of an underlying continuity – that of a historical-ontological destiny – that can allow Agamben, to cite Blumenberg, 'to identify

---

62   Ibid., 313.

the substance in its metamorphoses'. Against the idea of a history that is veiled to itself, of secularization as a kind of spell, which only the man of signatures could dispel by way of an archaeology of suspicion, it is worth reflecting on the suggestion that 'there exists a high degree of indifference between a concept and its history'[63] – that the persistence of ideas of authority, or justice, or salvation, which might have once been articulated in cultic or theological contexts, does not mark them with the sin of their origins.

Schmitt's own attempt to reply to Blumenberg's charges is instructive in this regard. *The Legitimacy of the Modern Age*, together with the broader debates on secularization and on the role of the Church after the Second Vatican Council, led Schmitt to produce *Political Theology II* as a sequel to the famous decisionist tract of 1922, where he had first put forward his own theory of secularization:

> All significant concepts of the modern theory of the state are secularized theological concepts not only because of their historical development – in which they were transferred from theology to the theory of the state, whereby, for example, the omnipotent God became the omnipotent lawgiver – but also because of their systematic structure, the recognition of which is necessary for a sociological consideration of these concepts. The exception in jurisprudence is analogous to the miracle in theology. Only by being aware of this analogy can we appreciate the manner in which the philosophical idea of the state developed in the last centuries.[64]

Counterposing his sociology of juridical concepts to any causal analysis, especially of a Marxist type, Schmitt employs a methodology which also plays a large role in the political religion literature: that of analogy, sometimes taken to the point of isomorphy, as when he writes: 'The metaphysical image that a definite epoch forges of the world has the same structure as what the world immediately understands to be appropriate

---

63   Hans Blumenberg, *The Legitimacy of the Modern Age*, trans. R. M. Wallace, Cambridge, MA: The MIT Press, 1983, 9, 15, 21.
64   Carl Schmitt, *Political Theology: Four Chapters on the Concept of Sovereignty*, trans. G. Schwab, Cambridge, MA: The MIT Press, 1985, 36.

as a form of its political organization.'[65] This approach, however, as Schmitt is at pains to show in his sequel half a century later, does not depend on the kind of functional identities or historical continuities posited by the narratives of secularization which underpin theories of political religion. Secularization is circumscribed to the relation between theology and the state, not founded on an anthropology of affect or a civilizational philosophy of history of the kind proposed by Voegelin.

Rather than adopting a linear narrative of the dissipation of religion by the expansion of the secular, or of the contraband presence of religious aspirations in political vehicles, Schmitt, whose conservative focus was always on the institutions and metaphysics of authority, on church and state, portrays a highly unstable situation which evades the grasp of any philosophy of history. More precisely, from his openly reactionary vantage point, he sees the emergence of revolutionary politics and of its subject, the working class, as breaking the bounds that determined the relationship between the temporal and the spiritual, the state and the church. From that point on, 'the spiritual-temporal, this world and the hereafter, transcendence-immanence, idea and interests, superstructure and substructure – can only be determined according to the struggle between subjects'.[66] What's more, 'given the changing friend-enemy constellations throughout history, theology can become a political tool of the revolution as well as the counter-revolution. This is a natural part of the ongoing change within political-polemical tensions and the formation of battle lines; it is just a question of intensity.'[67]

Though this last martial-vitalistic note raises far more questions than it answers, Schmitt's suggestion that the relationships between the political and the religious should be considered in terms of the contingencies and exigencies of political struggles which cannot be subsumed by a philosophy of history is worthy of note. His further argument, that the twentieth century ushered in a period where the anchoring of ideas of spiritual and secular authority in definite institutions is no longer

---

65   Ibid., 46.
66   Carl Schmitt, *Political Theology II: The Myth of the Closure of Any Political Theology*, trans. M. Hoelzl and G. Ward, Cambridge: Polity, 2008 [1970], 44.
67   Ibid., 42.

secure, also deserves attention. If 'we can no longer define the political from the state',[68] as Schmitt suggests, then our concepts of the articulation between religion and politics will also be transformed, as 'the walls collapse and the spaces which were once distinct [the religious and the political] intermingle and penetrate each other, as in a labyrinthine architecture of light'.[69] In this disorienting situation, is it only the intensity of friendship and enmity, association and dissociation that can guide us?[70] Even if we accept that politics and partisanship can't be disjoined, are polemic and conflict the only horizon for action?[71] If politics cannot be contained by the state, or overseen by spiritual authorities, what kind of universality can it attain?

Schmitt, who closely allies himself with the counter-revolutionary critique of the fanaticism of reason and equality put forward by the likes of De Maistre, Bonald and Donoso Cortés, is of course profoundly opposed to the communist assertion of a universalism beyond state and religion. Treating it, along with liberalism, as a pathologically abstract perception of politics, Schmitt too, despite the distance taken from the philosophy of history that underlies the political religion thesis, views communism as a messianism. Hinting at a critique of the Blochian theology of revolution, Schmitt writes of emancipatory tendencies in the contemporary world with the disdain of the wizened reactionary: 'I think that such a progressive, plurivalent, hominising society permits only that kind of eschatology which is immanent to the system and therefore also progressive and plurivalent. This kind of eschatology can therefore only be a *homo-homini-homo* eschatology. At most this eschatology is an utopia on the principle of hope, the content of which is an *homo absconditus* who produces himself and, moreover, produces the conditions for his own possibility.'[72] Unmoored from the transcend-

---

68 Ibid., 45.

69 Ibid., 97.

70 Ibid., 45.

71 On the emergence of the idea of 'party-fanaticism' in 1848, see Conze and Reinhart, 'Fanatismus'.

72 Schmitt, *Political Theology II*, 54. Taubes noted the 'purely hierarchical cataract' that prevented Schmitt in this book from grasping the radical, democratic dimensions of mysticism and messianism. Taubes, *The Political Theology of Paul*, 100.

ence of church and state, modern messianism moves from a hidden God to a hidden Man. In the end, humanism for Schmitt is a fanaticism, speculating on the intangible abstraction of Humanity and displacing antagonism from the realm of concrete conflicts to the struggle between mankind and its enemies, in either liberal or communist guises (whence his dictum *Humanität, Bestialität*).

UNIVERSAL REVOLUTIONS

An index of hubristic humanism, of levelling abstraction, and above all of fanatical faith, the identification of Marxism and communism with religion (though explored in affirmative tones by the likes of Bloch) is most often employed as a form of disqualification – by some for its perversion of religion's transcendence, by others on account of its iteration of religion's irrationality. But such analogies and isomorphism may elicit problems for the prosecutors themselves. As has been underscored with great acuity by Fredric Jameson, the depiction of Marxism by its detractors as a 'shamefaced religion, a religion that does not want to know its own name' is double-edged. Identifying Marxism with religion can also serve to reduce all religions to the standing of secular ideologies. Under the rubric of ideology, in effect, the very distinction between immanence and transcendence, secular and spiritual becomes far harder to maintain, and the uniqueness of religion difficult to defend. Jameson also points to the dangers for the non-believing critic of ascribing to religious belief 'some unique and specialized, intrinsically *other* type of psychological or spiritual experience' which secularism or scientific atheism might immunize us against. This, he argues, amounts to a kind of superstition.[73]

The blurring of the line between religion and ideology was in effect the 'blasphemous' dimension of the political religion thesis that Arendt, concerned to defend if nothing else the cultural elevation of Christianity, registered in Monnerot's work. It also lies at the source of the Marxist exploration of the 'religion of everyday life'. Jameson's warning against a psychologistic interpretation of atheism or Enlightenment is also

---

73   Jameson, *Marxism and Form*, 117.

particularly apposite. Accusations of fanaticism levelled at 'excesses' of rationality and claims of empirical realism made by defenders of religious faith suggest that the attempt to demarcate forms of legitimate subjective experience from pathological instances of conviction is scuppered by its reliance on categories that are not psychological, but cultural or political. Jameson's alternative suggestion, that we both historicize the comparison between Marxism and the Church and refer it to its material dimensions, opens up a more fertile avenue of research. Rather than invoke structures of experience or conceptual analogies, Jameson points out that both Marxism and Christianity emerged as 'material cultures' that tried to propagate universalist projects in the context of supra-national social settings (the Roman Empire, the capitalist world) already marked by high degrees of universality in their own right: 'What Marxism shares with Christianity is primarily a historical situation: for it now [in 1971] projects that claim to universality and that attempt to establish a universal culture which characterized Christianity in the declining years of the Roman Empire and at the height of the Middle Ages. It is therefore not at all surprising that its intellectual instruments should bear a structural similarity to those techniques . . . with which Christianity assimilated populations of differing and wholly unrelated cultural backgrounds.'[74] This insight has interesting affinities with one of the more influential analyses of the parallels between modern politics and religion, Tocqueville's discussion of the French Revolution as a 'religious revolution' in *The Ancien Régime and the Revolution*.

Tocqueville, whose narrative links the Revolution's irruption to the social processes of levelling and democratization that precede it – that is, to a kind of material universality that anticipates the universal ideals of rights and citizenship – finds the only ideological comparator for it in those world-transforming religious movements that, like Jacobinism, transgressed borders and particularisms, forging a project for humanity itself. While acknowledging the Revolution's fanatical excesses, its 'murderous maxims' and 'armed opinions',[75] Tocqueville nevertheless

---

74   Ibid., 117–18.
75   Alexis de Tocqueville, *The Old Regime and the Revolution*, F. Furet and F. Mélonio (eds), trans. A. S. Kahan, Chicago: University of Chicago Press, 1998, 94. It

does not make use of the religious analogy simply to treat the Revolution as a surrogate or usurper of legitimate faith. Rather, he identifies the radical novelty of the Revolution in its capacity for unlimited universalization, in its ability, unprecedented in political revolutions, to create 'a common intellectual homeland where men of all nations could become citizens'.

Though Tocqueville enumerates familiar analogies between religion and revolution – the role of preaching and propaganda, the importance of conversions and so on – it is universality which is foremost. Unlike previous political rebellions, where rights and freedoms were indexed to particular claims, to the fate of a specific nation, class or territory, the French Revolution, to the extent that it is addressed to 'human nature itself', is much closer to religious upheavals. This is indicated, for example, by the fact that the revolution 'preaches as ardently to foreigners as it acts passionately at home: think what a new sight this is!' For Tocqueville, among 'all the unheard-of things that the French Revolution presented to the world, this was certainly the newest'. Despite stressing the many hidden continuities between the *ancien régime* and the revolution, claiming that 'it innovated much less than is generally supposed',[76] Tocqueville is forced to recognize this absolute break with previous instances of political change. The foreigner can be welcomed by the revolution precisely on account of that feature, shared with religion, which for many of its detractors made it the very fount of fanaticism: abstraction. The 'more a religion has [an] abstract and general character', notes Tocqueville, 'the more it spreads, despite differences of laws, climate, and men'. Likewise, the French Revolution 'considered the citizen in an abstract manner, outside of any particular society, the same way that religion considers man in general, independently of time and place'.[77] Its concern was human nature and the 'general

---

should be noted that, alongside the sociological account of the bases of the Revolution, Tocqueville also adopts a more anthropological tack, seeing the origins of revolutionary fanaticism in the fact that anti-religious campaigns had, 'contrary to the natural instincts of humanity', left men 'empty' of the faith that had once filled them (203).
76   Ibid., 106.
77   Ibid., 100.

laws of human society',[78] the very things for which it was pilloried by the likes of Burke.

The expansive universality of revolution, and not the subjective quality of belief, is what grounds Tocqueville's own understanding of political religion. The analogy with Islam once again imposes itself. The Revolution 'took on that appearance of a religious revolution which so astonished its contemporaries. Or rather, it itself became a new kind of religion, an incomplete religion, it is true, without God, without ritual, and without a life after death, but one which nevertheless, like Islam, flooded the earth with its soldiers, apostles and martyrs.'[79] Like Hegel before him, Tocqueville finds an anticipation of the abstract enthusiasm and planetary ambition of revolutionary egalitarianism in the politics of Islam – worth musing on at a time when for many veteran or belated Cold Warriors, the menace posed to liberal capitalism by the Islam of the twentieth century (communism) has been relayed by the communism of the twenty-first (Islam). These analogies, however, suggest something more important, namely, that the crucial political dimension of fanaticism is not so much the psychological character of unyielding conviction – not a determinately political feature, and in any case one that too easily slips into invidious discussions of mental pathology – but its relationship to abstraction and universality.

From Burke to Monnerot, and including their twenty-first-century epigones, critics of revolution have fulminated against the rootless, geometrical character of ideas of universal emancipation, which ride

---

78   Ibid., 101.
79   Ibid. One of these astonished contemporaries was Edmund Burke, who stressed that the Revolution was 'one of doctrine and theoretick dogma. It has a much greater resemblance to those changes which have been made upon religious grounds, in which a spirit of proselytism makes an essential part.' Edmund Burke, 'Thoughts on French Affairs' (1791), in *Further Reflections on the Revolution in France*, D. E. Ritchie (ed.), Indianapolis: Liberty Fund, 1992, 208. This passage is discussed in Arno Mayer's account of the role of religion in the French Terror. For Mayer, in 'its uphill battle to desacralize the hegemony of throne and altar, the revolution eventually spawned a secular or political religion of its own. This bid for a substitute religion intensified the founding violence attending the drive to restore a single political sovereignty.' See *The Furies: Violence and Terror in the French and Russian Revolutions*, Princeton: Princeton University Press, 2000, 141 (also xvi, 146, 445).

roughshod over national differences, natural hierarchies and the limits of human possibility. Opponents of revolution with more liberal and cosmopolitan leanings have depicted the levelling abstractions of egalitarian fanaticisms as violent denials of the empirical complexities that only the joint work of representative institutions and market transactions is capable of coordinating. Whether refusing the conditioning of custom, or that of markets, the fanatic always seems to be marked out by a refusal of mediation, a 'religious' wish to bypass concrete differences.

The abiding character of this problem for a contemporary politics that desires to affirm universality while not exposing itself to anti-fanatical opprobrium, is perhaps most evident in the recent recourse to messianic and eschatological figures by a number of prominent radical thinkers such as Jacques Derrida, Giorgio Agamben and Alain Badiou. The ironies of this turn should be obvious by now. Although (bar notable exceptions like Bloch or Benjamin) much Marxist, communist or emancipatory thought has recoiled from the religious hermeneutics of suspicion which paints social revolution as a mere secularization of apocalyptic aspirations, it would appear that the recent trend has been to reverse that traditional defence and to embrace the religious dimension of revolutionary politics. My contention here is twofold: first, that political and philosophical invocations of religious ideas of redemption are at least in part to be understood as responses to the accusation of fanaticism; second, that they are symptomatic of the complex predicament of a thinking that wants to preserve the assertion of a politics of radical transformation while navigating between the Scylla and Charybdis of an untenable philosophy of history, on the one hand, and a resignation to the present, on the other.

THE ENDS OF KNOWLEDGE

These themes play a pivotal role in Jacques Derrida's *Specters of Marx*. Derrida's intervention becomes especially interesting in light of the overall problem of political religion, and specifically of Marxism as the foremost specimen of political messianism. Writing in the context of a return of the religious to the geopolitical arena (consider his hyperbolic statements on the 'world war' of monotheisms in Jerusalem), Derrida

stages the problem of critically inheriting Marx in terms of two tempo-
rally coded narratives that bind the religious to the political. The declaration of the 'teleo-eschatological good news'[80] of market democracy's
triumph over Marxism, embodied by Fukuyama's *The End of History
and the Last Man*, with its neo-liberal neo-evangelism, is shown to rely
on a link between termination and truth which, despite its nonchalant
secularism, is nothing short of apocalyptic[81] – in that it ties the sense of
an ending to the revelation of a truth: the truth of liberal democracy's
apotheosis as the only political system adequate to the post-historical
human animal. In bringing attention to the gap between liberalism's
standing as an ideal and its empirical crises – which Fukuyama papers
over with a makeshift Hegelianism reliant on Kojève's influential interpretation of the *Phenomenology of Spirit* – Derrida repeats one of the key
gestures of the Kantian critique of fanaticism. He demonstrates how a
particular philosophical position relies on treating what is purely regulative as determinate; how a moral truth is smuggled in as worldly knowledge. The counterpart, and perhaps the antidote, to this apocalyptic, and
fanatical, fusion of ideals and facts, truth (or faith) and knowledge, is the
other temporal and experiential mode that brings religious terminology
to bear on political hopes: the messianic. This term will prove pivotal
to Derrida's attempt to revive the 'spirit' of Marx (while, as many of his
critics note, jettisoning much of the letter).

On one level, despite the sophistication of much of his reading of
Marx, Derrida seems to subscribe to a variant of Löwith's thesis according to which Marx's *Weltsgeschichte*, his historical-materialist account
of the emergence and fatal contradictions of capitalism, is but a contraband *Heilsgeschichte*, a history of salvation. In Derrida's estimation:
'If analysis of the Marxist type remains, then, indispensable, it appears
to be radically insufficient there where the Marxist ontology grounding the project of Marxist science or critique *also itself carries with it and*

---

80 Derrida, *Specters of Marx*, 80.
81 'Whoever takes on an apocalyptic tone comes to signify to, if not tell, you something. What? The truth, of course, and to signify to you that it reveals the truth to
you. . . . Truth is itself the end, the destination, and that truth unveils itself is the
advent of the end.' Jacques Derrida, 'On a Newly Apocalyptic Tone in Philosophy',
in *Raising the Tone of Philosophy*, 151.

must carry with it, necessarily, despite so many modern or post-modern denials, a messianic eschatology.'[82] 'Ontology' is Derrida's bugbear. It denotes the idea that Marxism could have knowledge of the real — again, the Kantian legacy of an epistemological critique of *Schwärmerei* is in evidence.[83] The verdict here is really not so distant from the widespread view that Marxism was a pseudo-science that needed a religious supplement. But, instead of recommending that Marxist ontology be supplanted by a liberal empiricism, for Derrida this is all the more reason to affirm the messianic. In what could also be seen as a warding off of fanaticism, of the conviction that there could be a positive knowledge or immediate experience of truth, Derrida, faithful to his calls for a 'new Enlightenment', separates the 'messianic', understood as a non-religious structure of experience involving the wait without expectation for an event of justice, from 'messianism' as a determinate set of beliefs and practices.[84] Though anything but pejorative, this move, abstracting and purifying Marx of both scientific and religious 'contents', is uncomfortably reminiscent of the separation of religious form from specific historical content that made the anti-Marxist discourse of political religion possible. Derrida's operation is twofold: he wants to bracket the content of Marxism and religion to reveal the formal structure of promising which defines them both; and he wants to see in this form something that lies beyond critique, an undeconstructible hope for emancipation. Derrida advocates neither a scientific Marxism nor a transcendent religion, but a 'messianism without religion'.[85]

---

82   Derrida, *Specters of Marx*, 73.

83   A certain affinity with the critique of fanaticism can also be sensed in Derrida's tireless tracking down of any form of identity between thought and being, what Jameson has usefully captured in the idea that Derrida is carrying out a campaign against the 'unmixed': 'what is somehow pure and self-sufficient or autonomous, what is able to be disengaged from the general mess of the mixed, hybrid phenomena all around it and named with the satisfaction of a single conceptual proper name'. Fredric Jameson, 'Marx's Purloined Letter', in *Ghostly Demarcations*, M. Sprinker (ed.), London: Verso, 1999, 44–5.

84   On the 'universal structure' of the 'messianic appeal' and its difference from 'Abrahamic messianism', see *Specters of Marx*, 210. In his reply to critics, Derrida does recognize the difficulties involved in the separation of the messianic from messianism proper. See 'Marx & Sons', in *Ghostly Demarcations*, 213.

85   Derrida, *Specters of Marx*, 74.

What opponents of Marxism as a secular religion had identified as its original sin, its disavowed redemptive promise, is here transmuted into its saving grace. More, Derrida gleans from Marxism a purely formal concern with a future irreducible to the iterations of the present, with an otherness that no knowledge could anticipate, turning it into the very ethical motivation behind deconstruction. It is worth noting the very close bond between the move to a formal extraction of 'the messianic in general' and the idea of a politics of the event, and the related disparaging by Derrida of any political content as 'ontology'. Derrida will even speak of the 'quasi-atheistic dryness of the messianic', making much of its desert-like qualities.[86]

But, notwithstanding Derrida's protestations, the critique of Marxist knowledge in order to make room for a Marxian faith – understood as an opening to the promise of an 'impossible' event – risks stripping out any political substance from critique. The legitimate (though hardly original) desire to undo the securities of a teleology, to repeal the warrant the latter might give for instrumental violence justified by historical necessity and eventual victory, jettisons Marx's crucial insight that the politics of revolution – however precarious – must find its foothold in real social and economic tendencies. If communism is to be understood as a determinate negation of capitalism and its concrete forms of abstract domination – as concerned with what Engels called 'conditions of liberation' – then some (strategic, partisan, fallible) knowledge of the real is indispensable. After all, the Marxist notion of revolution – regardless of its particular historical embodiment – lies at the intersection between, on the one hand, the presence of a political capacity or force and, on the other, the idea that from the partisan perspective of that organized capacity, it is possible to know and practically to anticipate the real tendencies in the world that communism seeks – determinately and determinedly – to negate. For better or for worse, without some such articulation of power and knowledge – what Derrida might perceive as 'rush[ing] headlong toward an ontological content'[87] – there is no spirit of Marx, not even a spectre, only a simulacrum. In other words, though Derrida's opposition to dialectical and historical materialism repeats the Kantian proscription

---

86 Ibid., 211.
87 Ibid., 114.

against a positive knowledge or intellectual intuition of unexperience-able essences,[88] he seems to abrogate that link between emancipation and teleology which, orbiting around the event of the French Revolution, Kant bequeathed to dialectical thought. Derrida's contention that 'if one could *count* on what is coming, hope would be but the calculation of a programme'[89] places us before a false antinomy between instrumental certainty and pure otherness, the programme and the event, which is devoid of meaning for any politics working with both real constraints and real contingencies, whether these be catastrophic setbacks or fortu-nate opportunities.

It is beyond dispute that the often disastrous shortcomings of certain experiences of emancipatory politics have led many to look with distrust on historical materialisms of any stripe – regardless of the fact that, as we have seen, non-linear and non-deterministic visions of politics are not alien to the Marxist canon. Stinging defeats and bleak prospects have also played their part, as Jameson soberly reminds us:

> You would not evoke the messianic in a genuinely revolutionary period, a period in which changes can be sensed at work all around you; the messianic does not mean immediate hope in that sense, perhaps not even hope against hope; it is a unique variety of the species 'hope' that scarcely bears any of the latter's normal characteristics and that flourishes only in a time of absolute hopelessness, a period like the Second Empire, or the years between the Wars, or the 1980s and 90s, when radical change seems unthinkable, its very idea dispelled by visible wealth and power, along with palpable powerlessness.[90]

Though few philosophical positions are ever readily reducible to the status of symptoms, it would also be naïve to disregard the link between the recent period of capitalist restoration and the emergence of concern with the messianic and the event. At times it appears as if that which the situation

---

88   'No progress of knowledge could saturate an opening that must have nothing to do with knowing.' Ibid., 45.

89   Ibid., 212. This critique of the programmatic, and of any teleology whatsoever, is also linked to Derrida's wish – shared with many thinkers of his generation, includ-ing Badiou – to do without a concept of totality. See ibid., 33 and 45.

90   Jameson, 'Marx's Purloined Letter', 62.

painfully imposes – for instance, the seeming disappearance of movements bearing what Marx called the 'positive possibility' of change – is defensively valorized, as 'the impossible' turns from a grim recognition to a value that demands to be affirmed. Or, in a related gesture, the principal features of the attack on communism as a political religion, as a form of fanaticism – against its notions of totality, historical change, all-round revolution and so on – are incorporated into contemporary attempts to think radical change; radical thought seems to inoculate itself with conservative critique.

The turn to the figure of Paul, by philosophers such as Agamben, Badiou and Žižek, is particularly instructive here. The emphasis on faith over knowledge follows the trend, already evident in Derrida, to free the thinking of emancipation from a fallacious insight into the order of things, which would guide action 'like a programme'. This is a profoundly ambivalent move. In seeking to make itself immune from the charge of what the seventeenth century termed enthusiasm, it also puts the whole weight of political transformation on a wager, that is, on a resolute conviction and a radical separation from the status quo (coded in Pauline terms as 'the Law'), which – at least if we follow Taubes's view quoted in the epigraph to this chapter – can very well appear fanatical in its turn. But there is a more significant dimension of the debate on fanaticism that haunts these texts, and it is the one that I introduced, with Tocqueville and Jameson, in terms of the universality of religious revolutions. If political universality is not a matter of knowledge, can it still be sustained as universality?

This is the challenge that drives Badiou's book on Saint Paul, subtitled *The Foundation of Universalism*, a book replete with overt and implicit parallels between the Roman Empire of Paul's time and the American empire of today, but which also sees the question of political weakness as one that spans these otherwise distant moments. As Badiou writes, commenting on Paul's epistles, 'we can escape powerlessness'.[91] To attend to the nature of this 'foundation' is to try to evade the critiques of universalism as fanaticism while not giving up an iota of the radicality demanded by a transformative, oppositional and emancipatory political thought. Thus, though Badiou strenuously defends a conception of

---

91   Alain Badiou, *Saint Paul: The Foundation of Universalism*, trans. R. Brassier, Stanford: Stanford University Press, 2003, 88.

political truth that could easily be tagged as fanatical – with its emphasis on sameness and unconditionality – the model of universalism he seeks to draw from Paul is one that attempts to circumvent the arsenal of accusations with which we are by now familiar.

Like Derrida, Badiou – whose intellectual and political trajectory has of course been much more closely tied to the idea of communism – resorts to the concept of the event (or, in the Pauline lexicon, grace) to signal that universalizable truths or the advent of justice are not directly accessible by knowledge,[92] nor do they conform to a programme. A certain passivity functions here as an antidote to the censures that inevitably greet a Promethean subjectivity that seeks to change the world on the basis of a truth it claims to possess. Neither calculable nor knowable, the event as a political category is a mark of the distance taken from action that wants to draw its strength and legitimacy from historical tendencies, but also of the broader suspicion that has fallen on knowledge within the arena of politics. The resources for transforming the world, though not as such otherworldly, are also not to be found in any knowable processes. If action is to find a foothold it is in the lacunae and inconsistencies of the world, not in some present force or base: 'Only what is in immanent exception is universal.'[93]

Universality is not only radically contingent on an unexpected rending of the fabric of conformity, it is also configured in such a way that it cannot be achieved by the simple subsumption of difference. Conscious of Hegel's warnings about an enthusiasm of the abstract that would crush concrete difference for the sake of a consuming unity, Badiou, without wishing to relent on the absoluteness of truth, reclaims the category of tolerance. Since universality can only be attested and engendered by an egalitarian and collective dimension, by being addressed to all, and not only by its being individually experienced (this is the necessary passage from 'faith' to 'love', or, in Badiou's own Lacanian lexicon, from subjectivation to consistency), it must make its way through the world as it is, which is to say through difference.[94] Reflecting on Paul's tactical relation

---

92   The 'conditions of the universal cannot be conceptual'. Ibid., 108.
93   Ibid., 111.
94   'That every truth procedure collapses differences, infinitely deploying a purely

to the particularities he encounters (social institutions of sexual difference, ethno-religious identities), Badiou sees universality as 'an indifference that tolerates differences', and its maxim as that of 'combining
the appropriation of particularities with the immutability of principles'.[95]

The proposition that any militant production of truth is obliged to
subject itself to 'the ordeal of conformity' can also be read as a precaution
against universalism's fanatical drift – much like Badiou's considerations
on Terror in *Ethics*, or his related self-criticisms concerning the notion of
destruction in *The Century*.[96] What is worth stressing here Badiou's strategic focus on the universalizability of a truth, on the process of its collective organization. In an interesting echo of Jameson's reflections on the
analogies between Christian and Marxist militancy, Badiou declares that
the 'materiality of universalism is the militant dimension of every truth'.[97]
The singular absoluteness of the messianic event – its standing, to borrow
a formulation from Scholem, as 'an intrusion in which history itself
perishes' – is tempered by the historical labours of its universalization.[98]

---

generic multiplicity, does not permit us to lose sight of the fact that, in the situation
(call it: the world), *there are differences*. One can even maintain that there is nothing
else.' Ibid., 98.
95   Ibid., 99. Though Agamben's critique of the 'Catholic' form of universality taken
by Badiou's reading of Paul is suggestive, and rich in philological detail, his contention
that Badiou's notion of the universal is one that *subsumes* difference is problematic. The
idea that the production of truth is the production of a generic multiplicity, central to
Badiou's work ever since *Being and Event*, means that it cannot be the production of a
new (Christian) *identity* without collapsing back into the dimension of the statist representation and management of particularities, and the latter's capture by the mechanisms
of capital (the focus of the Introduction of *Saint Paul*, 'Paul: Our Contemporary'). For
Agamben's critique of the idea of Paul as universalist, see Giorgio Agamben, *The Time
That Remains*, 44–53.
96   'Thought is subjected to the ordeal of conformity, and only the universal, through
an uninterrupted labor, an inventive traversal, relieves it.' Badiou, *Saint Paul*, 110.
97   Ibid., 92.
98   Gershom Scholem, *The Messianic Idea in Judaism*, New York: Schocken, 1995, 10.

Conclusion

The idea of fanaticism has proven to be a remarkably resilient and adaptable weapon in a wide array of political and philosophical confrontations. Its constitutive ambivalence, which in many ways renders it an unreliable concept, turns into a strength when it comes to disqualifying or demonizing adversaries. Many of the pairings that structure our political thinking can easily be mapped onto fanaticism. The fanatic may be pathologically passive or manically active (or both, like the character of Séide in Voltaire's *Le Fanatisme*). Fanaticism may be a matter of individual delusion or crowd madness (or both, as in the Enlightenment image of fanaticism as a kind of 'swarming' affecting individual minds and assembled bodies alike). More importantly, the accusation of fanaticism may be levelled at excesses of abstraction and universality, but also directed towards the irredeemably sensuous and particular.

This is particularly evident in Hegel. In his *Philosophy of History*, fanaticism associated with the advent of Islam and the French Revolution, with Robespierre and Mohammed, is depicted as an 'enthusiasm for the abstract'. But fanaticism is also, in his infamous account of Africa as 'Unhistorical, Undeveloped Spirit', the dehumanizing lack of universality, the absence of all distinction, transcendence and individuality — not even religion, but simple fetishism. This is 'a physical rather than a spiritual enthusiasm'; the absence of ideas, rather than their unlimited sway.[1] At both extremes, though, fanaticism is culturalized

---

1   G. W. F. Hegel, *The Philosophy of History*, 98: 'Every idea thrown into the mind of the Negro is caught up and realized with the whole energy of his will; but this realization involves a wholesale destruction. These people continue long at rest, but suddenly

and contrasted with a proper measure of universality and mediation, whether as the abstract immediacy of the Islamic politics of the One or as the sensuous immediacy of 'the land of childhood'.

This book has been concerned above all with fanaticism as a politics of abstraction, universality and partisanship. This choice was informed by the belief that we have yet to shake off the effects of philosophy's long Cold War, that is to say of an anti-totalitarian discourse – liberally borrowed from the arsenal of Burkean counter-revolutionary rhetoric – which views unconditional conviction and principled egalitarianism with horror or contempt. Many today still perceive claims for radical emancipation as a mere displacement and corruption of religious desires, and those who make such claims as incorrigible 'abstractionists'. For them, as for Emil Cioran, 'when one refuses to admit the interchangeable character of ideas, blood is spilled'.[2] Hence the widespread tendency to celebrate a reasonable, liberal Enlightenment, while ignoring the latter's revolutionary potential: the fanaticism of reason for which his enemies castigated Kant.

Abstract passion and unconditional demands are an enduring dimension of politics, especially when the space for negotiation is absent – as in the case of abolitionism. Uncompromising partisanship is certainly a feature of the fanaticism that has often been associated with revolutionary thought. We can hear it in Saint-Just's plea for 'exaltation . . . in the stubborn resolution to defend the rights of the people'; in Paul Nizan's call that 'none of our actions be free from rage'.[3] But such partisanship need not preclude universality. The struggle to forge practices of antagonism that do not substantialize friendship and enmity is indeed one of

---

their passions ferment, and they are quite beside themselves. The destruction which is the consequence of their excitement, is caused by the fact that it is no positive idea, no thought which produces these commotions; – a physical rather than a spiritual enthusiasm.'

2   Emil Cioran, *Précis de Décomposition* (1949), in *Œuvres*, Paris: Gallimard, 1995, 582. The aphorism from which this quote is taken is entitled 'Genealogy of Fanaticism'.

3   Saint-Just, *Œuvres*, Paris: Gallimard, 2004, 762. Paul Nizan, *Aden Arabie*, Paris: La Découverte, 2002, 162. Nizan continues with these lines: 'We should not be afraid to hate. We should no longer blush for being fanatics.' See Georges Labica, 'Paul Nizan', *Europe*, 784–5 (1994).

the foremost challenges for a politics of emancipation.[4] If fanaticism is 'loyalty carried to a convulsive extreme', under what conditions is it to be an expansive rather than an exclusionary force?[5] If the nexus between partisanship and abstraction is not to result in the phobic separation from one's adversary, it will be necessary to revisit the idea of solidarity, which combines the reference to an abstract principle, collective action and a widening circle of allegiances.[6]

An assertion of the rights of the abstract in politics must nonetheless be accompanied by an effort to account for the emergence, autonomization and power of real abstractions. This is what Marx provides in his critical analyses of religion, the state, and capital as forms of abstract domination. Though Marx's views on the obsolescence of religion as a structuring principle of social life may have proved premature, the catastrophic re-enchantments of our modernity, as well as attempts to assert some abstractions (such as political equality) against others (such as monetary equivalence), require that we find ways of connecting a politics founded on the refusal of compromise with the openings or closures provided by contemporary capitalism. If one reason had to be identified as to why the question of fanaticism has gained such practical and theoretical significance, it is the contemporary difficulty in discerning concrete tendencies on which to base a project of liberation. The primacy of abstraction, conviction and partisanship – together with a certain messianism in the domain of radical theory – can also be regarded as the effect of a sense of historical closure.

Half a century ago, the American sociologist Daniel Bell declared the end of ideology, and of its principal advocate, the radical intellectual. He did so in terms familiar from our survey of the polemical uses to

---

4   See Badiou, *The Century*, 109–10.

5   William James, *Varieties of Religious Experience*, 271.

6   An instructive contemporary example of a political and theological vision of partisanship as absolute enmity is the Al Qaeda leader Ayman al-Zawahiri's 2002 communiqué, 'Loyalty and Separation', in *Al Qaeda in Its Own Words*, G. Kepel and J. P. Milelli (eds), trans. P. Ghazaleh, Cambridge, MA: Belknap Harvard, 2008, 206–34. I have dealt at greater length with the questions of solidarity and partisanship, respectively in 'A Plea for Prometheus' and 'Partisan Thought', *Historical Materialism*, 17: 3 (2009).

which the idea of fanaticism has been put – as 'an end to chiliastic hopes, to millenarianism, to apocalyptic thinking'.[7] A disenchanted diagnosis of our own time might perceive the reverse predicament: rather than the anachronism of fanatical thought in an age pacified by affluence and technology, we are faced with a critical, and for some potentially catastrophic, conjuncture which appears to exceed the resources of a common sense forged in a supposedly post-utopian age. Fanaticism, understood as a politics of passionate and unconditional conviction, is in many ways a child of crisis, of moments when the political compass is broken and militancy is more a matter of will and faith than the outgrowth of organic interests and clear prospects. This accounts both for its seemingly inexorable recurrence and for its ultimate weakness.

Writing of the emergence of Christianity in the Roman Empire, a period he portrays as one of social unravelling and political despotism, as well as of growing commerce and internationalism, Karl Kautsky remarked that only organizations founded on revolutionary idealism, rather than practical motives, stood a chance of surviving. 'Moralistic mysticism' allowed the individual to look beyond the grind of the day-to-day and aim at higher, collective goals. At such moments of disorientation and in conditions of immature development, a certain fanatical intolerance, the 'energetic rejection and criticism of every other view and energetic defense of one's own', could even be considered progressive.[8] Echoing his teacher Engels, however, Kautsky saw this as a historical, specific necessity, not to be replicated. Our own investigation of the role of crises and of anachronism in the debate over millenarian movements suggests that it might be not be so easy to assign fanaticism its proper moment and function in a linear history. One of the paradoxes of fanaticism is precisely this: its anti-historical rupture with historical time can be viewed as conditioning a modern understanding of history, and indeed of progress itself. In this regard the end of ideology and the end of history also spell the end of ends: the abandonment of any

---

7   Daniel Bell, *The End of Ideology: On the Exhaustion of Political Ideas in the Fifties*, rev. ed, New York: Collier, 1961, 393.
8   Karl Kautsky, *Foundations of Christianity*, London: Socialist Resistance, 2007, 84–5.

overarching political project of emancipation, and the derision of every vision of the millennium or intimation of catastrophe.

In the Introduction, I quoted Ruge's remark according to which as long as there are battles to be fought, there will be no history without fanaticism. Much the same could be said for crises, whether political, economic or otherwise. But it is precisely here that the limits of a politics of abstract, uncompromising and passionate conviction can be felt. Fanaticism is born of urgency and shock. This was how, in one of his notes on Machiavelli and the 'Modern Prince' (the Party), Gramsci depicted the regressive role of myth and individual charisma in modern politics. The 'heating up of passions and of fanaticism', which 'annihilated the critical sense and the corrosiveness of irony', followed from the perception of a great and imminent danger. But for Gramsci such fanaticism could never lead to a coherent and effective project of reshaping society. It could at most reorganize or restore, but never found a new polity. He juxtaposed this to the view whereby 'a collective will is to be founded *ex novo*, originally, and to be oriented towards concrete and rational goals, but of a concreteness and rationality which has yet to be verified and criticised by an actual and universally understood historical experience'.[9]

This is in a sense where we find ourselves today. Political disorientation and crisis mean that responses relying on passionate conviction alone – whether of a charismatic, religious or secular nature – are bound to proliferate. Cognizant of the long history of fanaticism as a term of abuse for emancipatory efforts, we should be wary of simply dismissing or pathologizing them: the refusal of compromise, the affirmation of principle and passionate partisanship are moments of any politics that seeks the radical transformation of the status quo. But politics is not reducible to the cry, the clash or the axiom. Urgency and intransigence must be coupled with patience and strategy, if there is ever to be a history without fanaticism.

---

9 Antonio Gramsci, *Quaderni del carcere*, V. Gerratana (ed.), Turin: Einaudi, 2007, 1558 (Notebook 13, § 1).

Acknowledgments

In preparing this book I have been able to rely on the knowledge, comradeship and scrutiny of a wide array of people. Benjamin Noys and Evan Calder Williams were indispensable and vigilant interlocutors throughout the writing, and my text bears the imprint of their own concurrent projects on negativity and apocalypse. Tom Penn's support for this project at Verso was unswerving, and his efforts to spare me from academic introversion valiant. I thank him and everyone at Verso involved in the production of the book. For their responses to written and spoken versions of the text, and their encouragement, I am thankful to Peter Hallward, Stathis Kouvelakis, Gilbert Achcar, Roland Boer, John Roberts, Massimiliano Tomba, Gil Anidjar, Petar Milat, Leonardo Kovacevic, Faisal Devji, Christopher Connery, Paolo Virno, Eyal Weizman, Jennifer Bajorek, Ray Brassier, Andrew Benjamin, Lorenzo Chiesa, Roberto Toscano and Francesca Lancillotti. For sharing their own writings on fanaticism, I am indebted to Joel Olson, Renzo Llorente and Ranabir Samaddar. I thank Peer Illner for his fine translation of Conze and Reinhart's entry on 'Fanatismus'. Commissions from Joan Copjec at *Umbr(a)* and Giancarlo Bosetti at *Reset*, and invitations from MAMA (Zagreb), the Workers' and Punks' University (Ljubljana), the International Marx Conference (Lisbon), the Cold War Research Network, the Yorkshire Theory Research Group, Kent Law School, Queen Mary Department of Politics, the Theory Reading Group at Cornell and the Birkbeck Institute for the Humanities gave me the opportunity to refine my thoughts on fanaticism. I thank all the organizers and participants at those talks. This book would have been a very different beast were it not for my comrades and co-workers on the editorial board of *Historical Materialism*, in particular Sebastian Budgen, Peter Thomas, Matteo Mandarini and Demet Dinler. Any deviations remain my responsibility.

Bibliography

Achcar, Gilbert, 'Marxists and Religion – Yesterday and Today', *International Viewpoint* (2004). Available at: <http://www.internationalviewpoint.org/spip.php?article622>.

Achcar, Gilbert, 'Religion and Politics Today from a Marxian Perspective', *Socialist Register 2008*, London: Merlin, 2007.

Adorno, Theodor W., *Notes to Literature*, Vol. 2, R. Tiedemann (ed.), trans. S. Weber Nicholsen, New York: Columbia University Press, 1992.

Afary, Janet and Kevin B. Anderson, *Foucault and the Iranian Revolution: Gender and the Seductions of Islamism*, Chicago: University of Chicago Press, 2005.

Agamben, Giorgio, *The Time That Remains: A Commentary on the Letter to the Romans*, trans. P. Dailey, Stanford: Stanford University Press, 2005.

Agamben, Giorgio, *Il Regno e la Gloria. Per una genealogia teologica dell'economia e del governo*, Vicenza: Neri Pozza, 2007.

Agamben, Giorgio, *Signatura rerum. Sul metodo*, Turin: Bollati Boringhieri, 2008.

Almond, Ian, *The New Orientalists: Postmodern Representations of Islam from Foucault to Baudrillard*, London: I.B.Tauris, 2007.

Althusser, Louis and Étienne Balibar, *Reading Capital*, London: Verso, 1997.

Anderson, Perry, *Arguments within English Marxism*, London: NLB, 1980.

Anderson, Perry, *Spectrum*, London: Verso, 2005.

Anidjar, Gil, *The Jew, the Arab: A History of the Enemy*, Stanford: Stanford University Press, 2003.

Anidjar, Gil, *Semites*, Stanford: Stanford University Press, 2008.

Anidjar, Gil, '*The Stillborn God*: A review in three parts', *The Immanent Frame*. Available at: <http://www.ssrc.org/blogs/immanent_frame/2007/12/26/a-review-in-three-parts/>.

Ansart-Dourlen, Michèle, *Le fanatisme. Terreur politique et violence psychologique*, Paris: L'Harmattan, 2007.

Arato, Andrew and Paul Breines, *The Young Lukács and the Origins of Western Marxism*, London: Pluto Press, 1979.

Arendt, Hannah, *The Human Condition*, Chicago: University of Chicago Press, 1958.

Arendt, Hannah, *Lectures on Kant's Political Philosophy*, R. Beiner (ed.), Chicago: University of Chicago Press, 1992.

Aron, Raymond, *L'opium des intellectuels*, Paris: Hachette, 2002 [1955].

Aron, Raymond, *Machiavel et les tyrannies modernes*, Paris: Éditions de Fallois, 1993.

Asad, Talal, *Formations of the Secular: Christianity, Islam, Modernity*, Stanford: Stanford University Press, 2003.

Asad, Talal, *On Suicide Bombing*, New York: Columbia University Press, 2007.

Badiou, Alain and François Balmès, *De l'idéologie*, Paris: Maspéro, 1976.

Badiou, Alain, *Saint Paul: The Foundation of Universalism*, trans. R. Brassier, Stanford: Stanford University Press, 2003.

Badiou, Alain, *The Century*, trans. A. Toscano, Cambridge: Polity, 2007.

Badiou, Alain, 'The Communist Hypothesis', *New Left Review*, 49 (2008), 29–42.

Badiou, Alain, *Theory of the Subject*, trans. B. Bosteels, London: Continuum, 2009 [1982].

Badiou, Alain, *L'hypothèse communiste*, Paris: Lignes, 2009.

Balakrishnan, Gopal, *Antagonistics: Capitalism and Power in an Age of War*, London: Verso, 2009.

Barth, Karl, *The Church and the Political Problem of Our Day*, New York: Scribner, 1939.

Bataille, Georges, *Visions of Excess: Selected Writings, 1927–1939*, A. Stoekl (ed.), Minneapolis: University of Minnesota Press, 1985.

Beiser, Frederick C., *The Fate of Reason: German Philosophy from Kant to Fichte*, Cambridge, MA: Harvard University Press, 1987.

Beiser, Frederick C., *The Sovereignty of Reason: The Defense of Rationality in the Early English Enlightenment*, Princeton: Princeton University Press, 1996.

Bell, Daniel, *The End of Ideology: On the Exhaustion of Political Ideas in the Fifties*, rev. ed, New York: Collier, 1961.

Benjamin, Andrew, 'Particularity and Exceptions: On Jews and Animals', *South Atlantic Quarterly*, 107: 1 (2008), 71–87.

Benslama, Fethi, *La psychanalyse à l'épreuve de l'Islam*, Paris: Aubier, 2002.

Berdyaev, Nicolas, *The Origin of Russian Communism*, trans. R. M. French, Ann Arbor: University of Michigan Press, 1960 [first ed 1937/ new ed 1948].

Berman, Marshall, 'Freedom and Fetishism' [1963], in *Adventures in Marxism*, London: Verso, 1999.

Bertrand, Michèle, *Le statut de la religion chez Marx et Engels*, Paris: Éditions Sociales, 1979.

Bhatt, Chetan, 'Frontlines and Interstices in the War on Terror', *Development and Change Forum 2007*, 38: 6 (2007), 1073–93.

Blickle, Peter, 'Social Protest and Reformation Theology', in *Religion, Politics, and Social Protest: Three Studies on Early Modern Germany*, K. von Greyerz (ed.), Boston: Allen & Unwin, 1984.

Blickle, Peter, *The Revolution of 1525: The German Peasants' War from a New Perspective*, trans. T. A. Brady, Jr. and H. C. E. Middlefort, Baltimore: Johns Hopkins, 1985.

Blickle, Peter, *From the Communal Reformation to the Revolution of the Common Man*, trans. B. Kümin, Leiden: Brill, 1998.

Bloch, Ernst, *Thomas Münzer als Theologe der Revolution*, 2nd ed, Frankfurt: Suhrkamp Verlag, 1989 [1962].

Bloch, Ernst, 'Aktualität und Utopie. Zu Lukács' "Geschichte und Klassenbewusstsein"', in *Philosophische Aufsätze*, Frankfurt: Suhrkamp Verlag, 1969.

Bloch, Ernst, 'Non-synchronism and the Obligation to Its Dialectics', trans. M. Ritter, *New German Critique*, 11 (1977), 22–38.

Bloch, Ernst, *The Principle of Hope*, Vol. 3, trans. N. Plaice, S. Plaice and P. Knight, Oxford: Basil Blackwell, 1986.

Bloch, Ernst, *Natural Law and Human Dignity*, trans. D. J. Schmidt, Cambridge, MA: The MIT Press, 1987 [1961].

Bloch, Ernst, *Spirit of Utopia*, trans. A. A. Nassar, Stanford: Stanford University Press, 2000 [1918/1923].

Blumenberg, Hans, *The Legitimacy of the Modern Age*, trans. R. M. Wallace, Cambridge, MA: The MIT Press, 1983.

Bodei, Remo, *Geometria delle passioni. Paura, speranza, felicità: filosofia e uso politico*, Milan: Feltrinelli, 1991.

Boella, Laura (ed.), *Intellettuali e coscienza di classe. Il dibattito su Lukács 1923–24*, Milan: Feltrinelli, 1977.

Bousquet, G.-H., 'Marx et Engels se sont-ils intéressés aux questions islamiques?', *Studia Islamica*, 30 (1969), 119–30.

Breckman, Warren, *Marx, the Young Hegelians, and the Origins of Radical Social Theory*, Cambridge: Cambridge University Press, 1999.

Bronner, Stephen Eric, *Reclaiming the Enlightenment: Towards a Politics of Radical Engagement*, New York: Columbia University Press, 2004.

Brown, Malcolm (ed.), *Plato's Meno*, New York: Bobb-Merrill, 1971.

Brown, Wendy, *Regulating Aversion: Tolerance in the Age of Identity and Empire*, Princeton: Princeton University Press, 2006.

Bull, Malcolm, *Seeing Things Hidden: Apocalypse, Vision and Totality*, London: Verso, 1999.

Bull, Malcolm, 'The Catastrophist', *London Review of Books*, 29: 21 (2007).

Burgat, François, *L'islamisme à l'heure d'Al-Qaida*, Paris: La Découverte, 2005.

Burke, Edmund, *Reflections on the Revolution in France*, L. G. Mitchell (ed.), Oxford: Oxford University Press, 1993 [1790].

Burke, Edmund, *Further Reflections on the Revolution in France*, D. E. Ritchie (ed.), Indianapolis: Liberty Fund, 1992.

Burke, Edmund, *The Writings and Speeches of Edmund Burke, Vol. III: Party, Parliament, and the American War, 1774–1780*, W. M. Elofson and J. A. Woods (eds), Cambridge: Cambridge University Press, 1996.

Burridge, Kenelm, *New Heaven, New Earth: A Study of Millenarian Activities*, Oxford: Basil Blackwell, 1971.

Calhoun, John C., *Union and Liberty: The Political Philosophy of John C. Calhoun*, R. M. Lence (ed.), Indianapolis: Liberty Fund, 1992.

Caygill, Howard, *A Kant Dictionary*, Oxford: Blackwell, 1995.

Chakrabarty, Dipesh, *Provincializing Europe: Postcolonial Thought and Historical Difference*, Princeton: Princeton University Press, 2000.

Chakrabarty, Dipesh, '*Subaltern Studies* and Postcolonial Historiography', *Nepantla: Views from the South*, 1: 1 (2000), 9–32.

Chiesa, Lorenzo and Alberto Toscano, 'Agape and the Anonymous Religion of Atheism', *Angelaki: Journal of the Theoretical Humanities*, 12: 1 (2007), 113–26.

Chomsky, Noam, *Rogue States*, London: Pluto, 2000.

Cioran, Emil, *Œuvres*, Paris: Gallimard, 1995.

Clemens, Justin, 'Man is a Swarm Animal', in *The Catastrophic Imperative*, D. Hoens, S. Jöttkandt and G. Buelens (eds), Basingstoke: Palgrave, 2009.

Cohn, Norman, *The Pursuit of the Millennium*, 2nd ed, London: Mercury Books, 1962.

Colas, Dominique, *Civil Society and Fanaticism: Conjoined Histories*, trans. A. Jacobs, Stanford: Stanford University Press, 1997.

Coleridge, Samuel Taylor, *Biographia Literaria*, New York: William Gowans, 1852 [1817].

Conze, Werner and Helga Reinhart, 'Fanatismus', in *Geschichtliche Grundbegriffe. Historisches Lexicon zur politisch-sozialen Sprache in Deutschland*, Vol. 2, O. Brunner, W. Conze and R. Koselleck (eds), Stuttgart: Klett-Cotta, 1975.

Critchley, Simon, *Infinitely Demanding*, London: Verso, 2007.

Critchley, Simon, 'Mystical Anarchism', *Critical Horizons*, 10: 2 (2009), 272–306.

Crossman, Richard (ed.), *The God that Failed*, New York: Bantam, 1959 [1950].

Cruise O' Brien, Conor, 'Edmund Burke: Prophet Against the Tyranny of the Politics of Theory', in Edmund Burke, *Reflections on the Revolution in France*, F. M. Turner (ed.), New Haven: Yale University Press, 2003 [1790].

da Cunha, Euclides, *Rebellion in the Backlands*, trans. S. Putnam, Chicago: University of Chicago Press, 1944 [1902].

David-Ménard, Monique, *La folie dans la raison pure. Kant lecteur de Swedenborg*, Paris: Vrin, 1990.

Davis, Mike, *Late Victorian Holocausts*, London: Verso, 2001.

Davis, Mike, *Dead Cities*, New York: The New Press, 2003.

Davis, Mike, 'Planet of Slums', *New Left Review*, 26 (2004), 5–34.

Davis, Mike, *Planet of Slums*, London: Verso, 2006.

De Martino, Ernesto, *La fine del mondo. Contributo all'analisi delle apocalissi culturali*, C. Gallini (ed.), Turin: Einaudi, 2002 [1977].

Derrida, Jacques and Gianni Vattimo (eds), *Religion*, Stanford: Stanford University Press, 1998.

Derrida, Jacques, *Specters of Marx: The State of the Debt, The Work of Mourning and the New International*, trans. P. Kamuf, London: Routledge, 2006 [1994].

Devji, Faisal, *The Terrorist in Search of Humanity: Militant Islam and Global Politics*, London: Hurst, 2008.

Dianteill, Erwann and Michael Löwy, *Sociologies et religion. Approches dissidentes*, Paris: PUF, 2005.

Dolar, Mladen, 'Freud and the Political', *Unbound*, 4: 15 (2008), 15–29.

Drayton, William, *The South Vindicated from the Treason and Fanaticism of the Northern Abolitionists*, Philadelphia: H. Manly, 1836.

Du Bois, W. E. B., *John Brown*, D. Roediger (ed.), New York: The Modern Library, 2001 [1909].

Elton, G. R., *Reformation Europe 1517–1559*, London: Collins, 1963.

Engels, Friedrich, *The Peasant War in Germany*, trans. M. J. Olgin, London: George Allen & Unwin, 1927 [1850].

Engels, Friedrich, *The Condition of the Working Class in England*, London: Penguin, 1987 [1845].

Étienne, Bruno, *Les combatants suicidaires* suivi de *Les amants de l'apocalypse*, Paris: L'Aube, 2005.

Fenves, Peter, *A Peculiar Fate: Metaphysics and World-History in Kant*, Ithaca: Cornell University Press, 1991.

Fenves, Peter (ed.), *Raising the Tone of Philosophy: Late Essays by Immanuel Kant, Transformative Critique by Jacques Derrida*, Baltimore: Johns Hopkins, 1993.

Feuerbach, Ludwig, *The Essence of Christianity*, trans. G. Eliot, New York: Harper & Row, 1956 [1841].

Finelli, Roberto, *Astrazione e dialettica dal romanticismo al capitalismo (saggio su Marx)*, Rome: Bulzoni Editore, 1987.

Finkielkraut, Alain, 'Fanatiques sans frontières', *Libération*, 9 February 2006.

Fisher, Andrew, 'Flirting with Fascism', *Radical Philosophy*, 99 (2000).

Flores, John, 'Proletarian Meditations: Georg Lukács' Politics of Knowledge', *Diacritics*, 2: 3 (1972), 10–21.

Foucault, Michel, *Language, Counter-Memory, Practice: Selected Essays and Interviews*, D. F. Bouchard (ed.), Ithaca, NY: Cornell University Press, 1977.

Foucault, Michel, *The Politics of Truth*, Los Angeles: Semiotext(e), 2007.

Freud, Sigmund, *The Complete Psychological Works of Sigmund Freud*, Vol. 9, J. Strachey (ed.), London: The Hogarth Press, 1959.

Freud, Sigmund, *The Future of an Illusion*, New York: Anchor Books, 1964.

Fukuyama, Francis. The End of

Furet, François, *Marx and the French Revolution*, trans. D. Kan Furet, Chicago: University of Chicago Press, 1988.

Gentile, Emilio, *Le religioni della politica. Fra democrazie e totalitarismi*, 2nd ed, Bari: Laterza, 2007.

Goertz, Hans-Jürgen, *Thomas Müntzer: Apocalyptic, Mystic and Revolutionary*, Edinburgh: T&T Clark, 1993.

Geoghegan, Vincent, *Ernst Bloch*, London: Routledge, 1996.

Geoghegan, Vincent, 'Religion and Communism: Feuerbach, Marx and Bloch', *The European Legacy*, 9: 5 (2004), 585–95.

Goody, Jack, *The Theft of History*, Cambridge: Cambridge University Press, 2007.

Gramsci, Antonio, *Quaderni del carcere*, V. Gerratana (ed.), Turin: Einaudi, 2007.

Gray, John, *Black Mass: Apocalyptic Religion and the Death of Utopia*, London: Allen Lane, 2007.

Grosrichard, Alain, *The Sultan's Court: European Fantasies of the East*, trans. L. Heron, introduction by M. Dolar, London: Verso, 1998.

Grjebine, André, *La guerre du doute et de la certitude. La démocratie face aux fanatismes*, Paris: Berg International, 2008.

Guha, Ranajit, 'The Prose of Counter-Insurgency', in *Subaltern Studies No. 2*, R. Guha (ed.), Delhi: Oxford University Press, 1983.

Guha, Ranajit, *Elementary Aspects of Peasant Insurgency in Colonial India*, Durham, NC: Duke University Press, 1999 [1983].

Halévy, Élie, *L'Ère des tyrannies. Études sur le socialisme et la guerre*, Paris: Gallimard, 1990 [1938].

Hall, Stuart, 'Religious Ideology and Social Movements in Jamaica', in *Religion and Ideology*, R. Bocock and K. Thompson (eds), Manchester, UK: Manchester University Press, 1985.

Hare, R. M., *Freedom and Reason*, Oxford: Oxford University Press, 1963.

Hart, William David, 'Slavoj Žižek and the Imperial/Colonial Model of Religion', *Nepantla*, 3: 3 (2002), 553–78.

Hart, William David, 'Can a Judgment Be Read?', *Nepantla*, 4: 1 (2003), 191–4.

Harvey, David, *A Brief History of Neoliberalism*, Oxford: Oxford University Press, 2005.

Hauerwas, Stanley, 'The Non-Violent Terrorist: In Defense of Christian Fanaticism', in *Incredible Forgiveness: Christian Ethics Between Fanaticism and Reconciliation*, D. Pollefeyt (ed.), Leuven: Peeters, 2004.

Haynal, André, Miklos Molnar and Gérard de Puymège, *Le fanatisme: ses racines. Un essai historique et psychanalytique*, Paris: Stock, 1980.

Hegel, G. W. F., *The Philosophy of History*, New York: Dover, 1956.

Hegel, G. W. F., *Lectures on the Philosophy of Religion, Vol. III: The Consummate Religion*, Berkeley: University of California Press, 1985.

Hegel, G. W. F., *Elements of the Philosophy of Right*, Allen W. Wood (ed.), trans. H. B. Nisbet, Cambridge: Cambridge University Press, 1991.

Heimonet, Jean-Michel, *Jules Monnerot ou la démission critique – 1932–1990. Trajet d'un intellectuel vers le fascisme*, Paris: Kimé, 1993.

Heine, Heinrich, *On the History of Religion and Philosophy in Germany*, T. Pinkard (ed.), trans. H. Pollack-Milgate, 2007 [1834/1852].

Heyd, Michael, *'Be Sober and Reasonable': The Critique of Enthusiasm in the Seventeenth and Early Eighteenth Centuries*, Leiden: Brill, 1995.

Herring, Ronald J., 'From "Fanaticism" to Power: The Deep Roots of Kerala's Agrarian Exceptionalism', in *Speaking of Peasants: Essays on Indian History and Politics in Honor of Walter Hauser*, W. R. Pinch (ed.), New Delhi: Manohar, 2008.

Higonnet, Patrice, 'Terror, Trauma and the "Young Marx": Explanation of Jacobin Politics', *Past and Present*, 191 (2006), 121–64.

Hill, Christopher, *The World Turned Upside Down: Radical Ideas During the English Revolution*, London: Penguin, 1975.

Hind, Dan, *The Threat to Reason*, London: Verso, 2007.

Hirschman, Albert, *The Passions and the Interests*, Princeton: Princeton University Press, 1977.

Hobsbawm, Eric J., *Primitive Rebels: Studies in Archaic Forms of Social Movement in the 19th and 20th Centuries*, New York: Norton, 1965 [1959].

Hollier, Denis (ed.), *The College of Sociology 1937–1939*, Minneapolis: University of Minnesota Press, 1988.

Hopkins, Nicholas S., 'Engels and Ibn Khaldun', *Alif: Journal of Comparative Poetics*, 10 (1990).

Hughes, Matthew and Gaynor Johnson (eds), *Fanaticism and Conflict in the Modern Age*, London and New York: Frank Cass, 2005.

Ileto, Reynaldo C., 'Philippine Wars and the Politics of Memory', *positions*, 13: 1 (2005), 215–34.

Israel, Jonathan I., 'Enlightenment! Which Enlightenment?', *Journal of the History of Ideas*, 67: 3 (2006), 523–45.

Israel, Jonathan I., *Enlightenment Contested: Philosophy, Modernity, and the Emancipation of Man 1670–1752*, Oxford: Oxford University Press, 2006.

James, William, *The Varieties of Religious Experience: A Study in Human Nature*, New York: Macmillan, 1961 [1902].

Jameson, Fredric, *Marxism and Form*, Princeton: Princeton University Press, 1971.

Kant, Immanuel, *Observations on the Feeling of the Beautiful and the Sublime*, trans. J. T. Goldthwait, Berkeley: University of California Press, 2003 [1764].

Kant, Immanuel, *Critique of Judgment*, trans. W. S. Pluhar, New York: Hackett, 1987 [1790].

Kant, Immanuel, *Theoretical Philosophy 1755–1770*, trans. and ed. D. Walford with R. Meerbote, Cambridge: Cambridge University Press, 1992.

Kant, Immanuel, *Religion and Rational Theology*, trans. and ed. A. W. Wood and G. Di Giovanni, Cambridge: Cambridge University Press, 1996.

Kant, Immanuel, *Critique of Practical Reason*, trans. W. S. Pluhar, 2002 [1788].

Kant, Immanuel, *Anthropology from a Pragmatic Point of View*, R. B. Louden (ed.), Cambridge: Cambridge University Press, 2006 [1798].

Kant, Immanuel, *Anthropology, History and Education*, R. B. Louden (ed.), Cambridge: Cambridge University Press, 2007.

Kautsky, Karl, *Foundations of Christianity*, London: Socialist Resistance, 2007 [1908].

Kepel, Gilles and Jean-Pierre Milelli (eds), *Al Qaeda in Its Own Words*, trans. P. Ghazaleh, Cambridge, MA: Belknap Harvard, 2008.

Klein, Lawrence E. and Anthony J. La Vopa (eds), *Enthusiasm and Enlightenment in Europe, 1650–1850*, San Marino, CA: Huntington Library, 1998.

Klemperer, Victor, *The Language of the Third Reich: LTI – Lingua Tertii Imperii: A Philologist's Notebook*, trans. M. Brady, London: Continuum, 2006.

Kouvelakis, Stathis, *Philosophy and Revolution: From Kant to Marx*, trans. G. M. Goshgarian, London: Verso, 2003.

La Barre, Weston, 'Materials for a History of Studies of Crisis Cults: A Bibliographic Essay', *Current Anthropology*, 12: 1 (1971), 3–44.

Labica, Georges, 'Paul Nizan', *Europe*, 784–5 (1994).

Laclau, Ernesto, *New Reflections on the Revolution of Our Time*, London: Verso, 1990.

Lafargue, Paul, *La religion du Capital*, Paris: L'Aube, 2006 [1887].

Walter Laqueur, *The New Terrorism: Fanaticism and the Arms of Mass Destruction*, Oxford: Oxford University Press, 1999.

Lanternari, Vittorio, *The Religions of the Oppressed: A Study of Modern Messianic Cults*, trans. L. Sergio, New York: Mentor, 1965.

La Rocca, Tommaso, *Es Ist Zeit. Apocalisse e storia: studio su Thomas Müntzer (1490–1525)*, Bologna: Cappelli, 1988.

Le Bon, Gustave, *The Crowd: A Study of the Popular Mind*, New York: The Macmillan Company, 1896.

Lefebvre, Henri, *The Sociology of Marx*, trans. N. Guterman, London: Penguin, 1972.

Lefort, Claude, *Complications: Communism and the Dilemmas of Democracy*, trans. J. Bourg, New York: Columbia University Press, 2007.

Leggett, William, 'Progress of Fanaticism' (1837), in *Democratic Editorials: Essays in Jacksonian Political Economy*, Indianapolis: Liberty Fund, 1984.

Lenin, Vladimir Ilyich, *Collected Works*, Vol. 17, Moscow: Progress Publishers, 1977.

Lewis, Bernard, 'The Roots of Muslim Rage', *Atlantic Monthly*, September 1990.

Lilla, Mark, *The Stillborn God: Religion, Politics and the Modern West*, New York: Vintage, 2008.

Lilla, Mark, 'Our Historical *Sonderweg*', *The Immanent Frame*, available at: <http://www.ssrc.org/blogs/immanent_frame/2008/01/04/our-historical-sonderweg/>.

Lincoln, Bruce, *Holy Terrors: Thinking about Religion after September 11*, 2nd ed, Chicago: University of Chicago Press, 2006.

Lindberg, Carter, 'Eschatology and Fanaticism in the Reformation Era: Luther and the Anabaptists', *Concordia Theological Quarterly*, 64: 4 (2000), 259–78.

Llorente, Renzo, 'Hegel's Conception of Fanaticism', *Auslegung*, 20: 2 (1995), 83–99.

Locke, John, *The Works of John Locke in Nine Volumes*, London: Rivington, 1824.

Lombroso, Cesare, *Les anarchistes*, 2nd ed, trans. M. Hamel and A. Marie, Paris: Ernest Flammarion, 1896.

Lombroso, Cesare, *Crime, Its Causes and Remedies*, trans. Henry P. Horton, London: W. Heinemann, 1911 [1899].

Lombroso, Cesare, *Criminal Man*, ed. and trans. M. Gibson and N. H. Rafter, Durham, NC: Duke University Press, 2006 [1876–97].

Lomonaco, Jeffrey, 'Kant's Unselfish Partisans as Democratic Citizens', 17: 3 (2005), 393–416.

Losurdo, Domenico, *Il revisionismo storico*, Bari: Laterza, 1996.

Losurdo, Domenico, *Nietzsche, il ribelle aristocratico. Biografia intellettuale e bilancio critico*, Turin: Bollati Boringhieri, 2002.

Losurdo, Domenico, *Hegel and the Freedom of the Moderns*, Durham, NC: Duke University Press, 2004.

Losurdo, Domenico, 'Towards a Critique of the Category of Totalitarianism', *Historical Materialism*, 12: 2 (2004), 25–55.

Losurdo, Domenico, *Controstoria del liberalismo*, Bari: Laterza, 2005.

Losurdo, Domenico, *Il linguaggio dell'impero. Lessico dell'ideologia americana*, Bari: Laterza, 2007.

Losurdo, Domenico, *Autocensura e compromesso nel pensiero politico di Kant*, 2nd ed, Naples: Bibliopolis, 2007 [1983].

Löwith, Karl, *Meaning in History*, Chicago: University of Chicago Press, 1949.

Löwy, Michael, 'Interview with Ernst Bloch', *New German Critique* 9 (1976), 35–45.

Löwy, Michael, *Georg Lukács – From Romanticism to Bolshevism*, trans. Patrick Camiller, London: NLB, 1979.

Löwy, Michael, *Redemption and Utopia: Jewish Libertarian Thought in Central Europe – A Study in Elective Affinity*, trans. H. Heaney, London: Athlone Press, 1992.

Löwy, Michael, *The War of the Gods: Religion and Politics in Latin America*, London: Verso, 1996.

Löwy, Michael, 'From Captain Swing to Pancho Villa: Instances of Peasant Resistance in the Historiography of Eric Hobsbawm', *Diogenes*, 48: 189 (2000), 3–10.

Löwy, Michael, 'Marxism and Religion: Opiate of the People', *New Socialist*, 51 (2005). Available at: <http://newsocialist.org/newsite/index.php?id=243>.

Löwy, Michael, 'Capitalism as Religion: Walter Benjamin and Max Weber', *Historical Materialism*, 17: 1 (2009), 60–73.

Lukács, Georg, *History and Class Consciousness: Studies in Marxist Dialectics*, trans. R. Livingstone, Cambridge, MA: The MIT Press, 1971.

Lyotard, Jean-François, 'The Sign of History' (1982), in *The Lyotard Reader*, Andrew Benjamin (ed.), Oxford: Basil Blackwell, 1989.

Lyotard, Jean-François, *L'enthousiasme. La critique kantienne de l'histoire*, Paris: Galilée, 1986.

MacIntyre, Alasdair, *Marxism and Christianity*, Harmondsworth: Pelican, 1971.

Mannheim, Karl, *Ideology and Utopia: An Introduction to the Sociology of Knowledge*, London: Routledge, 1936.

Marx, Karl, *A Contribution to the Critique of Political Economy*, New York: International Publishers, 1970.

Marx, Karl, *Early Texts*, D. McLellan (ed.), Oxford: Basil Blackwell, 1972.

Marx, Karl, *The Revolutions of 1848: Political Writings*, Vol. 1, London: Penguin, 1973.

Marx, Karl, *Grundrisse*, trans. M. Nicolaus, London: Penguin, 1973.

Marx, Karl, *The First International and After: Political Writings*, Vol. 3, D. Fernbach (ed.), London: Penguin, 1974.

Marx, Karl and Friedrich Engels, *Collected Works*, London: Lawrence & Wishart, 1975–2005.

Marx, Karl, *Capital: Volume 1*, trans. B. Fowkes, London: Penguin, 1990.

Marx, Karl, *Capital: Volume 3*, trans. D. Fernbach, London: Penguin, 1991.

Marx, Karl, *Early Writings*, trans. R. Livingstone and G. Benton, London: Penguin, 1992.

Marx, Karl (with Friedrich Engels), *The German Ideology*, New York: Prometheus, 1998.

Marx, Karl and Friedrich Engels, *The Communist Manifesto*, London: Penguin, 2002.

Marx, Karl, *Dispatches for the New York Tribune: Selected Journalism of Karl Marx*, J. Ledbetter (ed.), London: Penguin, 2007.

Mason, Richard, *Spinoza: Logic, Knowledge and Religion*, Aldershot: Ashgate, 2007.

Matheson, Peter (ed.), *The Collected Works of Thomas Müntzer*, Edinburgh: T&T Clark, 1988.

Mayer, Arno, *The Furies: Violence and Terror in the French and Russian Revolutions*, Princeton: Princeton University Press, 2000.

McLellan, David, *Marxism and Religion*, London: Macmillan, 1987.

McMahon, Darrin M., *Enemies of the Enlightenment: The French Counter-Enlightenment and the Making of Modernity*, New York: Oxford University Press, 2001.

Menand, Louis, *The Metaphysical Club*, London: Flamingo, 2002.

Mendes Sargo, David-Emmanuel, 'Martin Luther, Thomas Müntzer and the Birth of the Modern State: Reflections on the Status of the Lutheran Reform in the Historical Sociology of Protestantism', *Social Compass*, 36: 1 (1989), 105–31.

Miegge, Mario, *Il sogno del re di Babilonia. Profezia e storia da Thomas Müntzer a Isaac Newton*, Milan: Feltrinelli, 1995.

Monnerot, Jules, *Sociologie du communisme*, Paris: Gallimard, 1949.

Mufti, Aamir R., 'Fanatics in Europa', *boundary 2*, 34: 1 (2007), 17–23.

Negt, Oskar, 'The Non-Synchronous Heritage and the Problem of Propaganda', 9 (1976), 46–70.

Nietzsche, Friedrich, *The Will to Power*, W. Kaufmann (ed.), trans. W. Kaufmann and R. J. Hollingdale, New York: Vintage, 1968.

Nietzsche, Friedrich, *Beyond Good and Evil*, trans. W. Kaufmann, New York: Vintage, 1989 [1886].

Nietzsche, Friedrich, *Twilight of the Idols / The Antichrist*, trans. R. J. Hollingdale, London: Penguin, 1990 [1889/1895].

Nietzsche, Friedrich, *Human, All Too Human, I*, Stanford: Stanford University Press, 1995 [1878].

Nietzsche, Friedrich, *Daybreak: Thoughts on the Prejudices of Morality*, trans. R. J. Hollingdale, Cambridge: Cambridge University Press, 1982 [1881/1886].

Nizan, Paul, *Aden Arabie*, Paris: La Découverte, 2002 [1931/1960].

Olson, Joel, 'The Freshness of Fanaticism: The Abolitionist Defense of Zealotry', *Perspectives on Politics*, 5: 4 (2007), 685–701.

Olson, Joel, 'Friends and Enemies, Slaves and Masters: Fanaticism, Wendell Phillips, and the Limits of Democratic Politics', *Journal of Politics*, 71: 1 (2009), 82–95.

Olson, Joel, 'The Politics of Protestant Violence: Abolitionists and Anti-Abortionists', unpublished paper (2009).

Oz, Amos, *How to Cure a Fanatic*, Princeton: Princeton University Press, 2006.

Pareto, Vilfredo, *The Rise and Fall of Elites*, New Brunswick, NJ: Transaction, 2006 [1901].

Pick, Daniel, *Faces of Degeneration: A European Disorder, c. 1848–c. 1918*, Cambridge: Cambridge University Press, 1989.

Pocock, J. G. A., 'Edmund Burke and the Redefinition of Enthusiasm: The Context as Counter-Revolution', in F. Furet and M. Ozouf (eds), *The French Revolution and the Creation of Modern Political Culture, Vol. 3: The Transformations of French Political Culture, 1789–1848*, Oxford: Pergamon Press, 1989.

Pocock, J. G. A., *Barbarism and Religion, Vol. 2: Narratives of Civil Government*, Cambridge: Cambridge University Press, 1999.

Quarles, Benjamin (ed.), *Allies for Freedom & Blacks on John Brown*, Cambridge, MA: Da Capo, 2001 [1974/1972].

Rabinbach, Anson, 'Unclaimed Heritage: Bloch's *Heritage of Our Times* and the Theory of Fascism', *New German Critique* 11 (1977), 5–21.

Raines, John (ed.), *Marx on Religion*, Philadelphia: Temple University Press, 2002.

Rancière, Jacques, 'The Concept of "Critique" and the "Critique of Political Economy"', in *Ideology, Method and Marx*, A. Rattansi (ed.), London: Routledge, 1989.

Rancière, Jacques, *Le spectateur émancipé*, Paris: La Fabrique, 2008.

Roberts, John, 'The "Returns to Religion": Messianism, Christianity and the Revolutionary Tradition. Part I: Wakefulness to the Future', *Historical Materialism*, 16: 2 (2008), 59–84.

Roberts, John, 'The "Returns to Religion": Messianism, Christianity and the Revolutionary Tradition. Part II: The Pauline Tradition', *Historical Materialism*, 16: 3 (2008), 77–103.

Rodinson, Maxime, *Islam and Capitalism*, London: Penguin, 1977.

Rudin, Josef, *Fanaticism: A Psychological Analysis*, trans. E. Reinecke and P.C. Bailey, Notre Dame: University of Notre Dame Press, 1969.

Russell, Bertrand, *The Practice and Theory of Bolshevism*, London: George Allen & Unwin, 1920.

Said, Edward W. and Christopher Hitchens (eds), *Blaming the Victims*, London: Verso, 1988.

Said, Edward W., *Orientalism*, New York: Vintage, 1994.

Said, Edward W., *Freud and the Non-European*, London: Verso, 2003.

Said, Edward W., *Humanism and Democratic Criticism*, Basingstoke: Palgrave, 2004.

Samaddar, Ranabir, 'The Impossibility of Settled Rule – Lessons of the Colonial Time', unpublished manuscript, 2007.

Safouan, Moustapha, *Why Are the Arabs Not Free? – The Politics of Writing*, Oxford: Blackwell, 2007.

Saint-Just, *Œuvres*, Paris: Gallimard, 2004.

Sartre, Jean-Paul, *Cahiers pour une morale*, Paris: Gallimard, 1983.

Savater, Fernando, 'Fanáticos sin fronteras', *El País*, 11 February 2006.

Scarcia Amoretti, Biancamaria, *Tolleranʒa e guerra santa nell'Islam*, Florence: Sansoni (Scuola Aperta), 1974.

Schmidt, James (ed.), *What is Enlightenment? Eighteenth-Century Answers and Twentieth-Century Questions*, Berkeley: University of California Press, 1996.

Schmitt, Carl, *Political Theology: Four Chapters on the Concept of Sovereignty*, trans. G. Schwab, Cambridge, MA: The MIT Press, 1985.

Schmitt, Carl, *Political Theology II: The Myth of the Closure of Any Political Theology*, trans. M. Hoelzl and G. Ward, Cambridge: Polity, 2008 [1970].

Scholem, Gershom, *The Messianic Idea in Judaism*, New York: Schocken, 1995.

Scott, John T. and Ourida Mostefai (eds), *Rousseau and l'Infâme: Religion, Toleration, and Fanaticism in the Age of Enlightenment*, Amsterdam: Rodopi, 2008.

Scott, Tom and Bob Scribner (eds), *The German Peasants' War: A History in Documents*, Amherst, NY: Humanity Books, 1991.

Scurr, Ruth, *Fatal Purity: Robespierre and the French Revolution*, London: Vintage, 2007.

Seymour, Richard, *The Liberal Defence of Murder*, London: Verso, 2008.

Shanin, Teodor (ed.), *Late Marx and the Russian Road*, New York: Monthly Review Press, 1983.

Shorten, Richard, 'The Enlightenment, Communism and Political Religion: Reflections on a Misleading Trajectory', *Journal of Political Ideologies*, 8: 1 (2003), 13–37.

Shorten, Richard, 'The Status of Ideology in the Return of Political Religion Theory', *Journal of Political Ideologies*, 12: 2 (2007), 163–87.

Siblot, Paul, 'Les *fanatiques* et le discours colonial', *Mots. Les langages du politique*, 79 (2005), 73–81.

Sloterdijk, Peter, *Zorn und Zeit*, Frankfurt: Suhrkamp Verlag, 2006.

Sloterdijk, Peter, 'What Happened in the Twentieth Century? En Route to a Critique of Extremist Reason', *Cultural Politics*, 3: 3 (2007), 327–55.

Sloterdijk, Peter, *God's Zeal: The Battle of the Three Monotheisms*, trans. W. Hoban, Cambridge: Polity, 2009.

Sloterdijk, Peter, 'Rules for the Human Zoo: A Response to the *Letter on Humanism*', *Society and Space*, 27: 1 (2009), 12–28.

Smith, William, 'Fanum', in *Dictionary of Greek and Roman Antiquities*, W. Smith, W. Wayte and G. E. Marindin (eds), 2nd ed, London: John Murray, 1890.

Sprinker, Michael (ed.), *Ghostly Demarcations*, London: Verso, 1999.

Stengers, Isabelle, *Au temps des catastrophes. Résister à la barbarie qui vient*, Paris: La Découverte, 2009.

Sternhell, Zeev, *Les anti-Lumières. Du XVIIIe siècle à la guerre froide*, Paris: Fayard, 2006.

Stevens, Jacob, 'Exorcizing the Manifesto', *New Left Review*, 28 (2004), 151–60.

Stiegmann-Gall, Richard, 'Nazism and the Revival of Political Religion Theory', *Totalitarian Movements and Political Religions*, 5: 3 (2004), 376–96.

Stoker, Richard, 'Fanaticism and Heresy', *New International*, 14: 1 (1948), 31.

Talmon, J. L., *The Origins of Totalitarian Democracy*, London: Sphere Books, 1970 [1959].

Tarde, Gabriel, *L'opinion et la foule*, Paris: PUF, 1989 [1901].

Taubes, Jakob, *Abendländische Eschatologie*, Munich: Matthes & Seitz, 1991 [1947].

Taubes, Jakob, *The Political Theology of Paul*, trans. D. Hollander, Stanford: Stanford University Press, 2004.

Therborn, Göran, 'Nato's Demographer', *New Left Review*, 56 (2009), 136–44.

Thoreau, Henry David, *Civil Disobedience and Other Essays*, New York: Dover, 1993 [1849–63].

de Tocqueville, Alexis, *The Old Regime and the Revolution*, F. Furet and F. Mélonio (eds), trans. A. S. Kahan, Chicago: University of Chicago Press, 1998.

Toscano, Alberto, 'Fanaticism and Production: Schelling's Philosophy of Indifference', *Pli: The Warwick Journal of Philosophy*, 8 (1999), 46–70.

Toscano, Alberto, 'Communism as Separation', in *Think Again: Alain Badiou and the Future of Philosophy*, P. Hallward (ed.), London: Continuum, 2004.

Toscano, Alberto, 'Marxism Expatriated: Alain Badiou's Turn', in *Critical Companion to Contemporary Marxism*, Jacques Bidet and Stathis Kouvelakis (eds), Leiden: Brill, 2008.

Toscano, Alberto, 'The Open Secret of Real Abstraction', *Rethinking Marxism*, 20: 2, (2008), 273–87.

Toscano, Alberto, '*Ad Hominem*: Antinomies of Radical Philosophy', *Filozofski Vestnik* XXIX: 2 (2008), 137–53.

Toscano, Alberto, 'A Plea for Prometheus', *Critical Horizons*, 10: 2 (2009), 241–56.

Toscano, Alberto, 'Partisan Thought', *Historical Materialism*, 17: 3 (2009), 175–91.

Tosel, André, *Kant révolutionnaire. Droit et politique*, Paris: PUF, 1988.

Toynbee, Arnold J., *A Study of History: Abridgment of Volumes VII–X by D. C. Somervell*, Oxford: Oxford University Press, 1988.

Traverso, Enzo, *Il totalitarismo*, Milan: Bruno Mondadori, 2002.

Turcan, Robert, *The Gods of Ancient Rome*, London: Routledge, 2001.

Venturi, Franco, 'Un enciclopedista: Alexandre Deleyre', *Rivista Storica Italiana*, LXXVII: IV (1965), 791–824.

Virno, Paolo, *Scienze sociali e 'natura umana'*, Soveria Mannelli: Rubbettino, 2003.

Voegelin, Eric, *The New Science of Politics*, Chicago: University of Chicago Press, 1952.

Voegelin, Eric, *The Political Religions*, in *The Collected Works of Eric Voegelin, Volume 5: Modernity Without Restraint*, Columbia and London: University of Missouri Press, 2000 [1938].

Voltaire, *The Works of Voltaire: A Contemporary Version*, including a critique and biography by J. Morley, notes by T. Smollett, trans. William F. Fleming, New York: E. R. DuMont, 1901.

Voltaire, *Traité sur la tolérance*, Paris: Gallimard, 1975 [1763].

Voltaire, *Le Fanatisme, ou Mahomet le prophète*, Paris: Flammarion, 2004 [1741].

Wahnich, Sophie, *La longue patience du peuple. 1792. Naissance de la République*, Paris: Payot & Rivages, 2008.

Walzer, Michael, *The Revolution of the Saints: A Study in the Origins of Radical Politics*, New York: Atheneum, 1973 [1965].

Walzer, Michael, *Exodus and Revolution*, New York: Basic Books, 1985.

Walzer, Michael, 'Passion and Politics', *Philosophy and Social Criticism*, 28: 6 (2002), 617–33.

Whalen, Terence, *Edgar Allan Poe and the Masses: The Political Economy of Literature in Antebellum America*, Princeton: Princeton University Press, 1999.

Wittkower, Margot and Rudolf, *Born Under Saturn*, New York: New York Review of Books, 2007 [1963].

Wood, Allen W., *Kant*, Oxford: Blackwell, 2005.

Wood, Ellen M., *Democracy Against Capitalism*, Cambridge: Cambridge University Press, 1995.

Worsley, Peter, *The Trumpet Shall Sound: A Study of 'Cargo' Cults in Melanesia*, 2nd ed, London: Paladin, 1970.

Zammito, John H., *Kant, Herder and the Birth of Anthropology*, Chicago: University of Chicago Press, 2002.

Žižek, Slavoj, 'I Plead Guilty – But Where's the Judgment?', *Nepantla*, 3: 3 (2002), 579–83.

Žižek, Slavoj, *The Parallax View*, Cambridge, MA: The MIT Press, 2006.

Žižek, Slavoj, *How to Read Lacan*, London: Granta Books, 2006.

Žižek, Slavoj, *Violence*, London: Profile, 2008.

Žižek, Slavoj, *In Defense of Lost Causes*, London: Verso, 2008.

Index